Business and Society

Managing Corporate Social Performance

Business and Society

Managing Corporate Social Performance

Archie B. Carroll

The University of Georgia

Little, Brown and Company

Boston   Toronto

Library of Congress Catalog Card No. 80-83080
ISBN 0-316-130109

9   8   7   6   5   4   3   2   1

MV

Published simultaneously in Canada
by Little, Brown & Company (Canada) Limited

Printed in the United States of America

To my wife, Priscilla

Preface

We are in an age in which business must be concerned with much more than just its economic performance. Today, organizational success depends upon business's being able to adapt to its surrounding environment. In this time of adaptation, business is finding that the social and political environments are requiring modifications in its operating philosophy, in its attitudes toward constituent groups that have a stake in the business, and in the techniques that are used both to manage personnel and to deal with outside groups.

We could examine at length the social changes that are occurring and find numerous areas in which business is being required to make adaptations. One major event that has occurred sums up much of what has been happening for well over a decade. This was Big Business Day, which was held on April 17, 1980. The assault on corporate America on this day was the culmination of years of efforts to make business more accountable to its constituencies — consumers, shareholders, employees, and the community at large. On Big Business Day, Ralph Nader and a broad-based coalition of labor and public activists launched an unprecedented drive to curb the economic and political power of big companies.

If one considered the events of Big Business Day out of context, one might think that business had been totally unresponsive to the public's demands for more accountability. This is far from the truth. Business has made significant strides toward more social responsiveness in the past two decades. It seems, however, that the public's desire for more social responsiveness has exceeded the pace with which business has been responding.

Within the context of our rapidly changing social environment, business and managers at all levels, as well as in most of the functional areas, have felt great pressure to relate to societal expectations in a more effective way. As a result, in recent years there has been a proliferation of courses in business schools designed to better prepare the managers of tomorrow with the outlook, frame of reference, set of ethical values, skills, and approaches for dealing with the changing social scene as it is shaped by activist groups, governmental bodies, and other expressions of public interest.

This book is designed for such courses, which have variously been designated as "Business and Society," "Business and Its Environment," "Business and Public Policy," "The Environmental Setting of Business," and so on. The common thread in all of these courses is their focus on business's survival and success in dealing with its environment. Their common concern is with the management of corporate social performance, which this book pursues as its primary motif.

The Book's Structure

The book is organized into five parts. In Part I, we present an overview of the business and society relationship. In Part II, we discuss external publics and issues. In Part III, we consider internal publics and issues. The major managerial emphasis of the book is provided in Part IV — managing the business and society relationship. The book then closes with Part V, in which we consider trends now underway that will shape the future social role of business.

Acknowledgements

Sincere appreciation is extended to a number of people who have made direct or indirect contributions to the writing of this book. In the category of direct contributions, I must thank specifically the reviewers who made valuable suggestions concerning the manuscript. These persons include John Collins at Syracuse University, John Fleming at the University of Southern California, Sandra Holmes at the University of Texas at San Antonio, and Kenneth Newgren at Florida State University. Special appreciation is also extended to my colleague at the University of Georgia, James Lahiff, for his contribution of Chapter 14, Communicating the Business Social Role.

For the time, understanding, and professional support needed to complete a volume such as this, I want to thank William C. Flewellen, Jr., Dean of the College of Business Administration, and Richard C. Huseman, Chairman of the Department of Management, at the University of Georgia. For his help in coordinating materials and proofreading, I also thank my graduate assistant, Allen Payne. And for her unswerving attention to detail, I give a special thanks to Betty F. Brewer. Her contributions in editing, proofreading, and putting the total package together were invaluable.

Finally, I must express appreciation to my wife, Priscilla. Her continuous psychological support and willingness to make personal sacrifices over the three-year period the project was underway helped make all this possible.

Brief Contents

Contents

Business and Society

Managing Corporate
Social Performance

Part I:
The Business
and Society
Relationship

Basic Question   What is the subject of business and society all
                      about?

Objectives of Part I   To set the stage, provide historical context,
                            and define terms

                            To show how the responsiveness orientation
                            suggests a managerial approach

                            To study business ethics and its
                            management — a topic that pervades the study
                            of business and society

Chapters in Part I   1. An Overview of the Business and Society
                             Relationship

                          2. From Social Responsibility to Social
                             Responsiveness

                          3. Business Ethics and Management

INTRODUCTION TO PART I

The purpose of Part I is to introduce a number of concepts that are essential in understanding the relationship between business and society. In Chapter 1 we define terms, provide historical perspective, and outline the structure of the book. In Chapter 2 we discuss the evolution of the concept of social responsibility and trace how responsiveness has become an important focus in managing corporate social performance. In Chapter 3 we discuss business ethics and its management. Because ethical concerns permeate practically all the issues we discuss in the book, it is important to introduce this topic early. A particular focus in this chapter is on what managers can do to improve business ethics.

Taken together, these three introductory chapters lay the foundation for a closer look at the social issues business faces and at management's task of improving an organization's social performance.

An Overview of the Business and Society Relationship

Recent news stories about business and society included the following:

1. A charge by an investigative monthly magazine that banned drugs and dangerous birth-control devices were among faulty products being dumped in Third World countries by corporations from the United States.[1]
2. The dropping of sponsorship by General Motors of a two-part television drama as a result of pressure from a group of irate Protestant fundamentalists, although the company said that it found nothing objectionable in the program.[2]
3. A charge by a minister in Chicago that the Coca-Cola Company engaged in racial bias in one of its promotional schemes. The promotion sought to identify the PiBB Girl — the girl who most looks like a composite of five white American actresses.[3]
4. A charge by church groups and other activists that Switzerland-based Nestlé Company was contributing to infant mortality because of its sale of powdered-milk formula in less developed countries.[4]

One has only to read a daily newspaper or a magazine or two to find proof that the subject of business and society relationships is very current. Indeed, the actual cases cited above are typical of what is found in such reading. It is not our intent to judge the legitimacy of claims such as those above, but simply to offer them as illustrations of the widespread interactions between business and society that occur on an almost daily basis.

Aside from the question of legitimacy of the claims of these societal groups, the examples demonstrate the wide variety of charges being

---

[1]"Magazine Says Faulty Devices Dumped Abroad," *Atlanta Constitution,* October 12, 1979, p. A-19.

[2]"GM Bows Out on Jesus Show," *Atlanta Journal,* March 15, 1977, p. C-1.

[3]Evan Kossoff, "Coke Bottlers Here Noticed Bias, Rejected PiBB Contest," *Atlanta Journal and Constitution,* April 20, 1980, pp. 1-B, 6-B.

[4]"A Boycott Over Infant Formula," *Business Week,* April 23, 1979, p. 137.

3

brought against business today. In today's socially aware environment the business firm frequently finds itself on the defensive — that is, it finds itself in a position of having to admit that what it is doing is wrong, unethical, or otherwise inappropriate, or it simply may have to alter its behavior or actions because of the presssure brought by groups or individuals who wield an increasing amount of influence on public opinion.

Against this backdrop of growing turbulence in the business and society relationship, Chapter 1 presents an overview of the following major topics:

- Business and society defined
- The role of pluralism
- The evolving business and society relationship
- The concept of social responsibility
- The social contract
- Criticism of business today
- A managerial approach to business and society
- The structure of the book

BUSINESS AND SOCIETY DEFINED

Business is considered to be that collection of private, commercially oriented (profit-oriented) organizations which range in size from one-person sole proprietorships (Rogers TV Sales and Service, Tony's Restaurant, Pressley's Garage, and other small enterprises in a community) to corporate giants (General Electric, Procter and Gamble, Bethlehem Steel, or Sears, Roebuck and Company). Between these extremes, of course, are many medium-sized sole proprietorships, partnerships, and corporations.

When we speak of business in this comprehensive sense, we mean businesses of all sizes and in all types of industries; but as we embark on our discussion of business and society we will doubtless find ourselves speaking more of *big* business in *selected* industries, for a variety of reasons. Big business is highly visible. Its products and advertising are more widely disseminated and, consequently, it is more frequently in the critical public eye. In addition, people in our society often associate bigness with power, and the powerful are given closer scrutiny. Though it is well known that small businesses in our society far outnumber the larger ones, the impact, pervasiveness, power, and visibility of large firms keep them on the front page much more of the time.

With respect to different industries, some are simply more conducive to the creation of visible social problems than are others. Manufacturing firms, for example, may cause air and water pollution. Such firms, therefore, are more likely to be subject to criticism than, say, a life insurance company, which emits no obvious pollution. The auto industry is a particular case in point. Much of the criticism against GM and the other automakers is raised because of their high visibility as manufacturers (which, by nature, cause various forms of pollution), the products they make (which are the largest single source of air pollution), and the popularity of their products (nearly every family owns one or more cars). And, in the case of the auto industry, we have not yet worked out an ideal solution to the product-disposal problem; so we see unsightly pieces of metal and plastic on every roadside.

Some industries are highly visible because of the advertising-intensive nature of their products (Alka-Seltzer, Clorox 2, Die Hard Batteries, Budweiser), while other industries are examined because of the possible effect of their products on health (cigarettes, toys, food products), and still others because of their role in providing health-related products (pharmaceutical firms).

When we refer to business in its relationship with society, therefore, we may focus our attention too much on *large* businesses in *particular* industries. But we should not lose sight of the fact that small- and medium-sized companies also deserve special consideration because they, too, are important elements in our definition of business. In fact, problems have arisen over the last decade for small businesses because they have been subjected to many of the same regulations and demands as those imposed by government on larger organizations. In many instances, however, smaller businesses do not have the resources to meet the requirements for more accountability on many of the social fronts that we will discuss.

Society may be defined as a community, a nation, or a broad grouping of people having common traditions, values, institutions, and collective activities and interests. As such, when we speak of business and society relationships, we may, in fact, mean business and the local community (business and Los Angeles), business and the United States as a whole, or business and a group of people (consumers, minorities, stockholders).

When we refer to business and the entire society, we think of society as being comprised of numerous interest groups, more or less formalized organizations, and a variety of institutions. These groups, organizations, and institutions are purposeful units of people who have banded together because they represent a common cause or share a set of common beliefs about a particular issue. Examples of interest groups or purposeful organizations are numerous: Friends of the Earth, Common Cause, chambers of commerce, National Association of Manufacturers, Ralph Nader's activists.

THE ROLE OF PLURALISM

What is particularly notable about our society that makes for more interesting and novel business and society relationships than in other societies is its pluralistic nature. *Pluralism* is a condition in which there is diffusion of power among the society's many organizations. Joseph W. McGuire's straightforward definition of a pluralistic society is extremely useful for our purposes.

> A pluralistic society is one in which there is wide decentralization and diversity of power concentration.[5]

The key descriptive words in this definition are *wide* decentralization and *diversity* of power concentration.

In other words, power is dispersed; it is not in the hands of any single group (such as business, government, labor, or the military), or a small number of groups. Many years ago in *The Federalist Papers* James Madison speculated that pluralism was a virtuous scheme, and he correctly anticipated the rise of numerous organizations in our society as a consequence of it. Some of the many virtues of a pluralistic society are summarized in Exhibit 1-1.

All societal systems have their weaknesses, and pluralism is no exception. One weakness in a pluralistic system is that it creates an environment in which the diverse institutions pursue their own self-interests, with the result that there is no central direction to unify individual pursuits. Another problem or weakness is that groups or institutions proliferate to the extent that their goals tend to overlap, thus causing confusion as to what organizations best serve what functions. Related to this, pluralism forces conflict onto center stage because of its emphasis on autonomous groups, each pursuing its own objectives. In light of these concerns, a pluralistic system does not appear to be very efficient.

History and experience have indicated, however, that the merits of pluralism are such that most people in our society favor the situation that has resulted from it. Indeed, it has worked to achieve equilibrium in the balance of power of the dominant institutions that constitute the American way of life.

Knowing that society is comprised of so many different semi-autonomous and autonomous groups might cause one to question whether we can realistically speak of society in a broad term that has any agreed-upon meaning. We nevertheless do speak in such a term, knowing that unless we specify a particular societal subgroup, or subsystem, we are referring to all those persons, groups, and institutions that constitute a

---

[5]Joseph W. McGuire, *Business and Society* (New York: McGraw-Hill Book Company, 1963), p. 130.

EXHIBIT 1-1
The Virtues of a Pluralistic Society

1. A pluralistic society prevents power from being concentrated in the hands of a few.
2. A pluralistic society maximizes freedom of expression, action, and responsibility by striking a balance between monism (social organization into one institution) on the one hand and anarchy (social organization into an infinite number of persons) on the other.[a]
3. In a pluralistic society the allegiance of individuals to groups is dispersed.
4. Pluralism creates a widely diversified set of loyalties to many organizations and minimizes the danger that a leader of any one organization will be left uncontrolled.[b]
5. Pluralism provides a built-in set of checks and balances, in that groups can exert power over one another with no single organization (business, government) dominating and becoming overly influential.

[a]Keith Davis and Robert L. Blomstrom, *Business and Society: Environment and Responsibility,* 3rd ed. (New York: McGraw-Hill Book Company, 1975), p. 63.
[b]Joseph W. McGuire, *Business and Society* (New York: McGraw-Hill Book Company, 1963), p. 132.

society. This situation raises an important point: When we speak of business and society relationships we usually mean particular segments or subgroups of society (consumerists, women, minorities, environmentalists, youth), or we are referring to business and some system in our society (education, law, custom, religion, economics). These groups of people or systems may also be referred to in an institutional form (business and the courts, business and Common Cause, business and the church, business and the AFL-CIO, business and the Federal Trade Commission).

Figure 1-1 displays in pictorial form the points of interface between business and some of the multiple publics and systems with which it has social relationships. Note the overlapping of the groups themselves, symbolizing the concept of pluralism and interrelatedness.

If sheer numbers of relationships are an indicator of complexity, then we could easily argue that business's current relationships with different segments of society constitute a truly complex environment. And if we had the capacity to draw a diagram similar to Figure 1-1 that noted all the detail comprising each of those points of interface, it would be too overwhelming to comprehend. Management of businesses today cannot sidestep this problem as deftly as we can here, because management must live with these interfaces on a daily basis.

Having defined business, society, and pluralism, and having elaborated on these crucial concepts as a backdrop for this book, it is appro-

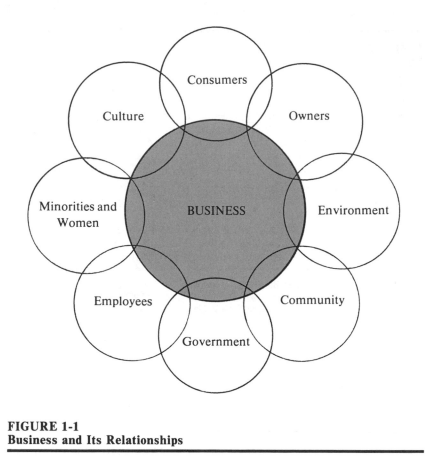

FIGURE 1-1
Business and Its Relationships

priate to ask now: Are not business and society the same as they always were? If not, what is the nature of the evolving business and society relationship?

THE EVOLVING RELATIONSHIP

To provide an overview of the evolving relationship between business and society, it is helpful to define at this point two crucial concepts — social responsibility and the social contract. (We will develop these two notions more fully in later chapters.) To avoid providing unique definitions for terms that have been ably defined elsewhere, let us use the brief definition of *social responsibility* that was set forth by Professor Raymond Bauer.

> Corporate social responsibility is seriously considering the impact
> of the company's actions on society.[6]

This definition is quite broad, but it does provide us with a frame of reference that suggests that business's responsibility to the society within which it exists goes beyond simply assuming an economizing or profit-producing role. This will take on importance as we discuss the various roles (socially expected behavior patterns) or functions that business has come to assume over time. Note that Bauer refers to *corporate* social responsibility in the same sense that we use the term *business* social responsibility.

The concept of the *social contract* is related to the roles or functions that are expected of an institution by other groups in a society, and what these institutions, in turn, expect of others. Let us define the social contract with reference to business and society as follows:

> The social contract refers to that set of two-way understandings or
> expectations that characterize the relationship of business with society.

To elaborate somewhat, the social contract is partially articulated through the laws or regulations that society has established as the framework within which business must operate, and it is partially manifested in the understandings shared by business and society as to what they expect of one another.

The concepts of social responsibility and the social contract help us depict how the relationship between business and society has evolved over time. We will see, for example, that business has seriously considered its impacts on society, to the extent of eventually factoring social considerations, as well as profits, into its matrix of objectives. We will also see how business and society have changed — sometimes reluctantly — their shared expectations of one another's role over time. In a real sense, then, the essence of the changes that have taken place in the relationship between business and society can be understood by examining the dynamics of social responsibility and the social contract.

To provide insight into how the business role in general, and the concepts of social responsibility and the social contract in particular, have evolved, it is useful to work within a frame of reference. Consider the historical categories of Robert Moore and Nicholas Eberstadt, as summarized in Table 1-1. They divide business history into five phases or periods.

---

[6]Quoted in John L. Paluszek, *Business and Society: 1976-2000* (New York: AMACOM, 1976), p. 1.

TABLE 1-1
Phases of Business History

Phase	Robert Moore	Nicholas Eberstadt
I	Pre-Business Capitalism (before 1100 A.D.)	Classical Period
II	Petty Capitalism (1100-1300)	Medieval Period (1000-1500)
III	Mercantile Capitalism (1300-1800)	Mercantile Period (1500-1800)
IV	Industrial Capitalism (1800-1900)	Industrial Period (1800-1930)
	Financial Capitalism (1890-1933)	
V	National Capitalism (1933-present)	Corporate Period (1930-present)

Phase I — Pre-Business Capitalism (Before 1100 A.D.)

Business in the modern sense did not flourish during this early time, though there was evidence of business activity taking place. One of the most advanced cultures of this early period, classical Greece, provides an interesting example of the low esteem in which business was held. The Greeks left business activity to slaves or second-class citizens. Though the Greeks frowned on business, they nevertheless expected business to serve the community. According to Raymond Bauer:

> The captains of industry of Miletus and Priene were subject to intense criticism from the upper classes of their societies if they failed to practice a standard of morality which went beyond common honesty, or if they failed to attend to the question of how they could use their wealth for the greater good ... The Greeks were particularly offended by the suggestion that material gains from business were to be used merely as the owners wished, without regard for the interests of the community.[7]

Evidence from the early Greeks, then, suggests that social responsibility and the social contract were such that commercial business was characterized by low esteem (not so much for the modern reasons but because such activity was not consistent with the value the Greeks placed on character development and nobility) and the expectation that business would provide services to the community.

[7]Quoted in Nicholas N. Eberstadt, "What History Tells Us About Corporate Responsibility," *Business and Society Review/Innovation,* Autumn 1973, pp. 77-78.

Though this period was not barren of economic activity, economic activity came to be represented by the cooperative collective economy that evolved in western Europe. The high point of the cooperative collective economy was manifested in manorialism and feudalism during the tenth century A.D. Then, after hundreds of years, this early period gave way to a period of petty capitalism. One of the primary reasons for this change was that the philosophy and approach of feudalism had become too narrow and inflexible. Even during this early period, as Moore asserts, "it lacked the universality to appeal to the heterogeneity of man and his desire for progress."[8]

Phase II — Petty Capitalism (1100 – 1300)

Credit is frequently given to the petty capitalists for introducing business to society. By so doing, they established the foundations for our present civilization. The major contribution of the petty capitalists was that they took over the task of individuals producing goods for themselves for survival. The petty capitalists, as small business people (merchants and shopkeepers), were individualists — they stressed the importance of independence, self-worth, and achievement through individual effort. They believed in working hard and offering opportunities for others to work, grow, and develop their own individual trades. They believed in democratic economic equality.[9]

To understand the context of business and society in which the petty capitalists existed, consider the significant role that the church assumed in these times in the development of economic doctrine and philosophy. The Catholic Church was extremely pervasive, powerful, and influential in defining acceptable and unacceptable practices for the petty capitalists. The view held during this medieval time was that God's hand was over all activities — there was to be "no division between church and state or between religion and business."[10]

Two of the most notable examples of the church's influence on business and economics appeared in the doctrines of just price and usury. St. Thomas Aquinas originated the concept of *just price*. He argued that everything has just one price: what it is worth. And what it is worth is inherent in the object — an objective value which is not determined by the individual purchaser. Aquinas held that there is one price for every item of purchase and that this price should not be subject to variation because of supply and demand, individual caprice, or skill in manipulat-

---

[8]Robert E. Moore, "Business Philosophy," *Business History Reivew,* 24 (December 1950), pp. 196-209.
[9]Moore, pp. 197-199.
[10]McGuire, pp. 17-18.

ing the market.[11] The price was termed "just" because it was a price that would leave both parties satisfied.

According to Aquinas, the just price of an item should be just enough to enable the merchant to recoup what he paid for the item plus whatever gain would enable him to maintain his standard of living. Trade was considered base if it permitted the merchant to improve his position. The church disapproved of any merchant who did not follow this pricing principle; thus the merchant's social responsibility was, in a very real sense, defined by the church's position on this important doctrine. It is useful to contrast the just price philosophy of this period with the market price's domination of modern business today.

Usury is the practice of lending money with an interest charge for its use. Aquinas was outspoken against this practice too. Basing his views on the Bible, Aristotle, and the Christian Fathers, his logic went as follows: One should not gain for letting another use his money for a period of time because all time belongs to God. Therefore, it is a sin to charge interest for something that is not one's own.

The economic doctrine of the church was perhaps the first formulated body of economic thought. The church branded the profit motive as anti-Christian and adopted what was basically an antibusiness attitude. Church influence on medieval culture was so pervasive that business people even came to doubt their own moral worth. Nevertheless, business went on and, though business people during these times often succeeded in circumventing society's high expectations of them, the business person was expected to have high morals and scrupulous principles.

It has been suggested that the medieval notion of social responsibility had one major defect: Its view of the community was narrow and it condoned the exploitation of outsiders.[12] Acceptance of this exploitation set the stage for what was to become a fundamental practice in the mercantile period of history.

Phase III — The Mercantile Period (1500 – 1800)

Though the petty capitalists did not disappear, some of them felt that a new system was necessary if business were to prosper and grow. This new approach required expansion into foreign markets. The mercantilists felt that international trade was good. Some countries tried to outdo one another in achieving a favorable balance of trade. The determination of a country to attain wealth through foreign trade became so paramount that it eventually led to a new social hierarchy of occupa-

[11]Moore, pp. 199-201.
[12]Eberstadt, p. 78.

tions. Agriculture was at the bottom, because farming brought no money into the country; manufacturing became especially important because of its creation of exportable goods.

Business during this time flourished and was supported by the state. It was also controlled by the state, and its energies were channeled into socially responsible behavior in some countries. England is a notable example; England's "harmony of interests" theory held that business should act in the national interest because the state supported it.[13]

During the latter part of the mercantile period the church lost power as Catholic dogma gave way to the doctrine of John Calvin and the Protestant reformation. At the same time, the economic scene also underwent changes. The economic philosophy of mercantilism brought government into the central role of financing and protecting trade to build strong national economies.[14] Mercantilism eventually fell because it tried to keep uneconomic enterprises alive, because it curbed individual initiative, because it buried itself in bureaucratic red tape, and because it fostered wars and trade rivalries that eventually destroyed the markets it was trying so hard to create.[15]

The economic thought of the physiocratic school, in particular that of Francois Quesnay, emerged to challenge the theory behind mercantilism. Unlike the mercantilists, the physiocrats argued that accumulation of gold and wealth was not as important as agricultural production. Quesnay also argued that laissez-faire capitalism (nonintervention of government) was the best economic system. This set the stage for Adam Smith's views, which were to be an important development in the period of industrial capitalism to come.

Phase IV — Industrial and Financial Capitalism (1800 – 1930)

Management historian Daniel A. Wren has suggested that a cultural rebirth was necessary to allow the industrial revolution to emerge. He posited a trinity of forces that combined to result in changed attitudes toward man, toward work, and toward profits. This "cultural trinity" consisted of the market ethic, the Protestant ethic, and the liberty ethic.[16] A brief look at each is useful for its value in understanding the industrial period.

[13]Eberstadt, p. 79.

[14]John Fred Bell, *A History of Economic Thought,* 2nd ed. (New York: Ronald Press, 1967), p. 53.

[15]Shepard B. Clough, *The Economic Development of Western Civilization* (New York: McGraw-Hill Book Company, 1959), Chapter 11.

[16]Daniel A. Wren, *The Evolution of Management Thought,* 2nd ed. (New York: John Wiley & Sons, 1979), pp. 27-40.

1. The Market Ethic. The market ethic represented a change in the economic sphere. Its main proponent was Adam Smith, a Scot. Though Smith was not a physiocrat per se, he subscribed to their idea of a natural harmony in economics. In his *The Wealth of Nations* he criticized the mercantilist view.[17] He felt that mercantilist policies impeded private enterprise. Smith advocated replacing state direction and power with market competition — the "invisible hand" — which would transform individual self-seeking into social well-being. The French cry of *laissez-faire, laissez-passer!* symbolized Smith's position: freedom of enterprise and movement.[18]

When Smith's writings appeared in the early days of the industrial revolution, his message was in tune with a growing number of would-be entrepreneurs seeking academic rationalization for their views. England thus found in Smith's writings a market ethic — an economic sanction for private initiative rather than mercantilism, competition rather than protection, innovation rather than economic stagnation, and self-interest rather than state interest — as a motivating force.[19]

2. The Protestant Ethic. Max Weber set forth a connection between the Protestant ethic and capitalism in his book *The Protestant Ethic and the Spirit of Capitalism.*[20] The stage was set for his book, however, in earlier writings and beliefs. The Protestant ethic, sometimes called the work ethic, had its beginnings in biblical times. St. Paul stated, "If any one will not work, let him not eat." The point of view of the medieval monks was that work was a glorification of God. St. Benedict's followers captured this same theme with their dictum, *Laborare est orare* ("to work is to pray").[21] At a later time, the stern Protestantism of John Calvin and Martin Luther provided additional religious sanction for work and achievement.[22] Specifically, the work ethic grew out of Luther's idea of a *calling* wherein God set a life task for each individual to demonstrate His grace. The calling gave earthly work a moral sanction. Belief in the calling and the Protestant ethic led to a spirit of capitalism, success, and improvement, as it fulfilled God's will for man to labor in this world. Religious sanctions for work led to capital ac-

---

[17]For an elaboration of this criticism see Douglas F. Dowd, *The Twisted Dream,* 2nd ed. (Cambridge, Massachusetts: Winthrop Publishers, 1977), pp. 5-14.

[18]Dowd, p. 7.

[19]Wren, p. 40.

[20]Max Weber, *The Protestant Ethic and the Spirit of Capitalism,* translated by Talcott Parsons (New York: Charles Scribner's Sons, 1958). Originally published in Germany (1905) and revised in 1920.

[21]Quoted in "Is the Work Ethic Going Out of Style?" *Time,* October 30, 1972, p. 96.

[22]For a discussion of the Protestant work ethic and modern behavior of youth see Archie B. Carroll, "Youth's Work Ethic: An Expectations Gap," *Personnel Administrator,* September/October 1973, pp. 11-14.

cumulation, economic growth, and a legitimization of the business person. In the Protestant (sometimes called the Puritan) ethic there was a fusion of spiritual and material views that encouraged busyness and worldly enterprise. [23]

3. The Liberty Ethic. The postulates of economic freedom (the market ethic) and the sanctions of individual rewards for worldly efforts (the Protestant ethic) can operate freely only in a political system that is conducive to individual liberty. The divine right of kings, the autocracy of the manor lord, the exercise of secular authority by the church, and serfdom were not ideas that favored the development of an industrialized society. According to the writings of John Locke and others, "the liberty ethic placed man in a participatory role in government, encouraged private property, discouraged rule by dictatorial whims, and introduced more freedom and individualism in all spheres of life." [24]

Taken together, these three ethics, Wren argues, set the stage for the industrial revolution and the growth in business that occurred during this period. As the industrial revolution developed in America in the nineteenth century, new attitudes toward business and business people emerged. This period also saw the emergence of the specialized industrial capitalist who used power machinery whenever possible, drove his employees hard, and sought to provide more goods for all at lower prices. The industrial capitalist was allowed to run free — building giant corporations, exploiting workers, engaging in fiercely competitive and sometimes unscrupulous practices. The thrust of the era was profit making and economic expansion.

Though there were many good business people during this period, we frequently think of the robber barons, who had very little conception of corporate social responsibility, as typical of the era's business people. Names such as Jay Gould, Daniel Drew, Jim Fisk, and William Vanderbilt come to mind as characteristic of the period.

A few examples of the underhanded business practices engaged in by these men illustrate the era. Daniel Drew was famous for having introduced the idea of watered stock. (The name derived from the practice of driving thirsty cattle to the market and then bloating them with water to increase their weight just before they were weighed for sale.) Another deception used by Drew was to create confusion on the floor of the stock exchange by mopping his forehead with a red bandanna and letting a slip of paper fall from his pocket. Another speculator would see

---

[23]Robert L. Heilbroner, *The Economic Transformation of America* (New York: Harcourt Brace Jovanovich, 1977), pp. 12-13.
[24]Wren, pp. 34-37.

this and pick up the note, on which were written Drew's instructions to his broker to buy or sell stocks. Thinking that he had discovered Drew's secret plans, he would place orders to take advantage of Drew's planned strategy. The problem was that it was all a hoax designed by Drew to outwit his opponents; he now knew what their transactions would be![25]

This was a period of great industrial expansion but very little corporate social responsibility. It was a turbulent age, with few instances of business taking responsibility for its actions. The Sherman Antitrust Act of 1890 and the Clayton Act of 1914 were responses to the emergence of the largest trusts of this time and their anticompetitive behavior. These laws were the first real attempt to establish a social contract with business, different from the loose expectations that had characterized the post-Civil War period of growth.

Moore characterized the period from 1890 to 1933 as one of financial capitalism. He suggested that this period saw the emergence of the financial capitalist — an individual who saw the benefits to business of mergers and the creation of large, diversified financial systems. Moore asserts that none of the systems of capitalism have been as widely condemned as financial capitalism. As we have mentioned, this period was also characterized by governmental regulations enacted to stem the rise of antisocial business behavior.

Phase V — National Capitalism (1933 – Present)

During this period much of the unrestrained business behavior of the earlier days came under government control. As a consequence of the trusts that had been established (for example, Vanderbilt in railroads, Carnegie in steel, Rockefeller in oil) and ruthless business behavior in general, concern now developed for equalizing the balance of power between business (both shareholders and management), the worker, and the consumer.

Numerous laws were passed in the first half of the twentieth century aimed at restraining corporate behavior and assuring a balance of power among various interest groups in society. In addition to the Sherman Antitrust Act of 1890, the Interstate Commerce Act of 1887, and the Clayton Act of 1914, business now faced a new and relentless manifestation of society's desire for a more equitable social contract. Society realized that the laissez-faire approach had not produced the desired results. Or perhaps it might be fairer to say that the industrial stimulus provided by laissez-faire was needed, but it had outlived its

[25]Heilbroner, pp. 72-73.

usefulness now that America was turning its attention to other, previously neglected facets of life.

Other significant business regulations that appeared during this period included the Federal Trade Commission Act of 1914 (preventing the formation and continuation of illegal trade combinations), the Robinson-Patman Act of 1936 (forbidding price discrimination), the Wheeler Act of 1938 (prohibiting false advertising of certain goods), as well as numerous pieces of labor legislation designed to establish some semblance of a balance of power between labor and business. This labor legislation included the 1926 Railway Labor Act, the 1932 Norris-LaGuardia Act, and the 1935 Wagner Act. Labor power was at its highest with the Wagner Act, which gave labor the right to bargain collectively with business management.

The history of this corporate period, as Eberstadt termed it, is characterized by the assumption that the corporation is an institution in our society that has a social role other than just profit making. One might think that with the increase in government regulation of business that occurred in this period, business would have institutionalized social concern and made it a part of its modus operandi. There is no evidence to suggest that this occurred, however. More precisely, even though business did become more socially responsive, it does not seem to have kept pace with society's expectations of it — as manifested through laws that had been passed, protests that had been made, lawsuits that had been filed against business, and public opinion polls that had been documenting societal concern with business's behavior and practices for quite some time.

The early 1970s witnessed what many would consider the most demanding social legislation known to business in recent decades in the form of the Environmental Protection Act, the Equal Employment Opportunity Act, the Occupational Safety and Health Act, and the Consumer Product Safety Act. Thus, although business's social responsibility and the social contract were changing in rather substantial ways, much of the impetus for the changes came in the form of new laws — not just understandings between business and society about newly agreed-upon concepts of one another's role.

Much more could be said about the changes in social responsibility that have occurred in recent years, but we will leave that subject for treatment when we examine business's specific interfaces with societal groups in Parts II and III of the book.

This overview and historical perspective of business's changing role should help to place modern business in its contemporary context. Perhaps a good way of summarizing much of this historical review of business's social role is to cite a statement made by Eberstadt about Ralph Nader's social activism, which began in the mid-1960s:

Nader's philosophy is not new. He is merely synthesizing over twenty centuries of Western civilization with our present environment, which is something of a post-industrial one.[26]

CRITICISM OF BUSINESS TODAY

By briefly examining some of the reasons for the widespread criticism of business today, perhaps we can gain a more accurate understanding of the nature of the contemporary relationship between business and society. As a point of departure we should note that practically every public opinion poll taken in recent years has documented a falling level of public confidence in business as an institution in our society. Although there are many reasons why criticism of business is so widespread today, we will highlight only a few of the more prominent ones.

1. General Disillusionment. This feeling about many of our major institutions — business, education, government, the military, the media — is partially due to the generally negative public attitude that has evolved as a result of many of society's problems (the Viet Nam war, Watergate, assassinations, the youth revolution, the energy crisis, and so on). This disillusionment can also be attributed to the public's perception that these institutions (especially business) are motivated by self-interest.

2. Increased Media Exposure. Extensive media coverage of both real and imaginary business abuses has heightened the public's awareness of and sensitivity to business-related social problems. Though the media claim fairness in their reporting of business, a number of executives argue differently. One business manager recently exclaimed:

> There is no doubt in my mind that there is antibusiness bias in a good deal of reporting. Television, notably the network news programs and documentaries, goes out of its way to exaggerate the flaws of business and minimize the achievements.[27]

In addition, business and business people have been consistently portrayed in the role of villain on many popular television shows.[28]

3. Rise of Society's Expectations. Increased affluence and higher levels of education have led the populace to expect more of business than ever before.

---

[26]Eberstadt, p. 81.

[27]Quoted in Leonard H. Orr, "Why Business Got a Bad Name," *Business and Society Review,* Fall 1976, p. 24.

[28]See, for example, Benjamin Stein, "Draculas in the Executive Suite," *Wall Street Journal,* May 27, 1976, p. 22.

Pepper... and Salt

"There's a $20,000 bonus for anyone who can come up with a euphemism for 'windfall profits'!"

SOURCE: From *The Wall Street Journal.* Permission Cartoon Features Syndicate.

4. Business Not Understood. Companies have not been effective in telling their side of the story. A classic illustration of this point is business's inability to convey to the public what profits are and how they are used. The accompanying cartoon presents a humorous version of how some people view business's efforts to communicate about profits.

5. Perpetuating Effect. Once the image of any institution has been tarnished, it is difficult to remove the tarnish simply by engaging in good behavior. One real problem here is that it is difficult for business, in the general sense, to act as a single entity; no one group has the power to enforce good behavior by all. Consequently, the acts of a few companies perpetuate the problem for business as a whole.

6. The State of the Economy and General Resource Shortages. These are blamed by many on business. People in our society feel that business causes inflation and shortages of such crucial resources as oil and other energy products.

7. Corporate Power and Autonomy. This is another reason why criticism has been levied against business. The public feels that business, particularly big business, is powerful, interested only in itself, and free to operate without accountability. The feeling that bigness brings power and that "bigness is badness" crops up time and again in surveys of the public's attitudes about business.

8. Poor Business Behavior. Hardly a day goes by that we do not hear of shoddy consumer goods, improperly labeled products, defective merchandise, misleading advertising, unethical business practices, or other unacceptable business activities. The major solution, of course, is for business to police itself. But even if it does, it still faces the problem of the perpetuating effect. The fact that there are actual business practices that demand rectification from a social responsibility standpoint in itself presents a formidable challenge for business.[29]

A MANAGERIAL APPROACH TO BUSINESS AND SOCIETY

We have given some examples of how societal groups are pushing companies to go beyond their traditional profit-making role. We have also defined business, society, and other key terms; we have looked at business's evolving relationship with society; and we have outlined a few of the reasons why criticism of business is so prevalent today. The picture we have painted may be dismal, but the situation is such that management of business firms in our society must address these issues in a more meaningful and pragmatic way than they have in the past.

There is abundant evidence that business firms are now accepting social goals and finding it economically feasible to combine these concerns with their profit-minded pursuits. Managers are raising questions, however, as to what short- and long-range implications the adoption of a socially responsible philosophy will have for them. As they accept such a myriad of goals, their decision processes become considerably more complex than in the past, and these newly accepted parameters of decision making do not lend themselves quite as nicely to conventional modes of analysis and prediction.

Managers, being the pragmatic beings that they are, have begun to deal with these social concerns in ways similar to those they have used to deal with traditional business issues — production, marketing,

---

[29]For an interesting discussion of this problem, see Robert Cushman, "Let's Put Our House in Order: A Businessman's Plea," *Business and Society Review,* Winter 1975-76, pp. 49-52.

finance, and so forth — in a rational, systematic, and administratively sound fashion. By viewing issues of social concern from a managerial frame of reference, managers have been able to reduce seemingly unmanageable social concerns to ones that can be dealt with in a rational fashion.

A managerial approach to the business and society relationship confronts the individual manager continuously with questions such as these:

- What changes are occurring or will occur in society's expectations of business that mandate business's taking the initiative with respect to particular societal problems?
- Did we have a role in creating these problems?
- What impact is social change having on the organization and how should we best deal with it?
- Can we reduce broad social problems to a size that can be effectively addressed from a managerial point of view?
- On which social problems can we act most effectively?
- What are the specific problems, alternatives for solving the problems, and implications of management's approach to dealing with social issues?
- How can we best plan for and organize for responsiveness to societally related business problems?

From the standpoint of urgency in managerial response, management is concerned with two broad classes of social issues. First, there are those issues that arise on the spur of the moment and for which management formulates a relatively quick response. These may be either issues that management has never faced before or issues they have faced but do not have time to deal with except on a short-term basis. A typical example might be a protest group that shows up on management's doorstep one day, arguing vehemently that the company withdraw its sponsorship of a violent television show scheduled to air the next week.

Second, there are issues or problems that management has time to deal with on a more long-term basis. These might involve environmental pollution, employment discrimination, product safety, or occupational safety and health. In other words, these are issues that will be of concern to society for a long time, and for which management must develop a reasonably sophisticated organizational response. It is true that issues like the ones just mentioned could also appear in the form of ad hoc problems necessitating an immediate response, but they should suffice to illustrate areas in which governmental legislation has matured somewhat. Management must thus be concerned with a short-term capability as well as a long-term capability to deal with social problems and the organization's social performance.

Our managerial aproach, then, will be one that, first, clarifies the nature of the social issues that affect organizations and, second, suggests alternative managerial responses to these social issues in a rational and systematic fashion. The test of success will be the extent to which we can improve an organization's social performance by taking the managerial approach rather than dealing with the issues on an ad hoc basis.

THE STRUCTURE OF THE BOOK

We begin by discussing the kinds of problems that business faces and must monitor in its relationship with society. We will then analyze how business manages the relationship through administrative technology — planning, organizing, controlling, policy design and implementation, and communication.

In Part I we present an overview of the relationship between business and society, and then discuss how and why the concept of social responsibility has matured to become one of social responsiveness. Implicit in this transition from responsibilty to responsiveness is a move to a managerial frame of reference. We also cover the subject of business ethics. Because all of the social issues treated in the book have an ethical dimension, it is important to discuss this facet of social responsibility early. It is also a topic that pervades management's relationships with both external and internal publics (audiences) and issues, discussed in the next two parts.

In Part II, major external publics and issues arc addressed. These include business's relationship with government, consumers, the environment, and the community. In Part III our focus turns to internal publics and issues. Here we direct our attention to business's relationships with employees, including special consideration of minorities, women, and other disadvantaged groups. Also important here is business's interaction with its ownership, an issue that is taking on renewed significance today.

Part IV, which assumes a knowledge and awareness of the issues, outlines the more enduring management responses that are essential to a well-conceived managerial approach. Here we will be concerned with generalizable management and organizational response patterns that have been proven effective in dealing with business problems and, to some extent, with social issues. Because the state of the art of managing the business and society relationship is still almost embryonic, this section will be merely descriptive and suggestive rather than definitive, in citing well-established principles.

The book ends on a futuristic note in Part V. What will the business and society relationship be in the future? How will the concept of social responsibility be viewed in the future? What will be the new areas of social concern for business, and how will management technology respond? These and other questions will be addressed as we attempt to place the present in perspective with the future.

SUMMARY

Business and society have both become more complex. This complexity is a consequence of many factors and has resulted in a changed social contract. In addition, the focus on social responsibility has become more acute. This is partly the result of criticism of business and of a maturing society, all of whose members have higher expectations. The major effect of these trends has been to increase the importance of a managerial approach to dealing with business and society relationships. To effectively survive today and in the future, management must both become aware of the nature and scope of social issues impinging on the organization, and develop mechanisms and modes of response that will best handle these demands, which seem to be increasing at an exponential rate. By so doing, management can convert social issues into managerial issues and thus handle them with the degree of effectiveness that has characterized other business operations in the past.

QUESTIONS FOR DISCUSSION

1. Define business. Define society. Why is the relationship between the two important?
2. What is meant by pluralism? What are its essential characteristics? What are the three most important virtues of a pluralistic society? What are its weaknesses?
3. Explain the relationship between the concept of the social contract and that of social responsibility.
4. Summarize the nature of the social contract during the period of pre-business capitalism.
5. Does the just price concept make more sense to you than market price? Why?
6. Summarize the nature of the social contract during the mercantile period.
7. What is the cultural trinity? Explain its significance.

8. Do you think that Daniel Drew's practice of watering stock was so-cially responsible? Explain. What about his red bandanna ruse? Discuss.

9. Explain Eberstadt's statement that "Nader's philosophy is not new."

10. Of the various reasons why criticism of business is so widespread, which two make the most sense to you? What are reasons you can suggest that were not mentioned?

11. What are the features of a managerial approach to the business and society relationship? Why is such an approach needed?

Cases

Exciting Games, Inc.:
People or Gremlins and Does It Matter?

Exciting Games, Inc., is an organization that has been in business for about seven years. It got started by offering game machines to various amusement galleries, bars, restaurants, and other organizations. A game they recently put on the market is called "Death Race." For 25 cents the player of this television-screen game can drive a small automobile and attempt to run down as many pedestrians as possible in 75 seconds. Each time the player "scores" by striking a pedestrian, the machine lets out a loud shriek and a small grave marker appears on the screen at the point of contact. The object, of course, is to maximize the number of "deaths" in 75 seconds.

The National Safety Council has called the game a "sick, sick product that would only be played by someone with sadistic impulses." Management of Exciting Games, Inc., asserts that the pedestrians are meant to be "gremlins," not people, and that this therefore takes the game out of the questionable category in which the Safety Council puts it.

The "Death Race" game was brought to the National Safety Council's attention by a group of concerned parents in South Bend, Indiana, who learned that their children were playing the game at a local amusement gallery in the city.

QUESTIONS

1. Identify and discuss the social issues involved in this case. Is there a business and society issue at stake?

2. What, exactly, is the firm's social responsibility in this case? Has a violation of the modern social contract occurred here?

3. How would you, as management, respond to the National Safety Council's accusations?

Down Goes Central Avenue

Unionville is a beautiful southern town with many antebellum homes. The state university and several "clean" industries are the main employers in the area. Unionville is a study in contrasts. Many of its citizens work to preserve its lovely old homes and southern traditions. At the same time it is a fast-growing town. A main thoroughfare of Unionville is Central Avenue. Many of the town's most beautiful homes are located there. Some of these homes have been converted into service businesses and reception centers. Citizens have tried to save and maintain the homes on the street. Several hamburger stands have been built on Central Avenue, and the Planning Commission, in an effort to save the street, has recommended a change in the zoning of the avenue to preserve its beauty and character. Final action on this zoning change has not been taken by the City Council.

At one time the city high school was located on Central Avenue. A new school has since been built and the original building abandoned. The building itself is a handsome white structure with Corinthian columns. Many old oaks and magnolia trees are on the lot. Azaleas are everywhere.

The Unionville Board of Education has accepted an offer of $160,000 from Build-a-Better Burger, a fast-growing hamburger chain, to buy the old school grounds. Build-a-Better Burger sees this as an excellent location for its first store in Unionville. Several other sites are available in town, two of which are on the outskirts of the city, in shopping centers. But B-B-Burger bought the school property because its central location in a high traffic area would make its first Unionville outlet more successful.

When the sale became public knowledge, there was a loud outcry. Citizens voiced their objection to the destruction of the original school building and the desecration of Central Avenue.

QUESTIONS

1. Identify the pluralistic interest groups involved here.
2. Considering the pride Unionville has in Central Avenue, does Build-a-Better Burger have a social responsibility to the town and its citizens?
3. Does the Board of Education have a responsibility to the town regarding this piece of property?

4. The real estate broker representing B-B-Burger is a native of Unionville. As a member of the Planning Commission he has worked actively to preserve the beauty of the town. He showed Build-a-Better Burger several other locations that were available at a lower cost. Does the broker have any other social responsibility in this case?

TV Violence — An Environmental Hazard?

Violence on television has become a major issue. The national Parent-Teachers Association, the American Medical Association, the National Citizens Committee for Broadcasting, the National Council of Churches, and the Southern Baptist Convention have all mobilized against it. These organizations are mustering a lot of support for their position, and the business community is being forced to respect it.

The AMA's House of Delegates in June 1976 called television violence an "environmental hazard" to the health of children. The chairperson of the NCCB cited it as "having disastrous social consequences." A NCCB study ranking the most violent shows on television, and listing the companies that most often sponsor them, received wide publicity. In addition, figures compiled by the J. Walter Thompson advertising agency show that 35 percent of TV viewers avoid violent programs and, among people with family incomes of $20,000 or more, 10 percent had considered not buying a product advertised on these programs. Whether out of civic spirit or self-interest, many businesses (Procter and Gamble, General Foods, Kraft, Bristol-Myers, Johnson and Johnson, and others) will not sponsor programs they consider too violent.

Not all businesses are complying gracefully with the pressure for television pacification. Companies that think the people in their target market prefer to view the more action-packed programs are reluctant to withdraw their sponsorship. There is also concern about censorship, the ability of advertisers to use their economic muscle to determine the content of programming, and the right of viewers to watch violent programs if they so desire.

But while this pacification drive goes on, script writers are pressing for freedom to write more realistically and more explicitly about drug use, abortion, rape, homosexuality, and other "serious" issues. There is also the argument that "sanitizing" violence, by eliminating the bloody scenes and leaving them implied, makes violence unrealistically palatable to viewers and may thus encourage violent behavior.

The view has been expressed that companies are using their concern about violence as a ploy to lower the cost of the time slots in which violent shows are usually scheduled; these companies will be much less concerned, it is said, when they can buy that time more cheaply.

Advertisers often buy shows sight unseen. It is difficult for them to learn much in advance how violent the episodes they are to sponsor will be. Companies sometimes do withdraw their sponsorship of episodes they consider too violent, and replacements are found, but, as one advertising director said, "Not everyone can buy 'The Mary Tyler Moore Show.'"

QUESTIONS

1. What are the social issues involved in this case?
2. Identify the various pluralistic interest groups and summarize their positions.
3. What are the social responsibilities of the sponsors and the networks? Have we seen the social contract change over the years with respect to this issue?
4. What action should be taken?

Big Business Day

Ralph Nader and his allies in a labor–consumer coalition were responsible for planning and organizing the first Big Business Day — April 17, 1980. Business was not particularly excited about this planned festive occasion, for its sponsors really intended it to be a day to criticize business and dramatize "crime in the suites." One coalition observer hoped that Big Business Day would do for the giant corporations what Three Mile Island did for nuclear energy.

Mr. Nader said that the goal of Big Business Day was to focus attention on abuses by large corporations. He thinks that big businesses are not delivering what they're supposed to — a prosperous economy. Some of the activities of Big Business Day included teach-ins, mock trials of companies, and "Corporate Halls of Shame" in about 135 cities to spotlight corporate abuses.

Business did not take all this sitting down, though there was no uniform response. Some companies ignored it, but others made plans to fight back. One corporate executive lashed out at what he called the "anti-big business zealots and their new crusade." Some companies countered the criticism by publicizing the virtues of the free enterprise system. One company appointed a task force to study possible countermeasures. One economics professor argued that business ought to make its point by having a No Business Day on April 17, with businesses closing factories and offices to emphasize that corporations are essential but cannot perform if they are going to be continuously harassed.

Some have argued that big business unwittingly assisted the Nader-inspired coalition by its overkill. One purpose of Big Business Day was to promote support for the Corporate Democracy Act of 1980, a bill the coalition drafted that would make corporations more accountable to employees, consumers, and others. Companies have spent thousands to purchase $10 copies of the proposed bill from the coalition. Nobody anticipates that Congress will act on the bill any time soon.[1]

QUESTIONS

1. What does the whole idea of this Big Business Day tell you about the status of the business and society relationship at the beginning of the 1980s?
2. Is this pluralism in action? Discuss.
3. What is your assessment of a Big Business Day as a means of dramatizing business abuses? How do you appraise business's response?

---

[1]This case was inspired by the article by Stan Crock, "Every Dog Has Its Day, But Big Firms Gladly Would Skip Theirs," *The Wall Street Journal*, April 9, 1980, pp. 1, 35. Reprinted by permission of *The Wall Street Journal*, © Dow Jones & Company, Inc., 1980. All rights reserved.

From Social Responsibility to Social Responsiveness

Today, business is undergoing the most intense scrutiny it has ever received by the public. As a result of the many charges being leveled at it — charges that it has little concern for the consumer, cares nothing about the deteriorating social order, has no notion of acceptable ethical behavior, is indifferent to the problems of minorities and the environment — concern is increasingly expressed as to what responsibilities business has to the society in which it resides. We call this problem the social responsibility issue.

The basic issue can be framed in terms of two key questions: Does business have a social responsibility? If so, how much and what kinds? Though the questions seem simple and straightforward, answers to them are not readily forthcoming. What is particularly paradoxical is that large numbers of business people have enthusiastically embraced the concept of social responsibility during the past decade, but no consensus has emerged about what social responsibility really means.

In this chapter, therefore, we intend to explore a number of different facets of the social responsibility question, and provide some insights to the questions raised above. We say insights because the dynamics of social change preclude our obtaining general agreement for any extended period on answers to these questions. We are dedicating an entire chapter to the issue of social responsibility because it is a core concept that underlies most of our discussions in this book.

The topics we will examine in this chapter include:

- How did social responsibility become an issue?
- What is meant by social responsibility?
- A four-part definition of social responsibility
- Arguments for and against social responsibility
- Areas in which social responsibility exists
- From social responsibility to responsiveness
- The limits of social responsibility

THE SOCIAL RESPONSIBILITY ISSUE

Continuing with our general understanding of social responsibility as presented in Chapter 1, let us briefly trace how social responsibility became an issue. We will develop the arguments favoring and justifying it more fully later in the chapter.

The concept of business responsibility that prevailed in the United States during most of our history was fashioned after the traditional or classical *economic model*. Adam Smith's concept of the "invisible hand" was its major point of departure. The classical view held that a society could determine its needs and wants through the marketplace. If business simply responds to this demand, society will get what it wants. If business is rewarded, as it is in the competitive marketplace, on the basis of its ability to respond to the demands of the market, the self-interest pursuit of that reward will result in society getting what it wants. Thus, the "invisible hand" of the market converts self-interest into societal interest. Unfortunately, though the marketplace did a reasonable job in deciding what goods and services should be produced, it did not fare as well in ensuring that business always acted fairly and ethically.

At a later time, when laws began to proliferate to constrain business's behavior, it might be said that a *legal model* prevailed. Society's expectations of business changed from being strictly economic in nature to encompassing aspects that had been at business's discretion. We outlined a number of these laws in the previous chapter.

In practice, though business subscribed early to the economic emphasis and was willing to be subjected to an increasing number of laws imposed by society, the business community later did not fully live by the tenets of even these early conceptions of business responsibility. As James W. McKie observed, "The business community never has adhered with perfect fidelity to an ideologically pure version of its responsibilities, drawn from the classical conception of the enterprise in economic society, though many businessmen have firmly believed in the main tenets of that creed."[1]

There were at least three areas in which there was a modification of the classical formulation of the economic model in practice: philanthropy, community obligations, and paternalism.[2] There is evidence that even during periods characterized by the traditional view, business people did engage in philanthropy — contributions to charity and other worthy causes — and voluntary actions aimed at community improvement, beautification, and uplift. One example of this was the coopera-

---

[1]James W. McKie, "Changing Views," in *Social Responsibility and the Business Predicament* (Washington, D.C.: The Brookings Institution, 1974), p. 22.
[2]McKie, p. 22.

tion between the railroads and the YMCA immediately after the Civil War to provide community services in areas served by the railroads. Though, as one might observe, these services economically benefited the railroads, they nevertheless were philanthropic to a degree.[3]

There were many examples of paternalism during the latter part of the nineteenth century and even into the twentieth century. Paternalism appeared in many forms, one of the most visible being the company town. Though business's motives for beginning company towns (for example, the Pullman/Illinois experiment) were mixed, business had to do a considerable amount of the work in governing them. Thus, social responsibility was thrust upon the company.[4]

The emergence of large corporations during the late 1800s played a major role in hastening the movement away from the classical economic view. As society evolved from the economic structure of small, powerless firms primarily governed by the marketplace to large corporations in which power was concentrated, questions of responsibility to society surfaced.[5]

Though social responsibility had not fully developed in the 1920s, managers even then had a more positive view of their role. Community service was in the forefront — the most visible example of this was the Community Chest movement, which received impetus from business. Morrell Heald suggests that this was the first large-scale endeavor in which business leaders became involved with other nongovernmental community groups for a common, nonbusiness purpose, necessitating their contribution of time and money to community welfare projects.[6] Social responsibility, then, had received further broadening of its meaning.

The 1930s signaled a transition from a predominantly laissez-faire economy to a mixed economy, in which business found itself but one of the constituencies monitored by a more activist government. From this time well into the 1950s business's social responsibilities grew to include employee welfare (pension and insurance plans), concern for safety, medical care, retirement programs, and so on. McKie has suggested that these new "developments were spurred both by governmental compulsion and by an enlarged concept of business responsibility."[7]

The period from roughly the 1950s to the present may be considered part of the modern era in which the concept of social responsibility

---

[3]See Morrell Heald, *The Social Responsibilities of Business: Company and Community, 1900-1960* (Case Western Reserve University Press, 1970), pp. 12-14.
[4]McKie, p. 23.
[5]Ibid., p. 25.
[6]Heald, p. 119.
[7]McKie, pp. 27-28.

gained considerable acceptance and a broadening of meaning. During this time the emphasis moved from philanthropy to an awareness of social and moral duties to a period in which particular issues, such as urban decay and racial discrimination, were emphasized. The issue orientation then gave way to the more recent focus on social responsiveness, which we will discuss later in this chapter. But rather than attempt to recount all that occurred during this most socially turbulent period, we will wait until we have examined each of the areas in Parts II and III of this book — which, when taken together, enhance our understanding of what social responsibility has come to mean today in operational terms. First, however, we can expand the modern view of social responsibility by examining various definitions or understandings of the term that have prevailed in recent years.

SOCIAL RESPONSIBILITY: A NUMBER OF VIEWPOINTS

Let's now return to the basic question, "What does social responsibility really mean?" To this point we have been operating with Bauer's definition of social responsibility as presented in Chapter 1: "Social responsibility is seriously considering the impact of the company's actions on society." Though this definition has inherent frailties, we will find that most of the definitions presented by others also have weaknesses. Part of the difficulty in obtaining a definition on which we might get consensus is the problem of determining, operationally, what the definition implies for management. This poses an almost insurmountable problem because organizations vary in size, in the types of products they produce, in their profitability and resources, in their impact on society and so on. Since this is the case, the ways they all practice social responsibility will vary too.

One might ask, "Why is this so?" Are there not absolutes, areas in which all firms must be responsible? Yes, there are, and these are nearly equivalent to those items or expectations society has translated into legal aspects of the social contract. But as we will suggest here, social responsibility goes beyond simply (although it frequently is not so simple) abiding by the law. In the realm of activities over and above abiding by the law, the variables (size of the firm, etc.) become more relevant.

A second definition is worth looking at. Keith Davis and Robert Blomstrom define social responsibility as follows:

> Social responsibility is the obligation of decision makers to take ac-

tions which protect and improve the welfare of society as a whole along with their own interests.[8]

This definition is somewhat more pointed. It suggests two action aspects of social responsibility — protect and improve. To protect implies avoiding negative impacts on society. To improve implies creating positive benefits for society.

Like the first definition, the second contains a number of words that are perhaps unavoidably vague. For example, words from both definitions that might permit managers wide latitude in interpretation include *seriously, considering, protect, improve,* and *welfare of society.* The intention here is not to be critical of these good, general definitions, but rather to show that business people and others are quite legitimately confused when trying to translate the concept of social responsibility into practice.

A third definition, one by Joseph McGuire, is also quite general but, unlike the previous two, it places social responsibilities in context vis-a-vis economic and legal objectives. McGuire asserts:

> The idea of social responsibility supposes that the corporation has not only economic and legal obligations, but also certain responsibilities to society which extend beyond these obligations.[9]

Though this statement is not fully operational either, its attractiveness is that it acknowledges the primacy of economic objectives and the secondary importance of legal obligations while it also encompasses a broader conception of the firm's responsibilities.

A FOUR-PART DEFINITION
OF SOCIAL RESPONSIBILITY

At the risk of subjecting our own definition to the same sort of criticism, it is nevertheless time to set it forth. This four-part definition attempts to place economic and legal expectations of business in perspective by relating these concerns to more social concerns.[10] In a

---

[8]Keith Davis and Robert L. Blomstrom, *Business and Society: Environment and Responsibility,* 3rd ed. (New York: McGraw-Hill Book Company, 1975), p. 39.

[9]McGuire, p. 144.

[10]Archie B. Carroll, "Social Responsibility as an Objective of Business: Evolving Toward a Model of Corporate Social Performance," in William F. Glueck, *Business Policy: Strategy Formation and Management Action,* 3rd ed. (New York: McGraw-Hill Book Company, 1980), pp. 62-70. See also Archie B. Carroll, "A Three-Dimensional Conceptual Model of Corporate Social Performance," *Academy of Management Review,* October 1979, pp. 497-505.

sense, our definition, which includes four kinds of responsibility, builds upon the definition proposed by McGuire.

First, there are business's *economic responsibilities*. It may seem odd to call an economic responsibility a social responsibility, but this is, in effect, what it is. First and foremost the American social system calls for business to be an economic institution. That is, it should be one whose orientation is to produce goods and services that society wants and to sell them at a fair price — a price that society feels represents the value of goods and services delivered and that provides the business with adequate profit for its perpetuation, growth, and reward to its investors.

Second, there are business's *legal responsibilities*. Just as society has sanctioned our economic system by permitting business to assume the productive role mentioned above, as a partial fulfillment of the social contract, it has also laid down the ground rules — the laws — under which business is expected to operate. It is business's responsibility to society to comply with these laws. If business does not agree with laws that have been passed or are about to be passed, our society has provided a mechanism through the political process for dissenters to be heard.

Third, there are business's *ethical responsibilities*. Though the first two categories embody ethical norms, this area — called by many the grey area — involves behaviors and activities that are not embodied in law but still entail performance expected of business by society's members. This area is more amorphous; consequently, it is one of the most difficult areas for business to deal with. Because it is so important, we devote the entire next chapter of the book to it. Suffice it to mean for the moment, however, that ethical responsibilities are those areas in which society expects certain performance but which it has not yet been able to articulate in the form of laws.

Fourth, there are business's *discretionary responsibilities*. Perhaps it is a misnomer to call these responsibilities, for they are completely guided by business's discretion — it's choice or desire. These activities are purely voluntary, guided only by business's desire to engage in social activities that are not mandated, not required by law, and not generally expected of business in an ethical sense. These might include training the hard-core unemployed, giving to charitable causes, providing day-care centers for working mothers, and conducting in-house programs for drug abusers.

In essence, then, our definition forms a four-part social responsibility conceptualization that may be summarized as follows:

> The social responsibility of business encompasses the economic, legal, ethical, and discretionary expectations placed on organizations by society at a given point in time.

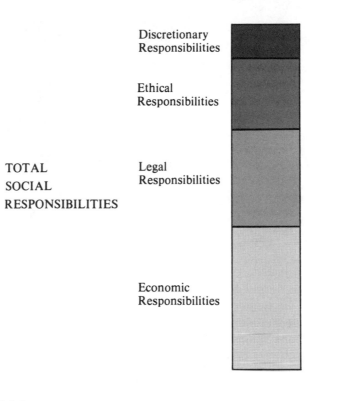

TOTAL
SOCIAL
RESPONSIBILITIES

Discretionary
Responsibilities

Ethical
Responsibilities

Legal
Responsibilities

Economic
Responsibilities

FIGURE 2-1
Social Responsibility Categories

SOURCE: Archie B. Carroll, ''A Three-Dimensional Conceptual Model of Corporate Social Performance,'' *Academy of Management Review,* October 1979, p. 499. Reprinted by permission.

This four-part definition, it is suggested, provides us with categories within which to place the various expectations that society has of business. With each of these categories considered as one facet of the total social responsibility of business, we have a conceptual model which more completely describes what society expects of business. One real advantage of the model is that it can accommodate those who have argued against social responsibility by characterizing an economic emphasis as separate and apart from a social emphasis. This model offers these two facets along with two others that collectively comprise social responsibility. Figure 2-1 depicts the model as it might appear when one superimposes it on a scale denoting all of the social responsibilities of business.

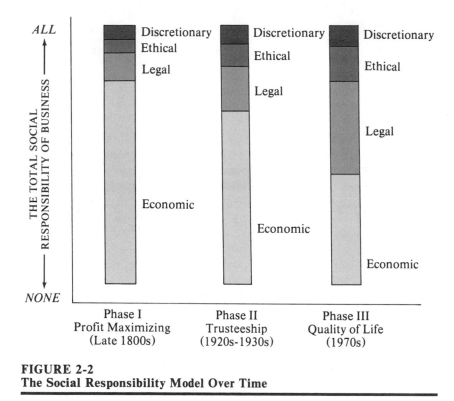

FIGURE 2-2
The Social Responsibility Model Over Time

Figure 2-2 depicts the model as it might have evolved from the late 1800s to today. The periods chosen represent what Robert Hay and Ed Gray have termed the three historical phases through which the social responsibilities of business managers have evolved.[11] These are the profit-maximizing management phase, the trusteeship management phase, and the quality-of-life management phase. The estimates of the influence of the various facets of social responsibility as seen in Figure 2-1 are not from Hay and Gray but are ours. They represent symbolic proportions rather than any empirical study of how these facets have evolved in relative importance. It should be stressed that the proportions shown in the pictorial model are intended only to illustrate the relative importance of the various facets at a point in time. As in all models, this one perhaps oversimplifies the interconnectedness of the facets, and indeed it should be noted that the four facets of the model are not mutually exclusive.

[11]Robert Hay and Ed Gray, "Social Responsibilities of Business Managers," *Academy of Management Journal*, vol. 17, no. 1 (March 1974).

Nor was the basic four-part model built completely independently of other efforts. For example, George Steiner presents a model that is similar in that it shows business's total social responsibilities ranging from traditional production efficiency; through government dictation and demands of outside groups, and met by business under presssure; through a voluntary area; and to expectations beyond reality.[12] In a similar vein but with a slightly different focus, Keith Davis and Robert Blomstrom suggest a widening circle of business responsibilities ranging from an inner circle representing the traditional economic responsibilities, through an intermediate circle representing responsibilities that arise from performance of basic functions, to an outer circle that suggests responsibilities for aid with general social problems.[13]

It is hoped that by using the four-part social responsibility model presented, the reader will have a more comprehensive and accurate view of all that is involved with the social responsibility concept. As we study the evolution of business's major areas of social concern, as presented in various chapters in Parts II and III of this book, we will indeed see how our model's four facets (economic, legal, ethical, and discretionary) provide us with a coherent framework for conceptualizing these issues. The social contract between business and society is to a large extent formulated from mutual understandings that exist in each area of our basic model. But it should be noted that the ethical and discretionary categories, taken together, more nearly capture the essence of what people generally mean today when they speak of social responsibility. Situating these two categories relative to the legal and economic obligations, however, keeps them in necessary perspective.

ARGUMENTS AGAINST AND FOR SOCIAL RESPONSIBILITY

In an effort to provide a balanced view of the corporate social responsibility issue, we should consider the arguments that have been raised against and for it. It should be stated at the outset, however, that those who argue against social responsibility are not using the comprehensive social responsibility model presented above in their considerations. Rather, it appears the critics are viewing social responsibility more narrowly — as only the efforts of the organization to pursue social, non-economic goals (our ethical and discretionary categories). It should also be stated that only a few business people or academics argue against the

[12]George A. Steiner, *Business and Society,* 2nd ed. (New York: Random House, 1975), p. 169.
[13]Davis and Blomstrom, pp. 7-8.

fundamental notion of social responsibility today. The debate among business people has more often centered on the *kinds* and *degree* of social responsibility, than on the basic question of whether business has it or not. As for academics, economists are probably the easiest group to single out as being against the pursuit of social goals, but even some economists no longer resist social responsibility on grounds of economic theory.

Arguments Against Social Responsibility

Nevertheless, let us look at the arguments that have surfaced over the years from the "anti" school of thought. Most notable has been the classical economic argument. This traditional view holds that management has one responsibility: to maximize the profits of its owners or shareholders. This classical economic school, led by economist Milton Friedman, argues that social matters are not the concern of business people and that these problems should be resolved by the unfettered workings of the free market system.[14] They hold, further, that if the free market cannot solve the social problem, then it falls upon government and legislation to do the job. Friedman softens his argument somewhat by his assertion that management is "to make as much money as possible while conforming to the basic rules of society, both those embodied in the law and those embodied in *ethical customs.*"[15] The latter part of this comment seems to leave room for broad interpretation. In any event, it is clear that the economic argument views social responsibility more narrowly than we have articulated it in our conceptual model.

A second major objection to social responsibility is that business is not equipped to handle social activities. This position holds that managers are oriented toward economics and production and do not have the necessary expertise (social skills) to make social decisions.[16] Closely related to this argument is a third: If managers were to pursue social responsibility vigorously, it would tend to dilute business's primary purpose.[17] The objection here is that social responsibility would put business into fields not related, as F. A. Hayek has stated, to their "proper aim."[18]

[14]Milton Friedman, "The Social Responsibility of Business Is to Increase Its Profits," *New York Times,* September 1962, sec. 6, p. 126.
[15]Ibid., p. 33 (emphasis added).
[16]Christopher D. Stone, *Where the Law Ends,* (New York: Harper Colophon Books, 1975), p. 77.
[17]Keith Davis, "The Case For and Against Business Assumption of Social Responsibilities," *Academy of Management Journal,* vol 16, no. 2 (June 1973), pp. 312-322.
[18]F. A. Hayek, "The Corporation in a Democratic Society: In Whose Interest Ought It and Will It Be Run?" in H. Ansoff (ed.), *Business Strategy* (Middlesex: Penguin, 1969), p. 225.

A fourth argument against social responsibility is that business already has enough power.[19] According to this view, business already has considerable power — economic, environmental, technological — so why should we place in its hands the opportunity to wield additional power? As it is, the influence of business permeates society. By giving to business decision-making opportunities in the social domain, would we not be aggravating the balance of power problem that already exists in our society?

One other argument that merits mention is that by pursuing social responsibilities we might be placing our business in a deleterious position in terms of international balance of payments. One consequence of being socially responsible is that business must internalize costs that it formerly passed on to society — in the form of dirty air, unsafe products, consequences of discrimination, and so on. The increase in the costs of products caused by including social considerations in the price structure would necessitate raising the price of products, making them less competitive in international markets. The net effect might be to dissipate the country's competitive advantages gained previously through technological advances.

Other arguments against social responsibility could be given, some of which were included in a study of managers' attitudes toward corporate social responsibility. Figure 2-3 presents some of these arguments and the importance attributed to them by both top managers and operating managers of Fortune 500 corporations. None of the arguments against social responsibility presented in this survey were viewed by business managers as being very important.

The arguments we have discussed constitute the principal claims made by those who oppose the social responsibility concept. Many of the reasons given appear quite rational. Value choices as to the type of society the citizenry would like to have become, at some point, part of the total social responsibility question. Let us now examine some of the main arguments given in favor of this concept.

Arguments for Social Responsibility

It is worthwhile to summarize Thomas Petit's statement as our point of departure in discussing support of the social responsibility doctrine. Petit synthesizes the thoughts of such intellectuals as Elton Mayo, Peter Drucker, Adolph Berle, and John Maynard Keynes. He asserts that though their ideas on this matter vary considerably, they agree on two fundamental points:

[19]Davis, p. 320.

In your opinion, how important are the following arguments against corporate social action or responsibility policies and programs?

Top Management ━━━━━

Operating Management ●●●●●●

Society is better advised to ask only that corporations maximize their efficiency and profits.

The costs of involvement in social problems will drive marginal firms out of business.

Corporate executives lack the perceptions, skills, and patience for solving society's problems.

Getting involved in solving social problems merely dilutes the primary strengths and purpose of business.

Spending money and time on social problems will drive up costs and hurt our exports.

Corporations have more than enough power now without also allowing them to remold society.

Corporations aren't held accountable to an electorate the way politicians are and therefore shouldn't start trying to transform society.

Since there is considerable disagreement among the public as to what should be done, corporations will be criticized no matter what is attempted.

Governments should merely pass the laws they want followed, not expect corporations to go beyond the law in solving society's problems.

If society wants to get corporations involved in solving its ills, the government should use tax incentives or subsidies to make it happen.

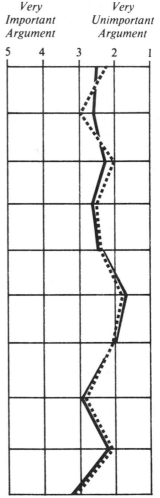

Very Important Argument		*Very Unimportant Argument*	
5	4	3	2	1

FIGURE 2-3
Survey of Arguments Against Corporate Social Responsibility

SOURCE: ©1977 by the Regents of the University of California. Reprinted from Lyman E. Ostlund, "Attitudes of Managers Toward Corporate Social Responsibility," *California Management Review,* vol. XIX, no. 4., p. 39, by permission of the Regents.

(1) Industrial society faces serious human and social problems brought on largely by the rise of the large corporation, and (2) managers must conduct the affairs of the corporation in ways to solve or at least ameliorate these problems.[20]

This generalized justificaton of social responsibility is appealing. It actually comes close to what we might suggest as a first argument for social responsibility — namely, that it is in business's long-range self-interest to be socially responsible. This argument provides an additional dimension by suggesting that it was partially business's fault that these social problems arose in the first place and that, consequently, business should assume a role in remedying past problems. It might be inferred from this that deterioration of the social condition must be halted if business is to survive and prosper in the future.

The long-range self-interest view is basically that if business is to have a healthy climate in which to exist in the future, it must take actions now that will ensure its longer-term viability. Perhaps the reasoning behind this is that society's expectations are such that if business does not respond on its own, its role in society may be altered by the public.

It is frequently difficult for managers who have a short-range orientation to appreciate that their rights and roles in the economic system are determined by society; that if they do not assume the roles that society desires over the long term, their charter to exist as they currently do may be in jeopardy. Business, in other words, must be responsive to society's expectations over the long term if it is to survive in its present or in a less restrained form. Davis and Blomstrom articulated this major concern in what they called the Iron Law of Responsibility: "In the long run, those who do not use power in a manner which society considers responsible will tend to lose it."[21] They argue that the position of business today could hardly be expected to continue unless it assumes its social responsibilities. Business would retort, of course, that it is "difficult to anticipate what socially responsible public opinion will demand next."[22] This is a valid objection, but it does not override the basic concern as already expressed.

Perhaps the most pragmatic reason for business's assuming social responsibility is to ward off future government intervention and regulation. There are numerous instances today of areas in which government

[20]Thomas A. Petit, *The Moral Crisis in Management* (New York: McGraw-Hill Book Company, 1967), p. 58.

[21]Keith Davis and Robert L. Blomstrom, *Business, Society, and Environment: Social Power and Social Responses,* 2nd ed. (New York: McGraw-Hill Book Company, 1971), p. 95.

[22]R. Joseph Monsen, *Business and the Changing Environment* (New York: McGraw-Hill Book Company, 1973), p. 111.

In your opinion, how important are the following arguments against corporate social action or responsibility policies and programs?

Top Management ▬▬▬
Operating Management ▪▪▪▪▪

	Very Important Argument		Very Unimportant Argument

It is in the long-run self-interest of the business to get directly involved in social issues.

Corporate social action programs create a favorable public image for the corporation.

Corporate social action programs will help preserve business as a viable institution in society.

Corporate social action programs help avoid more government regulation.

Society already expects companies to act.

Other institutions have failed, so business must now try.

Business has the necessary money and talent to engage in social action programs.

Solving social problems can be profitable.

It is better to start now and thereby prevent further social problems.

Making at least a token effort on social policies is wiser than holding out on principle.

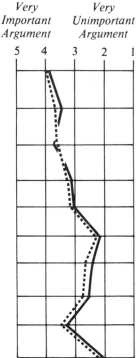

FIGURE 2-4
Arguments for Corporate Social Responsibility

SOURCE: ©1977 by the Regents of the University of California. Reprinted from Lyman E. Ostlund, "Attitudes of Managers Toward Corporate Social Responsibility," *California Management Review,* vol. XIX, no. 4, p.38, by permission of the Regents.

intruded with an expensive, elaborate regulatory apparatus to fill a void left by business's inaction. To the extent that business polices itself, with self-disciplined guidelines, future government intervention can be somewhat forestalled. We will discuss later some areas in which business could have prevented intervention and simultaneously ensured greater freedom in decision making had it imposed higher standards of behavior on itself.

Two arguments presented by Keith Davis deserve mention together: "Business has the resources," and "Let business try."[23] These two views maintain that because business has a reservoir of management talent, functional expertise, and capital, and because so many others

[23]Davis, p. 316.

have tried and failed to solve general social problems, business should be given a chance. These arguments have some merit, as there are some social problems that can be handled *only* in the final analysis, by business. Examples include avoiding discrimination, providing safe products, and engaging in fair advertising. Admittedly, government can and does assume a role in these areas, but business must make the final decisions.

One other view is that "proacting is better than reacting." This position holds that if business proacts (anticipates and initiates), this is a more practical and less costly posture than that of simply reacting to problems once they have developed. Environmental pollution is a good example of this, particularly business's experience with attempting to clean up rivers, lakes, and other waterways that were neglected for years. In the long run, it would have been wiser not to allow the environmental deterioration to occur in the first place.

Some of the other arguments that have been given in support of the social responsibility concept were included in the survey of Fortune 500 companies mentioned previously. Figure 2-4 presents these arguments and how they were viewed by the managers studied. It should be noted that the most important argument indicated was that it is in the long-term self-interest of business to get directly involved in social issues.

Many of the arguments presented are interconnected. Taken together they represent the bulk of public opinion today that business has responsibilities to society that exceed the traditional role business once played. Managers are assuming social responsibilities and are, at the same time, putting forth' their best public relations image. Business today is considered to be a multipurpose social institution, one that has more roles to assume than just that of the profit machine as viewed by many in the past.

AREAS OF SOCIAL RESPONSIBILITY

The question was posed earlier concerning the areas in which business has a social responsibility. Unfortunately, there are no current survey data that provide clear answers. It would be easy to suggest that business has a social responsibility in every area in which there exists a constituency that has some interaction with business. This answer would not be entirely wrong, either, for with each passing day we encounter vociferous exhortations by new protest groups, headlined demands in business periodicals and daily newspapers, and new government legislation.

Let us report in an evolutionary fashion some results of studies and surveys of recent years, keeping in mind that these areas seem to

---

EXHIBIT 2-1
Spectrum of Current Corporate Activities

Economic growth and efficiency	Education
Employment and training	Civil rights and equal opportunity
Urban renewal and development	Pollution abatement
Conservation and recreation	Culture and the arts
Medical care	Government

SOURCE: CED, *Social Responsibilities of Business Corporations* (New York: Committee for Economic Development, 1971), pp. 37-40. Used with permission.

expand and increase in number just as a stone tossed into a pond creates an ever-widening ripple effect. In a sense this analogy is not far from what has happened in the social responsibility arena.

The first item we will report that suggests areas in which business has a social responsibility comes from a landmark document published by the Committee for Economic Development (CED) in 1971. Most significantly, their *Social Responsibilities of Business Corporations* was put together by a group of business people — not protestors, not academics, not journalists. The CED posed a number of study questions, among which was: "What is the appropriate scope of corporate social involvement from the standpoint of management — considering the limitations of company resources, cost-benefit ratio, and good judgment about balancing the primary needs of the business with efforts to help improve social conditions?"[24]

In answer to their question they listed "the sorts of things being done by business in the aggregate," with the suggestion that individual companies must select those activities that they can most effectively pursue. Exhibit 2-1 summarizes the CED's list.

Several years later, John Corson and George Steiner conducted a wide-ranging survey for the CED in which they asked corporations to report those activities from the original CED list in which they had made "significant commitments of money and/or resource time."[25] Table 2-1 presents a summary of those activities companies indicated most frequently. This survey has to be viewed cautiously for, as Corson and Steiner point out:

> ... the list presumes that the corporation is meeting the consumers' demand for the safety and reliability of the product; it does not ask whether the company is recording and reporting the num-

[24]Committee for Economic Development, June 1971, p. 36.
[25]John J. Corson and George A. Steiner, *Measuring Business's Social Performance: The Corporate Social Audit* (New York: Committee for Economic Development, 1974), pp. 26-29.

TABLE 2-1
Social Responsibility Activities

The following is a rank-order listing of those activities which were noted *most frequently* to involve significant commitments of money and/or personnel time.

Rank*		Number of Responses
1	Ensuring employment and advancement opportunities for minorities.	244
2	Direct financial aid to schools, including scholarships, grants, and tuition refunds.	238
3	Active recruitment of the disadvantaged	199
4	Improvement of work/career opportunities.	191
5	Installation of modern pollution abatement equipment.	189
6	Increasing productivity in the private sector of the economy.	180
7	Direct financial support to art institutions and the performing arts.	177
8	Facilitating equality of results by continued training and other special programs (civil rights and equal opportunity).	176
9	Improving the innovativeness and performance of business management.	174
10	Engineering new facilities for minimum environmental effects.	169

*Rank 1 indicates highest commitment.

SOURCE: These data were summarized from information presented in John J. Corson and George A. Steiner, *Measuring Business's Social Performance: The Corporate Social Audit* (New York: Committee for Economic Development, 1974), pp. 27-29. Used with permission.

ber of products or service complaints received or potential liabilities ensuing from them.[26]

Corson and Steiner also mention some other assumptions that, to a certain extent, render the list of topic areas incomplete.

In another study, Henry Eilbirt and Robert Parket sought to determine the areas in which business recognized a social responsibility. They surveyed the extent to which firms were engaging in various activities and presented their data in a comparative fashion, juxtaposing larger firms with smaller firms. Their results are presented in Figure 2-5.

[26]Ibid., pp. 26-29.

Activity   Percent of Firms Engaged in Activity

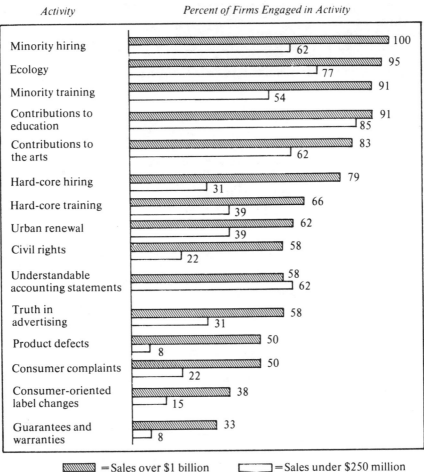

FIGURE 2-5
Comparison of Social Responsibility Activities

SOURCE: Henry Eilbirt and I. Robert Parket, "The Practice of Business: The Current Status of Corporate Social Responsibility," *Business Horizons,* August 1973, p. 11. Copyright, 1973, by the Foundation for the School of Business at Indiana University. Reprinted by permission.

In a more recent survey of executives in a number of different industries, the top five areas of social involvement of firms were identified.[27] Table 2-2 presents these top areas, classified according to industry.

[27]Sandra L. Holmes, "Adapting Corporate Structure for Social Responsiveness," *California Management Review,* Fall 1978, p. 51.

TABLE 2-2
Top Five Areas of Social Involvement Across Five Major Industrial Classifications

		INDUSTRY			
	Oil and Gas	*Finance, Insurance, and Real Estate*	*Wholesale and Retail*	*Manufacturing*	*Transportation, Communication, and Utilities*
Top five areas of social involvement within each major industrial group, in ranked order of importance	1. Pollution control	Charities	Community affairs	Charities	Charities
	2. Conservation of resources	Community affairs	Charities	Education	Recruitment/ development, racial/ ethnic minorities
	3. Education	Education	Recruitment/ development, females	Pollution control	Education
	4. Recruitment/ development, racial/ethnic minorities	Recruitment/ development, females	Recruitment/ development, racial/ethnic minorities	Recruitment/ development, racial/ethnic minorities	Community affairs
	5. Charities	Urban renewal and development	Consumer protection	Community affairs	Pollution control

SOURCE: ©1978 by the Regents of the University of California. Reprinted from Sandra L. Holmes, ''Adapting Corporate Structure for Social Responsiveness,'' *California Management Review*, vol. XXI, no. 1, p. 51, by permission of the Regents.

Note the variation in what constitutes the top areas of social concern depending upon the industry surveyed.

Finally, it is worth looking at what some managers think the future will hold for social responsibility issues. The American Management Association (AMA) surveyed 644 company presidents, asking them to indicate what the emerging priorities are among their companies' social responsibility programs. Table 2-3 reports the findings of this survey.

The inescapable conclusion from these managers' responses is that American business plans to do much more in its own back yard in the future. By this we mean that the executives expect the most increased activity in the following areas:

1. Response to changing aspirations of minority groups and female employees
2. Improvement of physical working conditions
3. Job enrichment programs
4. Better consumer relations
5. Increased employee participation in decision making

The sole purpose of these listings is to give the reader a sense of where thinking has been concerning business's social responsibilities. More inclusive lists could be created, but none would capture precisely and completely the pulse of where business, collectively, stands today. Our thinking about what constitutes the most significant areas of social responsibility is reflected in the choice of chapter topics in Parts II and III of this book, and we will speculate about where the concept of social responsiblity is heading in the last chapter. As the CED suggested, individual companies will decide which areas are most important to them as they examine factors relevant to them.

THE SOCIAL RESPONSIVENESS VIEW

We have discussed the evolution of social responsibility, a model for viewing social responsibility, the arguments for and against it, and examples of areas in which some companies think a social responsibility exists. It is now important to address a concern that has arisen in recent years over the use of the term *responsibility*.

The general argument that has been taking shape over the last five years or so states that the term responsibility is too suggestive of efforts to pinpoint accountability or obligation, and therefore is not dynamic enough to fully describe the social performance of business that resulted from whatever motivation stimulated business to act in the

TABLE 2-3
The Future Direction of Corporate Social Responsibility

What are the emerging priorities among your organization's social responsibility programs?

	Expect Increased Activity	Expect Decreased Activity	Expect to Remain about the Same	Does Not Apply
Reduction of damaging environmental effects	39%	4%	26%	32%
Improvement of physical working environments (OSHA, etc.)	55	2	36	7
Response to changing aspirations of minority groups and female employees	59	2	35	4
Increased employee participation in decision making	43	1	51	5
Employee "voluntarism programs" (sabbaticals, etc.)	21	2	48	29
Job enrichment programs	53	3	38	6
Product safety improvement	42	—	25	33
Better consumer relations	52	—	31	16
Truth in advertising/marketing	29	—	49	22
More purchasing from "minority vendors"	16	2	54	29
Improved relations with socially oriented investors (churches, universities, foundations, etc.)	16	1	47	36
Contributions to urban or community improvement	41	2	51	6
Support to education	37	2	55	6
Support to the arts	19	4	63	14
Support to other philanthropies	14	5	68	13
Other	76	—	24	—

SOURCE: Reprinted with permission from John L. Paluszek, *Business and Society: 1976-2000,* an AMA Survey Report (New York: AMACOM, a division of American Management Associations, 1976), p. 34.

first place. For example, Robert Ackerman and Raymond Bauer criticize the term by stating, "The connotation of 'responsibility' is that of the process of assuming an obligation. It places an emphasis on motivation rather than on performance." They go on to say, "Responding to social demands is much more than deciding what to do. There remains the management task of doing what one has decided to do, and this task is far from trivial."[28] They then argue that, as the title of their book suggests, "social responsiveness" is a more apt description of what is essential. Their point is well made. Responsibility, taken quite literally, does imply more of a state or condition of having assumed an obligation, whereas responsiveness connotes a dynamic — action-oriented — condition. It should not be overlooked, however, that much of what business has done and is doing has resulted from a particular motivation — an assumption of obligation — whether *assigned* it by government, *forced* on it by special interest groups, or *voluntarily* assumed. Perhaps business, in some instances, has failed to accept and internalize the obligation, and thus it may seem strange to refer to it as a responsibility. Nevertheless, some motivation had to be there that led to social responsiveness, even though, in some cases, it was not admitted to be a responsibility or obligation.

S. Prakash Sethi takes a slightly different, but related path in getting from social responsibility to social responsiveness. He proposes a three-stage schema for classifying corporate behavior in responding to social or societal needs: social obligation, social responsibility, and social responsiveness.

Social *obligation,* Sethi argues, is corporate behavior in response to market forces or legal constraints. Corporate legitimacy is very narrow here, and is based on legal and economic criteria only. Social *responsibility,* Sethi suggests, "implies bringing corporate behavior up to a level where it is congruent with the prevailing social norms, values, and expectations."[29] He argues that whereas the concept of social obligation is proscriptive in nature, social responsibility is prescriptive in nature. Social *responsiveness,* the third stage in his schema, suggests that what is important is "not how corporations should respond to social pressure, but what should be their long-run role in a dynamic social system."[30] He suggests that here business is expected to be "anticipatory" and "preventive." It should be noted that his obligation and responsibility categories embody essentially the same message we were attempting to convey with our four-part conceptual model.

To summarize the evolution from social responsibility to social responsiveness, it is useful to present a conceptualization set forth by Patrick Murphy. He suggested that the evolution of corporate social responsibility moved through four eras: philanthropic, awareness, issue, and responsiveness. Table 2-4 summarizes these eras and their

[28]Robert Ackerman and Raymond Bauer, *Corporate Social Responsiveness: The Modern Dilemma* (Reston, Va: Reston Publishing Company, 1976), p. 6.

[29]S. Prakash Sethi, "Dimensions of Corporate Social Performance: An Analytical Framework," *California Management Review,* Spring 1975, pp. 58-64.

[30]Ibid., pp. 62-63.

TABLE 2-4
Corporate Social Responsibility Eras

Era	Dates	Primary Characteristics
Philanthropic	To early 1950s	Concentration on charitable donations
Awareness	1953-1967	Recognition of overall responsibility
		Involvement in community affairs
Issue	1968-1973	Concern about urban decay
		Correction of racial discrimination
		Alleviation of pollution problems
		Assessment of the social impact of technology
Responsiveness	1974-present	Alteration of boards of directors
		Examination of ethics and corporate behavior
		Utilization of social performance disclosures

SOURCE: Patrick E. Murphy, "An Evolution: Corporate Social Responsiveness," *University of Michigan Business Review,* November 1978, p. 20. Reprinted by permission.

primary characteristics. Though our description of the responsiveness era departs somewhat from Murphy's statement of primary characteristics, his depiction of these periods is very helpful as a summary of one point of view.

The Managerial View Again

Both the Ackerman and Bauer position and the Sethi position highlight some very fundamental points regarding moving social responsibility into the action sphere. This author, too, attempted to suggest this same movement with the title of his earlier book, *Managing Corporate Social Responsiblity,*[31] and, indeed, that is the theme picked up and carried through the present volume. In the earlier volume, for example, it was argued that what is important is

> how social responsibility considerations *impacted management* and how *management was responding* to accommodate the increasing number of social expectations emanating from various environmental sectors.[32]

---

[31]Archie B. Carroll (ed.), *Managing Corporate Social Responsibility* (Boston: Little, Brown and Company, 1977).
[32]Ibid., p. v.

The social responsiveness issue, then, argues for a managerial posture as we outlined briefly in Chapter 1. It stems from the premise that business does assume a social role in society, and it addresses ways business might more adequately ascertain what this role is, what it ought to be, and how it might be achieved. If there is any dominant thread of continuity or emphasis that should be assumed to run through this book, this is it. In the meantime, we will not haggle over whether we should use the term *social responsibility, social responsiveness,* or, as some have suggested, *social performance.* We will assume that we are concerned with diagnosis, anticipation, prevention and action as we use these various terms throughout the volume.

LIMITS OF SOCIAL RESPONSIBILITY

Though we have argued in this chapter in favor of social responsibility — or at least have been biased toward it — there are, indeed, limits to social responsibility. We should add at this point that we are referring to special parts of social responsibility as portrayed in the social responsibility model — not the entire model. To repeat, when most people speak of social responsibility, they are speaking of either (1) the legal, ethical, and discretionary parts of our model (excluding economic, as that is presumed to be an economic and not a social responsibility), or (2) the ethical and discretionary parts of the model (again excluding economic, and also excluding legal because it is obligatory).

Though we prefer the first understanding because it includes the legal facet — and though actions are required by law, they still frequently possess an ethical dimension (letter versus spirit of the law) — the present discussion of the limits of social responsibility best relates to the second interpretation. This is because more general debate has surrounded business's delving into ethical and discretionary activities, with questions always being asked about how business can legitimize its behavior in these nonprofit or nonrequired realms.

The main reason questions are raised about the limits of social responsibility is that a firm's management could conceivably use a leadership position to aggressively pursue social problems and, consequently, permit the organization to erode and lose economic viability through neglect. Such an event is highly unlikely, however, and cannot be said to have occurred in any but the most remote cases, if at all.

It must be constantly reiterated that the major function of business is economic, and care must be taken to ensure that the firm's basic survival or minimum profitability requirements are not violated. As Peter Drucker articulates this, the manager's ". . . first task is to make the institution . . . perform the function and make the contribution for the sake of which it exists."[33] Stated another way, Drucker argues: "Performance of its function is the institution's first social responsibility."[34] It should be noted that this latter quote is perfectly consistent with the spirit of the social responsibility model presented earlier.

Without question the business firm must draw limits on its social responsibilities, just as any individual must draw limits on how much time and money to give to social causes in the community. On the other hand, it is increasingly imperative if the corporate form of business organization is to survive that it not repeatedly seek its legitimacy by attending only to the wishes of its stockholders. As Neil Chamberlain asserts about business:

> Less and less it can rest its claim to power on a fictional stockholder election; more and more it is forced to seek legitimacy by demonstrating its responsiveness to its publics . . .[35]

In conclusion, though we acknowledge limits to social responsibility which derive from necessity for survival, maintenance of profits, competition, and other cost-benefit calculations, the business firm must set aside its narrowly conceived role of the past and recognize the convergence between economic and social orientations that inevitably transpires in a modern society.

SUMMARY

The issue of social responsibility has become important partially because of the intense scrutiny business has been getting in recent years. Society now expects more of business than it once did. Not only is business expected to fulfill its economic role and comply with legal and regulatory mandates, it is expected to be responsive to ethical concerns as well. Beyond this, business has discretionary responsibilities that extend into the purely voluntary realm of social behavior and deeds. Taken together, these four kinds of responsibilities — economic, legal, ethical, and discretionary — comprise a comprehensive definition of social responsibility.

The four can also be viewed as constituting a conceptual model, which has changed over time. During the profit-maximizing phase, the

---

[33]Peter F. Drucker, *Management: Tasks, Responsibilities, Practices* (New York: Harper and Row, Publishers, 1974), Chapter 26, "The Limits of Social Responsibility," p. 343.
[34]Ibid.
[35]Neil W. Chamberlain, *The Limits of Corporate Responsibility* (New York: Basic Books, 1973), p. 204.

economic responsibility dominated and the other three were less important. In the trusteeship phase, the legal, ethical, and discretionary components grew in importance. This same trend continues into the present-day quality-of-life phase. In modern times we place heavy emphasis on legal, ethical, and discretionary responsibilities, while still acknowledging the primacy of economic viability.

A brief review of the arguments for and against social responsibility (viewed primarily as ethical and discretionary responsibilties) revealed some interesting stances. The arguments against the concept included (1) the classical economic argument, (2) that business is not equipped to handle social activities, (3) that it would dilute business's primary purpose, (4) that business already has enough power, and (5) a predicted deleterious impact on the international balance of payments. Arguments for the concept included (1) that it is in business's long-range self-interest, (2) that society expects it, (3) that it can ward off future government regulation, (4) that business has the resources, (5) that it is time to let business try, and (6) that proacting is better than reacting.

Surveys have shown a multitude of areas in which business has been or should be exercising its social responsibilities. Perhaps the most important today include consumer issues, discrimination, environmental protection, culture and the arts, product safety, and concern for the individual.

Though we have concentrated on social responsibility, the modern concern is with social responsiveness as well. This focus suggests that the action phase, that of management and the organization putting into practice its concern for the social environment, is of utmost importance. This represents the managerial view.

Our orientation in this chapter and throughout this book is of business responding to society. It must be constantly reiterated, however, that the major function of business is economic and that a firm's basic survival or minimum profitability requirements cannot be sacrificed; thus, business must place limits on its social responsibilities. At the same time, business must set aside its narrowly conceived role of the past and recognize that the convergence between economic and social orientations undergirds its continuing legitimacy as an institution. When this enlightened view prevails, business *and* society will be the ultimate benefactors.

QUESTIONS FOR DISCUSSION

1. Discuss the significance of the following: "The business community never has adhered with perfect fidelity to an ideologically pure

version of its responsibilities, drawn from the classical conception of the enterprise . . .''

2. Summarize, from a historical perspective, how social responsibility became important.

3. Define *social responsibility*. Be sure you understand the major features of each definition presented in the chapter.

4. Give examples of ways business can protect and improve the welfare of society, and yet benefit itself.

5. Give examples of each part of the four-part social responsibility model presented.

6. Summarize the common arguments in favor of social responsibility. What understanding of social responsibility is being used in the presentation of these arguments? Which argument do you think is most powerful?

7. What are the major arguments against social responsiblity? Rank in order of importance the arguments as you see them.

8. Does Friedman's quote concerning ''those embodied in ethical norms'' seem to contradict his basic profit argument? Discuss.

9. Does it make sense to you that ''proacting is better than reacting''? Is this always the case? Give illustrations of your answer.

10. Carefully examine the list of social responsibilities presented by the CED in Figure 2-3. Which seem most appropriate and which most inappropriate? Give your reasons.

11. What is your analysis of the social responsibilities reported in Figure 2-4? Do you note any significant patterns among the items? Discuss.

12. Differentiate between social responsibility and social responsiveness. How is each related to the managerial view?

Cases

Bar the Candy Bar

Action for Children's Television, a public-interest organization, filed a petition with the Federal Trade Commission (FTC) stating that many candy commercials contain misleading information about candy nutrition and that advertised sweets can cause tooth decay, but that children under twelve lack the sophistication to realize it. The petition asks the FTC to bar television commercials aimed at selling candy to children. The organization also filed individual complaints against four leading candy makers.

The group cites as precedent an FTC consent order in which Hudson Pharmaceutical Corporation agreed to stop advertising their Spider-Man vitamins in comic books or on TV programs aimed at children. The FTC charged that such advertising could persuade children to believe "the endorsed product has qualities and characteristics it doesn't have" and induce them to take "excessive amounts of vitamins."[1]

QUESTIONS

1. What are the social issues involved in this case?
2. What are the social responsibilities of the individual firms and the FTC in this case? Do any of their social responsibilities conflict?
3. What response should be made by these two groups?

The Blue Skies Airlines

After forty years as a regional carrier, Blue Skies had finally gone transcontinental. The Civil Aeronautics Board (CAB) had just approved their application for a new, very lucrative route connecting Los Angeles and Miami. In addition, there were high hopes of getting another long-haul route between Seattle and Tokyo.

Along with the good news, however, came the bad news: The Blue Skies operations manager announced that in light of the new developments, their aging Boeing 727s and 707s should be replaced as soon as possible. The main reason for the urgency of the replacement decision was the fact that there was fierce competition for the new routes, demanding the upgrading of the company's fleet.

Competing bids were received from various aircraft manufacturers. After careful evaluation of the engineering specifications and the financial terms that each bid offered, Blue Skies management narrowed the field to two jet airliners: the European Airbus A300 and the McDonnell-Douglas DC10.

The Airbus is produced by Airbus Industries, which is 50 percent owned by a French manufacturer and 50 percent by West German companies. The plane is assembled in France, while the fuselage is built in Germany, the tail in Spain, and the wings in Britain. The DC10, which is manufactured entirely in the United States, is a tri-engine jet seating about 254; the Airbus is a twin-engine seating 230. The fact that the European airplane had only two engines suggested reduced

---

[1]From "Bar to TV Ads for Candy Aimed at Children Asked," *The Wall Street Journal*, April 7, 1977, p. 24. Reprinted by permission of *The Wall Street Journal*, © Dow Jones & Company, Inc., 1977. All rights reserved.

maintenance costs, as well as simplified maintenance procedures and schedules. In addition, the Airbus's price was $7 million below the DC10's, and it was offered under more favorable financial terms.

At the time, it was understood that the board of directors of Blue Skies favored the Airbus option. Several powerful union leaders, however, approached the company and demanded that Blue Skies "buy American" and thus protect thousands of jobs.

QUESTIONS

1. As a company spokesman, how would you respond?
2. How many claimants can you identify in this situation?
3. A Blue Skies director held a press conference during which he argued: "After all, the United States has sold lots of planes to the Germans and the French, so why shouldn't we buy some from them?" How do you react to this statement? Was the press conference advisable?
4. As chairman of the board of a corporation, would you see "buying American" as a strictly social responsibility, above financial considerations? Why or why not?
5. What kind(s) of social responsibility does the company have in this case? Economic? Legal? Ethical? Discretionary?

Power's Profits or Consumers' Pockets?

In December of 1976, Georgia Power Company and thirteen other Atlanta businesses each contributed $25,000 to help save the Atlanta Flames hockey team. This action by Georgia Power was protested by those who felt that power consumers were being made to pay for the company's generosity.

Georgia Power stated that the Flames contribution was taken out of company profits and was paid by stockholders at the rate of about 0.02 of a cent per share and, furthermore, that the ratepayers were not penalized by the donation. The company also maintained that without financial support the team would have to fold, resulting in a loss of jobs and revenue. It has been estimated that every dollar paid in salaries to Atlantans is turned over six times before it leaves Atlanta.

QUESTIONS

1. What responsibility, if any, has Georgia Power for the continued financial well-being of the Flames and other area businesses?

2. Do you believe Georgia Power's contention that ratepayers were not affected by this action?
3. What exactly are the company's social responsibilities in this case?
4. What would be Georgia Power's proper course of action?

A Legal Race?

Ron Smith retired at thirty-two as a millionaire. His hobbies included speed-boat racing. This hobby and a desire to win led him into the manufacture of the world's fastest racing boats. His handcrafted boats reach speeds in excess of 90 mph and sell for $100,000 and up.

The quality of Ron's boats and their reputation for speed have led to a large portion of the boats being purchased by narcotics smugglers in the Gulf of Mexico. Ron knows this. He says he has "mixed emotions" about his boats being used by criminals. He feels that it hurts his reputation that the underworld is using his boats, which they call "grasshoppers." He adds, however, that it is good business when law enforcement agencies also buy the boats. "If the law breakers go fast, so must the law enforcers."

QUESTIONS

1. Is there an issue of social responsibility in this case? Explain.
2. Should Ron be required by law not to sell his boats to smugglers?

Business Ethics and Management

The evidence is clear that the ethics of business people are, once again, on the minds of everyone. We say once again because the past several decades have been marked by an ebb and flow of interest in business ethics. In the modern period, the interest in business ethics was stimulated by the 1960 electrical conspiracy cases in which a number of electrical equipment manufacturers were indicted for alleged conspiracy to fix prices and restrict competition for the sale of their equipment. The following year, the United States Secretary of Commerce formed a Business Ethics Advisory Council, which had as its objective the voluntary improvement of business conduct.

The year 1961 was also the year Raymond Baumhart published his now classic work, "How Ethical Are Businessmen?"[1] Though his survey of 1,700 *Harvard Business Review* readers did not indicate a prevalence of unethical practices in the private sector, executives did admit and point out numerous generally accepted practices in their industries which they considered unethical.

A number of books and articles on the subject of business ethics were published in the middle and late 1960s, but preoccupation with ethical behavior did not set in again until Watergate and its aftermath. Since that time a profusion of headline stories has suggested a near obsession with the ethical behavior of business people. Several headlines illustrate: "Corruption in the U.S.: Do They ALL Do It?" "After Watergate: Putting Business Ethics in Perspective," "Watergate as a Case Study in Management," "Stiffer Rules for Business Ethics," and "Bribery and Slush Spur Ethics Courses at Business Schools."

Because of renewed interest in corporate and managerial behavior in the wake of Watergate and ensuing scandals, such as the Equity Funding fraud, corporate payoffs and bribes abroad, illegal campaign slush funds and contributions and, even, the General Services Administra-

---

[1]Raymond C. Baumhart, "How Ethical Are Businessmen?" *Harvard Business Review,* July-August 1961, p. 6ff.

tion fraud in government, we must address careful attention to this vital topic. Most of the issues discussed in this book have an ethical dimension, so our examination here should help us understand all of them more fully.

In this chapter, then, we will examine the nature of ethics in business, its consequences for business organizations, and some of the ways business people can learn to manage business ethics. Specifically, we intend to cover the following topics:

- Business ethics versus social responsibility
- What is meant by business ethics?
- What is the current state of business ethics?
- The source of a manager's values
- Managing business ethics

Though the topic of business ethics can hardly be dealt with as it should be in so short a space, we hope the coverage provided will help to clarify the issue and its ramifications for modern business organizations and society.

BUSINESS ETHICS VERSUS SOCIAL RESPONSIBILITY

One of the first issues we need to address is the distinction between business ethics and social responsibility. These two terms are frequently used interchangeably, and a few words of clarification are needed. Because each concerns the appropriateness of business behavior, it is impossible to completely separate the two concepts. Social responsibility issues do, indeed, have an ethical dimension to them. Both social responsibility issues and ethics involve what *ought* to be done by business.

The distinction we are making here for discussion purposes hinges on whether we are primarily addressing organizational concerns (corporate social responsibility) or individual concerns (business or managerial ethics). This separation is not as neat and clean as we would like it to be. We all know that a firm's social responsibility posture stems from the position its key managers take, and it is therefore a corporate policy, position, or philosophy only because individuals have made it so. Nevertheless, we propose to draw a distinction between social responsibility as primarily a corporate or organizational phenomenon, and business ethics as primarily the concern of the individual business decision maker. (Technically, it is impossible to enforce this distinction, but it is a fairly common one in the literature.)

BUSINESS ETHICS: ITS MEANING

When we speak of business ethics we refer to the rightness and wrongness of the behavior or actions of people who work in business organizations. It becomes immediately obvious why questions of business ethics are so difficult to deal with. Questions arise such as "Who determines what is right or wrong?" "Are there degrees of right?" "Are there degrees of wrong?"

Unfortunately, we can raise the questions but cannot provide clear answers. If we recall our definition of social responsibility offered in Chapter 2, specifically in the four-part model, we can conclude that ethical behavior is that kind of behavior *expected* by society or specific groups, over and above legal requirements. That still is not the whole solution, but it does narrow our focus somewhat. If society in general had a clear concept of appropriate business behavior, we would have an answer. That, unfortunately, is not the case.

When decisions are made about what is ethical (right), there is room for variability on several counts (see Figure 3-1). Three key elements go into the decision. First, we have the behavior or act that has been committed. Second, we compare the act with prevailing norms of acceptability — that is, society's standards of what is right or wrong. Third, we must recognize that *value judgments* are being made by someone as to what really occurred (the actual behavior) and what society's norms of acceptability really are. What this means is that two different

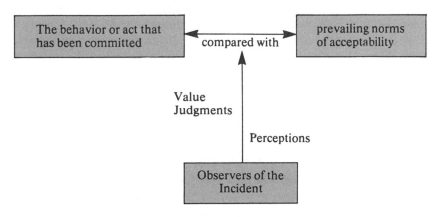

FIGURE 3-1
Elements that Go into the Determination of Ethics

persons may look at the same behavior, compare it with their concept of what society's norms are, and reach different conclusions as to whether the behavior was ethical or not. This becomes quite complex as perceptions of what is ethical inevitably lead to the difficult task of ranking different values against one another.

If we can put aside for a moment the fact that perceptual differences about an incident do exist, and the fact that we differ among ourselves because of our personal philosophies of right and wrong, we are still left with the problematical task of determining society's prevailing norms of acceptability of business behavior. As a whole, members of society generally agree at a very high level of abstraction that certain behaviors are wrong, but the consensus tends to disintegrate as we move from abstract to specific situations.

Let us illustrate with a business example. We might all agree with the general dictum that "You should not steal someone else's property." At a high level of abstraction (as a general precept) we would have consensus on this. But as we look at specific questions our consensus tends to disappear: Is it acceptable to take pencils home from work? Pens? Paper clips? Paper? Staplers? Adding machines? Calculators? Is it acceptable to use the company telephone for personal calls? Long distance? Is it acceptable to use company gasoline for private use? Pad expense accounts? What if everyone else is doing it?

What is interesting in this example is that we would likely get more consensus in principle than in practice: a number of people who would say these practices are not acceptable would privately engage in them. Furthermore, a person who would not think of shoplifting even the smallest of items from a local store would take pencils and paper home from work on a regular basis. A recent cartoon of the "Born Loser" is related to this discussion. In the first panel the father admonishes his son Wilberforce in the following way: "You know how I feel about stealing. Now tomorrow I want you to return every one of those pencils to school." In the second panel, Father says to Wilberforce, "I'll bring you all the pencils you need from work."

Determinations of what is ethical and what is not, then, involve judgments being made on three counts:

1. What is the true nature of the event, act, or decision that occurred?
2. What are society's prevailing norms of acceptability?
3. What value judgments are being made by someone about the event, and what are that person's perceptions of society's norms?

Thus, the human factor in the situation introduces the problem of perception and values.

Other Definitions

We have given an initial definition of business ethics and discussed the major variables that go into the making of ethical judgments. Now let us present two other definitions that are helpful. The first is a general definition of ethics and the second personalizes ethics to the business situation.

Clarence Walton, who has studied business ethics quite extensively, offers:

1. Ethics involves critical analysis of human acts to determine their rightness and wrongness in terms of two major criteria: truth and justice.
2. Business ethics extends the range of criteria whereby human actions are judged to include such things as societal expectations, fair competition, the aesthetics of advertising and the use of public relations, the meaning of social responsibilities, reconciling corporate behavior at home with behavior abroad, the extent of consumer sovereignty, the relevance of corporate size, the handling of communications, and the like.[2]

Walton's first definition is somewhat more pointed than our earlier one in that it specifies criteria of judgment by which critical analysis is to be guided. Those two criteria in their broadest interpretation truly embrace most of the behaviors on which judgment must be made. Several illustrations are helpful. Listed below are several behaviors that might be examined for their ethicalness by the criterion of *truth.*

- Falsifying time/quality/quantity reports
- Claiming credit for someone else's work
- Calling in sick to take a day off
- Concealing one's errors

Below are several behaviors that might appropriately be examined for their ethicalness by the criterion of *justice.*

- Pilfering company materials and supplies
- Using company services for personal use
- Accepting gifts/favors in exchange for preferential treatment
- Doing personal business on company time[3]

---

[2]Clarence C. Walton (ed.), *The Ethics of Corporate Conduct* (Englewood Cliffs, N.J.: Prentice-Hall, 1977), p. 6.
[3]This list of behaviors comes from John W. Newstrom and William A. Ruch, "The Ethics of Management and the Management of Ethics," *MSU Business Topics,* Winter 1975, p. 31.

In some instances, of course, the criteria of both truth and justice apply. These two concepts are employed quite often by philosophers. In business situations, as Walton's second definition suggests, the range of criteria may be extended to encompass those specific considerations mentioned. His second definition particularizes the first to the business predicament and is, as a result, a better working definition.

No definition of business ethics, unfortunately, captures the essence of all that is important in examining this critical issue. From our social responsibility model presented earlier, keep in mind that we are talking about behavior, acts, and decisions that exceed those required by law. Though it may be somewhat unclear as to how far, exactly, good ethics requires one to go, the principle is clear. The philosophy expressed by Caterpillar Tractor Company in its code of *Worldwide Business Conduct* supports this view.

> The law is a floor. Ethical business conduct should normally exist at a level well above the minimum required by law.[4]

Nevertheless, well-intentioned managers still have considerable difficulty reaching consensus on precisely what that level of conduct should be. This dilemma is what makes the study of business ethics fascinating to the observer of the business scene, although quite frustrating to those who are on the firing line every day.

THE CURRENT STATE OF BUSINESS ETHICS

If one makes judgments about the current state of business ethics based on reading daily newspapers, business news magazines, or watching "60 Minutes" on television, the conclusion might quickly be reached that it is in a shambles and that behind every business door an evil-minded individual is lurking.

It is true that we are hearing today unprecedented reports of bad business ethics — or lack of business ethics — in the private sector. The questions that should be raised, however, are whether business's ethics have really deteriorated; whether the media are simply reporting scandal more frequently and vividly than before; or whether it is society that is really changing, so that once-accepted practices are now considered unacceptable by the public.

Many business managers subscribe to this third hypothesis. W. Michael Blumenthal, former United States Secretary of the Treasury

---

[4]Cited in Walton, p. 5.

and chief executive officer of the Bendix Corporation, for example, is one of the leading advocates of this third view. He argues:

> It seems to me that the root causes of the questionable and illegal corporate activities that have come to light recently . . . can be traced to the sweeping changes that have taken place in our society and throughout the world and to the unwillingness of many in business to adjust to these changes.[5]

He goes on to say:

> People in business have not suddenly become immoral. What has changed are the contexts in which corporate decisions are made, the demands that are being made on business, and the nature of what is considered proper corporate conduct.[6]

Though it would be difficult to prove Blumenthal's thesis, it is attractive. One does not have to investigate some of today's business practices long to realize that a good number of what are now called unethical practices are ones that were at one time acceptable. Or, it may be that they never really were acceptable to the public but that, since they were not known, they were tolerated and caused no moral dilemma for the public.

The second question we raised was whether the media are reporting ethical problems more vigorously than before. There is no doubt that this is true. Spurred on by Watergate and the post-Watergate moral climate, the media have found in business ethics — and, indeed, ethics questions among all institutions — a subject of sustaining interest.

The first question we raised was whether business's ethics have really deteriorated. Unfortunately there is no scientific way to determine this. Max Ways' description of a statistical analysis (the twentieth century's favorite kind of investigation) aimed at answering the question, "How widespread is corporate misconduct?" is enlightening. He says that to describe such a project would demonstrate its impossibility. He argues that the researcher would have to count the trangressions publicly exposed in a certain period of time. Then the total of known misdeeds would have to be correlated with the trillions and trillions of business transactions that occur daily. He concludes:

> If we assume (recklessly) that a believable estimate of total transactions could be made, then the sum of the publicly known malfeasances almost certainly would be a minute fraction of the whole. At

---

[5]From Michael Blumenthal, "Business Morality Has Not Deteriorated — Society Has Changed," *The New York Times,* January 9, 1977. ®1977 by The New York Times Company. Reprinted by permission.
[6]Ibid.

this point the investigator would have to abandon the conclusion that the incidence of business misconduct is so low as to be insignificant.[7]

In fact, no such study has ever been attempted. The closest one might come to research into the current state of business ethics might be the public opinion polls, which show a decline in the level of public confidence in business's ethics. If one looks at surveys of business managers themselves, asking whether their ethics are better now than in the past, one gets divided results. Let us look at the question raised by the author in his 1975 survey of managers. Presented to a random sample of 400 managers, 238 of whom responded (59 percent response rate), was the proposition below; the results are also shown:[8]

Proposition: Business ethics today are far superior to ethics of earlier periods.

Response	No.	Percent
Disagree	60	25.2
Somewhat disagree	52	21.8
Somewhat agree	78	32.8
Agree	48	20.2
Totals	238	100.0

It should be noted that 47 percent disagreed and 53 percent agreed with this proposition.

Steven Brenner and Earl Molander in a 1977 study asked somewhat the same question in a different way. Their study was of *Harvard Business Review* readers. Five thousand were surveyed and 1,227 responded — a 25 percent response rate. Their question was:

How do you feel ethical standards in business today compare with ethical standards 15 years ago?

The respondents split fairly evenly as follows:[9]

Standards are lower	32%
Standards are about the same	41%
Standards are higher	27%
Total	100%

In both of these studies we see an almost even split between those who feel today's business ethics are lower or higher than those of the

[7]Max Ways, "A Plea for Perspective," in Walton, p. 108.
[8]Archie B. Carroll, "Managerial Ethics: A Post-Watergate View," *Business Horizons,* April 1975, pp. 75-80.
[9]Steven N. Brenner and Earl A. Molander, "Is the Ethics of Business Changing?" *Harvard Business Review,* January-February 1977, pp. 57-71.

past. The disagreement suggests the kind of response one would get if the nation's football fans were asked who would win a football game between the current Super Bowl champs and the Green Bay Packers under the leadership of the late Vince Lombardi. Any response is speculative, emotional, highly judgmental, and, in the final analysis, simply not verifiable.

In sum, it seems safest to conclude that (1) we have no real evidence that business ethics today are lower than in the past, (2) media exposure probably results in business's transgressions getting more coverage than in the past, and (3) society's concept of what is acceptable behavior on the part of business has become more demanding in recent times.

The subject of business ethics is on the minds of managers, employees, and the public alike, and thus constitutes an extremely significant dimension of the relationship between business and society.

SOURCE OF A MANAGER'S VALUES

Ethics and values are intimately related. We referred earlier to ethics as the rightness or wrongness of behavior. More precisely, ethics is the set of moral principles or values that drives behavior. Thus, the rightness or wrongness of behavior really turns out to be a manifestation of the ethical beliefs held by the individual. Values, on the other hand, are the individual's concepts of the relative worth, utility, or importance of certain ideas. Values reflect what the individual considers important in the large scheme of things. One's values, therefore, shape one's ethics. Since this is so, it is important to understand the many different value-shaping forces that influence managers.

The increasing pluralism of the society in which we live has exposed managers to a large number of kinds of values (concepts of relative worth or importance), and this has resulted in ethical diversity. We can examine the source of a manager's values by considering both forces that come from outside the organization to shape or influence the manager and those that emanate from within the organization. This, unfortunately, is not as simply done as we would like, for some sources are difficult to pinpoint. It should lend some order to our discussion, however.

External Forces

By external forces we refer to those broad sociocultural values that have evolved in society over a long period of time. Though current events (kickbacks, fraud, bribery cases) seem to affect these historic values by bringing specific ones into clearer focus at a given time, these values are rather enduring and change slowly.

George Steiner has stated that "every executive is the center of a web of values" and that there are five principal repositories of values influencing business people. These five include religious, philosophical, cultural, legal, and professional values.[10]

Religion has long been a basic source of morality in American society, as in most societies. Religion and morality are so intertwined that William Barclay relates them for definitional purposes: "Ethics is the bit of religion that tells us how we ought to behave."[11] The biblical tradition of Judeo-Christian theology forms the core for much of what we believe today about the importance of work, the concept of fairness, and the dignity of the individual.[12]

Philosophy and various philosophical systems are also an external source of the manager's values. Beginning with preachments of the ancient Greeks, philosophers have claimed to demonstrate that reason can provide us with the principles of morals in the same way it gives us the principles of mathematics. John Locke argued that morals are mathematically demonstrable, though he never explained how.[13] Aristotle with his golden rule and doctrine of the mean, Kant with his categorical imperative, Bentham with his pain and pleasure calculus, and modern-day existentialists have shown us time and again the input of various kinds of reason to ethical choice.

Culture, that broad synthesis of societal norms and values emanating from everyday living, has also had an impact on the manager's thinking. The melting-pot culture of the United States is a potpourri of norms, customs, and rules that defy summarization.

The *legal* system has been and continues to be one of the most powerful forces defining what is ethical and what is not for managers. This is true even though (as we stated earlier) ethical behavior is that which is over and above legal dictates. The law represents the codification of what the society considers right and wrong. Though we as members of society do not completely agree with every law in existence, there is typically more consensus for law than for ethics. Law, then, "mirrors the ideas of the entire society."[14] Law represents a minimum ethic of

[10]George A. Steiner, *Business and Society* (New York: Random House, 1975), p. 226.

[11]William Barclay, *Ethics in a Permissive Society* (New York: Harper and Row, Publishers, 1971), p. 13.

[12]For a more complete discussion of values see Gerald F. Cavanagh, *American Values in Transition* (Englewood Cliffs, N.J.: Prentice-Hall, 1976).

[13]Marvin Fox, "The Theistic Bases of Ethics," in Robert Bartels (ed.), *Ethics in Business* (Columbus, Ohio: Bureau of Business Research, Ohio State University, 1963), pp. 86-87.

[14]Carl D. Fulda, "The Legal Basis of Ethics," in Bartels, pp. 43-50.

behavior but does not encompass all the ethical standards of behavior. Law addresses only the grossest of violations of society's sense of right and wrong, and thus is not adequate to completely describe all that is acceptable or unacceptable. Since it represents our official, consensus ethic, however, its influence is most persuasive.

Professional values are those emanating, for the most part, from professional organizations and societies that represent various jobs and positions. As such, they presumably articulate the ethical consensus of leaders of those professions. For example, the Public Relations Society of America has a code of ethics which public relations executives have imposed upon themselves as their own guide to behavior. The National Association of Realtors adopted its "Rules of Conduct" in 1913. Compliance with the code was first recommended for voluntary adoption and then made a condition of membership in 1924.[15] Professional values thus exert a more particularized impact on the manager than the four broader values discussed.

In addition to Steiner's five values, there is another classification of values that deserves mention. This is the set of six kinds of values orientation identified by Edward Spranger, a German philosopher. First, there is the *theoretical* man, who is primarily oriented toward the discovery of truth and the systematic ordering of his knowledge. Second, there is the *economic* man, whose focus is on what's useful — the practical affairs of the business world. Third, there is the *aesthetic* man, whose chief interest is in the artistic aspects of life. He values form and harmony. Fourth, there is the *social* man, who loves people — the altruistic or philanthropic aspect of love. Fifth, there is the *political* man, characteristically oriented toward power, not necessarily in politics. And, finally, there is the *religious* man, one "whose mental structure is permanently directed to the creation of the highest and absolutely satisfying value experience."[16]

Spranger's classification of values served as the theoretical underpinning for a study conducted by William Guth and Renato Tagiuri. They sought to measure, quantitatively, the relative strength of each of the six value orientations in an individual. Using a select group of high-level executives in the United States as their sample, they obtained the following average value profile (values ranked according to their strength within the individual):[17]

---

[15]H. Jackson Pontius, "Commentary on Code of Ethics of National Association of Realtors," in Ivan Hill (ed.), *The Ethical Basis of Economic Freedom* (Chapel Hill, N.C.: American Viewpoint, 1976), p. 353.

[16]*Types of Men*, translated by P. Pigors (Halle, Germany, 1928).

[17]William D. Guth and Renato Tagiuri, "Personal Values and Corporate Strategy," *Harvard Business Review*, September-October 1965, pp. 123-132.

Value	Score
Economic	45
Theoretical	44
Political	44
Religious	39
Aesthetic	35
Social	33

It is interesting to note that economic and political values rank in the top three, and religious, aesthetic, and social values are placed lower. The usefulness of this ranking is that it gives us an average profile of managers' values and thus helps to explain why managers are the way they are when they must act and make decisions.

It should also be noted that the values of executives, on the average, are different from those of persons in other professions. A sample of ministers, for example, ranked the values in the following order of decreasing importance: religious, social, aesthetic, political, theoretical, and economic.[18]

In sum, a number of external sources of values bear on the manager. In addition to those mentioned, the manager is influenced by family, friends, acquaintances, and social events of the day. The manager thus comes to the workplace with a personal philosophy that is truly a composite of numerous interacting values that have shaped his or her view of the world, life, and business.

Internal Forces

The external forces — broad social values and existing attitudes — described above constitute the broad background or milieu against which the manager or employee behaves or acts. They affect the person's personal view of the world and business and help to formulate what is acceptable and unacceptable. There are, however, a number of less remote factors that help to channel the individual's behavior, and these grow out of the specific organizational experience itself. These internal (within the business organization) forces constitute more immediate and direct influences on one's behavior and decisions.

When one joins an organization — goes to work for an organization — a socialization process takes place in which the individual assumes the predominant values in that organization. The individual learns rather

[18]Adapted from G. W. Allport, P. E. Vernon, and G. Lindzey, *Manual for the Study of Values* (Boston: Houghton-Mifflin Company, 1960), p. 14.

quickly that to survive and to succeed, certain norms must be perpetuated and revered. There are a number of norms that are prevalent in business organizations, including respect for the authority structure, loyalty, conformity, and performance (results).

Each of these factors can assume a major role in a person who subordinates his or her own concept of ethics to those of the organization. In fact, it will be suggested here that these internal forces play a much more significant role in shaping business ethics than the host of external forces we considered first.

The authority structure, loyalty, conformity, and performance results have been historically almost synonymous with survival and success in business. When these concepts are operating together they form a composite ethic which is extremely persuasive in its impact on individual and group behavior. These values form the central motif of organizational activity and direction.

Underlying the other three is the focus on results. Carl Madden referred to this as the "calculus of the bottom line."[19] One does not need to study business organizations for long to recognize that the bottom line — profits — is the sacred value that seems to take precedence over all others. "Profits now" rather than later seems to be the orientation that spells success for managers and employees alike. Respect for authority, loyalty, and conformity become means to an end — though one could certainly find organizations and people who see these as legitimate ends in themselves.

Let us examine two research efforts that suggest that some of these concerns, particularly the hierarchical authority relationship, assume an important place in determining ethical behavior in organizations. The thesis basically is that it is the local organizational environment and especially the superior-subordinate relationship that shape the modern business person's ethical standards and behavior. Also at the core of the issue are the different understandings and perceptions that the various levels of management have about ethical questions.[20] Though it is difficult to prove this causality link, there is evidence to suggest that such a hypothesis is plausible.

Two findings, in particular, from the research survey conducted by the author suggest the importance of hierarchy.[21] In a national study conducted soon after the Watergate incident, the author surveyed managers in an effort to ascertain the validity of certain current ideas concerning the relationship between business ethics and political ethics.

[19]Carl Madden, "Forces Which Influence Ethical Behavior," in Walton, pp. 31-78.
[20]Archie B. Carroll, "Linking Business Ethics to Behavior in Organizations," *S.A.M. Advanced Management Journal,* Summer 1978, pp. 4-11.
[21]Carroll, *Business Horizons,* April 1975, pp. 77-79.

The questionnaires went to 400 managers chosen from various levels of management, and were designed to elicit responses indicating the extend of a respondent's agreement or disagreement with selected propositions. Of the 400 questionnaires sent, 238 were completed and returned. Two of the ten propositions tested are pertinent here, and the results of each item suggest a hierarchical pattern of response.

The first proposition and response were as follows:[22]

Proposition 1: Managers today feel under pressure to compromise personal standards to achieve company goals.

Response	No.	Percent
Disagree	58	24.6
Somewhat disagree	26	11.0
Somewhat agree	102	43.2
Agree	50	21.2
Total	236	100.0

It is insightful to consider the management level of the 64.4 percent (43.2 + 21.2) who agreed with the proposition. The results are:

Top management	50% agreed
Middle management	65% agreed
Lower management	85% agreed

Notice the pattern: the lower the respondents were in the organization, the more they tended to feel that "managers today feel under pressure to compromise personal standards to achieve company goals."

The second proposition and response in the Carroll study were as follows:[23]

Proposition 2: The junior members of Nixon's reelection committee who confessed that they went along with their bosses to show their loyalty did just what young managers would have done in business.

Response	No.	Percent
Disagree	58	24.6
Somewhat disagree	38	16.1
Somewhat agree	84	35.6
Agree	56	23.7
Total	236	100.0

[22]Ibid., p. 77.
[23]Ibid., p. 78.

In examining the 59.3 percent of respondents who agreed with this proposition, by management level, we find a response pattern similar to the first:

Top management	37% agreed
Middle management	61% agreed
Lower management	85% agreed

In each case we see that the lower the respondents were in the managerial hierarchy, the more they perceived ethical problems as prevalent. There were other propositions that suggested this same pattern of response. For another example: "I can conceive of a situation where you have sound ethics running from top to bottom but, because of pressures from the top to achieve results, the person down the line compromises." The pattern of findings on this proposition was similar to the other two.

What is particularly troublesome about these findings is the pattern of response. It seems that the lower one is in the hierarchy, the more one perceives pressures toward unethical conduct. Though there are a number of plausible explanations for this phenomenon, one explanation seems particularly attractive because of its agreement with conversations the author has had with a number of different managers. This interpretation is that top-level managers just do not know how strongly their subordinates feel pressures to go along with their bosses. These differing perceptions at different levels in the managerial hierarchy suggest that higher-level managers may not be tuned in to how pressure is received at lower levels. There seems to be a gap in the understanding of higher managers and lower managers regarding the pressures toward unethical behavior that exist, especially in the lower echelons. This breakdown in understanding, or lack of sensitivity by top management to how far subordinates will go to please them, can be conducive to lower-level subordinates behaving unethically out of a real or perceived fear of reprisal, misguided sense of loyalty, or distorted concept of the job.

Supporting this view that the superior-subordinate relationship is at the core of much unethical behavior are the findings by Brenner and Molander in their survey of 1,227 *Harvard Business Review* readers. They conclude that

> . . . relations with superiors are the primary category of ethical conflict. Respondents frequently complained of superiors' pressure to support incorrect views, sign false documents, overlook superiors' wrongdoing, and do business with superiors' friends.[24]

[24]Brenner and Molander, p. 68.

Though the above citations do not represent an exhaustive search of the literature, they do point in the direction of hierarchy being implicated as a source of ethical problems today. If managers are at the core of the problem, as data suggest they are, this constitutes a useful point of departure for discussing actions managers can take to effectively address this problem, which has serious implications for organizations and society at large.

MANAGING BUSINESS ETHICS

It has been widely assumed for years that ethics are personal, that they cannot be legislated, and that ethics cannot be managed. Starting from our reasoning that many ethical problems evolve out of the superior-subordinate relationship, in particular, and the organizational environment, in general, it seems logical that there are some actions that can be taken by managers to improve both their own ethics and the ethics of their subordinates.

It is useful to suggest a model that can aid our thinking about the various levels on which the ethics problem can be addressed. We can suggest actions on at least five increasingly comprehensive levels that can be taken to improve ethical behavior. Figure 3-2 diagrams these levels.[25]

First, there is the level of the *individual*, for questions of ethics ultimately reside with the individual decision maker. The second (moving toward more inclusive systems) is the level of the *organization*. The third level is that of *associations* — groups of organizations that have banded together for mutual benefit. Next is the *societal* level. Last, action can be taken at the *international* level to improve business ethics. As we move from the smallest unit of analysis — the individual — to the largest — the international environment — it becomes increasingly difficult to pinpoint actions managers can take that will affect business ethics. It is worthwhile, however, to look more closely at management actions that can be employed at each of these five levels. Our primary focus will be on the first three levels because this is where management is more apt to be effective in bringing about improved behavior.

Individual Level

By individual level we are suggesting that individuals as persons, whether they are managers or nonmanagers, can take certain steps to

[25]Much of this material is taken from Carroll, *S.A.M. Advanced Management Journal,* Summer 1978, pp. 6-11.

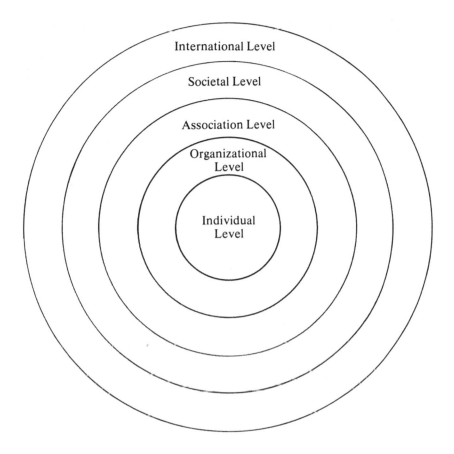

FIGURE 3-2
Levels at Which the Improvement of Business Ethics Can Be Addressed

SOURCE: Reprinted with permission from Archie B. Carroll, "Linking Business Ethics to Behavior in Organizations," *S.A.M. Advanced Management Journal,* Summer 1978 (New York: S.A.M., a division of American Management Associations, 1978), p. 7.

improve the quality of their own behavior. To do this they can pose certain tests for their behavior which will raise questions individuals should ask before engaging in an action. One's answers to the questions should help determine the ethicalness of the behavior and/or its advisability.

Test of Common Sense. Here the individual simply asks, "Does the action I am getting ready to take make sense?" When one thinks of behavior that may have ethical implications, it is logical to consider the practical consequences. If one would surely be caught doing a questionable practice, for instance, the act does not meet this test.

Will the Action Hurt Someone? Here the individual simply poses the question to help illuminate the impact the action will have on others. It should lead one to assess the degree and the kinds of negative impact the action would have on someone else.

Test of One's Best Self. Each person has a self-concept. As a decision or act is being considered, this test would have you question whether it is compatible with your concept of yourself at your best. If it is not, the act is questionable.

Test of Making Something Public. This is one of the most powerful tests. If you are getting ready to do something that is questionable, ask: "How would I feel if others knew I was doing it?" This questions whether your actions can withstand public scrutiny.[26] In a recent survey of over 500 managers on whether legislation would stop bribes abroad, most felt that publicity (public exposure) would be more effective. Arjay Miller, former president of Ford, has called this the Watergate TV test.

Test of Ventilation. This asks whether an idea or a proposed action can hold up under exposure to others' views and criticisms. This test suggests that you should not isolate yourself with your dilemma but seek other views; you should talk with others about a proposed action before engaging in it.

Beware of the Purified Idea. Do not let your superior's values or judgment or that of a lawyer or accountant be the final arbiter of what is right and wrong. An idea or action is not sanctified or purified simply because someone else knows about it or says it is appropriate. If you look hard enough you can always find a lawyer or CPA who will endorse almost any idea or plan if it is worded in just the right way. The idea or action may still be questionable even though someone has said it is permissible.[27]

The Gag Test. This test was provided by Judge Peter Beer of the Louisiana Court of Appeals. He asserted that as a manager your clearest signal that a dubious assignment is going too far is when you simply gag at the prospect of carrying it out.[28]

None of these tests alone offers a perfect way to question the ethical-

---

[26]Gordon L. Lippitt, *The Leader Looks at Ethics,* pp. 12-13.
[27]"Stiffer Rules for Business Ethics," *Business Week,* March 30, 1974, p. 88.
[28]Frederick Andrews, "Corporate Ethics: Talks with a Trace of Robber Baron," *New York Times,* April 18, 1977, sec. C, pp. 49-52.

ness of a decision or act. If several are used together, especially the more powerful ones, they do provide a means for examining proposed actions before engaging in them. This assumes, however, that the person really wants to do what is right and is looking for assistance; to the fundamentally unethical person, on the other hand, these tests would not be of much value.

Organizational Level

This is the level at which managers are best able to influence business ethics. By taking specific actions here, managers can shape the environment in which others are often most tempted to do something unethical. It is because of specific organizational misdeeds that the current interest in ethics has become so pronounced. What, then, can be done at this level? Let us discuss some major strategies or actions that should be considered.

Provide Leadership from the Top. It has become almost a cliche but it must be established at the outset: The moral tone of an organization is set by top management. This is true because all managers and employees look to the highest level for their cues as to what is acceptable. Top management is in the best position to establish the pattern of behavior, decisions, and actions. All formal organizational activities are derivative from those taken at the top.

Stressing the point that top management assumes a vital role, L. W. Foy, chairman of Bethlehem Steel Corporation, has asserted that

> It is a primary responsibility of business management to instruct, motivate, and inspire their employees to conduct themselves with honesty, probity, and fairness. Starting at the top, management has to set an example for all the others to follow.[29]

Top management, through its capacity to set a personal example and to shape policy, is in the ideal position to provide a highly visible role model. The authority and ability to shape policy — both formal and implied — forms one of the vital characteristics of the leader's job in any organization. An illustration of a manager who set the wrong kind of example will make this point clear.

In one of his consulting experiences, the author encountered a situation in a small company where a long-time employee was identified as having embezzled about $20,000.00 over a fifteen-year period. When approached and questioned as to why she had done this, she explained that she thought it was all right because the president had led her to be-

[29]L. W. Foy, "Business Ethics: A Reappraisal," Distinguished Leaders Lecture Series, Columbia University Graduate School of Business, January 30, 1975, p. 2.

lieve it was. She further explained that any time during the fall when the leaves had fallen and he needed them raked, he would simply get company personnel to do it. When the president needed cash, he would take it out of the company's petty cash box or get the key to the soft drink machine and raid its coin box. When he needed stamps to mail his personal Christmas cards, he would just take them out of the company stamp box. The woman's perception was that it was all right for her to take the money because the president did it frequently. Therefore, she felt it was an acceptable practice for her![30]

This is a vivid example of how the leader's actions and behavior become implied policy for others in the organization. In the absence of knowing what to do, some employees look to the leader's behavior for their cues as to acceptable conduct.

In other decision and policy situations management also has the chance to articulate good ethical standards and conduct. Four recommendations by Lee Morgan, president and chief operating officer of Caterpillar Tractor Company, illustrate this point. Morgan suggests the following actions for top management:

1. Create clear and concise policies that define its business ethics and conduct.
2. Select for employment only those people and firms whose character and ethics appear to be in keeping with corporate standards.
3. Promote people on the basis of performance and ethical conduct and beliefs.
4. Company personnel must feel the obligation and the opportunity to report perceived irregularities in ethics or in accounting transactions.[31]

Thus, management has at its disposal a number of methods for exercising leadership in creating a sound ethical climate. Fred Allen, chairman and president of Pitney-Bowes, Inc., summarizes this point well: "It is up to the leader to make sure that ethical behavior permeates the entire company."[32] Ethical policy in organizations must be clearly and systematically established at the top, for if it is not, it will be set haphazardly as the need arises lower in the organization.

Set Realistic Objectives. Closely related to leadership being exercised

[30]Archie B. Carroll, "Business Ethics and the Management Hierarchy," *National Forum: The Phi Kappa Phi Journal,* Summer 1978, p. 39.
[31]Lee L. Morgan, "Business Ethics Start with the Individual," *Management Accounting,* March 1977, pp. 14, 60.
[32]Fred T. Allen, "Corporate Morality: Is the Price Too High?" *Wall Street Journal,* October 17, 1975, p. 16.

from the top is the necessity that managers at all levels set objectives or goals that are realistic. A manager may quite innocently and inadvertently create a condition leading to unethical behavior on a subordinate's part. Take the case of a marketing manager setting a sales goal of a 25 percent increase for next year when a 15 percent increase is all that could be realistically expected, even with outstanding performance. In the absence of clearly established and communicated ethical norms, it is easy to see how a subordinate might feel that he should go to any lengths to achieve the 25 percent goal. With the goal having been set too high, the salesperson faced a situation that is conducive to unethical behavior in order to please the superior.

Fred Allen reinforces this point:

> Top management must establish sales and profit goals that are realistic-goals that can be achieved with current business practices. Under the pressure of unrealistic goals, otherwise responsible subordinates will often take the attitude that "anything goes" in order to comply with the chief executives' target.[33]

The point here is that there are ethical implications to even the most routine managerial decisions, such as goal setting. Managers must be keenly sensitive to the possibility of innocently creating situations in which others may perceive a need or an incentive to do the wrong thing.

Establish Codes of Ethics. One of the classic suggestions in discussions of business ethics is that one establish a code of ethics or a code of conduct. A recent survey of business suggests that most codes of ethics were issued or revised in the past decade or so. Table 3-1 presents a summary of dates a number of such codes were issued or revised. Codes of ethics have been abused by many organizations. One of the primary forms of abuse is that they seem to be enforced only after a major ethical scandal, rather than being employed on a regular basis.[34]

Codes of ethics are usually employed on the level of either the organization or the industry. Organization or company codes are of interest to us here. When we discuss the association (third) level, we will look more closely at industrywide codes. Though some have suggested that there is a need for business in general to have a uniform code of ethics,[35] attention has centered around company and industry codes.

The purpose of a company (internal) code of ethics is to demonstrate to all organization members general ethical precepts to guide decision

---

[33]Ibid.

[34]"How Companies React to the Ethics Crisis," *Business Week,* February 9, 1976, p. 79.

[35]See, for example, Paul L. Wilkins, "The Case for Ethical Absolutes in Business," *Business and Society Review,* Spring 1975, pp. 61-63.

TABLE 3-1
Year Codes Were Issued or Revised

Year	Aggregate		BUSINESS SECTOR Top Industrials		Other Industrials		Non-Industrials	
	%	N	%	N	%	N	%	N
1978-1979	8.4	(10)	2.9	(1)	7.7	(4)	15.2	(5)
1977	10.9	(13)	20.6	(7)	7.7	(4)	6.1	(2)
1976	2.9	(51)	50.0	(17)	55.8	(29)	15.2	(5)
1975	9.2	(11)	8.8	(3)	5.8	(3)	15.2	(5)
1970-1974	10.9	(13)	2.9	(1)	9.6	(5)	21.2	(7)
1969 or earlier	1.7	(2)	—		—		6.1	(2)
	84.0	(100)	85.3	(29)	86.5	(45)	78.8	(26)
Not dated	16.0	(19)	14.7	(5)	13.5	(7)	21.2	(7)
Totals	100.0	(119)	100.0	(34)	100.0	(52)	100.0	(33)

SOURCE: Donald R. Cressey and Charles A. Moore, *Corporation Codes of Ethical Conduct,* A Report to the Peat, Marwick and Mitchell Foundation; February 1, 1980, p. 7. Reprinted by permission.

making and behavior. Exhibit 3-1 illustrates what one business management hopes to communicate to its employees in a code of ethics. It is the letter from the chairman of the board to Standard Oil of California employees promulgating the company's conduct principles and practices.

Codes of ethics can be quite general or very specific. Research tends to show that managers prefer general codes to specific ones.[36] General codes are less valuable from the standpoint of answering questions about specific behavior. Specific codes, on the other hand, can overly constrain people, and probably never are specific enough to handle every contingency that arises.

There have been both success and failure reported with organizational codes of ethics, but the acid test seems to be to make them "living documents," not just platitudinous public relations statements that are put into a file drawer upon dissemination. As Theodore Purcell has noted, "Ethical codes are no panacea . . . but they help to clarify ethical thinking and to encourage ethical behavior."[37] Wallace Booth, presi-

[36]Brenner and Molander, p. 66.
[37]Theodore V. Purcell, "A Practical Guide to Ethics in Business," *Business and Society Review,* Spring 1975, pp. 43-50.

EXHIBIT 3-1
Standard Oil Code of Ethics

TO ALL EMPLOYEES:

Over the years, Standard Oil Company of California employees have established a record of unexcelled integrity in their business conduct and relationships. This exemplary record is fundamental to the Company's reputation for doing business worldwide in a fair and honest way. The business reputation of our employees and the Company is one of the most valuable assets we have and should be a source of pride to all those who helped achieve it. We value this reputation, and it is management's intention to ensure that it is maintained — even improved — in the years ahead.

The concept of corporate responsibility is by no means new to us as a Company, but in view of recent publicity about questionable payments by other corporations and increased public concern over business ethics, we believe it is timely to review, restate and draw together our major Company policies in this area. This booklet, which summarizes the Company's policies on specific issues related to business conduct, reaffirms our continuing commitment to integrity as our way of doing business.

It is, of course, the policy of the Company for all employees to comply fully with the law at all times in their conduct of the Company's business. However, the policy of the Company goes beyond this. Our business should be conducted not only in compliance with the legal rules, but voluntarily in accordance with the highest standards of business integrity and honest dealing. While community standards of ethics may vary at different times and different places, the strict standards of honesty and integrity are a basic and continuing cornerstone of our business in all areas and functions and at all times.

Company management takes the matter of corporate responsibility and business ethics very seriously, and it is our policy to foster cooperative and forthright relationships with employees, shareholders, dealers, suppliers, unions, local communities, customers and governments. Our Company realizes that its longterm success depends, to an important degree, on its responsiveness to society's evolving needs and expectations, to the creation of a climate of trust in our business dealings and to a work environment for its employees which assumes high ethical standards of conduct.

While management recognizes its obligation to establish and monitor standards of conduct for the entire organization, and to carry out its own responsibilities in a manner beyond reproach, all employees share this responsibility. The Company desires to create an environment that encourages and rewards individual initiative and achievement, not only in results, but also in how they are achieved. In the final analysis, the ethical conduct of a corporation depends on the understanding, judgment and actions of its employees. All employees are asked to review their respective roles in light of the principles set forth in this booklet and to give their full cooperation in conducting themselves according to the high standards expected by our Company.

Harold J. Haynes
Chairman of the Board
April 20, 1979

SOURCE: Reprinted by permission of Chevron U.S.A., Inc. (Standard Oil Company of California).

TABLE 3-2
Policy Areas Discussed in Codes of Ethics[a]

Policy Area	Aggregate	
	%	N
A. Conduct on behalf of the firm		
1. Relations with U. S. governments[b]	76.7	(89)
2. Relations with customers/suppliers	75.0	(87)
3. Employee relations	52.6	(61)
4. Relations with competitors	50.0	(58)
5. Relations with foreign governments	42.2	(49)
6. Relations with investing public	41.4	(48)
7. Civic and community affairs	34.5	(40)
8. Third-party commercial transactions[c]	26.7	(31)
9. Environmental affairs	19.8	(23)
10. Host country commercial relations	12.1	(14)
11. Other	2.6	(3)
B. Conduct against the firm		
1. Conflict of interest	69.0	(80)
2. Other white-collar crimes[d]	16.4	(19)
3. Personal character matters	9.5	(11)
4. Other	1.7	(2)
C. Integrity of books and records[e]	49.1	(57)
Codes discussing specific policy areas	97.5	(116)
No differentiation of policy areas	2.5	(3)
Totals	100.0	(119)

[a]Percentages are based on the number of codes discussing specific policy areas. Percentages do not total 100 percent because most codes discuss more than one policy area.

[b]Includes participation in public life (e.g., office-holding).

[c]Includes transactions with agents, consultants, and distributors.

[d]Crimes other than those relating to conflict of interest (e.g., embezzlement).

[e]Includes discussion of off-book accounts, false or misleading records and supporting documents, and candor with internal and independent auditors.

SOURCE: Donald R. Cressey and Charles A. Moore, *Corporation Codes of Ethical Conduct,* A Report to the Peat, Marwick, and Mitchell Foundation; February, 1980, p. 10. Reprinted by permission.

BUSINESS SECTOR					
Top 100 Industrials		*Other Industrials*		*Non- Industrials*	
%	N	%	N	%	N
87.9	(29)	74.5	(38)	68.8	(22)
81.8	(27)	66.7	(34)	90.6	(26)
54.6	(18)	51.0	(26)	53.1	(17)
51.5	(17)	52.9	(27)	43.8	(14)
66.7	(22)	37.3	(19)	25.0	(8)
45.5	(15)	43.1	(22)	34.4	(11)
30.3	(10)	25.5	(13)	53.1	(17)
38.4	(13)	25.5	(13)	15.6	(5)
27.3	(9)	19.6	(10)	12.5	(4)
24.2	(8)	9.8	(5)	3.1	(1)
—		3.9	(2)	3.1	(1)
72.8	(24)	62.8	(32)	75.0	(24)
15.2	(5)	11.7	(6)	25.0	(8)
9.1	(3)	3.9	(2)	18.8	(6)
3.0	(1)	—		3.1	(1)
48.5	(16)	57.5	(30)	34.4	(11)
97.1	(33)	98.1	(51)	97.0	(32)
2.9	(1)	1.9	(1)	3.0	(1)
100.0	(34)	100.0	(52)	100.0	(33)

dent of United Brands, adds, "If you have a formal code you have less chance of getting into trouble unknowingly."[38] Brenner and Molander conclude: "The mere existence of a code, specific or general, can raise the level of ethical behavior because it clarifies what it meant by ethical conduct."[39] Table 3-2 illustrates the range of issues that are addressed in modern-day codes, according to a recent survey. Specific information in these areas should help clarify ethical dilemmas employees and managers face.

[38] *Business Week,* February 9, 1976, p. 79.
[39] Brenner and Molander, p. 66.

If a company code is established, it must be made clear by management and the board that economic results will not excuse violations of the code. Effective sanctions for violations must exist so there is no question that the code represents company policy and is not just a public relations charade. Moreover, the company board should create a committee or group independent of management to oversee the operation of the code.[40]

To be effective, codes of ethics must embody the thinking and policy beliefs that management and employees alike desire in the organization and, as such, they should represent sincere communication efforts to guide employees' acts and behavior in questionable situations. If they are anything less than this they tend to become mere symbolic gestures, which are probably not worth having.

Discipline Violators of Ethics Standards. To bring about an ethical climate that all organizational personnel will come to believe in, management must punish violators of its accepted ethical norms. A major reason the general public, and even employees in many organizations, have questioned business's sincerity in desiring a more ethical environment has been business's unwillingness to discipline violators. There are numerous cases of top management personnel who behaved unethically and were retained in their positions. At lower levels there have been cases of top management overlooking or failing to punish unethical behavior of subordinates. These evidences of inaction on management's or the board's part represent implicit approval of the individual's behavior.

It is argued by Fred Allen that an organization should respond forcefully to the individual who is guilty of deliberately or flagrantly violating its code of ethics:

> From the pinnacle of the corporate pyramid to its base there can only be one course of action: dismissal. And should actual criminality be involved, there should be total cooperation with law enforcement authorities.[41]

Phillip Blumberg supports this general line of reasoning with his assertion that "there should be effective sanctions for violations so that there is no doubt that the code really represents corporate policy and that the effort is more than a public relations charade."[42]

The effort has to be complete in communicating to all, by way of dis-

[40]Phillip I. Blumberg, "Corporate Morality and the Crisis of Confidence in American Business," *Beta Gamma Sigma Invited Essay* (St. Louis: Beta Gamma Sigma, January 1977), p. 7.
[41]Allen, p. 16.
[42]Blumberg, p. 7.

ciplining offenders, that unethical behavior will not be tolerated in the organization. It is management's tacit approval of violations that has seriously undermined efforts to bring about a more ethical climate in many organizational situations.

Create an Ethics Advocate Role. A creative proposal by Theodore Purcell is that each organization appoint or hire an ethical devil's advocate — a top-level corporate manager whose responsibility is to serve as an ethical catalyst for management by constantly asking probing questions regarding the organization's actions and posture. For example, whereas a strategic planner might ask with respect to a certain decision, "What would our market share be?" or "What would our discounted cash flow be?" the ethics advocate might ask, "How will this decision affect the rights of our employees versus the rights of the corporation?"[43]

One possible serious problem with this proposed organizational position is that managers might be inclined to delegate ethical concerns to the advocate and not worry about the ethical dimension themselves. This must be carefully guarded against. Very little experience exists to show whether the ethics advocate concept might work in practice; however, it does represent innovative thinking.

Provide a Whistle-Blowing Mechanism. One of the problems that frequently leads to the covering up of unethical acts by persons in an organization is that they do not know how to react when they observe a questionable practice. An effective ethical climate is contingent on employees having a mechanism for (and top management support of) "blowing the whistle" on violators. Allen has summarized this point as follows: "Employees must know exactly what is expected of them in the moral arena and how to respond to warped ethics."[44]

It frequently happens that unethical practices or, indeed, crimes come to the attention of organization members several layers down in the organization's structure. John McCloy, who served as chairman of the Special Review Committee to study the use of corporate funds by Gulf Oil Corporation, found that some boards of directors of companies have "adopted and disseminated throughout their companies a policy which encourages any employee who observes a criminal act to report the incident to his or her superior. If the superior is not responsive, the employee then has direct access to the board, usually through its audit committee."[45] This would illustrate the functioning of a whistle-blow-

[43]Purcell, p. 47.
[44]Allen, p. 16.
[45]Myles L. Mace, "John J. McCloy on Corporate Payoffs," *Harvard Business Review,* July-August 1976, p. 28.

ing mechanism. Extreme care should be exercised, however, in use of this approach, as there is considerable evidence of whistle blowing backfiring.[46]

Train Management in Business Ethics. For several years there has been debate and controversy about whether managerial ethics can and should be taught. One school of thought assumes that ethics are personal, already embedded within the manager and, hence, not alterable or teachable. A growing school of thought, on the other hand, argues that instruction in business ethics should be made a part of management training, development programs, and seminars.

In fact, this latter course of action is taking place in a number of organizations in the United States today. What might be the purposes or objectives of such ethics training? A number of purposes have been suggested:

1. To increase the manager's sensitivity to ethical problems
2. To encourage critical evaluation of value priorities
3. To increase awareness of organizational realities
4. To increase awareness of societal realities
5. To improve understanding of the importance of public image and public/society relations[47]

To this list we might add some desirable goals:

6. To examine the ethical facets of business decision making
7. To bring about a greater degree of fairness and honesty in the workplace
8. To respond more completely to the organization's social responsibilities

There will doubtless be difficulties in training managers in such an amorphous subject as ethics. These difficulties, however, should not preclude serious attempts and experimentation with case studies, incidents, role playing, and discussion of crucial ethical issues. With respect to the teaching of ethics, John Adair has asserted: "A good teacher can help managers to become generally aware of their values and to compare them with the consensus of value judgments in a particular company, industry, or profession."[48] We believe, therefore, there is merit

---

[46]For example, see the accounts cited in "Disclosing Misdeeds of Corporations Can Backfire on Tattlers," *Wall Street Journal,* May 5, 1976, p. 1. See also Charles W. Stevens, "The Whistle Blower Chooses Hard Path, Utility Story Shows," *Wall Street Journal,* November 8, 1978, p. 1ff.

[47]Ron Zemke, "Ethics Training: Can We Really Teach People Right from Wrong?" *Training HRD,* May 1977, p. 39.

[48]John E. Adair, *Management and Morality: The Problems and Opportunities of Social Capitalism* (London: David & Charles, 1974), p. 143.

in management training and development in ethics as a viable aid to bringing about more ethical organizational behavior.

Though we have not touched on all that can be done at the organizational level to improve or manage business ethics, the actions suggested can move management a long way toward improving the organization's ethical climate. By taking specific steps as suggested, many behaviors or decisions that might otherwise have been wrong have a greater chance of being in line with leadership's ethical standards. Thus, ethics can be managed and managers do not have to treat value concerns as matters totally out of their control. On the contrary, managers can intercede and improve the organization's ethical climate.

Association (or Industry) Level

There are literally tens of thousands of associations in the United States. These are groups of firms in a particular industry or occupation that join together to achieve common purposes. Each trade and professional association has a paid staff to run the organization along with voluntary assistance from the membership. In addition to programs on such topics as governmental relations, lobbying, education, and research, they also are in an ideal position to help their respective memberships undertake efforts to improve the level of ethics in their industry or field.

It makes sense for associations to exert leadership in the ethical arena because they have individuals in the same field of work, all of whom are wrestling with fundamentally the same problems. It is natural, therefore, for voluntary associations to take the initiative in raising the standards of ethics within the professional and commercial community. Moreover, it is one of the most useful kinds of leadership that associations can give at a time when both the private and the public sector are being questioned as never before.[49]

Associations are in an excellent position to provide the following:

1. A code of conduct or set of guidelines for the membership
2. A process, a method, or an arrangement of steps to be taken by the organization to encourage compliance and to discourage or even penalize noncompliance
3. Professional leadership to provide the essential planning, the procedures, and, most importantly, the sustained action that is so vital[50]

The commitment to raise the standards of ethics within a professional or trade group requires dedication to the belief that internal monitoring

[49]Arch N. Booth, "Introduction to Codes and Commentaries," in Hill, p. 260.
[50]Ibid., pp. 257-258.

of the affairs of association members is preferable to the risk of loss of their freedom to government control. Arch Booth, former president of the Chamber of Commerce of the United States stated this point well:

> We must take voluntary action to increase the number of people practicing honesty or ethics — or find our freedom repressed by centralized authority and coercive regulation.[51]

Research has shown that the ethical climate of industry is a very important factor in preventing or causing unethical behavior.[52] It follows, then, that steps taken at this level to improve business ethics should be beneficial. Though there are no statistics proving the success of associations in improving the ethics or the ethical climate in particular lines of work, observers of associations indicate that there are indeed positive results from the serious efforts being made. Associations that have reported successes with their efforts include the Direct Selling Association, Public Relations Society of America, National Association of Broadcasters, and the National Association of Realtors.[53]

Societal Level

Once we leave the level of associations, we remove ourselves from the realm of collective activities where business can most directly and specifically influence ethics. At the societal level, business ethics is shaped most by pressures on business from particular segments of society (pluralism at work) and by law. The impetus at this level comes primarily through local, state, and federal legislation.

It is not our intent to discuss this level in detail here; however, it should be noted that in our social responsibility model in Chapter 2, legal responsibilities and ethical responsibilities were closely related to one another. There are many examples of actions that society, through the legislative process, has removed from the ethical category and placed in the legal category. This is the primary means by which society, collectively, expresses its statement of ethics. Through the legislative mechanism, society's values and norms are brought to bear on organizations. Society's primary ethical agents are, then, the court system, the SEC, the FTC, the EPA, and so on.

International Level

Once national or cultural boundaries are crossed, agreement on what constitutes acceptable and ethical conduct becomes exceedingly diffi-

---

[51]Ibid., p. 261.
[52]Brenner and Molander, p. 66.
[53]See Hill, pp. 263-386, for a discussion of the activities of these groups.

cult. The consensus that may have been reached on the national level tends to disintegrate once it is exposed to the multitude of ethical precepts held by various nations of the world.

Progress has been made, though the progress may be considered minuscule when placed alongside the problem. To the average person the enormity of the problem is a shock. In the last several years improper or questionable payments to foreign government officials, to agents acting on their behalf, or to other business people have been revealed that suggest the staggering magnitude of international payoffs and bribes. As of 1978, more than 400 companies — most of them among the nation's largest 500 — have disclosed nearly $800 million in questionable payments.[54] These payments, representing only what has been disclosed by United States corporations as a result of SEC and Justice Department prodding, are believed by some experts to be only the tip of the iceberg. All this has occurred despite steps taken since at least 1975 by international-level organizations attempting to halt such questionable practices.

In July 1975 the Permanent Council of the Organization of American States adopted the following resolution:

> To condemn in the most emphatic terms any act of bribery, illegal payment or offer of payment by any transnational enterprise; any demand for or acceptance of improper payments by any public or private person . . .[55]

In that same year, the United Nations General Assembly condemned all corrupt practices, including bribery by transnational and other corporations in violation of the regulations and laws set down by host countries.[56] In July 1976 the Council of Ministers of the Organization of Economic Cooperation and Development (OECD) — which is composed of the leading non-Communist industrial nations — adopted a Declaration on International Investment and Multinational Enterprises. Among other statements contained in the declaration is the following:

> Multinational enterprises should not render — and they should not be solicited or expected to render — any bribe or other improper gift, direct or indirect, to any public servant or holder of public office.

[54]Barry Richman, "Stopping Payments Under the Table," *Business Week,* May 22, 1978, p. 18.
[55]Organization of American States, Permanent Council Resolution CP/Res 154 (167/75), July 10, 1975.
[56]Blumberg, p. 6.

The United States was a signatory to this declaration, and it received the support of the Senate.[57]

The United States State Department has entered into bilateral agreements with twelve countries providing for the exchange of vital information on illegal corporate practices. It is also calling for an international treaty prohibiting corrupt practices which would be mandatory rather than voluntary, as is the case with the OECD declaration.

Though Jack Behrman has concluded that national rather than international action is more effective in dealing with corporate bribery and corruption,[58] Phillip Blumberg suggests that "international codes and treaties have a useful function to supplement national legislation by host and home countries."[59] Such agreements symbolize international concern for the problem and might lead to more effective implementation and enforcement of national legislation. In addition, inclusion of such provisions on corrupt practices might "provide an element of universality, encourage the harmonization of national legislation, and lead to intergovernmental cooperation on enforcement."[60]

SUMMARY

It remains difficult to define precisely what is meant by business ethics, but there is consensus that the term refers to concern for good, fair, and just business behavior. Business ethics are of utmost concern today, as reflected by the proliferation of articles and studies on the subject, the self-admitted transgressions of the country's largest corporations, and the results of numerous public opinion polls. It is not clear whether business ethics today are any better or worse than in previous years, but it does seem clear that the public's expectations of business behavior are higher and more demanding.

Managers today are at the center of a complex web of values. These values come from such external sources as religion, philosophy, culture, the law, and the professions. In addition, internal forces in an organization affect the manager's values and actions. These forces include the authority structure, loyalty, conformity, and pressure for results. Research suggests that these internal forces are more influential than the external forces in channeling employee and managerial be-

---

[57]S. Res. 516, 94th Congress, 2nd Session, adopted October 1, 1976.
[58]Jack N. Behrman, "Code for Transnational Enterprises," in Hill, pp. 125-128.
[59]Blumberg, p. 6.
[60]Ibid.

havior. Indeed, it is believed that one's relationship with one's superiors (the superior-subordinate relationship) is the most potent of the internal forces.

The improvement of ethics in business can be addressed at five increasingly broader levels. First, there are tests that individuals can use who sincerely want to improve their ethics. Second, companies can employ strategies to provide a more ethical climate. Third, trade and professional associations can display leadership among individuals and firms that have much in common. Fourth, society can improve business ethics with its laws, regulations, and opportunities to put other kinds of pressure on business. Fifth, international organizations can pass resolutions, reach agreements, provide for treaties, and so on, that address the ethical aspect of transactions across national boundaries. In sum, business ethics can be influenced, shaped, and, in fact, managed.

QUESTIONS FOR DISCUSSION

1. What is meant by business ethics? What are the three key elements that go into making ethical determinations?
2. Give several examples, other than those mentioned in the text, of ethical precepts on which we have consensus at a high level of abstraction but which tend to become controversial as we move from the abstract to the specific.
3. Do you feel that most behavior can be judged right or wrong by the criteria of "truth" or "justice"? Discuss and give examples.
4. In what way is "using company services for personal use" a violation of the criterion of justice?
5. What is your analysis of the Caterpillar Tractor Company view that "the law is a floor"? Discuss how a company might operationalize that statement of belief.
6. Do you agree that it's impossible to tell whether modern business ethics are better or worse than ethics of years ago? Do you agree that the public's concept of what is right and wrong has changed more than business's actual behavior and practices? Discuss.
7. Summarize the external sources of a manager's values. Which of those external sources seem most potent in influencing behavior? Rank in order the five mentioned in terms of their impact on people and be prepared to defend your ranking. What problems did you have in doing the ranking?

8. Speculate as to which of Spranger's values would come out on top (and then on the bottom) for each of these persons:

   purchasing manager   sales manager
   business school professor   engineer
   business school student   liberal arts student

9. What are the internal forces that have an impact on an employee's or manager's value system? Which are most important? What role does the superior-subordinate relationship play in affecting one's ethical behavior?

10. Discuss the various levels at which actions can be taken to improve the quality of business ethics.

11. Of the various tests the individual may employ to improve ethical behavior, rank them in order according to their power or ability to affect behavior. Be prepared to justify your ranking.

12. Of the various strategies management may employ to improve ethics at the organizational level, rank in order the three which you feel are most important. Be prepared to discuss your ranking. Which of the suggestions presented seem least pragmatic?

13. Do you really think students and managers can be trained to be more ethical? Discuss the pros and cons of this.

14. What major difficulties do you envision in attempting to develop an international code of business conduct? What basic approach would you take to create such a code?

Cases

Mother's Milk Is Best

The Infant Formula Action (INFACT) Coalition and other groups have urged American consumers to boycott the products of Nestlé Alimentana, the colossal Switzerland-based food company (1979 sales of $12 billion). The groups accuse Nestlé, the leading seller of powdered infant formula in underdeveloped countries, of contributing to the death of Third-World babies by promoting its formula to people who are unable to use it properly. Illiterate and uneducated mothers often prepare the formula in an unsanitary manner or dilute it excessively in order to economize.

INFACT would like Nestlé and other companies that sell powdered infant formula in underdeveloped countries to stop promotion of the formula and distribution of free samples. They say these marketing techniques make the formula available to the people who are least able to afford it and use it properly.

Though the infant formula producers acknowledge and advertise that breast-feeding is better, the companies and some health officials insist there is a need for the formula as a supplement for malnourished mothers who breast-feed and as an alternative for mothers who choose to bottle-feed. Nestlé contends that its formula is promoted in larger cities where mothers are better educated and able to afford the formula; a concentrated sales promotion in rural areas where people would be unable to afford the product would be economically infeasible. In addition, Nestlé and other infant food producers have adopted an ethical code which requires that promotional materials used in underdeveloped countries adequately educate illiterate consumers.[1]

QUESTIONS

1. What are the ethical issues in this case? Do you feel Nestlé has been unethical? Discuss your rationale.
2. What is the extent of Nestlé's obligation to educate the users of its product?
3. What action, if any, should Nestlé take on the boycott?
4. Should Nestlé discontinue (or change) its marketing practices for infant formula? What if the product were something other than infant formula — coffee, vitamins, or soap?

What's in a Name?

Two large car makers, Chrysler Corporation and Ford Motor Company, have been juggling names of cars for the new model year (1977). This practice has been done before. Few substantial product changes have been made. A mid-sized car once known as the Dodge Coronet now sells under the name of Monaco. The Monaco, formerly the large-sized luxury model, is now named the Royal Monaco. A Ford LTD keeps the same name, but the smaller Torino is now the LTD II. Mid-sized Mercurys are now Cougars, which have traditionally been larger luxury models.

Such name shifting has not been adopted by all United States auto makers this year. General Motors has redesigned some of its large cars into different smaller models.[2]

[1]This case was prepared by Betty F. Brewer.

[2]Based on "What's in a Name?" *Consumer Reports*, January 1977, vol. 42, no. 1, p. 40. Copyright 1977 by Consumers Union of United States, Inc., Mount Vernon, N.Y. 10550. Excerpted by permission from *Consumer Reports* (January 1977).

QUESTIONS

1. Is this a case involving the discretionary, ethical, legal, or economic realm of business responsibility? Discuss.
2. As long as the consumer can see what he or she is buying, does the businessman have a right to call a product whatever he chooses?
3. Would it have made a difference in this case if the product had been a mousetrap instead of a car? Why?
4. What ethical responsibility does the individual car dealer have? What approach would you take in marketing these new cars?

The Trauma of Docu-Dramas

Docu-dramas are causing the TV networks a lot of problems. They are historical novels for television, a hybrid of documentary and drama. They attempt to tell a true story, but where the real story does not neatly fit into a made-for-TV package, the facts may be altered.

Opposition to these productions centers around this mixing of fact and fiction. Teachers report that students regard the docu-dramas as accurate representations of history. Many other viewers suffer the same misconception. After the program "They've Killed Mr. Lincoln," for example, one CBS executive recalls, "We got a good many phone calls and letters from people wanting to know where we got that rare historical movie footage of the assassination of Lincoln."

In creating these shows, there is the persistent temptation to create events or powerful statements to improve their dramatic quality. The problem of historical accuracy is a difficult one. Even historians disagree on many points, and those who write the scripts must choose and face the consequences. Events are often telescoped and characters consolidated in order to simplify the plot. Tony Converse, CBS vice president for special programs, said, "What we hope to avoid is any major flaws in presenting the feeling of the event." Irwin Siegelstein, vice president for programming at NBC, said, "Docu-dramas depart from reality but they are not intended to deceive."

Television executives maintain there is a rigid distinction between news and entertainment, but with docu-dramas the division is becoming difficult to define.

The docu-dramas are popular; they receive much higher Nielsen ratings than documentaries, as illustrated by the different networks' offerings on the Entebbe rescue. The CBS documentary received a rating of 15, while the ABC docu-drama received a 20.8 rating (even when shown opposite the Bob Hope Christmas Special), and the NBC docu-drama received a 28.8 rating. The higher ratings for docu-dramas make them attractive to sponsors and complicate any network decision regarding them.[3]

QUESTIONS

1. What are the networks' social and ethical responsibilities in the case of docu-dramas?
2. Where and how distinct should be the division between fact and entertainment?
3. Based on this division, what is permissible in the dramatization of a documentary?
4. Based on your answers, what actions(s) should the networks take in response to those who are critical of them?

Give a Little, Take a Little

From company to company one can find varying policies about business gifts. A survey of 1,200 purchasing agents found that the same management may frown on accepting gifts but has no problem with offering them.

The survey, conducted by the National Association of Purchasing Management, found that 75 percent of the buyers questioned said their bosses wanted them to maintain higher standards of ethics about accepting gifts than other departments. But 80 percent said their own sales departments gave largesse to the buyers they called on.

What guidelines did the purchasing agents themselves follow? Theater or sports tickets were considered acceptable by 60 percent (although only 19 percent said they had ever actually received them from salesmen). Golf outings were considered acceptable with 47 percent (33 percent had accepted them). Items considered taboo included vacation trips, clothing, and appliances. The majority of the agents saw nothing wrong with lunch, dinner, or a souvenir pen and pencil set.[4]

QUESTIONS

1. What is your analysis of the findings of this survey of business ethics?
2. Do you see a difference between giving and receiving gifts?
3. What underlying thinking do you suppose led the purchasing agents to develop the guidelines discussed above? How are sports tickets different from clothing?

---

[3]Developed from "Is Television Rewriting History?" *Atlanta Journal and Constitution*, March 19, 1977, pp. 1-A, 6-A; and "Drama Comes First, Facts Second," *Atlanta Journal and Constitution*, March 20, 1977, pp. 1-A, 14-A. Reprinted by permission.

[4]From "Give and Take," *Forbes*, May 14, 1979, p. 19. Reprinted by permission.

Part II:
External Publics
and Issues

Basic Question

What are the specific issues concerning external publics?

Objectives of Part II

To introduce business's relationship to government, a topic that directly touches on the next six chapters

To discuss how concern for consumers, the environment, and the community is causing managers to look differently at their jobs and their approaches to doing business

Chapters in Part II

4. Business and Government

5. Business and the Consumer

6. Business and the Environment

7. Business and the Community

INTRODUCTION TO PART II

The purpose of Part II is to develop an understanding of the issues and the publics that are outside of business but with which business must interact on a regular basis. Of particular concern are the social issues created as a result of the interaction between business and each of the societal publics. In Chapter 4 business and government interaction is dealt with first. It is essential to gain an appreciation of the increasingly complex business-government relationship if other topics in the book are to be comprehended. The topic of Chapter 5 is business and the consumer. More social issues have arisen in recent years due to this relationship than to any other. In Chapter 6 we discuss business and the environment. Because the environment was the source of some of the first conflicts between business and society, it is necessary that we study this relationship carefully. Finally, in Chapter 7, we treat the important topic of business and the community. Here we see a whole host of social issues that involve the business-community relationship.

As social issues, business's dealings with external groups and publics preceded its concern with internal publics and issues. Today, however, social relationships are strained from both without and within. Our treatment of the external groups will furnish a background for reviewing business's relationships with its internal publics.

Business and Government

Few issues today seem to excite business people as much as government's role in society. This was not always so. In recent years, however, the depth, scope, and direction of government's involvement in business affairs has made the business-government relationship one of the most hotly debated issues of modern times. In the last several years the general public has been rebelling against government encroachment also. An important step in the public's involvement occurred in 1978 with the passage of Proposition 13 in California by a 65 percent plurality. Proposition 13 was designed to reduce the size of government by slashing property taxes — the lifeblood of state government.[1]

It is obvious from the passage of Proposition 13 that not only is business alarmed over the growing size and influence of government (and the taxes it takes to keep government going), but so is the citizenry. Whether at the federal, state, or local level, there are widespread indications that many people wish the old maxim "he governs best who governs least" would be revitalized.

In this chapter we will mainly examine the relationship between business and government, though the general public will assume an important role in the discussion. Exploring this relationship carefully, however, will give you an appreciation of the complexity of the issues surrounding business-government interactions. From the prospective manager's standpoint, one needs a rudimentary understanding of the forces and factors that are involved in these issues before one can begin to talk intelligently about strategies for dealing with them. Unfortunately, more is known about the nature of the problem than about the nature of solutions, as is common when dealing with complex social issues.

In developing this awareness of the importance of the business-government relationship, we intend to cover the following topics:

[1]"The Big Tax Revolt," *Newsweek,* June 19, 1978, p. 20ff.

99

- A brief history of government's role
- An overview of the issues
- The interaction of government, business, and the public
- Government's influence on business
- Problems with government's influence
- Business's influence on government
- Improving the business-government relationship

A BRIEF HISTORY OF GOVERNMENT'S ROLE

The philosophy with which our country began was one of either leaving business alone or encouraging it. In the early days of the United States the government supported business in the form of tariffs for fledgling industries. In the second half of the 1800s government gave large land grants as incentives for private business to build railroads. During that same period, however, the relationship took on a new dimension when government began to concern itself with curbing certain business practices because it was not felt that they were in the public interest.[2]

The end of the laissez-faire period was marked by the passage of such significant legislation as the Interstate Commerce Act of 1887, in which freight rates were fixed by government, and the Sherman Antitrust Act of 1890. As mentioned in Chapter 1, this latter act was intended to curb concentrations of economic power that were emerging, especially in the form of trusts. This was followed in 1914 by the Clayton Act and the Federal Trade Commission Act, which, as we noted in Chapter 3, was an antitrust law at first but was broadened later to permit its application against "unfair or deceptive acts."

Another great wave of regulation occurred during the Depression and the subsequent New Deal of the 1930s. Significant legislation included the Securities Act of 1933 and the Securities and Exchange Act of 1934. These laws were aimed at curbing abuses in the stock market, stabilizing markets, and restoring investor confidence.[3] Significant labor legislation during this same period signaled government's involvement in a new area. Several examples that we noted in Chapter 1 were the 1926 Railway Labor Act, the 1932 Norris-LaGuardia Act, and the 1935 Wagner Act.

During the New Deal period in the 1930s, government also took on a new dimension in its relationship with business, as it actively assumed

---

[2]John T. Conner, "The Changing Pattern of Business-Government Relations," *The Conference Board Record*, May 1971, pp. 23-24.
[3]Ibid., p. 24.

responsibility for restoring prosperity and promoting economic growth through public works programs. In 1946 this new role of government was formalized with the passage of the Full Employment Act.[4]

This brings us to the present period, in which government has passed legislation involving itself deeply in the affairs of business. Prior to the mid-1950s most congressional legislation affecting business was *economic* in nature. Since that time, however, legislation has sought *social* goals as well. Much legislation of the last two decades has very often been concerned with the quality of life.[5] Several illustrations of this come to mind: the Civil Rights Act of 1963, Water Quality Act of 1965, Occupational Safety and Health Act of 1970, Consumer Product Safety Act of 1972, and Warranty Act of 1975.

Just as the kinds of areas in which government has chosen to initiate legislation have changed, the multiplicity of roles that government has assumed has increased the complexity of its status. George Steiner has outlined a number of the varied roles that government has assumed in its relationship with business. These are worth looking at because they suggest the influence, interrelationship, and complexity that characterize the business-government nexus. Government:

1. prescribes the rules of the game for business.
2. is a major purchaser of business's products and services.
3. uses its contracting power to get business to do things it wants.
4. is a major promoter and subsidizer of business.
5. is the owner of vast quantities of productive equipment and wealth.
6. is an architect of economic growth.
7. is a financer of business.
8. is the protector of various interests in society against business exploitation.
9. directly manages large areas of private business.
10. is the repository of the social conscience, and redistributes resources to meet social objectives.[6]

After examining and assessing these various roles, one can perhaps begin to appreciate the crucial interconnectedness between business and government, and the difficulty both business and the public have in fully understanding (much less prescribing) what government's role ought to be vis-a-vis business.

[4]Ibid.

[5]Alfred L. Seelye, "Societal Change and Business-Government Relationships," *MSU Business Topics,* Autumn 1975, pp. 5-6.

[6]George A. Steiner, *Business and Society,* Second ed. (New York: Random House, 1975), pp. 359-361.

THE MAJOR ISSUES

Though we do not intend to philosophize in this chapter on the proper role of government vis-a-vis business, as that is outside of our managerial frame of reference, we will strive for an understanding of current major issues as they pertain to this vital relationship.

The fundamental question underlying our entire discussion of business-government relationships is: What should be the respective roles of business and government in our socioeconomic system? This question is far easier to ask than to answer, but as we explore it some important basic understandings may emerge.

The issue could be stated in a different fashion: Given all the tasks that must be accomplished to make our society work, which of these should be handled by government and which should be handled by business? This poses the issue clearly, but there are other questions that remain to be answered. If we decide, for example, that it is best to let business handle the production and distribution roles in our society, the next question pertains to how much autonomy we are willing to allow business. If our goals were simply the production and distribution of goods and services, we would not have to constrain business severely. In modern times, however, other goals have been added to the production and distribution functions: a safe working environment for those engaging in production, equal employment opportunities, fair pay, clean air, safe products, and so on. With these goals superimposed on the basic economic goals, the task of business becomes very difficult.

Since these latter, more socially oriented goals are not automatically factored into business decision making and processes, it ultimately falls on government to ensure that these goals that reflect the public interest are achieved. Thus, whereas the marketplace dictates economic production decisions, government becomes the citizenry's designated representative to articulate and protect the public interest.

This clash of emphasis partially forms the crux of the antagonistic relationship between business and government. L. Earle Birdsell has termed the problem "a clash of ethical systems."[7] The two ethical systems include the "individualistic" ethic of business and the "collectivistic" ethic of government. Table 4-1 summarizes the characteristics of these two philosophies.[8]

The clash of these two ethical systems partially explains why the cur-

---

[7]L. Earle Birdsell, "Business and Government: The Walls Between," in Neil H. Jacoby (ed.), *The Business-Government Relationship: A Reassessment* (Santa Monica, Calif.: Goodyear Publishing Co., 1975), pp. 32-34.

[8]Ibid., pp. 32-34. A summary of Birdsell's discussion.

TABLE 4-1
The Clash of Ethical Systems

Business	*Government*
Individualist ethic	Collectivist ethic
Maximum concession to self-interest	Subordination of individual goals and self-interest to group goals and group interests
Minimizing the load of obligations society imposes on the individual (personal freedom)	Maximizing the obligations assumed by the individual and discouraging self-interest
Emphasizes inequalities of individuals	Emphasizes equality of individuals

rent business-government relationship is adversary in nature. Beyond this basic distinction in nature or philosophical orientation, perhaps government's function must be that of policing obedience of the laws.

One of the most important seminars of the past decade on business-government relations was held in 1974 at the UCLA Graduate School of Management. In summarizing the view of all those present at the seminar, Neil Jacoby indicated that the current business-government relationship could be described as adversary in nature. He went on:

> Officials of government characteristically look upon themselves as probers, inspectors, taxers, regulators, and punishers of business transgressions. Businessmen typically view government agencies as obstacles, constraints, delayers, and impediments to economic progress, having much power to stop and little to start.[9]

Not only did the participants at the UCLA seminar conclude that the business-government relationship is adversary, but they also agreed that the relationship has been deteriorating. The goals and values of our pluralistic society have become more complex, more numerous, more interrelated, and consequently, more difficult to reconcile. The result has been increasing conflicts among diverse interest groups, with trade-off decisions becoming harder to make. In this process it has become more difficult to establish social priorities, and consensus has in many cases become impossible to achieve.[10]

As one attempts to find out why all this has happened, it is only natural to look to changes in the social and technological environments for some explanations. Four major changes since World War II, according

[9]Jacoby, p. 167.
[10]Ibid., p. 168.

to Daniel Bell, have had a profound impact on American society in general, and on the business-government relationship in particular. First, out of local and regional societies a truly national one has arisen.[11] Second, we have seen a "communal society" arise, characterized by a greater emphasis on public goods and the internalization of external costs. Third, the revolution of rising expectations has brought with it the demand for "entitlements" — good jobs, excellent housing, and other amenities. Fourth, a rising concern has emerged for an improved "quality of life."[12]

In addition to these, Alfred Seelye has suggested six other societal value changes that are now shaping the course of business-government relations. These are the youth movement, the consumer protection movement, the ecology movement, the civil rights movement, the women's liberation movement, and the egalitarian movement.[13]

In a sense, the last movement — the egalitarian — embraces all of the others in an effort to create an equitable balance of all facets of what is good in life in the United States. Thus, the value changes that have taken place "have multiplied the number of *political* decisions that have to be made relative to the number of decisions made in markets."[14] And to the extent that these political decisions affect business — and they do to a great extent — we can understand the basic conflict arising once again in a clash between individualist and collectivist ethics. Government's responses to changes taking place in society put it directly in opposition to business's philosophy and mode of operating.

INTERACTION OF BUSINESS, GOVERNMENT, AND THE PUBLIC

A brief examination is offered of the influence relationships between business, government, and the public — the major parties we are concerned with in this chapter. This should be helpful in understanding both the nature of the process by which societal decisions are made and the current problems that characterize the business-government relationship. Figure 4-1 illustrates the influence relationships.

We will not concern ourselves until later chapters with the relationships between the public and government nor between the public and

[11]For a view somewhat counter to this, see Kevin Phillips, "The Balkanization of America," *Harper's,* May 1978, pp. 37-47.
[12]Daniel Bell, "Too Much, Too Late: Reactions to Changing Social Values," in Jacoby, pp. 17-19.
[13]Seelye, pp. 7-8.
[14]Jacoby, p. 168.

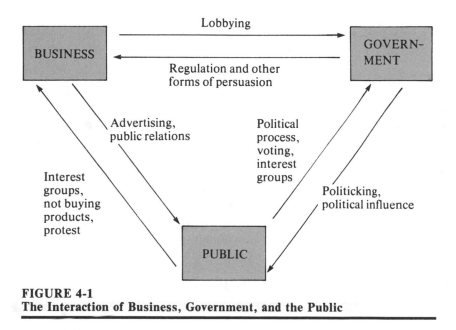

FIGURE 4-1
The Interaction of Business, Government, and the Public

business. Our interest here is in the bilateral relationships of influence between business and government. First, we will discuss the many ways in which government influences business to do what it wants; also, we are concerned with the problems that have been caused by these efforts. Second, we will examine ways business influences government, and the problems that have arisen from those efforts. Most of the major current issues concerning business and government are embedded in these relationships.

GOVERNMENT'S INFLUENCE ON BUSINESS

Most citizens would agree that it is up to government to establish rules for businesses operating in our society. The important question becomes, then, to what extent government should control or regulate business and how. Government represents the people, at least in theory, and it must employ whatever legal techniques are available to direct business's behavior in directions the people desire.

Nonregulatory Influences

Though outright regulation is the most potent and frequently used approach to controlling business's behavior, there are many ways short of this that government uses. We shall examine some of these approaches briefly, and then discuss more fully the alternative of outright regulation.

One tactic that government uses is *moral suasion,* sometimes called jawboning. *Jawboning* is a generalized form of government appeal — for example, to business in general or specific industries to hold down prices or to labor to be restrained in their wage demands. Jawboning usually begins with the President of the United States calling for business's cooperation in the public interest. *Voluntary standards* or guideposts represent a more specific governmental effort to control business. In this approach government sets standards and then appeals to business to comply voluntarily. President Jimmy Carter recently tried to stabilize wages and prices by imposing voluntary guidelines.

These two approaches may be supplemented by various forms of government *pressure* or coercion, which can range from public chastisement of individual organizations to veiled threats to terminate government contracts or other benefits.[15] Formal wage and price *controls* go beyond the voluntary standards and have been used only as a last resort to handle an inflationary situation that has gotten out of hand.

Government also controls business's behavior through the use of *subsidies* (with qualifications attached) and *procurement contracts,* in which government spells out the goods and services to be delivered along with requirements that must be met (hiring and training minority groups, favoring depressed areas or small business, and so on).

The government also uses the tax system to provide incentives for business to comply with its wishes. The Internal Revenue Service grants *tax credits* for hiring certain categories of people (unskilled, minorities), tax *deferrals* for income derived from exports, and tax *reductions* for investment in capital goods.[16]

The government in its role of financier also is able to channel business behavior in directions that help it achieve national objectives. Three programs stand out as illustrations. First, *direct loans* are made by federal departments and agencies, such as low-interest loans by the Rural Electrification Administration. Second, loans are *guaranteed* and *insured* by federal departments and agencies. These are more frequently used today and entail no expenditure of federal funds except in cases of default; the government simply guarantees and backs loans made by private lenders. Third, loans are made by federally sponsored *agencies* such as the Federal National Mortgage Association, the Federal Home Loan Banks, and the farm credit agencies. These low-interest loans

---

[15]Murray L. Weidenbaum, *Business, Government, and the Public* (Englewood Cliffs, N.J.: Prentice-Hall, 1977), p. 20.
[16]Ibid.

have increased sharply since the mid-1960s and now represent the major form of federal loan assistance to the private sector.[17]

Because of its visibility and recent controversy, we will treat outright government regulation in a separate section.

Regulation by Government

Some have argued that the increase in government regulation in the United States reflects a failure of the market system to achieve national goals: a cleaner environment, safer products, a safer workplace, and fairer employment opportunities. Government regulation does not evolve in a vacuum. Rather, it evolves as a political response to problems that do not seem to be solvable by market forces alone. The net consequence is that government is thrust deeper and deeper into what were formerly private business decisions.

It is the explosive growth of government regulation that has drawn the ire of business people and consumers alike in the last decade. More recently, widespread criticism of government regulation may also be the direct result of a new form of regulatory model. Early efforts at government regulations were in the pattern of such organizations as the Interstate Commerce Commission (ICC), the Civil Aeronautics Board (CAB), and the Federal Power Commission (FPC). Each of these organizations regulated a specific industry. The newer form of regulation, termed by some as functional regulation, attempts to monitor and control a specific feature of business activity, such as product safety, labor relations, pollution, or the work environment.[18] Rather than applying to specific industries, *functional regulation* is concerned with a specific segment of operations in all companies. The net result of these new regulations, best illustrated by the Environmental Protection Agency (EPA), Consumer Product Safety Commission (CPSC), Equal Employment Opportunity Commission (EEOC), and the Occupational Safety and Health Administration (OSHA), is a matrix of functional regulations superimposed upon the original industry-related regulations. Figure 4-2 illustrates the resulting regulatory pattern.

To help us appreciate what has happened in the regulatory environment to provoke the ire of business and the public alike, let us examine some of the data regarding these new government regulations. First, data showing the increase in spending by major economic and social regulatory agencies illustrate one dimension of the problem. As Figure

---

[17]Ibid., pp. 132-135.
[18]Jacoby, p. 171.

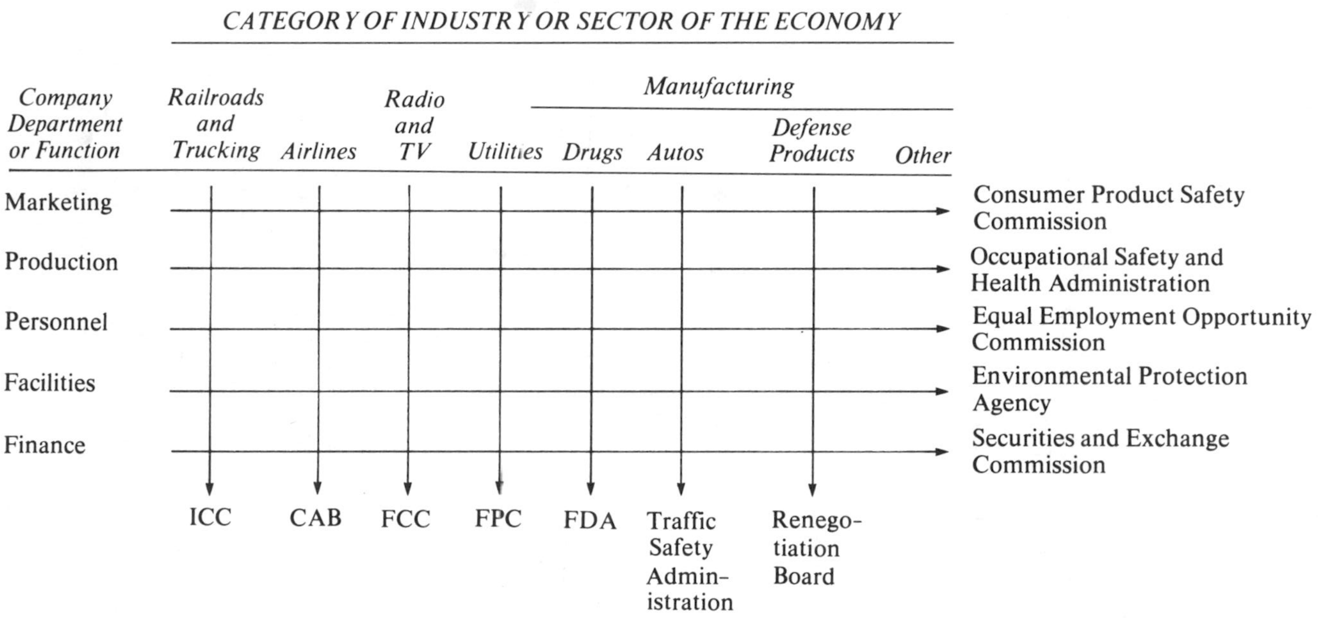

CATEGORY OF INDUSTRY OR SECTOR OF THE ECONOMY

Company Department or Function	Railroads and Trucking	Airlines	Radio and TV	Utilities	Manufacturing — Drugs	Autos	Defense Products	Other	
Marketing								→	Consumer Product Safety Commission
Production								→	Occupational Safety and Health Administration
Personnel								→	Equal Employment Opportunity Commission
Facilities								→	Environmental Protection Agency
Finance								→	Securities and Exchange Commission
	ICC	CAB	FCC	FPC	FDA	Traffic Safety Administration	Renegotiation Board		

FIGURE 4-2
The Matrix of Government Regulations

SOURCE: Murray L. Weidenbaum, *Business, Government, and the Public,* © 1977, p. 14. Reprinted by permission of Prentice-Hall, Inc., Englewood Cliffs, New Jersey.

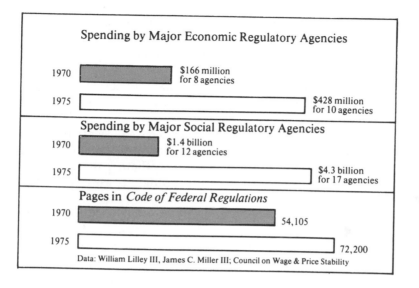

FIGURE 4-3
The Rising Tide of Federal Regulation

4-3 illustrates, spending increased about two and one-half times for economic agencies and over three times for social agencies during just the five-year period indicated.[19] As an expansion of these data, Murray Weidenbaum estimated that expenditures of the major regulatory agencies increased from $2 billion in fiscal 1974 to $3.8 billion in fiscal 1978.[20]

These aggregate data do not tell the complete story. We can look at the experiences of individual companies to appreciate how all this affects them. General Motors, for example, estimates that the documents it had to file in connection with certification of its cars for sale in a single year would make a stack fifteen stories high.

Most companies, like GM, can report only fragmentary statistics to illustrate the impact government regulations have on them. Dow Chemical, however, established a ten-person task force in 1976 to assess its costs of meeting government regulations. Using a conservative approach, the company categorized its various regulatory expenses as "appropriate," "questionable," and "excessive." As a result of its

[19]"Government Intervention," *Business Week,* April 4, 1977, p. 47.
[20]Ibid.

analysis, Dow Chemical decided that of the $147 million spent to meet government regulations, more than one-third was "excessive," and 41 percent (excessive + questionable) was less than appropriate.[21] Managers of the company admit that it is the law rather than the specific agencies that they are upset with, but are nevertheless unhappy with these figures and hope they can use their study to demonstrate to Congress that they are being over-regulated.

A recent study estimated that $300 was added each year to the cost of automobiles as a result of federal requirements from 1968 to 1974.[22] In the final analysis, no one can really calculate whether these increased expenditures are "worth it," but their magnitude is worth knowing.

In addition to the many overt costs of regulation, there are a number of hidden costs that do not appear so neatly as readily identifiable dollar expenditures. Irving Kristol, for example, is concerned about pollution-control filtering equipment being counted as a capital investment and being carried on the books as an asset of a corporation. He argues that a capital investment is supposed to promise an increase in production or productivity but that pollution-control equipment may do none of this, and may actually decrease productive capacity and productivity.[23]

There are other hidden costs as well. The pharmaceutical industry provides an interesting example. Economists are now assembling data that show that stringent regulations by the Food and Drug Administration (FDA) seriously hinder innovation in the drug industry. The deleterious result, of course, is the seriously slowed pace at which new drugs arrive on the market: whereas in 1966 it took 2.7 years for a new drug to be approved for use, it required 6.6 years by 1973.[24] In looking at the average annual number of new chemical entities approved by the FDA from 1957 to 1961 and from 1972 to 1975, one sees a decline from about sixty to fourteen.[25] While government regulation cannot be entirely blamed for this decline and the resulting economic consequences, economists have argued that "by ignoring the economic impacts of regulation the FDA is having a devastating effect on the drug industry."[26]

A final hidden cost worth mentioning is the detrimental effect that the rapidly rising number of regulations is having on small businesses.

[21]Ibid., p. 50.

[22]Murray Weidenbaum, "The High Cost of Government Regulation," *Business Horizons,* August 1975, p. 46.

[23]Irving Kristol, "The Hidden Costs of Regulation, " *Wall Street Journal,* January 12, 1977, p. 14.

[24]The Hidden Cost of Drug Safety," *Business Week,* February 21, 1977, p. 80. See Also J. E. S. Parker, "Regulating Pharmaceutical Innovation: An Economist's View," *Food Drug Cosmetic Law Journal,* April 1977, pp. 160-181.

[25]Ibid.

[26]Ibid.

SOURCE: Cartoon by Jeff MacNelly, "Small Business, Inc." (1977). Reprinted by permission of the Chicago Tribune-New York News Syndicate, Inc.

Because they do not have the slack in their organizations to absorb the impact of government regulations, small business people protest the burden of regulation more bitterly than do large corporations. They do not have the money to purchase new equipment, cannot cope with the amount of paperwork, and do not have the managerial staff to handle the responsibilities. The accompanying cartoon illustrates the dilemma of small businesses.

Failings of Regulation. Though it is somewhat difficult to separate the high and hidden costs of government regulation from what might be termed the failings of regulation, an effort will be made here to do so. In particular we will look briefly at two sets of criticisms. First, some of the major causes of poor federal performance as seen by two former employees of the Federal Trade Commission will be examined. Second, some of the adverse effects of governmental regulation as seen by Roger G. Noll will be considered.

Norman Kangun and Charles Moyer worked for the FTC and the Department of Commerce during 1973-74. Based on their experiences, they cite four particular failings of regulation. First, they charge regulatory bodies with "excessive reliance on classical economic models as a basis for public policy actions.''[27] Here they argue that "effective regulation requires a more holistic view of social impacts, not just one dominated by classic static partial equilibrium models.''[28] They also criticize regulatory agencies for using a simplistic "economic man" model of consumer behavior. Second, they say that the dominance of lawyers in the formation of public policy is a failing. The training, habits, and analytical tools of lawyers, they argue, are inadequate for effective policy making. Lawyers also do not have the appropriate finance and economics training.

Closely related to the problem of dominance by lawyers is their third point: There is a misallocation of agency resources and an overemphasis on "winning" without carefully considering the economic significance of winning. As an illustration, very few lawyers would be willing to commit several years of their careers to a large antitrust case against the medical industry if the estimated probability of success was only 40 percent. The expected social gain from such a case, however, might far surpass the smaller, more winnable cases of little significance.[29] The final failing of regulation named by Kangun and Moyer is agency insulation from external judgment and review.[30]

The adverse effects, or failings, of regulation as seen by Roger Noll are also four in number, and merit brief mention. First is *Penncentralization.* This is the tendency of the regulatory process to destroy incentives for business to operate efficiently. In the Penn Central Railroad case, regulation by the ICC left scant incentive to minimize operating costs or to make innovations that would reduce costs or make new services possible. Regulation has thus insulated or protected inefficient firms from competition with more efficient ones.[31]

The second failing is *Lockheedization*— the tendency of government to subsidize large, poorly managed firms which might not otherwise survive. Not only does this encourage slothful and inefficient management, but it can create an entirely new industry that might be called the "failure business.''[32] If a firm's success depends significantly on whether government subsidizes or guarantees its loans, managers may become so dependent on such subsidies or guarantees that they no longer calculate their risks closely enough.

Third, *legalization* is an undesirable effect. This is the "tendency of

[27]Norman Kangun and R. Charles Moyer, "The Failings of Regulation," *MSU Business Topics,* Spring 1976, p. 5.

[28]Ibid., p. 6.

[29]Ibid., pp. 5-10.

[30]Ibid., pp. 11-12.

[31]Roger G. Noll, "The Social Costs of Governmental Intervention," in Jacoby, 1975, p. 56.

[32]Ibid.

the regulatory process to become a labyrinth of procedural complexities that imposes mountainous costs and endless delays on the regulated firms."[33] In a sense, this failing is very similar to that mentioned by Kangun and Moyer.

The final failing is termed *consultantization* — the "tendency of the regulatory process to divert scarce creative talent from productive pursuits to redistributive activities."[34] This is a subtle failing, in that it assumes that consultants called in to help represent companies before government agencies would otherwise be spending their time creating new productivity, and not just becoming a party to government's efforts to redistribute wealth.

There are other failings; however, those given represent a fair sampling of the kinds of objections that have been raised against government regulation. Other failings or weaknesses in the system that could be mentioned include the paperwork burden imposed, the conflict and duplication caused (ecology versus product safety, ecology versus equal employment opportunity),[35] and the more recent concern about how to regulate the regulators.[36] And, if certain managers were to be queried, they would add the increasing extent to which the law is closing in and holding them personally responsible for corporate violations.[37] These kinds of concerns need to be weighed against the benefits of regulation, to derive a fair picture of the roles of regulatory bodies in society.

Toward Solutions. When President Jimmy Carter took office in January 1977, he pledged to reverse the 200-year trend toward more government intervention in the economy.[38] Recent data, however, indicate that the trend is accelerating.[39]

Following the efforts to control government regulations begun by President Gerald Ford, President Carter expressed particular interest in reducing the "nonproductive" interventions by government. Thus, improving the quality of intervention was one of his goals.[40] Toward this end, on November 18, 1977, the White House published a proposed executive order concerned with "improving government regulation." This was the first time an executive order had ever been released

---

[33]Ibid., p. 57.
[34]Ibid.
[35]See Weidenbaum, 1977, pp. 154-160, for a discussion of these types of conflicts.
[36]"How to Regulate the Regulators," *Time,* October 21, 1974, p. 58; Timothy D. Schellhardt, "The Watchdog of the Watchdogs," *Wall Street Journal,* June 18, 1975.
[37]"The Law Closes in on Managers," *Business Week,* May 10, 1976, pp. 110-115. See also "When Investigators Knock," *Business Week,* November 8, 1976, pp. 52-55.
[38]"Government Intervention," *Business Week,* April 4, 1977, p. 42.
[39]"Federal Regulation of Business on Rise, Budget Study Shows," *Wall Street Journal,* March 14, 1978, p. 18.
[40]"Government Intervention," *Business Week,* April 4, 1977, p. 42.

in tentative form for public comment before being finalized.[41] The major features of this order may be summarized as follows:

1. Regulations should be set forth simply, clearly, should be effective and efficient, and should not impose any unnecessary burdens.

2. The order applies to all "significant" regulations issued by both the executive branch and independent agencies.

3. Each agency must publish a semi-annual agenda of the regulations it is proposing; its staff must provide agency heads with a clearly detailed plan for each regulation; agencies must more effectively solicit public participation in the process; agency heads must approve all significant regulatory proposals.

4. A regulatory analysis of regulations that may have "major consequences" must be prepared. The analysis must provide a succinct statement of the problem and of the major alternatives for solving the problem, must analyze the economic consequences of the proposal and the alternatives (similar to President Ford's Economic Impact Statement) and must explain why one approach was chosen over others.

5. Important regulations now on the books must be reviewed by agencies to insure they are clear, effective, and unburdensome.

6. All regulatory proposals underway on the date the order becomes effective are exempt from the proposed standards. The order, unless extended, expires on June 15, 1980.[42]

The proposed program, which went beyond any efforts previously offered, would be supplemented by a Regulatory Analysis Review Group. The group, chaired by the Council of Economic Advisers, would include representatives from the major economic and regulatory agencies.[43] Earlier proposals had also included a "sunset" requirement — that is, some date by which any new legislation would be allowed to expire unless action were taken to extend it.[44]

[41]Allan L. Otten, "War in the Bureaucratic Trenches," *Wall Street Journal,* February 2, 1978, p. 14.
[42]Summarized from "After Economic Impact Statements — What?" *Regulation,* January-February 1978, pp. 12-13.
[43]Ibid., p. 13.
[44]*Business Week,* April 4, 1977, p. 63.

BUSINESS'S INFLUENCE ON GOVERNMENT

It has been argued that "American business corporations have been, *are,* and, in the foreseeable future, will undoubtedly continue to be involved in the political process."[45] Stated another way, it is inevitable that business will be involved, like so many other interest groups, in attempting to influence election outcomes and legislation. Business has a major interest in ensuring that its viewpoint is heard regarding potential legislation that may be adverse to its interests, and that it receives ample opportunity to advocate legislation that it feels would be consistent with and most supportive of its interests.

In attempting to influence the public policy process, business is exercising the same right as other interest groups in society. Indeed, this is the process by which public decisions in our society are made. Since politics may be considered the "process of allocating resources and values,"[46] business's efforts are aimed at imposing its concept of values and resource allocations on public policy leaders.

Business has several major purposes in its efforts to shape public policy decision making, and it employs a variety of approaches to achieve these ends. In the process, questions arise about the legitimacy of business's activities in the political sphere and about its power vis-a-vis other groups in this process.

Major Purposes

Among the many goals that business hopes to achieve in its struggles with government are to:

1. maintain an environment favorable to business,
2. inject rational thinking into government,
3. counterbalance union power and influence,
4. promote political interests of managers, and
5. counterbalance the power of groups with objectives contrary to those of business (e.g., consumerists, environmentalists).[47]

In its efforts to achieve these purposes, business operates through the electoral process, the legislative process, and the judicial process. Although there are some restrictions on the types of activities business can engage in to influence elections and place people it wants into of-

---

[45]Edwin M. Epstein, *The Corporation in American Politics* (Englewood Cliffs, N.J.: Prentice-Hall, 1969), p. 6.

[46]Carol S. Greenwold, *Group Power: Lobbying and Public Power* (New York: Praeger Publishers, 1977), p. 23.

[47]Steiner, pp. 382-385.

fice, the 1974 campaign law has enabled business to be extensively involved in politics. As for its legislative efforts, business has had mixed
success over the years. Most astute observers believe that business has
not been as effective as labor has.[48] Its efforts through the judicial process have had mixed results, too, with business frequently having to use
legal procedures to forestall unfavorable governmental activity.

Approaches to Influence

Business tries to influence government decision making through the
legislative process by lobbying, the electoral process through campaign
contributions, and the judicial process through lawsuits.

Lobbying, in one form or another, represents business's most significant influence activity. A lobby is defined as "a political interest group
. . . whose shared activities include attempts to influence decisions
made within the public policy-making system."[49] Lobbying thus refers
to the dynamic process of influencing public policy. Over the years
various combinations of business groups have been formed to influence
government decision making. Groups of a general nature that have
lobbying as one of their many activities incude the National Association
of Manufacturers (NAM) and the Chamber of Commerce of the United
States. Groups that represent a more specific or limited interest include
lobbyists for individual companies, trade associations, the Business
Roundtable, the Committee of One Hundred, and the National Federation of Independent Business.

The NAM and the Chamber of Commerce are considered by many to
be the old-line outfits. Both have been around for many years and
represent such a broad constituency that their effectiveness is sometimes impaired. They are credited, however, with being a part of successful efforts to stave off legislation unfavorable to the free enterprise
system. In addition to these groups, firms have for many years maintained individual Washington offices which attempt to sell the companies' viewpoints and to serve as a two-way information conduit between government and business.[50]

Perhaps the most effective lobbying groups in Washington in recent
years have been the Business Roundtable and trade associations.
Formed in 1972, the Business Roundtable is a confederation of almost
200 chief executives of blue-chip corporations, including such recognizable giant firms as GM, U.S. Steel, DuPont, GE, and Sears,

---

[48]Alan L. Otten, "Business in Politics," *Wall Street Journal,* April 28, 1977, p. 20.
[49]Greenwald, p. 15.
[50]Epstein, p. 90.

Roebuck.[51] One of the reasons the Roundtable has been so successful is that it is the chief executives themselves who are involved, not lower-level managers who sometimes are active in other groups, Thus, the Roundtable commands access to politicians and the political process that eclipses the lobbying power of some of the old-line groups.[52]

The initial purpose of the Roundtable was to match the lobbying power of labor organizations in Washington.[53] It has been held by many that labor has been much more effective in the political arena, historically, than has business. Despite the fact that it has had to follow the lead set by labor, the Roundtable and other goups have been credited with blocking some legislation. In recent years, this includes killing the proposed consumer protection agency, and defeating bills that would broaden picketing rights of construction workers and allow class-action suits against companies violating FTC orders.[54]

The Roundtable is not without its critics, some of whom believe its power extends too far. One critic recalls that in the fall of 1975 Vice President Nelson A. Rockefeller held a private briefing for Roundtable members on a proposed report by the National Commission on Water Quality. In the briefing, Rockefeller presented a draft of the report, allowed Roundtable members to offer alternative proposals, and these were later accepted word for word as the recommendations of the commission. The nonbusiness members of the commission were not invited.[55]

Trade associations also carry on extensive lobbying efforts, representing specific industries or businesses. The *Encyclopedia of Associations* lists thousands of national associations in the United States, with the largest category being trade, business, and commercial. The American Society of Association Executives has over 5,500 members representing every conceivable industry and trade group.[56] In the book *Principles of Association Management* we find a succinct expression of the association's role vis-a-vis government:

> The role of the association in government relations is to represent members by presenting their views on issues and problems where they are needed.[57]

[51]"Business' Most Powerful Lobby in Washington," *Business Week,* December 20, 1976, p. 60.

[52]Ibid.

[53]Ibid.

[54]Robert W. Merry and Albert R. Hunt, "Business Lobby Gains More Power as It Rides Antigovernment Tide," *Wall Street Journal,* May 17, 1978, p. 1.

[55]*Business Week,* December 20, 1976, p. 60.

[56]"Latching on to a Good Thing," *Forbes,* October 15, 1976, p. 110.

[57]American Society of Association Executives and Chamber of Commerce of the United States (Washington, D.C., 1975), p. 159.

Associations as lobby groups attempt to educate lawmakers regarding their points of view on the thousands of bills that will be introduced in a legislative session. Examples of association lobbying efforts include the United Fresh Fruit and Vegetable Association's attempt to influence the FDA's guidelines pertaining to nutritional labeling; the Boating Industry Association's efforts to obtain standardized identification numbers throughout the fifty states; and the National Paint and Coating Association's fight against what it considers "harsh and uninformed restrictions on the use of lead in house paints."[58] Because association members feel that government regulation and intervention will increase in all areas up to at least 1985, government relations will continue to be a very important function of associations.[59]

A recent development in business's efforts to influence government is the success of groups that represent small business. This may be due in part to a backlash against the hugeness of big business lobbying. One successful group illustrating this trend is the National Federation of Independent Business (NFIB). Using modern, sophisticated means, including computers, the NFIB has its half-million membership list categorized according to congressional district and type of business. Computer printouts even show which members know their congressmen personally. As a result, they can marshal a pointed and immediate lobbying effort.[60] The small business group is only one of the groups to use modern approaches to lobbying. The NAM, Chamber of Commerce, and others are beginning to combine the "power of new coalitions in Washington with grass-roots organizations that reach into virtually every congressman's home district.[61]

In addition to lobbying efforts, business also employs electoral and judicial efforts to advocate its viewpoints. Though we will not discuss the various judicial battles business engages in to forestall unfavorable government activity, its attempts to influence elections deserve a brief look.

Though the federal criminal code forbids business contributions to candidates in federal elections, business nevertheless still strives to place its favored candidates in office. (Yet, despite the laws, an unprecedented number of companies were indicted for illegal contributions in the 1972 presidental election campaign.) Though direct corporate contributions are illegal in national elections, there are a number of permissible actions a firm can take to shape the electoral process, including those below.

[58]Jean Briggs, "The Countergovernment," *Forbes,* October 15, 1976, p. 106ff.
[59]Robert M. Fulmer, *Managing Associations for the 1980's* (Washington: American Society of Association Executives, 1972), p. 54.
[60]*Wall Street Journal,* May 17, 1978, p. 1.
[61]"A Potent New Business Lobby," *Business Week,* May 22, 1978, pp. 64-69.

1. Encourage stockholders and employees to register to vote, although it may not suggest *how* they should vote.
2. Permit candidates to tour company premises to meet or greet employees. If it does this, however, it must grant all candidates this privilege.
3. State its position on public issues affecting its well-being, including legislation currently pending congressional decisions.[62]
4. Communicate information to its employees and stockholders concerning candidates for office, including voting records of members of Congress.
5. Provide political education programs for employees. A firm can promote on a nonpartisan basis its employees' voluntary involvement in direct political action on their own time. Also, an employee may be granted a leave of absence without pay to work in a political campaign.[63]

The 1974 campaign law opened the door for further legitimate business involvement in elections by permitting establishment by corporations of *political action committees* (PACs). These committees can make periodic presentations to company officials and stockholders on behalf of particular candidates and can collect campaign contributions to distribute later.

One outspoken critic of business's use of PACs is David Keene, recognized as one of the most competent young political operatives today.[64] Keene argued that business had a prime opportunity in the 1976 election but "missed the boat." After the 1974 campaign act, more than 400 business-oriented PACs were formed. Most of the money collected by business in 1976, however, came from just 40 of them, with one-third of the groups raising less than $1,000 each.

Though vagueness and complexity in the 1974 law made many firms cautious about violations, Keene argues that business's political efforts were inept, especially in contrast to the success of labor unions. In contrast to 1976, however, a number of politicians expect business to be a more effective force in the future.[65]

Current statistics indicate that PACs are, indeed, multiplying rapidly. In 1978 there were an estimated 525 PACs, and some enthusiasts predicted that as many as 1,500 other companies would set up such com-

---

[62]For an interesting discussion of the corporation's rights to speak out, see "Corporation's Rights to Disseminate View on Political Issues Backed by High Court," *Wall Street Journal,* April 27, 1978, p. 4.

[63]Weidenbaum, 1977, pp. 273-274. See also Lewis Freeman, "Permissible Political Activities," *NAM Reports,* September 9, 1974, p. 10.

[64]Alan L. Otten, "Business in Politics," *Wall Street Journal,* April 28, 1977, p. 20.

[65]Ibid.

mittees in 1978-79.[66] Figure 4-4 illustrates the percentage of the *Fortune* top 1000 industrial companies that had PACs, and Figure 4-5 shows in which types of industry these corporate PACs were found, based upon a 1979 Conference Board survey.

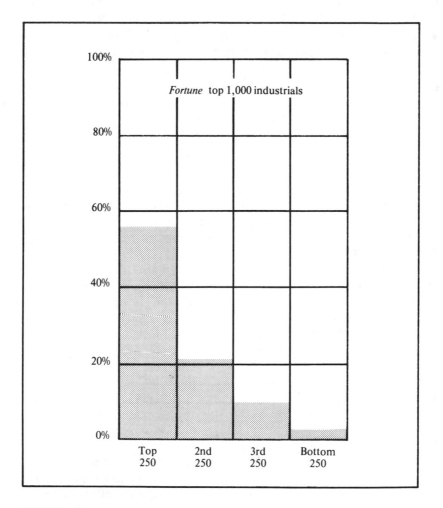

FIGURE 4-4
Percent of Largest Companies with at Least One PAC

SOURCE: "Economic Road Maps, Political Action Committees," Nos. 1868-1869 (New York: The Conference Board, December 1979), p. 2. Reprinted by permission.

[66] "Big Year for Company Political Action," *Dun's Review,* March 1978, pp. 100-105.

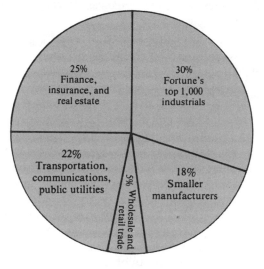

FIGURE 4-5
Corporate PACs by Number of Committees (767 Committees=100%)

SOURCE: "Economic Road Maps, Political Action Committees," Nos. 1868-1869 (New York: The Conference Board, December 1979), p. 2. Reprinted by permission.

Status of Business's Political Power

The question that is inevitably raised in discussions of attempts by business to influence government is whether business possesses inordinate political power. Some experts — Ralph Nader and Mark Green, for example — have forcefully argued that business does have excessive political power.[67] Others have advocated this viewpoint also.

There is considerable support, too, for the opposing view. Neil Jacoby concludes, for example, that "the notion that corporate enterprise 'dominates' or unduly influences the American government simply does not withstand examination."[68] His view is that both business and unions have lost political power in the postwar era as environmentalists, consumerists, civil rights groups, and other such organizations have successfully applied influence that resulted in social legislation.

Edwin Epstein, who has carefully studied corporate political power for some time, also does not feel there is sufficient evidence to support

[67]Ralph Nader and Mark Green (eds.), *Corporate Power in America* (New York: Grossman Publishers, 1972).
[68]Jacoby, p. 157.

the view that business's power is excessive relative to that of other groups in society. He concludes:

> ... contentions that corporations control the American political order have yet to be proven. While, on occasion, the critics have been helpful in highlighting particular, dangerous examples of excessive corporate political power, all too frequently they have presented mere caricatures of reality.[69]

Taking all positions into consideration, it does not appear that business has excessive political power. But this is a difficult question because management techniques of power are simply not very sophisticated. And the exercise of political power should not necessarily be viewed with disdain, as it represents the dynamic process by which a pluralistic society works. Business, along with labor, education, farmers' associations, and most other groups in society are politicized in that they attempt to influence public policy. As Jacoby has said, "In a pluralistic society, every institution has a right — if not a duty — to do what it can to survive. Pressure upon government for this purpose is a legitimate expression of a fundamental drive."[70]

The overall view of society should be to keep the balance of power among competing interest groups such that groups are not denied access to the political decision-making process. Our laws are designed to do this. Beyond the law, however, we get into the area of what is ethical for business and other groups; unfortunately, there has been no emergence of a set of guidelines or principles governing organizations. As a consequence, situations have to be carefully examined as they arise, and out of this process a consensus might evolve concerning what is acceptable. This can then serve in future decision making. In the meantime, vigilance must be the watchword.

TOWARD AN IMPROVED BUSINESS-GOVERNMENT RELATIONSHIP

Most of what has been concluded about improving business-government relations is quite general in nature. Because this is so, and because the matter is so broad in perspective that the average student of business and society will probably never be directly involved in such determinations, the temptation is not to discuss it at all. This temptation will be avoided, because even a brief treatment of the subject can go far toward communicating current thinking.

---

[69]Edwin M. Epstein, "Dimensions of Corporate Power, Pt. 2," *California Management Review,* Summer 1974, p. 44.
[70]Jacoby, p. 150.

A decade ago the Committee for Economic Development was formed as "a government-business partnership for social progress."[71] In 1974 the UCLA Seminar on Business-Government Relations ranked "conditions of business-government collaboration in resolving social problems" as second in importance only to reform of governmental regulation of business.[72] In 1977, Charles W. Robinson was calling for more business-government cooperation as "business and government face the future."[73] Pleas such as these have been numerous. They have been more successful in calling attention to the need for such cooperation, however, than they have been in actually getting new forms of cooperation into effect. This is not a condemnation. It simply reflects the fact that we are dealing with highly complex issues that are not easily resolved.

Whereas most agree that the basic government-business relationship is adversary in nature, and some agree that this is the way it must be, most commentators call for new forms of government-business cooperation as a means for solving societal problems. The fundamental questions keep resurfacing: In a complex society such as ours, what functions or roles should be performed by business, by government, or by both working in concert? Where is the dividing line to be drawn?

Though we seem to keep asking questions and not providing clear answers, this is a commentary on the state of our understanding. George Steiner reasons that there are some distinct barriers inhibiting business-government cooperation that need to be recognized initially. These include an antipathy between business and government, growing out of their past philosophical attitudes; the inability of government officials to foresee emerging problems (such as energy shortages) and take necessary action; and the absence of a suitable body of tested practices and principles to guide the relationship.[74] He therefore recommends as a first step cross-sectional research on business-government cooperation. This would entail: systematic forecasting to identify major future problems which, if delineated, would instigate present actions; an investigation of ways to avoid abuses that can develop from too close cooperation; research on incentives for business; and research designed to identify specific areas in which the public expects business-government cooperation.[75]

[71]Committee for Economic Development, *Social Responsibilities of Business Corporations,* 1971, pp. 50-61.

[72]Jacoby, p. 173.

[73]Charles W. Robinson, "Business and Government Face the Future," in Lillian W. Kay' (ed.), *The Future Role of Business in Society* (New York: The Conference Board, 1972), pp. 23-31.

[74]George A. Steiner, "Creating a Cooperative Interface Between Business and Government," in Jacoby, pp. 112-113.

[75]Ibid., pp. 113-115.

Michael Blumenthal asserts, in this connection, that the issues deserving the highest priority include the following:

1. Redefining the role of private business
2. Business-government collaboration on social projects
3. Setting standards of business behavior
4. Educating for leadership in business and government
5. Financing of political campaigns
6. Auditing the regulatory agencies[76]

The agendas of both Steiner and Blumenthal would, if pursued, represent logical starting points in moving toward an understanding of what the business-government relationship ought to be. These are not calls to move us toward a planned society as in some socialist countries, but they are efforts to move us toward a "planning society."[77] It is only by applying management knowledge and techniques that have been so successful in building the economic and productive aspects of our present system that we will begin to find rational and feasible avenues for dealing with the host of problems that require business and government to act in concert. Yet, at the same time, caution must be exercised lest the "bureaucratic symbiosis" of business and government living off one another to their mutual advantage, as John Kenneth Galbraith has warned, becomes more of a reality than a caricature.

Indications are that the increased role of government, which has been accelerating for years, will not diminish.[78] Thus, business has every incentive to anticipate the areas, depth of involvement, and possible modes of intervention that it will face. By acting sooner rather than later, management will be in the best position to enforce its input into public policy decision making and, as we suggested earlier, this is not only its right but its responsibility.

SUMMARY

Few issues today are of more concern to business than its relationship with government — especially the federal government. Historically, business has become more and more affected by government, as social legislation has increased relative to economic legislation. The relation-

---

[76]W. Michael Blumenthal, "Correcting Flaws in the Business-Government Interface," in Jacoby, pp. 96-98.

[77]Ibid., p. 116.

[78]For example, see Jon G. Udell, Gene R. Laczniak, and Robert F. Lusch, "The Business Environment of 1985," *Business Horizons,* June 1976, p. 53.

ship between business and government has been complicated further by the multitude of roles government assumes in its interaction with business. The major question seems to be: What should be the respective roles of business and of government in our socioeconomic system?

A close look shows that government does attempt to influence business and vice versa. Government employs a number of nonregulatory and regulatory approaches in its efforts. Moral suasion, voluntary standards, coercion, formal controls, subsidies, the tax system, and financing are among the most often used nonregulatory strategies employed. Direct regulation has exploded in terms of its size and its impact on business. Functional regulation superimposed on traditional industry regulation has produced a matrix effect, resulting in a complex regulatory pattern. The impact of regulation has manifested itself in both overt and hidden costs. Though solutions to the regulatory problem have been pursued, business still thinks that the maze of regulations is excessive and counterproductive.

Business also attempts to influence government and the political process. Although business has a multitude of objectives in this endeavor, it basically desires a climate more favorable to its growth and prosperity. Business attempts to influence government decision making through the legislative process by lobbying, through the electoral process with campaign contributions, and through the judicial process with lawsuits. Newly formed groups such as the Business Roundtable, the Committee of One Hundred, and political action committees seem to hold the most immediate promise for organized activity that can influence government. This is supplemented by Washington offices, lobbyists, and the efforts of associations.

Though the basic business-government relationship is best characterized as adversary, many suggestions have been made for more business-government cooperation. Indications are that the increased role of government, which has been accelerating for years, will not diminish; thus business, along with government, has every incentive to pursue new models of cooperation for their mutual benefit.

QUESTIONS FOR DISCUSSION

1. Give a brief overview of the history of government's role in business's evolution. When were the key turning points?
2. Outline the various roles government has assumed in its relationship with business. Do some of these roles seem counterproductive for an efficient and effective system?

3. Why are business-government relations often termed a "clash of ethical systems"? Indicate the dimensions of this clash. Is this the way it must be, given our basic system?
4. What are some of the value changes that have been occurring in society that help explain the increased role of government in our system? Could these value changes have been accommodated in a system without increased government? Discuss.
5. In what sense does the egalitarian movement embrace all of the other value shifts that are occurring?
6. Discuss the paths of influence that exist among business, government, and the public.
7. Rank in order the various nonregulatory approaches used by government to influence business in terms of your perception of their potential effectiveness. Can you present some evidence supporting the validity of your ranking?
8. Differentiate between traditional industry regulation and functional regulation. Which is more recent and which represents greater potential impact on business? How do the two types combine to create a matrix?
9. Identify and discuss some of the hidden costs of government regulation. Give specific examples. What are the major failings of regulations?
10. Discuss the major means used by business to influence government. Which seem to have the most future potential?
11. What are the differences between such old-line business groups as the NAM and the Chamber of Commerce, and such modern groups as the Business Roundtable? Which seem to have the most future potential?
12. Does business have excessive political power? Discuss.
13. Outline and discuss initial steps that can and should be taken in moving toward an improved business-government relationship.

Cases

PAC-Rats

National Technologies Corporation (NTC), a manufacturer of such products as elevators, helicopters, and aircraft engines, has formed one of the most active Political Action Committees (PACs) in the United States. PACs are a legal method by which businesses may contribute to politicians without using their own money. When employees, usually middle and top managers of a company, are organized into PACs, they may then contribute their own money to politicians. PACs are business's response to the highly successful COPEs (Committees on Political Education), formed by labor unions.

In 1976 alone, NTC's PAC contributed $120,000 to twenty-five Senate and ninety-five House candidates. It seemed that Democrats received about half of the money even though Republicans are typically perceived as being more probusiness and conservative.

Critics of PACs and COPEs have accused both business and labor of trying to wield too much power and influence over government by buying the votes of politicians. Business claims that labor has been doing this for years and, thus, has had an unfair advantage. Both business and labor, however, see no ethical problems in pursuing their own interests in such a manner, as the practice is deemed entirely legal by the Federal Election Commission. The contributions of both PACs and COPEs reached an all-time high in the 1980 election.

QUESTIONS

1. Though PACs and COPEs are legal, do you see any potential in them for unethical abuses?
2. Is a company acting socially responsible by allowing its employees time off to work on PACs when they might otherwise be engaged in such beneficial projects as working on a new pollution abatement system?
3. Assume, hypothetically, that you learned that NTC's top management was putting pressure on its managers to give to the company's PAC. How do you analyze this situation from the standpoint of acceptable ethics?
4. Does it seem to you that PACs and COPEs are reasonably fair mechanisms for management and labor to employ in their efforts to influence government?

The Chrysler Bailout

In June 1979 the Chrysler Corporation, the nation's third largest auto manufacturer, informed government officials that the company would probably suffer a $300 million loss. Chrysler blamed the federal rules relating to fuel economy, safety, and emissions, which add about $640 to a new Chrysler as compared to $340 for a GM or Ford car. GM and Ford are able to spread these costs of meeting government regulations over a wider base, thus reducing the cost per car. The third quarter of 1979 brought Chrysler a $460 million loss, the largest one-quarter operating loss for a company in the country's history. Instead of seeking only a relaxation of regulatory rules, as was initially proposed, the company, lead by chief executive officer Lee Iacocca, approached the federal government with a plea for loan guarantees. The Chrysler executives asked Treasury Secretary William Miller for loan guarantees of $500 million plus standby loan guarantees of $700 million if they are needed. Iacocca warned that if Chrysler went bankrupt, reverberations would be felt throughout the economy and thousands of American jobs would be lost.

The concept of loan guarantees is not new. Currently, federal loans go to steel companies and shipbuilders, students, home buyers, railroads, and minority business people. Even if Chrysler did not get a cent, the amount of federal loans outstanding in 1980 would be more than $550 billion. The federal government, however, is not obligated to save every failing company. Pan Am was denied help a few years ago. The free enterprise system is based on competition and survival of the fittest. The regulatory burdens aside, Chrysler has proven itself a marginal competitor due to management weaknesses and lack of responsiveness to the marketplace. Chrysler wanted to become a global corporation and continued its European operations even though the company was obviously losing money in Europe. Chrysler delayed capital spending for the production of fuel-efficient cars when soaring fuel costs made the consumers energy conscious. When arguing that federal regulations have all but crushed Chrysler, its executives failed to explain how foreign car manufacturers smaller than Chrysler meet these regulations and earn profits.

After Chrysler had already trimmed $560 million a year from its operating budget, Congress passed a $3.5 billion aid package in December 1979, which includes $1.5 billion in loan guarantees. Chrysler had to obtain the remainder by raising money from auto dealers, suppliers, banks, and other sources in states where Chrysler had operations. Included as part of the arrangement were concessions of $446 million from the United Auto Workers Union over the next three years. Chrysler was also required to distribute $162.5 million of its common stock over the next four years. Iacocca wanted to maintain a full line of cars to compete with Ford and GM; he admits that this is expensive, but he believes it is worth the price. Privately, a group of bankers believed that to remain a full-line manufacturer, the company may well require additional infusions of aid running as high as $2 or $3 billion. In any event, Iacocca may have to abandon his goal of competing head to head with his old friends at Ford.[1]

[1] This case was prepared by Allen Payne from Peter Bohr, "Chrysler's Pie-in-the-Sky Plan for Survival," *Fortune*, October 22, 1979, pp. 46-52. Reprinted by permission.

QUESTIONS

1. Should the federal government back loans to private corporations? What are the implications of this both for now and in the future? What role, if any, should government assume with companies, like Chrysler, that are about to fail?

2. What kind of society are we developing that allows for these kinds of loan guarantees? Is it capitalism or free enterprise any more? Discuss.

3. Under what circumstances, if any, should federal loan guarantees be made?

4. How can you have a system that allows for federal bailouts in some cases but not in others? With such a system in place, will companies not calculate their risks as closely because they know the government may intervene and support them?

Business and the Consumer

A recent survey of 2,400 metropolitan household consumers revealed that one in five purchases of products and services results in consumer dissatisfaction with something other than price, and about one in three of the complaints made by those surveyed ended with an unsatisfactory resolution of the problem.[1]

Is it any wonder, then, that the issue of business and the consumer (or customer) is at the forefront of discussions about business and its relationships with and responsibility to the society in which it exists. Products and services are the most visible manifestation of business in society. It is for this reason that the whole issue of business and the consumer deserves a very close examination.

In this chapter we propose to examine the following topics:

- The consumer orientation — the paradox
- The consumer's Magna Carta
- Consumerism — What is it? Why has it come about?
- Business responsibility for product information
- Business responsibility for products
- How is business responding to consumerism?

THE CONSUMER ORIENTATION: THE PARADOX

If one studies the history of business in America, one sees how business has evolved through what some marketing experts have termed

---

[1] Alan R. Andreasen and Arthur Best, "Consumers Complain — Does Business Respond?" *Harvard Business Review,* July-August 1977, p. 93. For a further discussion of consumer dissatisfaction, see Hiram C. Barksdale and William D. Perreault, Jr., "Can Consumers Be Satisfied?" *MSU Business Topics,* Spring 1980, pp. 19-30.

different eras in the evolution of marketing. In fact, it has been said that recent changes could be characterized as a revolution in marketing.[2] Basically, this revolution stems from the idea that the customer is the focus of business, and not the company as was once thought.

The focus, in other words, has shifted from problems of production to problems of marketing. The product business *can* make is no longer as important as the product the consumer *wants* business to make.[3] Robert Keith, using the Pillsbury Company as a model, suggests that it went through four eras — which he suggests also typifies American business in general. The first era was that of manufacturing, in which the company philosophy was product-oriented. Second came the sales-oriented era, when the focus was on having a first-rate sales organization that could dispose of all the product (in Pillsbury's case, flour) that could be made. The third era was marketing-oriented. The philosophy here was consumer-oriented: "We make and sell products for consumers." The fourth era followed a philosophy of marketing control, articulated as, "We are moving from a company which has the marketing concept to a marketing company."[4]

The consumer orientation, which prevails today, is at the heart of the "marketing concept."[5] The paradox of the marketing concept — the consumer orientation — however, is that in a period when practically all marketing theorists and practitioners proclaim a consumer orientation, we see a concomitant rise in the voice of the consumer exclaiming that business does not care about the consumer. Indeed, the consumer movement of the last decade or so, marching under the banner of "consumerism," seems to fly in the face of the marketing concept. *Business Week* magazine expressed this concern a number of years ago when they asserted:

> In the very broadest sense, consumerism can be defined as the bankruptcy of what the business schools have been calling the "marketing concept."[6]

We will return to the subject of consumerism later, but a number of fundamental questions have already emerged, the most important of which is: What does business owe the consumer? Or, stated differently, what does the consumer have a right to expect from business?

---

[2]Robert J. Keith, "The Marketing Revolution," *Journal of Marketing,* January 1960.
[3]Ibid.
[4]Ibid.
[5]Martin L. Bell and C. William Emory, "The Faltering Marketing Concept, *Journal of Marketing,* October 1971.
[6]"Business Responds to Consumerism," *Business Week,* September 6, 1969, p. 95.

THE CONSUMER'S MAGNA CARTA

Many marketing experts have chosen to indicate what business owes the consumer by reciting what Holloway and Hancock termed the "consumer's Magna Carta" — those four basic consumer rights spelled out by President John F. Kennedy in his 1962 Special Message on Protecting the Consumer Interest.[7] Those rights were the right to safety, the right to be informed, the right to choose, and the right to be heard.

The *right to safety* is concerned with the fact that many products are dangerous (insecticides, foods, drugs, automobiles, appliances). The *right to be informed* is intimately related to the marketing and advertising function. The consumer's right here is to know what a product really is, how it is to be used, and what cautions must be exercised in its use. It also includes the whole array of marketing: advertising, labeling, and packaging. The *right to choose,* though perhaps not as great a concern as the first two, refers to the assurance that competition is effectively working. The fourth right, the *right to be heard*, was proposed because of the view of many consumers that they cannot effectively communicate to business their desires and, especially, their grievances.[8] Considerable evidence exists, including the study cited at the beginning of this chapter, that the business environment is not receptive to consumer complaints and their rectification.

Though the four basic rights articulated by President Kennedy do not embody all the responsibilities that business owes to consumers, they do capture the essence of business's social responsibilities to consumers.[9] They provide an excellent first approximation of those responsibilities; and they accept the fact that business has on numerous occasions violated basic consumer rights, thus contributing to the emergence and development of the consumer movement.

THE CONSUMER MOVEMENT: CONSUMERISM

There have been outcries for decades that the consumer was mistreated.[10] The contemporary wave of criticism, however, started to build in the late 1950s, took form in the 1960s, and continues even today. The

[7]Robert J. Holloway and Robert S. Hancock, *Marketing in a Changing Environment,* 2nd ed. (New York: John Wiley & Sons, 1973), pp. 558-565. For additional discussion, see Robert M. Estes, "Consumerism and Business," *California Management Review,* Winter 1971, pp. 5-12.

[8]Ibid., pp. 565-566.

[9]For an excellent discussion of how one large company, Giant Food, Inc., responded to these four basic rights, see Esther Peterson, "Consumerism as a Retailer's Asset," *Harvard Business Review,* May-June 1974, pp. 91-101.

[10]Robert O. Herrmann, "Consumerism: Its Goals, Organizations, and Future," *Journal of Marketing,* October 1970, pp. 55-60.

following definition of consumerism captures the essence of the consumer movement:

> Consumerism is a social movement seeking to augment the rights and powers of buyers in relation to sellers.[11]

Though the consumer movement is often said to have begun in the 1960s with the publication of Ralph Nader's criticism of General Motors in *Unsafe at Any Speed,*[12] the impetus for the movement was actually a complex combination of circumstances. With respect to consumerism, Philip Kotler asserts:

> The phenomenon was not due to any single cause. Consumerism was reborn because all of the conditions that normally combine to produce a successful social movement were present.[13] These conditions are structural conduciveness, structural strains, growth of a generalized belief, precipitating factors, mobilization for action, and social control.[14]

Kotler then goes on to specify the major factors within each of these categories that contributed to the rise of consumerism in the 1960s. These factors are presented in Exhibit 5-1. A close examination of this exhibit will help explain the rise of consumerism.

Kotler argues that consumerism is, indeed, a beneficial movement, and that it promises to deliver real gains in the long run — both to business and the consumer. It will force business to reexamine its role in society, challenge business people to scrutinize problems that are easily ignored, and challenge managers to look at ends as well as means.[15]

Beyond these beneficial concerns there may be a number of other practical gains for consumers and business people, such as the following:

1. *Product information* will be increased as a consequence of consumerism. This will result in consumers buying more efficiently, obtaining more value for money spent, and therefore being able to buy more total goods and services.

2. *Legislation* will emerge that places a limit on promotional spending, which is for the purpose of increasing market share rather than total demand. Thus, such appeals as trading stamps, games, and other gimmickry may be severely curtailed.

[11]Philip Kotler, "What Consumerism Means for Marketers," *Harvard Business Review,* May-June 1972, pp. 48-57.
[12]Ralph Nader, *Unsafe at Any Speed* (New York: Brossman Publishers, 1965).
[13]Kotler, p. 50.
[14]Kotler states that these conditions were proposed by Neil J. Smelser, *Theory of Collective Behavior* (New York: The Free Press, 1963).
[15]Kotler, p. 53.

EXHIBIT 5-1
Factors Contributing to the Rise of Consumerism in the 1960s

1. *Structural Conduciveness*
   Advancing incomes and education
   Advancing complexity of technology and marketing
   Advancing exploitation of the environment

   ↓

2. *Structual Strains*
   Economic discontent (inflation)
   Social discontent (war and race)
   Ecological discontent (pollution)
   Marketing system discontent (shoddy products, gimmickry, dishonesty)
   Political discontent (unresponsive politicians and institutions)

   ↓

3. *Growth of a Generalized Belief*
   Social critic writings (Galbraith, Packard, Carson)
   Consumer-oriented legislators (Kefauver, Douglas)
   Presidential messages
   Consumer organizations

   ↓

4. *Precipitating Factors*
   Professional agitation (Nader)
   Spontaneous agitation (housewife picketing)

   ↓

5. *Mobilization for Action*
   Mass media coverage
   Vote-seeking politicans
   New consumer interest groups and organizations

   ↓

6. *Social Control*
   Business resistance or indifference
   Legislative resistance or indifference

SOURCE: Reprinted by permission of the *Harvard Business Review.* Exhibit from "What Consumerism Means for Marketers," by Philip Kotler (May-June 1972), p. 51. Copyright © 1972 by the President and Fellows of Harvard College; all rights reserved.

3. *Absorption of social costs* will be required of manufacturers. This will result in goods with high social costs selling for more and therefore selling in less volume, and goods with lower social costs selling for less and therefore selling in more volume.
4. A *reduction* in unsafe/unhealthy products will lead to more satisfied, healthier consumers.[16]

The consumer movement came somewhat as a shock to many business people, for they believed that because they had created the most advanced productive machinery known, they were beyond consumer criticism. Indeed, even today, some business people still express disbelief that the movement continues to flourish despite all they have done for the world and for the consumer. But before we examine business's response to the consumer movement, it seems appropriate first to examine more closely what has happened in recent years in two categories of activities that are central to much of the discussion about business's social responsibilities to the consumer. These two broad categories relate to the *information* that business transmits about products and services in the form of advertising, promotion, and packaging; and the *product itself* that business makes, sells, and, in some instances, guarantees.

RESPONSIBILITY FOR
PRODUCT INFORMATION

Why have complaints been raised about business's social responsibilities in the area of product information? Most consumers know why. Consider, for a moment, the following actual cases:

> A cemetery in a large city advertised, as a "special," double burials at a seemingly good price. The double burial turned out, however, to be two coffins stacked in one plot, rather than in two side-by-side plots, as the average customer might expect!
>
> A large automobile dealer not too long ago signed a "voluntary compliance assurance" with a state's office of consumer affairs, agreeing that he would stop using the term "bank sale" in ads unless the cars in that sale actually resulted from repossessions or otherwise were obtained from a bank. The explanation this particular auto dealer gave for his use of the term was that he had stored some of his new cars in the basement of a bank!
>
> A large national motel chain used in its billboard advertising the statement, "Under 18 — Lodge Free," without any conditions

---

[16]Ibid., p. 53.

specified. Upon registering, one found that there was an extra
charge for any beds, cots, or cribs used by those under 18!

These cases are actual examples of the questionable use of product or
service information. And it is widely alleged that the public is exposed
to as many as 500 to 1,500 similar advertisements each day.[17] Admittedly, the companies involved in the cases above were willing to cease
their misleading advertising once an officer of consumer affairs ordered
them to, but one might suspect in reading these cases some effort to
deceive. Whether the motive was there or not, business has an ethical
responsibility to *fairly* and *accurately* provide information on its products or services. The primary form of product information abuse by
business falls in the realm of advertising. In addition to this, business
has a responsibility in the information-related areas of warranties and
guarantees, packaging, labeling, and instructions for use.

Advertising

Advertising is the lifeblood of the American free enterprise system. It
stimulates competition and makes available information consumers can
use in comparison buying. It also provides competitors with information against which to respond in a competitive way, and contains a
mechanism for immediate feedback in the form of sales response.
Advertising, in sum, provides social and economic benefits to the
American people and the free enterprise system.

Unfortunately, advertising also has drawbacks. The frequently heard
phrase, "the seamy side of advertising," alludes to the economic and
social costs that derive from advertising abuses, such as those illustrated earlier, and to which the reader is probably able to supply ample
additions. These abuses are usually designated as deceptive, exaggerated, distorted, misleading, or unsubstantiated advertising. No attempt
will be made to differentiate among these advertising abuses, but collectively they form a pastiche of abuses which severely undermine the
public's confidence in business in our society.

Interconnected with the abuses listed is the problem of advertising
puffery, perhaps one of the more subtle forms of questionable advertising and certainly one of the most widespread. Eli Cox defines *puffery* as
"the practice by a seller of making exaggerated or deceptive claims
about a product or service."[18]

---

[17]C. H. Lushbough, "Advertising: Consumer Information and Consumer Deception," *California Management Review,* Spring 1974, pp. 80-82.
[18]Eli P. Cox, "Deflating the Puffer," *MSU Business Topics,* Summer 1973, p. 29.

Cox argues that puffery is practiced at great social and economic costs, and is one of the chief disadvantages of our economic system. What are these costs? Four are worth considering.

1. Counterproductivity of Consumer Benefits. Puffery induces people to buy things that do them no good or things that can be harmful. For example, if the Federal Trade Commission's (FTC) assertion that Geritol's advertising contributed to delay in people seeking needed medical attention was valid, this is potentially serious. Puffery may also cause people to alter their priorities. Do you think, for example, there is a possibility that strong deodorant advertising may lead someone to stop buying and using soap? Puffery might also beget puffery, Cox suggests, by stimulating competitive advertising — the net effect of which is to drive up the costs of similar products.[19]

2. Loss of Advertising Efficiency. When advertising credibility declines due to puffery, it requires a larger expenditure to achieve the same objective. Studies have demonstrated that public confidence in advertising is decreasing. A Gallup poll showed that the consumer sees very little difference between the credibility of advertising claims made for products and services and those made for political candidates.[20] This skepticism is not limited to adults, apparently. In a study conducted among 11- and 12-year-old children, researchers found that "three-quarters of them felt that advertising is sometimes designed to 'trick' the consumers." The study concluded, "Most children have already become cynical (by age 11) — ready to believe that, like advertising, business and other social institutions are riddled with hypocrisy."[21]

3. Bad Advertising Drives Out the Good. Consumers are usually unable to test advertisers' claims, and are therefore likely to purchase the products for which the most exaggerated claims are made. If businesses are able to get away with this (and in some cases they have), competitors who expect to stay in business may have to resort to similar practices. Since administrative agencies have limited resources, it is possible that they would have to spend their time on the worst offenders and leave free to operate those who just hover around the line between legality and illegality.[22] The consumer pays in cases such as this.

4. Loss of Faith in the System. The average American develops his view of the economic system from the clues he gets from advertising

[19]Ibid., pp. 32-33.
[20]Ibid., p. 33.
[21]Morton C. Paulson, "What Youngsters Learn on TV," *National Observer,* May 29, 1976, p. 10.
[22]Cox, p. 33.

about products, services, and the companies that produce them. The pervasiveness of advertising — its ubiquitousness — gives it an enormous influence in shaping the consumer's view of business. The magic tube and the glossy magazine capture and shape perceptions. Advertising seems to put business's worst foot forward, and the result is frequently a serious injustice. As Cox continues,

> Distorted advertising claims cheapen good products and discredit their producers. They also tell our young people that the system is based on greed, deception, and sharp practice and that those who supply us also exploit us. It makes it easy for people to fall prey to arguments that we should scrap the system and build another from the ground up.[23]

The deleterious effects of misleading advertising are therefore clear and numerous. And, in the long run, the last cost society and business pay — loss of faith in the system — may be the most significant. When this occurs, a multitude of events may lead inevitably to new forms of government intervention or, more dramatically, to new institutions in which society would carry out its commercial function.

Packaging

Packaging and labeling are other dimensions of business's responsibility in providing consumer information. Abuses in this area were fairly frequent until the truth-in-packaging act, the formal name of which is the Fair Packaging and Labeling Act, was passed by Congress in 1967. The purpose of the act was to assure the consumer of an adequate supply of product information through product labeling. The act's usefulness is discussed further:

> The moving force behind the Fair Packaging and Labeling Act is to help the consuming public make the best buy, price-quality wise, from retail store shelves in this day of promotion through packaging. Disclosure of those factors helping it to make buying decisions is the method used. While prevention of deception underlies much of the law, the theme of disclosure permeates the entire law.[24]

The question of product information is but one facet of the packaging issue. Though not related to information, the issue of packaging and its effect on the environment has also become a concern that business must address. Waste package material — crushed cartons, broken glass, and bent cans — create litter in the streets and choke municipal dumps

---

[23]Cox, p. 35.
[24]Fair Packaging and Labeling Act with Explanation (Chicago: Commerce Clearing House, 1966), p. 3.

and incinerators.[25] On another front, then, we see consumerism raising another social issue — environmental protection.

Warranties

Though warranties were initially used by manufacturers to limit the length of time they were expressly responsible for products, they came to be viewed by consumers as devices to protect the buyer against a faulty or defective product. Most consumers have had the experience of buying a hair blower, refrigerator, washing machine, chain saw, or any of thousands of other products only to find that it did not work properly or did not work at all. Then when the buyer reads the fine print on the warranty it is found to include so many qualifications and exceptions as to make the manufacturer's promise to remedy the defect just about useless.

Much of this was changed with the passage of the Warranty Act of 1975. This act was aimed at clearing up some misunderstandings about manufacturers' warranties — especially as to whether a "full" warranty was in effect or whether certain parts of the product or certain types of defects were excluded from coverage. Also at issue was whether the buyer had to pay shipping charges when a product was sent to and from the factory for servicing a defect.[26]

The new federal law sets standards for what must be contained in a warranty and the ease with which consumers must be able to understand it. If a company, for example, claims that its product has a "full" warranty, it must contain certain features, including repair "within a reasonable time and without charge."[27] The law holds that anything less than this unconditional assurance must be promoted as a "limited" warranty.

There is some speculation in the business community as to whether calling attention to an unwillingness to offer a full warranty might scare off buyers. A midwestern producer of auto replacement parts, for example, was so afraid that a warranty labeled "limited" would be counterproductive that it dropped warranties from its entire line.[28] Similarly, Fisher-Price toy makers dropped written warranties on music boxes rather than use the word "limited."[29] Many products, on the other hand, need the warranty as an aid to sales (as in the area of "big-ticket" items), and thus companies like General Electric and Whirlpool continue to offer full warranties.

[25]William N. Gunn, "Packagers and the Environmental Challenge," *Harvard Business Review,* July-August 1972, pp. 103-111.

[26]"Marketing: Anti-Lemon Aid," *Time,* February 1976, p. 76.

[27]"The Guesswork on Warranties," *Business Week,* July 15, 1975, p. 51.

[28]Ibid.

[29]*Time,* February 1976, p. 76.

The Role of the Federal Trade Commission (FTC)

We have discussed three main areas of product information — advertising, packaging, and warranties. It is important now to look carefully at the federal government's major instrument — the FTC — for ensuring that business lives up to its responsibilities in these areas. Actually, the FTC has broad and sweeping powers, and it delves into a number of other areas which we will refer to throughout the book.

The FTC is one of the oldest of the federal agencies charged with responsibility for overseeing commercial acts and practices. It was created in 1914, originally as an antitrust weapon, and broadened in 1938 to permit the agency to pursue "unfair or deceptive acts or practices in commerce."[30] Over the years Congress has given the FTC enforcement responsibility in a number of consumer-related fields, including the important Truth-in-Lending Act, Fair Packaging and Labeling Act, Fair Credit Reporting Act, and Equal Credit Opportunity Act. Congress actually designed the FTC's mission broadly: to protect the consumer from "unfair or deceptive acts or practices." This broad power was given because of fear that any specification of a list of prohibitions might lead business to reason that it could do anything not on the list. Exhibit 5-2 is the goal statement of the Federal Trade Commission, as seen in one of its recent annual reports.

The FTC actually did relatively little from 1941 to 1969, a period called by Thomas G. Krattenmaker the "decades of neglect." But 1970 to 1973 were the "years of promise" for the FTC.[31] The agency became "activist" when President Richard Nixon appointed Miles Kirkpatrick chairman. Kirkpatrick and his staff of eager young lawyers put the FTC on the map, so to speak, and since that time the agency has become so aggressive that it has created "an escalating struggle" between itself and business.[32] The source of the struggle has been the FTC's zealousness, its fuzzy and broad powers, its lack of consistency in its own administration, and its concept of what constitutes proper business conduct — or at least so business charges.

Congress does permit the FTC to monitor a wide range of consumer issues. It probes everything from deceptive advertising to antitrust violations. Since we have suggested deceptive advertising to be the major problem in the product information area, let us look at the FTC's activities there.

At one time, the FTC's role in monitoring advertising was somewhat

---

[30]"The Escalating Struggle Between the FTC and Business," *Business Week,* December 13, 1976, p. 52.
[31]Thomas G. Krattenmaker, "The Federal Trade Commission and Consumer Protection," *California Management Review,* Summer 1976, pp. 94-95.
[32]*Business Week,* December 13, 1976, pp. 52-59.

EXHIBIT 5-2
A Goal Statement of the Federal Trade Commission

THE GOAL: A Vigorous and Honest Free Market

The FTC's congressional mandate — a legacy from Theodore Roosevelt, Woodrow Wilson and Louis Brandeis, among other great Americans — is to root out abuses of market power and enhance the role of competition and the sovereign informed consumer as regulators of the marketplace. This mandate enbodies a strong faith in the ability of the marketplace to allocate goods and services efficiently, and a determination that the market mechanism must not be distorted by those who would prefer to control markets to their own ends, whether under the protective umbrella of government regulation or by private regulation through price-fixing, collusion, or other anticompetitive restraints.

Today, as inflation takes an increasingly heavy toll on our economy, this mandate acquires renewed force. The Commission has thus concentrated its activities on those sectors where consumer sovereignty has been most frustrated, where inflation has done the most damage to the consumer's pocketbook. In each area, the FTC's objective is the same: to arm the consumer with the knowledge and the ability to command the lowest price and highest quality goods and services which a competitive marketplace can produce.

SOURCE: Annual Report of the Federal Trade Commission for the Fiscal Year Ended September 30, 1978 (Washington, D.C.: Superintendent of Documents), p. 1.

innocuous. It concentrated only on the most blatant cases of deception. Advertisers, knowing basically what the FTC would do from past experience, freely engaged in what is now called puffery, or unsubstantiated claims. In recent years, though, the FTC has intervened in cases where deception was not nearly as clear. Examples of its intervention include the Chevron gas, Wonder Bread, Hi-C, and Firestone tire cases — products familiar to us all. The Chevron case was one in which Standard Oil of California was accused of implying that its gas contained an additive that would eliminate pollution. Advertisements for Wonder Bread were accused of implying that it was more nutritious than other breads. The Coca Cola Company was accused of implying that Hi-C was more nutritious than orange juice. And Firestone was accused of implying that their "safe tire" was safe under any conditions.[33] Though the FTC experienced mixed success in these cases, it was not deterred from vigorously pursuing deceptive advertising practices.

Perhaps one of the FTC's most controversial moves has been its *cor-*

---

[33]Gary M. Armstrong and Frederick A. Russ, "Detecting Deception in Advertising," *MSU Business Topics,* Spring 1975, p. 22. See also "Wonder, F-310 Cases Sent to FTC Judges," *Advertising Age,* October 2, 1972, p. 34; "Hi-C Ads Lauded as FTC Judge Rules They Didn't Mislead," *Advertising Age,* October 2, 1972, p. 1; "FTC Rules Firestone Ads Deceptive, " *Advertising Age,* October 9, 1972, pp. 1, 77.

rective advertising program, designed to remedy promotional deceptions. Under this program, the FTC would force companies to publish paid ads that admitted past false or misleading statements, and then go on to tell the consumer what the truth really is — or the truth as it has been negotiated with the FTC.[34] Companies such as International Telephone and Telegraph, Amstar, Matsushita Electric, Ocean Spray Cranberries, and twenty-five chemical firms are among those that have had to recant some of their advertising claims.

Warner-Lambert, on the other hand, decided to take the FTC to court to argue that the agency was overstepping its lawful authority in ordering corrective advertising. The FTC wanted Warner-Lambert to run corrective advertising on its Listerine mouthwash ads, which it felt were misleading. The outcome of this case, won by the FTC, will be important to both business and government for a long time to come.

The FTC is also becoming assertive in the areas of nutritional claims and drug advertising. It wants to develop specific rules that all firms will have to follow, rather than deal with companies on a case-by-case basis. In the nutrition area, for example, it wants to set down three rules that will govern nutritional claims, stating that certain foods must meet these rules before being called nutritious, energy-giving, or wholesome. Two of the three rules would require that a list of specific nutrients be included in advertising.

The FTC is also asserting itself by raising questions about professional groups that do not permit advertising, on the ground that it inhibits competition. Professions that the FTC is looking at closely include optometry and medicine. In one other interesting case, the FTC ordered Hudson Pharmaceutical Corporation to stop advertising its Spider-man Vitamins to children because the firm was using a hero figure to boost sales.[35] This case was just the first in a series of attacks by the FTC and consumer groups on advertising of children's products, aimed at children.

There is evidence, however, that the FTC believes some of its own rules may have been dysfunctional, having caused consumers more harm than good. An example of this is the "unavailability" rule, which requires retailers to stock "reasonable" quantities of goods they advertise at sale prices. Though on its face this appears to be advantageous to consumers, the FTC now sees some drawbacks. The agency suggests that this rule may (a) discourage retailers from having sales, and (b) result in higher operating costs due, for example, to higher inventories and food spoilage. The FTC plans to undertake more such self-analysis

---

[34]"Back on the Warpath Against Deceptive Ads," *Business Week*, April 19, 1976, p. 148.
[35]"The FTC's Ad Rules Anger Industry," *Business Week*, November 1, 1976, p. 30.

"impact evaluations" in the future, and perhaps such evaluations may become a standard part of the government's regulatory approach.[36]

Self-Regulation in Advertising

In addition to using governmental or compulsory approaches to improving the honesty and fairness of advertising, self-regulation is an option also available to business. This would entail business policing itself, either through organized bodies or as individual firms acting alone. In a later section we will examine ways individual firms have responded to consumerist pressures, including those on advertising. Let us first examine the option of self-regulation through group-of-industry mechanisms.

The most prominent instance of self-regulation in the advertising industry is the program sponsored by the National Advertising Review Council. Their two-tiered program consists of an independent National Advertising Review Board (NARB) and a National Advertising Division (NAD) within the revitalized Council of Better Business Bureaus.

Any complaints received about national advertising are first referred to the NAD, which performs the staff functions of reviewing, evaluating, and negotiating charges in advertising. Should the complainant's position be supported, and the advertiser make required changes, the case is closed at this level. The advertiser may appeal to the second tier, the NARB, if it does not concur with the staff decision.

The NARB serves an appellate function through a five-member panel. There is no appeal at this level. If a complaint is not resolved with the advertiser, the case is disclosed to the public and referred to the appropriate governmental agency.[37]

The NAD was formed in mid-1971; it had heard 964 cases by 1976. These involved such highly visible companies and products as Schick vs. Remington and Pledge vs. Behold. This self-regulation has probably prevented greater governmental restrictions in the advertising area. Efforts by local communities to emulate this national effort have met with some difficulty, though. In Denver, when the Rocky Mountain Better Business Bureau (BBB) set up its own ad-study board and went after a local health studio, it ran into trouble. After having no success with the health studio, the BBB told its story to the local media. The local health studio responded immediately with a suit against the BBB for restraint of trade. During years of litigation, serious questions were

---

[36]"The FTC Reviews Its Own Consumer Rules," *Business Week,* March 28, 1977, p. 92.
[37]Howard H. Bell, "Self-Regulation by the Advertising Industry," *California Management Review,* Spring 1974, pp. 58-63.

raised as to whether local ad boards could reasonably expect to bring about change with small offenders who were inclined to file nuisance suits.[38]

The national effort has gone far in regulating advertising, however, and it is interesting to note some results the NARB has achieved. One interesting area, with nothing to do with deception, pertains to ads that can possibly foster unsafe practices. The NARB has held, for example, that though tire commercials showing cars driven over roads strewn with broken glass and nails may document performance, they do not encourage safe consumer practices. The board has also held that ads showing children grilling hot dogs in a microwave oven without an adult present, and parents placing insect sprays on the edge of tables within easy reach of children do not foster safe consumer practices and should not appear.[39]

Among the board's findings:

1. "Advertisers and agencies occasionally fail to 'think safety' during the planning, creation, and review of national advertising."
2. "From time to time, common sense safety considerations are overlooked completely in the production of advertising, or are sacrificed for some desired dramatic effect."
3. Safety in advertising requires the same attention "paid by advertisers and agencies to matters of legality, truth and accuracy, and minority group representation."[40]

RESPONSIBILITY FOR PRODUCTS

In addition to deceptive advertising, meaningless warranties, and a host of other consumer-related issues, another area in which the public feels business has an important social responsibility to the consumer is that of unsafe or impure products. This situation moved to the forefront in the 1970s, as indicated by court cases and the activities of the newly founded Consumer Product Safety Commission (CPSC).

The problem of business's responsibility for its products and services is not a small one. According to the National Commission on Product Safety, a government study group that several years ago investigated injuries associated with hazardous household products, twenty million Americans are injured annually as a consequence of incidents involving

---

[38]"Pulling the Teeth of the Local Watchdogs," *Business Week,* February 9, 1976, p. 34.
[39]Kay Mills, "Ads Can Foster Unsafe Practices," *Atlanta Constitution,* July 18, 1974, p. B-11.
[40]Ibid.

consumer products around the home. Of these people, 110,000 are permanently disabled and 30,000 were killed (excluding automobile accidents).[41]

Armed with the above figures and other alarming statistics, along with strong consumer lobbying, Congress passed the Consumer Product Safety Act in 1972. In just the short time since the commission's formation, it has created and enforced product safety rules in a multitude of areas, such as aspirin bottles, refrigerator door latches, children's pajamas, and the distance between the slats of cribs. It has also issued warnings about such products as mobile homes, tricycles, and sandals made of water-buffalo hide (which can cause a rash).[42]

Prior to the existence of the CPSC, there was very little evidence that business was taking upon itself the monitoring and regulation of product safety. The commission grew out of escalating reports of product dangers and accident statistics compiled by various government bodies. Now, the CPSC has a sophisticated product-injury data-gathering operation that receives and analyzes daily teletype reports from 119 scientifically selected hospital emergency rooms around the country. The data system, called NEISS (National Electronic Injury Surveillance System), is the heart of the commission's efforts to gather and catalog injury statistics. One of NEISS's findings is that the ten most dangerous items (those most often involved in accidents, excluding automobiles) today are the following:

1. Bicycles and bicycle equipment
2. Stairs, ramps, and landings
3. Nonglass doors
4. Cleaning, caustic compounds
5. Nonglass tables
6. Beds
7. Football
8. Playground apparatus
9. Liquid fuels
10. Architectural glass[43]

The CPSC may be the most powerful regulatory agency ever created by Congress.[44] The commission has jurisdiction over practically every consumer product except food, automobiles, and several others that are regulated by other agencies. It has the power to ban products, order the redesign of products, publicize the dangers of products, inspect manufacturing facilities, gather extensive product information, and otherwise place great pressures on business.[45]

[41]R. David Pittle, "The Consumer Product Safety Commission," *California Management Review,* Summer 1976, pp. 105-109.

[42]Paul H. Weaver, "The Hazards of Trying to Make Consumer Products Safer," *Fortune,* July 1975, pp. 133-140.

[43]Listed in Weaver, p. 135.

[44]"Hold onto Your Hats," *Wall Street Journal* (editorial), August 31, 1973, p. 4.

[45]Weaver, p. 133, and *Wall Street Journal,* August 31, 1973, p. 4.

The whole question of *product liability* has become one of the most important social concerns of business in recent years. One of the primary reasons for this is that since the mid-1960s the courts have moved toward a doctrine of "strict liability," which holds the manufacturer responsible for any defects in products that result in injury.[46] To see how far the courts will carry this concept, consider several cases that occurred not too long ago.

> A worker in Texas won $50,000 in damages from a bench-saw maker for injuries received while using a saw which had been originally delivered, complete with safety equipment, to the U.S. Navy in 1942. After buying the saw as surplus, a dealer rebuilt it and resold it without the safety guard to a private operator. The original manufacturer was held liable.[47]

> A high school student in Florida won a $5.3 million suit from the maker of his football helmet, which was held to be the cause of injury, when he was paralyzed by an injury.[48]

In some cases product liability awards seem justified; in others they do not. Nevertheless, this "sue syndrome" and the increasing frequency and size of court-ordered awards is resulting in skyrocketing premiums for product liability insurance — especially among manufacturers of industrial machinery, industrial chemicals, and other high-risk consumer goods.[49]

"Let the seller beware," indeed, is replacing the old adage of "caveat emptor" (let the buyer beware) as a watchword for business today in the product safety and liability area. What has been business's response? Increasingly protective — which is understandable, as many small companies are being driven out of business by large awards. One representative of the American Insurance Association facetiously queried: "Will manufacturers of safety pins one day have to label their product with a warning not to swallow when open?"[50] This may not be very far-fetched. The manufacturer of a child's jumprope felt it necessary to warn the purchaser that it should not be used for climbing, and that it should be inspected before each use. Similarly, the maker of a child's beanbag warns that it is not intended for use by children under three years old.[51]

---

[46]"The Way to Ease Soaring Product Liability Costs," *Business Week*, January 17, 1977, p. 62.

[47]Paul C. Hood, "Product Liability: It'll Raise Prices, but . . . Let the Seller Beware," *The National Observer*, February 12, 1977, pp. 1, 12.

[48]Ibid.

[49]*Business Week*, January 17, 1977, p. 62.

[50]John Cunniff, "Threat to Small Business? Product Liability Called Scourge," *Atlanta Journal*, March 28, 1977, p. C-2.

[51]Ibid.

Given the attitude of the courts, the increasing number of consumer complaints, the possibility of being driven out of existence by huge awards, and the increasing zealousness of the CPSC, business will have to pay considerably more attention to its responsibilities for product safety and performance in the future. The net effect of these trends may be continuing inflation and a decrease in the rate of innovation, along with increasing standardization of products. But these seem to be prices a consuming public concerned about the quality of life is willing to pay.

BUSINESS RESPONSE TO CONSUMERISM

Business's response to consumerism has been mixed. It has ranged from poorly conceived public relations ploys at one extreme to well-designed and implemented departments of consumer affairs at the other extreme. The history of business's response to consumerism parallels business's perceptions of the seriousness, pervasiveness, effectiveness, and longevity of the consumer movement. When the consumer movement first began, business's response was casual, perhaps symbolic, but hardly effective. A 1969 study by Cohen of the communication systems between management and the consumer, for example, showed that whereas such communication did exist, it was not used in managerial decision making.[52]

Today the consumer movement has matured and gained strength, and is assumed by practically everyone to be a continuing part of the business environment. Regarding the success of the consumer in recent years, Ken Bernhardt and Steve Weisbart have concluded, after researching the effectiveness of consumer complaints, that:

1. Consumers today are more persistent than in the past.
2. Consumers are more assertive.
3. Consumers are more likely to utilize or exhaust all appeal channels before being satisfied.[53]

The two researchers conclude that "Ralph Nader has made complaining respectable."

Now armed with considerable influence, consumer activists have been a primary stimulus to more sincere responses from business. These responses have included efforts to improve communication be-

[52]D. Cohen (ed.), *Communication Systems Between Management and the Consumer in Selected Industries* (Hofstra University Yearbook of Business, series 6, vol. 2, 1969).
[53]Sarah Cash, "With Complaints: Consumer Now More Effective," *Atlanta Journal,* January 19, 1977, p. B-3.

tween companies and consumers; the integration of consumer input into marketing decisions; the designation of specific consumer affairs officers; and the creation of specific organizational units, or departments, to handle consumer affairs.

Even when such seemingly sophisticated efforts are undertaken, questions can still be raised as to whether they represent valid attempts by management to improve or are mere public relations gestures. In a 1973 study of *Fortune* 500 companies, for example, F. E. Webster found that although many firms had created departments of consumer affairs, a number of them were just for public relations purposes.[54] More recent evidence seems to indicate that in a growing number of companies, corporate consumer professionals are exerting more significant influence on such crucial functions as product development and marketing campaigns. Several examples are illustrative:

- At Pennsylvania Power & Light Company the consumer and community affairs department is planning regular utility-consumer meetings to exchange information.
- Polaroid Corporation maintains a 300-person consumer services department to perform such functions as rewriting potentially misleading ads and making quality checks on camera repair centers. The department also makes sure that the company's toll-free service phone number is printed in large type on every product.
- Whirlpool Corporation spends one-half million dollars annually operating a toll-free complaint line, which it feels is resulting in repeat business.[55]

Many other makers of consumer goods with highly recognizable names are engaging in similar efforts to be responsive to consumers. There are many reasons for this new responsiveness; but one must be the recent Harris poll in which 46 percent of the respondents felt that "most manufacturers don't really care about giving customers a fair deal," and 59 percent responded that companies are "too concerned about profits to care about quality."[56]

Additional evidence of business's response to consumerism is found in the Barksdale and French survey of chief marketing executives in 1,080 business firms, which shows that:

1. The consumer movement has caused top management to take a more active part in the review and approval of advertising campaigns.

[54]F. E. Webster, Jr., "Does Business Misunderstand Consumerism?" *Harvard Business Review*, September-October 1973, pp. 89-97.
[55]"Corporate Clout for Consumers," *Business Week*, September 12, 1977, p. 144.
[56]Ibid., p. 148.

2. The consumer movement has caused top management to take a more active role in the handling of consumer complaints.[57]

The researchers also sent their questionnaire to a sample of 149 consumer advocates, and their replies were similar to those of the marketing executives.

One more facet of business response to consumerism ought to be mentioned — the issue of improving the exchange of information and shared understanding between business and consumers. William Nickels and Noel Zabriskie call this the "marketing correspondence function." They argue that too many companies today spend too much time talking to potential customers and very little time "listening to and reacting to customer inquiries and complaints."[58] They assert:

> Firms must learn to anticipate and resolve potential consumer problems before they are reflected in the market. Marketing correspondence must be viewed as an active attempt to respond to consumer inquiries and complaints, not as a defensive measure to muffle critics.[59]

David Aaker and George Day reached the conclusion that despite internal barriers and external threats, firms and trade associations are making progress in their response to consumerism pressure.[60] We are entering a new era in business's response. Consumerism pressures do not seem to be letting up — indeed, they are intensifying — and more corporate executives are beginning to take the movement seriously. One motivation for this is, of course, the desire to avoid additional governmental intervention, with its multitude of inflexibilities, uneven applications, and high costs.

In addition, executives see an opportunity to capitalize on consumerism as a competitive marketing tool, one through which profits can be generated. A study by Stephen Greyser and Steven Diamond concludes that (a) consumerism is a positive force in the marketplace, (b) company investment in consumer service and satisfaction will typically pay for itself, and (c) it is good for both the consumer and business.[61]

Two observations are worth making regarding this "new" view of consumerism and business's response: (1) It would be naive to think that business would or should shy away from a social issue in which it

[57]Hiram C. Barksdale and Warren A. French, "Response to Consumerism: How Change Is Perceived by Both Sides," *MSU Business Topics,* Spring 1975, pp. 55-67.

[58]William G. Nickels and Noel B. Zabriskie, "Corporate Responsiveness and the Marketing Correspondence Function," *MSU Business Topics,* Summer 1973, pp. 53-58.

[59]Ibid., p. 58.

[60]David A. Aaker and George S. Day, "Corporate Responses to Consumerism Pressures," *Harvard Business Review,* November-December, 1972.

[61]Stephen A. Greyser and Steven L. Diamond, "Business Is Adapting to Consumerism," *Harvard Business Review,* September-October 1974, p. 38ff.

clearly sees the opportunity for more profit. (2) Given this position, it seems strange that business is still being attacked in an unprecedented fashion for not adequately concerning itself with the consumer.

We see again the enigmatic paradox mentioned at the beginning of this chapter, for which there are several possible explanations. One might be that since consumers wanted low prices, business moved more and more to mass production. When this shift away from custom-made goods occurred and the trend toward low-priced products took hold, business almost guaranteed that some customers would be unhappy. Whereas some customers wanted low prices, others wanted high quality and safer products. Because mass-produced goods some-times cannot fulfill all of these characteristics, there will always be some unhappy consumers who will complain.

Another explanation must lie in the fact that even though business and consumer views have converged in recent years, there is still a gap in their perceptions or understandings of what the ideal business-consumer relationship should be. As long as this gap exists, the business-consumer relationship is bound to be a heated issue.

SUMMARY

The business and consumer relationship is one of the most important, for everyone is a consumer and thus is in contact with business every day. Selling products and services to someone is business's reason for existing. Evidence suggests that though business is more consumer-oriented than ever before, the public is still not satisfied.

Behind the modern consumerism movement are concern for the consumer's rights to safety, to be informed, to choose, and to be heard. The consumerism movement has arisen for many reasons, but its focus has always been basically the same — to augment the rights and powers of buyers in relation to sellers.

Business's social responsibilities to the consumer may be classified into two broad categories — responsibility for information, and responsibility for products and services. The first is involved with issues of advertising, packaging, and warranties, for which the FTC assumes the primary governmental role of regulating. In addition, business monitors itself through such organizations as the National Advertising Review Board.

The extent of business's responsibility for its products has been one of the most heated consumer issues of the decade. The Consumer Product Safety Commission, in particular, has provided the impetus for holding companies to more rigorous standards of product safety. The doctrine of strict liability, in part, has made "Let the seller beware" the watchword for modern business.

Business's response to consumer pressure has been mixed. It has ranged from simple public relations ploys at one extreme to sophisticated information systems and organizational changes at the other. In general, as the consumer movement matured and gained strength, business's response became more deliberate and sincere. The consumer movement has caused top management to take a more active role in the marketing function. But despite all business's attempts to be responsive, the issue does not go away — it is too fundamental to our system.

QUESTIONS FOR DISCUSSION

1. What is referred to as the paradox surrounding business's orientation to the consumer? Discuss.
2. Outline the eras through which organizations have evolved to their present consumer orientation.
3. What are the rights outlined in the "consumer's Magna Carta?" Would you include any other rights? Justify your position.
4. Define consumerism. Discuss the factors that contributed to its rise in the 1960s. Which factors appear to be most significant?
5. Discuss business's social responsibilities in the area of product information and safety.
6. Indicate the major disadvantages of puffery. On balance, do you think puffery is just something we must learn to live with? What is the alternative?
7. Describe the FTC and its role in monitoring business practices. Do you get the impression the FTC has gone too far? Discuss.
8. What future do you see in self-regulation by business in the area of advertising? Do you see self-regulation becoming more common than FTC regulation in the future?
9. Has the CPSC gone too far? What do you see as its future? What does the future hold for product liability lawsuits? Are you pleased with the trend?
10. Has "Let the seller beware" replaced "Let the consumer beware" as the business watchword? Discuss.
11. Outline the range of business's response to consumerism, indicating advantages and disadvantages of the various postures.
12. Where do you think the business-consumer relationship is heading? Support your prediction with evidence.

Cases

"Gentlemen, Switch Your Engines"

The General Motors Corporation has been hit by a series of legal actions (and much criticism) since the discovery that it has allowed engines made by various GM divisions to be installed in cars bearing the brand names of other divisions without the knowledge of the buyer. This matter came to light when an Illinois buyer found that his 1977 Oldsmobile Delta 88 had a Chevrolet engine rather than the engine he thought was in the car.

Most of the legal actions accuse GM, maker of Chevrolet, Oldsmobile, Pontiac, Buick, and Cadillac automobiles, either of violating consumer fraud laws or engaging in false and deceptive advertising by allowing engines to be marketed as if they were made by the same division that manufactured the car. In most cases, suits seek some sort of compensation from the company, and courts are being asked to order the company to make full disclosure to customers in the future of anything unusual under the hood of a particular car. The Federal Trade Commission instituted a preliminary investigation into the engine-switching practice to determine if any federal laws were violated.

In a recent statement responding to demands for financial restitution, GM said: "Because the engines are substantially identical in performance, it is our position that the customer received equal value regardless of what engine he received. Thus, financial restitution would not be appropriate." General Motors has begun a program of posting signs in car dealerships showing which engines are available in various car lines, and in advertisements has suggested that potential buyers ask dealers what engines are available in specific cars.[1]

QUESTIONS

1. Do you think GM was socially responsible in not revealing what engines were being put in specific cars? Why or why not?
2. What else would you recommend that GM do to (a) try to avoid legal actions, and (b) to be socially responsible in the future?

To Advertise or Not to Advertise, That Is the Question

According to recent issues of the *Wall Street Journal* and *Broadcasting* magazine, some corporations that pay for network television advertising

[1]Based on "Engine-Trading Reaction Mounts," *Atlanta Constitution*, April 12, 1977, p. 6-C. Reprinted by permission.

have withdrawn their commercials from the most violent movies and dramatic series. Such corporations as Best Foods, a $24 million-a-year television advertiser, cite "the growing number of letters from viewers who have criticized our commercials for being on programs they consider as violent" as at least one reason for this new advertising policy. One advertising analyst, however, suggests that some advertisers "are using their stated concern over violence as a lever to try to drive down sky-high prices for TV time."

The whole issue of violence on TV came to a head when the National Citizens Committee for Broadcasting, a Washington-based media-reform group, released a study ranking TV series in terms of violent content, and named sponsors most often associated with violent programs. In spite of these reports and subsequent ad pull-outs by some corporations, the networks seem firm in their intent to keep some violence on TV. They may tone it down but they will not eliminate it, because "violence and conflict have always been an integral part of literature and drama." In addition, "action" shows still attract audiences that some advertisers want to reach.

Although many viewers are critical of violence on TV simply because it is there, some criticize the networks for "sanitizing" violence and thus "making it unrealistically palatable to reviewers." Network censors routinely edit bloody scenes out of programs to help reduce the depiction of violence.

QUESTIONS

1. What is business's social responsibility to the consumer in this issue?
2. Do you think corporations have a genuine social concern when they pull ads from excessively violent shows?
3. Are there other means that the sponsors or viewers have used (or can use) to reduce violence on television? Explain.
4. According to this case, are the networks being socially responsive? If not, how can they be? If they are, can they be more socially responsible? How?

Continental Casket Company

Continental Casket Company is the largest maker of burial caskets in the United States. The firm has expanded at a phenomenal compounded annual rate of 18 percent since 1968. The company now accounts for 10 percent of all coffins sold in this country. Continental has a high level of consumer service and educational activities, running seminars for funeral directors and giving special programs at mortuary schools. A highlight of the effort, according to its annual report, is the consumer-education film program to "assist the funeral director in communicating with customers."

The merchandising of caskets determines a funeral director's profits: funeral services are sold as package deals, but the only difference between the cheapest and the most expensive is the grade of the casket. Hence, strategems to promote the sale of higher-priced coffins are frequently used.

A recent FTC study of the funeral industry disclosed several such tactics employed by funeral directors: comparison shopping is discouraged by the jumbling together of caskets of different prices and styles; price tags are seldom attached, and the bereaved may be made to feel cheap if they inquire about the cost; salesmen habitually refer to the cheaper coffins as "boxes" and express shock if price is considered a factor in a family's decision.

The results of color preference studies are widely utilized by the industry. The FTC states: "Expensive caskets are displayed in warm hues while the inexpensive units are presented only in colors that are cold, pallid, or garish." Plain wooden boxes are often concealed in an inner room, viewable only on request; these rooms will likely be darker and colder than the glow of the regular showroom.

The allure of modern caskets lies in their "silk linings, satin pillows, and Beautyrest mattresses." They are often sold with the intimation that the more expensive ones will preserve the body longer. Acutally, the contemporary airtight coffins (including Continental's new "air- and water-resistant protective Monoseal model") seal in anaerobic bacteria and hasten decomposition. Embalming is routinely done, with funeral directors often stating that it is required for public health reasons. It is required, however, only if the body is to be shipped by common carrier, or in cases of certain contagious diseases.

QUESTIONS

1. The FTC's proposed trade rule would require that all caskets be displayed in solemn hues, and that customers be given price lists in showrooms. Would you support such a regulation? Do you have any further suggestions for regulations?
2. As the Continental Casket Company marketing director, how would you defend your educational activities and programs to the FTC?
3. Analyze this situation from the standpoint of the public; of the funeral directors. How would you draw the line between legitimate marketing strategies necessary for sales, and deception?
4. What, in the final analysis, is the funeral director's social responsibility to the customer?

Forgers Find a Friend?

Forgers have now found a new playtoy that is costing government and business a lot of money. This new toy is the Xerox 6500 Color Copier. People are forging everything from payroll checks and stock certificates to postage stamps.

Financial institutions and other businesses that print stocks and bonds and other negotiable instruments are alarmed. A California company was forced to redesign its payroll checks after a former employee made copies of her last pay check and started cashing them. FBI agents are looking for a District of Columbia resident who bought a $10,000 Cadillac from a Virginia resident, paying for the car with a color reproduction of a cashier's check. Secret Service agents last March arrested a 42-year-old Detroit pharmacist who was using the Xerox color copier to duplicate United States currency.

Concern about the counterfeiting has spread abroad. European bankers have held two meetings to discuss the copier, and Spanish government officials are considering restricting its use in their country.

The machine costs $19,000, accepts various types of paper, and the quality of its reproductions is excellent. Xerox will not discuss how many of the copiers are in use, but government sources say there are more than a thousand in this country and an additional hundred or so overseas.

Federal officials and people in the financial community have asked Xerox to add a printing device to their copier to mark each reproduction as a copy. They also suggested that Xerox consider making a copier that makes poorer reproductions.

Xerox won't budge. One official was quoted as saying, "These people want us to debase the very thing we're trying to accomplish — making excellent copies."[2]

QUESTIONS

1. Discuss, in detail, the social issues raised by this case.
2. What product-related social responsibilities does the company have?
3. As president of Xerox, how would you react to the government's concerns? Does the government have a right to restrict the use of your copier?

---

[2]From Timothy D. Schellhardt, "Forgers Find a Friend in Color Copier: Widespread Abuses Alarming Companies," *The Wall Street Journal*, February 10, 1977. Reprinted by permission of *The Wall Street Journal*, © Dow Jones & Company, Inc., 1977. All rights reserved.

Business and the Environment

The 1970s began as the decade of ecology. Since Earth Day 1970, the issues of environment and ecology have received more public attention than in all prior years. Before 1970 only a few biologists and conservationists wrote about problems of the environment. Since that time, however, there has been a veritable flood of publications about environmental isues. President Richard M. Nixon set the stage for this concern by signing into law the National Environmental Policy Act, the purpose of which was "To declare a national policy which will encourage productivity and enjoyable harmony between man and his environment . . ." The 1970s, the President asserted, " . . . absolutely must be the years when America pays its debts to the past by reclaiming the purity of its air, its water, and our living environment."

The health of the environment is not a new problem; but like many of the social issues discussed in this book, society has only recently taken it seriously. Nor can it be said that business is the single major cause of environmental deterioration. But because business and society is the focus of this book, we will concentrate on business's role in creating some of the environmental problems we face today and their impact on the rest of society. We will also look at the impact environmental issues are having on business and how business is responding to the environmental ethic.

In sum, we plan to discuss the following topics in this chapter:

- Causes of environmental deterioration
- Types of environmental pollution
- The EPA and its role
- The cost versus benefit issue
- The impact of plant closings
- Environment versus energy
- Impact on innovation, production, and profit
- Other problems
- Business's response to the environmental problem

156

CAUSES OF ENVIRONMENTAL DETERIORATION

It is difficult to determine the root causes of any phenomenon, especially one as complex as that of environmental deterioration, which has been so pronounced since World War II. It is commonly held, however, that several major social forces have combined to create much of the problem. These forces include affluence and the rising standard of living, population growth and concentration, and technological progress.

Affluence

The unprecedented and continuously rising standard of living in the United States is one of the contributors to our difficulties.[1] Government statistics show that real personal income per capita almost doubled during the two decades from 1950 to 1970.[2] During this time, the American public bought more goods, traveled more miles, generated more waste, and, paradoxically, changed its ideas about the quality of life. The American "consumption machine" must therefore be considered a major contributor to the environmental problem of pollution.

Business, in responding to society's desire for more goods, services and greater conveniences, has become a party to the consumption ethic, the heart of escalating public demands. With rising incomes, Americans have become less concerned with the durability of goods; the public's demands, along with business's supply, have lead to a "throwaway" mentality, causing solid waste disposal problems, specifically, and environmental degradation, generally. Discarded automobiles, aluminum cans, glass bottles, and other litter attest to the scope of this social problem.

Population Growth and Concentration

Population increases and their concentration in urban centers have exacerbated the environmental problem. The sheer numbers of people result in stress and produce crowding effects that both reduce the quality of life and strain the physical environment.

The rapid population increase following World War II gave rise to problems that today continue to aggravate the environmental situation. This is described by Rex Campbell and Jerry Wade:

---

[1]Richard A. Tybout, *Environmental Quality and Society* (Columbus: Ohio State University Press, 1975), p. 8.

[2]U.S. Bureau of the Census, *Statistical Abstract of the United States, 1971* (Washington: U.S. Government Printing Office, 1971), p. 17.

At first, hospitals were overcrowded, and the diaper business boomed. Then the first wave of baby boom children hit the elementary schools, and bond issue after bond issue was passed to add classrooms. The wave engulfed high schools ... At the same time, the typical new American house grew from two or three bedrooms to three, four, and even five. The number of cars per household increased ... Now pressure is on for more housing, highways, employment, and other improvements ...[3]

Although in the past decade there has been a decrease in the birthrate,[4] population increases continue to put pressure and strain on the environment. Americans, however, long assumed that population is something that other, less developed countries should worry about, not us. After all, we are the richest nation in the world. But now many Americans are becoming aware of the problems created by population increases everywhere, such as worldwide shortages in natural resources and energy availability.

The dense concentration of population in certain areas is another facet of the issue. For years people in the United States have been moving away from certain parts of the country — most notably, from the "corn belt" of the plains states — and going to such areas as the "sun belt" of the Southwest and the Southeast, the Gulf Coast, and the eastern seaboard. In a sense, the concentration of people causes more problems than just the sheer numbers, as Neil Jacoby notes:

... this overwhelming tendency of people to concentrate in cities has worsened the environment through crowding, traffic congestion, delays and loss of time, and the overloading of transportation, marketing, and living facilities.[5]

Taken together, sheer numbers of people and where they have tended to gravitate constitutes what S. Fred Singer has termed a "popullution" problem of enormous proportions.

An essential point should be stressed in the relationship between population growth and environmental degradation. This point concerns waste. While we have always had waste, it becomes *pollution* when it is found where we do not want it. Population growth not only gives us more waste, it also leaves us with fewer places to put it. As a result, the environment is perceived to be deteriorating because we find more waste where we do not want it.

[3]Rex R. Campbell and Jerry L. Wade, *Society and Environment: The Coming Collision* (Boston: Allyn and Bacon, 1972), pp. 213-214.

[4]Lawrence A. Mayer, "U.S. Population Growth; Would Slower Be Better? in Campbell and Wade, pp. 238-245. See also Wayne H. Davis, "Overpopulated America," *The New Republic,* January 1970, pp. 13-14.

[5]Neil H. Jacoby, *Corporate Power and Social Responsibility* (New York: Macmillan, 1973), p. 208.

Technology

Technology has been accused as the main villain in aggravating the environmental problem. As a villain, technology has two faces. One, in the form of machinery, factories, and productive equipment (for example, the high-polluting aluminum and chemical industries), leads *directly* to pollution of the air and water. The other is technology's *indirect* effect on pollution by placing in consumers' hands products that, when carelessly used, result in deterioration of the environment. Soap, for example, has been displaced by phosphate detergents, aluminum throwaway cans have replaced returnable glass bottles, nondegradable plastics have replaced paper, and so on.[6]

Some people blame technology as a contributor to environmental deterioration more than others. The Sierra Club, Environmental Action, and other special interest groups, for example, have suggested that a "technological determinism" is in control of our society. Stated differently, if we were capable (had the technological means) of producing a product, we did it, "without due regard to the social consequences."[7] An example of this, they might argue is the Concorde, a supersonic transport that may be a socially destructive application of technology because of the noise that it emits and the large quantity of fuel that it uses.

Though technology is without question a contributing factor in the environmental problem, it might also be a possible savior. A *Business Week* commentary makes this point well:

> Properly directed by business and government, it (technology) can undo much of the environmental damage it once wrought.[8]

And, indeed, we must believe that this is the case. For without technology, and without new attitudes about economic growth, consumption, and quality of life, environmental pollution would eventually doom mankind.

TYPES OF ENVIRONMENTAL POLLUTION

Very briefly, to provide a context for our discussion of business's role with respect to the environment, let us consider each of the following types of pollution we face today:

1. Air pollution

---

[6]"Technology Isn't the Villain — After All," *Business Week*, February 3, 1973, p. 38.
[7]Ibid.
[8]Ibid.

"Now they say we can't dump our industrial wastes in the river anymore! What's a river for?"

SOURCE: From *The Wall Street Journal,* Permission Cartoon Features Syndicate.

2. Water pollution
3. Solid waste pollution
4. Chemical pesticides
5. Noise pollution
6. Visual pollution
7. Odor pollution

Air pollution is certainly one of the most visible forms of pollution, and is probably the type that most Americans can most easily identify. Though we now know that the automobile is one of the most serious air polluters, citizens still look at the belching smokestacks of factories — spewing particulate matter and gases of various kinds — as the main cause of society's air pollution problems. In reality, however, there are four major sources of air pollution combining to cause today's problem: (1) electric power generation by utilities, (2) transportation (especially automobiles), (3) industry, and (4) household and commerce activities in general.[9]

Water pollution is also highly visible. Like air, water has been assumed since our country was founded to be a "free good," plentiful in quantity, and hence not requiring much concern.

---

[9]Robert U. Ayres, "Air Pollution in Cities," in *Politics and Environment,* Walt Anderson (ed.) (Santa Monica, Calif.: Goodyear Publishing Co., 1970), pp. 80-81.

This lack of concern for our water resources has been obvious. We foul lakes and rivers with bottles, cans, and garbage as well as with toilet effluent from boats. Our municipalities and businesses casually discharge raw sewage and industrial wastes into waterways — Lake Erie, for example, has been called a big sewage reservoir.[10] In recent years there have been a large number of oil spills in our oceans, such as the one from the widely publicized *Torrey Canyon,* whose broken hull lies at the bottom of the sea after running aground and dumping 118,000 tons of crude oil.[11] Our waters are also fouled by thermal (heat) pollution from nuclear-powered generating plants and by chemical pollution due to the widespread agricultural use of herbicides and pesticides. As a consequence of all these forms of water pollution, we face a water crisis of unimaginable proportions unless we change our uses of the world's waterways.

Solid waste disposal has also been a cause of considerable concern in recent years. Modern packaging of food products and other consumer goods, combined with the throwaway mentality and planned obsolescence of products, have resulted in great accumulation of solid waste. Municipalities around the country are finding it increasingly difficult to handle and dispose of these wastes. This problem is aggravated further when garbage strikes occur in large, congested cities.

Chemical pesticides have long been a problem, but it was not until Rachel Carson's *Silent Spring* was published in 1962 that public awareness of the situation became widespread. Even after Carson's book, it was so difficult to prove the danger of such chemicals as DDT that it took seven years for DDT to be prohibited. Like many other social issues, chemical pesticides have both advantages and disadvantages. As a source of environmental pollution, pesticides must be monitored continuously for their side effects on animals and humans.

The effects of *noise, visual,* and *odor* pollution are relatively minor compared to those problems already discussed. The concern for noise in the workplace has led to considerable debate in recent years, sometimes even between government agencies, about establishing noise standards. The Environmental Protection Agency (EPA) and the Occupational Safety and Health Agency (OSHA), for example, have disagreed as to what standards are desirable and reasonable. Nevertheless, business can expect more constraints on allowable noise in the future.[12] And although very little has been written about visual pollution and odor pollution, they are also important social issues that business must face.

[10]Donald E. Carr, "The Politics of Pollution," in Campbell and Wade, pp. 80-87.

[11]Robert Rienow and Leona Train Rienow, "The Oil Around Us," *New York Times Magazine,* June 4, 1967, p. 25ff.

[12]"Workplace Noise Rules Appear Headed for Lengthy Dispute," *Industry Week,* May 12, 1975, p. 13.

Some communities, for example, have enacted ordinances restricting the size and placement of signs and billboards, thereby reducing visual pollution that defaces or degrades the environment. And as a result of its emission of foul odors, a pulp and paper company in San Francisco had to expend $28 million on odor control technology to meet guidelines of the state's Air Resources Board.

THE EPA AND ITS ROLE

Having described some of the contributing causes of environmental deterioration and the various types of environmental pollution, it is now important to present the history of environmental regulations with which business must contend.

Prior to the 1970s little action had been taken by business or anyone else to protect the environment. Although a number of laws existed, they were, for the most part, quite ineffectual. The situation changed, however, with the ecology movement of the late 1960s and with the creation of the Council on Environmental Quality (CEQ) and the EPA in 1970.[13] The CEQ was designed to consider policy on new environmental legislation and programs, and the EPA was charged with responsibility for administering a wide range of environmental protection programs, including air pollution control, water pollution control, solid waste management, and the control of radiation, pesticides, and noise.[14]

The activities of the EPA center around its power to establish and then enforce standards in the above areas. When the agency observes a violation of these standards, it has available several avenues of enforcement, including the seeking of voluntary compliance, court action, fines, and even jail sentences.

Though the EPA has regulatory authority over the types of pollution mentioned earlier, its biggest impact on business has been in the realm of air and water pollution, probably the most serious of the environmental issues we face today. With respect to air pollution, the EPA draws its strength from the Clean Air Act of 1970. Under this legislation, the agency has the power to set emergency standards for air quality from common pollutants (such as sulfur oxides, particulates, carbon monoxide), for new plants, for motor vehicle emissions, and for fuel.[15]

---

[13]Stahrl Edmunds and John Letey, *Environmental Adminstration* (New York: McGraw-Hill Book Company 1973), pp. 79-80.
[14]Murray L. Weidenbaum, *Business, Government, and the Public* (Englewood Cliffs, N.J.: Prentice-Hall, 1977), pp. 74-75.
[15]Ibid., pp. 75-76.

Apparently the Clean Air Act and the EPA's powers of enforcement have resulted in improvements; between 1970 and 1974, air-borne particulates decreased 14 percent, sulfur oxides were down 25 percent, and other pollutants were reduced or stabilized.[16]

In the area of water pollution, a fundamental shift in thought about environmental problems occurred in 1972 with the passage of the Federal Water Pollution Control Act, for which the EPA has regulatory responsibility. This law also draws into clearer focus the conflict that has arisen in recent years between business and the EPA.

Prior to 1972, the only major water law was one that had been passed in 1965. In the 1965 law, Congress employed the water quality approach, sometimes called the "pollution dilution" approach because it assumed that at least one proper function of waterways was to absorb waste. Using this thinking, the states set water quality standards and then converted these into specific limits on effluents. These limits varied, depending on such factors as the assimilative capacity of a body of water, the nature of the pollutant, and whether the waterway was to be used for recreational purposes.[17]

The water quality approach seemed sensible, but inherent in it were a number of difficulties. These difficulties led the Senate Public Works Committee to change to direct effluent limits, an approach that had "zero discharge" as its ultimate goal. This was a revolutionary change in thinking, overturning the long-held view that waterways should be used to assimilate waste.

In addition to requiring companies to obtain permits to discharge waste, the 1972 water pollution law established the following deadlines and requirements that business would have to meet:

Deadline	Requirement
July 1, 1977	Companies must have installed the "best practicable" control technology
July 1, 1983	Companies must have installed the "best available" control technology
1985	"Zero discharge" is the goal—the complete elimination of water pollution

According to the EPA, "best practicable" means a "level of control achieved by the least polluting plants in any given industry." If, for example, several paper mills have used a type of technology to achieve a high level of control, then all paper mills would be required to have that same kind of technology in 1977. "Best available" technology, on the

---

[16]"The Clean Air Act Will Keep Its Teeth," *Business Week, July 14, 1975, p. 92.*
[17]*"A Costly New Challenge for Water Polluters," Business Week,* October 28, 1972, p. 42.

other hand, is even more demanding. According to this concept, if "only one plant in a given industry has a highly advanced waste control system, then that will probably become the standard for all plants in that industry.[18]

EPA's strong pressures to force businesses to abide by the above requirements and deadlines have created a continuing controversy between affected industries and the agency. The issue is a complex one, with business arguing on the one hand that the EPA is attempting to do too much too quickly, but with EPA arguing forcefully on the other hand that compliance is essential. If we are to understand the complexities of this environmental problem, it is necessary to look closely at some of the challenges associated with cleaning up the environment.

THE COST VERSUS BENEFIT ISSUE

In terms of aggregate costs to industry, environmental protection represents one of the government's most costly interventions into business activities. On top of that is the complex question of pollution expenditures. In addition to the tremendous sums of money involved, there is the difficulty of justifying the cost in terms of the benefits derived, assessing their contribution to inflation, and determining the validity of cost figures supplied by companies to various government and industry sources.

The total sums of money spent by industry on pollution control increased considerably in the 1970s. One publication estimated that American business spent $6.2 billion in 1973 to control air and water pollution, 38 percent more than in 1972 and nearly double the 1971 figure.[19] The CEQ estimated that business spent $16 billion in 1976. In addition to business's share, consumers spent $7 billion that year, primarily for smog control devices on cars and related expenses.[20] The CEQ's projection for the period 1975-84 comes to $127 billion, with water pollution control accounting for $65 billion.[21]

Even larger are the figures that have been projected by the National Commission on Water Quality (NCWQ), a panel of private experts and members of congress. After spending two-and-one-half years analyzing the impact of the 1972 water pollution legislation, the NCWQ con-

[18]Ibid.

[19]"Catching Up on the Cleaning Up," *Business Week,* May 19, 1973, p. 78.

[20]Gladwin Hill, "Pollution: Cost Becomes a Factor," *New York Times,* January 9, 1977.

[21]Tom Alexander, "It's Time for New Approaches to Pollution Control," *Fortune,* November 1976, p. 131.

cluded that the total public and private expenditures for pollution control could be in the range of $160 billion to $670 billion.[22]

Cost figures of this magnitude are hard for the average individual to comprehend. Perhaps a specific illustration would be helpful. In one federally attested case in Atlanta, the NCWQ states that it costs $5,300 a day to purify the Chattahoochee River, of industrial effluent, as per 1977 standards. To bring the purity up to 1983 standards would cost an additional $13,000 per day. The 1977 level of control improves water quality by about one part per million, while the 1983 level would improve it by only another 0.3 part per million. Thus, a tripling of the original expenditure would result in only a 30 percent additional improvement![23]

Thus the cost versus benefit issue is one of the most serious problems in achieving the EPA's 1977 and 1983 deadlines. In many cases substantial expenditures have to be made to bring about a very small increment of improvement in environmental quality. One representative of the federal Council on Wage and Price Stability reflected a genuine concern for this problem with the following observation:

> When the iron and steel industry eventually meets the 1977 water-discharge standards, their pollutants will be down 97.3% from the no-control level. Meeting the 1983 standards will result in a 99% reduction. Yet the cost to the industry of going down from the 1977 standards to the 1983 standards will be two-thirds the cost of meeting the 1977 standards. Is it going to be worth it?[24]

The fact is that there is an inescapable tendency for costs to increase disproportionally as pollution control standards become more demanding. One consequence of this is, of course, continuing debate between business, government, and policymakers as to where the balance ought to be achieved.

THE IMPACT OF PLANT CLOSINGS

Because not all attempts by business to comply with the pollution laws now in existence are successful, some businesses are being driven out of existence. It is difficult to obtain precise figures on how many plant closings have occurred as a direct consequence of pollution requirements, but some estimates and actual figures are available to help grasp the magnitude of the problem.

[22]Ibid.
[23]Hill.
[24]Cited in Alexander, p. 230.

TABLE 6-1
Executive Responses to Impact of Pollution Laws

Percent	n	Pollution control laws have caused:
36.5	50	1. A few companies to close in the last five years (less than 100 nationwide)
23.4	32	2. A "moderate" number of companies to close (approximately 500)
36.5	50	3. Many companies to close (over 1,000)
3.6	5	4. No response
100.0	137	

SOURCE: James S. Bowman, "Business and the Environment: Corporate Attitudes and Actions in Energy Rich States," *MSU Business Topics,* Winter 1977, p. 43. Reprinted by permission of the publisher, Division of Research, Graduate School of Business Administration, Michigan State University.

According to a 1972 estimate by Chase Econometrics Associates, a subsidiary of Chase Manhattan Bank, 200-300 plants in key industries would be closed by 1976 because of failure to meet pollution requirements.[25] A 1976 EPA survey, however, reported only eighty-one industrial plants closed, either partly or completely, becuse they could not meet requirements with existing equipment or could not afford new equipment.[26] But this figure included only plants with twenty-five or more employees, yet many smaller operations are known to have closed.

In a recent survey of business firms, James Bowman asked the respondents what impact pollution laws have had on company closings. His data appear in Table 6-1. As seen from these data, estimates vary widely on plant closings. Although the validity of these aggregate data is questionable, they do suggest the magnitude of the problem as business executives perceive it.

The impact of pollution control costs is greater on some industries than on others. The foundry industry was having difficulties even before the intervention of the EPA — from 1968 to 1974, 427 foundries were forced to close. Though a number of reasons account for the closings, pollution-abatement requirements are near the top.[27]

The steel industry, which is among the worst of the polluters, has

[25]"Turning Pollution Control into an Asset," *Business Week,* September 9, 1972, pp. 96-97.

[26]Alexander, p. 130.

[27]Robert E. Curran, *The Foundry Industry* (Washington, D.C.: U.S. Department of Commerce, Bureau of Domestic Affairs, March 24, 1975).

problems that are most expensive to remedy. This industry is faced with a critical question: Should the companies invest millions of dollars in adapting aging mills that they perhaps plan to replace soon anyway? Because many steel executives do not think so, this has been the source of a bitter battle with EPA. EPA holds that steel's requests for exemptions for older plants with limited life are too vague and thus should not be granted. [28]

One of the serious social consequences of this "clean up or close up" predicament is the loss of jobs and the economic impact on a community whose main employer is a steel firm that is forced to close. Steel companies in Youngstown, Ohio, and Bethlehem, Pennsylvania, have been fighting with the EPA for years. Basically, they must choose to (a) upgrade their mills' pollution devices, (b) shut their old mills, or (c) fight to win exemptions from state and federal rules. [29]

In several cases, business has been able to convince the EPA to provide exemptions from water pollution control requirements. But this approach backfired in one significant case. U.S. Steel, Republic Steel, and Youngstown Sheet and Tube convinced the EPA to grant them exemptions for eight plants situated along a twenty-four-mile stretch of the Mahoning River in Ohio. The EPA granted the exemptions in March 1976 because severe economic and employment disruptions would have resulted if the agency pressed its case. The steel firms welcomed the exemptions, of course, because they did not think the eight plants, which were discharging oil, grease, heavy metals, and other pollutants into the Mahoning River, were profitable enough to justify the requested $140 million for pollution controls. [30]

The Sierra Club, an environmentalist group, and the State of Pennsylvania challenged the exemptions. Their argument was that similar exemptions might be granted elsewhere based on this precedent. Although the court held that some flexibility by the EPA was appropriate, exemptions from effluent limits were not permissible. Thus, both EPA and business received a clear message from the courts as to just how far they could go to reach a settlement on this sensitive issue.

Though it is not evident whether these steel plants will be forced to close eventually, it is ironic to note that other plant closings now occurring are resulting in a significant benefit — higher productivity. This is so because those plants being forced to close are marginal ones that probably would have been closed soon anyway. As one illustration, after International Paper Company closed an old mill and replaced it

[28]"Steel: Clean Up or Close Up," *Business Week*, April 6, 1974, pp. 72-73.
[29]Ibid., p. 72.
[30]"EPA Exemption for 8 Steel Plants Ruled Invalid," *Wall Street Journal*, September 9, 1977, p. 14.

with a $76-million facility, productivity went up 70 percent.[31] Some executives are concluding, therefore, that there is a positive side to what is happening, and that perhaps the net effect will be beneficial.

ENVIRONMENT VERSUS ENERGY

Since the advent of the environmental issue, another social problem has arisen which in many respects is in direct conflict with pollution control. This is the problem of energy and its conservation. Energy is an important issue that affects everyone's life on a daily basis, and may assume even greater importance as it is viewed in conflict with environmental considerations.[32]

There has been considerable speculation on the relationship between the environment and energy, and a few studies conducted. One study by Kefalas and Carroll sought to obtain views by executives on possible causes of the energy crisis, and it was interesting to note where environmental standards ranked in the survey, as shown in Table 6-2. While environmental standards were not considered the most significant cause of the energy crisis, its relatively high ranking indicates its importance to the executives surveyed nationwide. Also, it is difficult to know how much environmental standards were included in excessive governmental regulation, which ranked first.

Many directors of environmental control at major American corporations are of the opinion that cleaning up the environment is an obstacle to energy conservation. One study conducted by Research Planning Associates, a consulting firm in Cambridge, Massachusetts, concluded that "environmental controls will force the (iron and steel) industry to use 10% more energy."[33] This conclusion is consistent with the Arthur D. Little, Inc., report that the steel industry would have to increase energy consumption by 11 percent to meet 1983 pollution control requirements.[34] Though there is some controversy over the accuracy of these figures, with some people feeling that they overstate the impact of environmental protection on increased energy consumption, it is clear that the problem is real, even if the magnitude may not have been fairly portrayed. In any event, an energy crisis exists, and concern must be expressed by business and policymakers as they seek solutions for both

[31] *Business Week,* September 9, 1972, p. 97.
[32] See, for example, Jean A. Briggs, "The Price of Environmentalism — The Backlash Begins," *Forbes,* June 15, 1977, pp. 36-40.
[33] "Does Pollution Control Waste Too Much Energy?" *Business Week,* March 29, 1976, p. 72.
[34] Ibid.

TABLE 6-2
Most Likely Causes of the Energy Crisis

Cause	Rank
Excessive governmental regulation	1
Price controls	2
Environmental standards	3
Population growth	4
Business shortsightedness	5
U.S. foreign policy	6

SOURCE: Asterios G. Kefalas and Archie B. Carroll,
"U.S. Business and the Energy Crisis," *Energy Policy,*
September 1976, p. 269. Reprinted by permission.

environmental and energy needs. A survey of business executives by Bowman shows that 87 percent of the executives polled do feel that "protection of the environment should be a major concern when we develop new energy resources."[35] The conflict between the environmental protection and energy conservation still exists, making the environmental issue more complex for business, government, and society to solve. But the conclusion reached by the Committee for Economic Development, a national group of business people, holds promise that business will give this matter serious consideration in their problem-solving efforts. They state:

> Reasonable energy and environmental objectives need not be irreconcilable. Piecemeal, duplicating, and overlapping approaches to environmental protection and energy resources, with frequent recourse to arbitrary and extreme standards, should be replaced by a systematic and realistic analysis of risks and benefits. The need for energy must play a major role in environmental decisions.[36]

IMPACT ON INNOVATION, PRODUCTION, AND PROFIT

It has been asserted that environmental protection may also conflict with business innovation, production, and profits. This concern was manifested as early as 1969, when a survey was taken for *Fortune* maga-

[35]James S. Bowman, "Business and the Environment: Corporate Attitudes, Actions in Energy-Rich States," *MSU Business Topics,* Winter 1977, p. 39.
[36]Committee for Economic Development, *Key Elements of a National Energy Strategy* (New York: CED, June 1977), pp. 14-15.

zine by Daniel Yankelovich, Inc.[37] One part of this survey, related to the above problems, was replicated by Kefalas and Carroll in 1974,[38] and again in 1976 by Bowman.[39] Basically, the question sought business managers' views on the environment vis-a-vis innovation, production, and profit. Table 6-3 summarizes the findings of the three studies.

Though the survey groups differed somewhat in the three studies, those of 1969 and 1974 were national samples and the 1976 was a more limited sample, the trends noted in the data are quite interesting. They document that business is more willing to take care of the environment if it means just slowing down on innovation (slowing the introduction of new products), but the results are mixed when it comes to business's willingness to forego an increase in production or to reduce profits. Another interesting pattern is the decline in willingness to do all three as the surveys moved from 1969 to 1976. Thus, when the factors of innovation, production, and profits are combined, their total impact makes the whole environmental matter more complex for business and society to resolve.

OTHER PROBLEMS

The issues mentioned above constitute some of the major difficulties that business faces in the area of environmental protection. When these are combined with the five additional problems described below, the situation becomes even more complex.

Inflation and Unemployment

Determining the precise cost of environmental protection poses a difficult challenge. In their *Fifth Annual Report* CEQ estimated the inflationary effect of environmental control at 0.5 percent.[40] Because, according to modern economic theory, unemployment is closely tied to inflation, some experts have raised the question about the impact of environmental protection on the employment rate. Both the EPA and the CEQ have, however, shown that "environmental impacts have contributed

---

[37]R. S. Diamond, "What Business Thinks About the Environment," in *The Environment: A National Mission for the Seventies,* ed. by editors of *Fortune* (New York: Harper and Row, Publishers, 1970).

[38]Asterios G. Kefalas and Archie B. Carroll, "Perspectives on Environmental Protection: A Survey of the Executive Viewpoint," *Journal of Environmental Systems,* vol. 6, no. 3 (1976-77), pp. 229-242.

[39]Bowman, p. 40.

[40]Council on Environmental Quality, *Fifth Annual Report* (Washington, D.C.: Superintendent of Documents, December 1974).

TABLE 6-3
Environmental Restrictions and Corporate Operations[a]

"Should environmental problems be taken into consideration if it means:	Yes			No			Uncertain/ No response		
	1976	1974	1969	1976	1974	1969	1976	1974	1969
1. slowing the introduction of new products	72.3	[83.6][b]	(88)	10.2	[8.6]	(8)	17.5	[7.8]	(8)
2. foregoing an increase in production	58.4	[79.3]	(84)	11.7	[16.4]	(9)	29.9	[13.3]	(7)
3. reducing profits?"	57.7	[64.6]	(85)	15.3	[22.3]	(9)	27.0	[13.1]	(6)

[a]Figures are given in percentages: η = 137.
[b]Numbers in brackets refer to the 1974 Kefalas and Carroll study; in parentheses to the 1969 *Fortune* survey.

SOURCE: James S. Bowman, "Business and the Environment: Corporate Attitudes and Actions in Energy-Rich States," *MSU Business Topics*, Winter 1977, p. 40. Reprinted by permission of the publisher, Division of Research, Graduate School of Business Administration, Michigan State University.

171

negligibly to inflation or unemployment."[41] Hence the problem may not be one of major magnitude.

Control Produces Pollution

Only recently have we learned that the very process of pollution control itself causes pollution. Several years ago a group of researchers investigated the environmental impact of a highly advanced new sewage-treatment plant at South Lake Tahoe, California, and uncovered some interesting problems. They found considerable pollution in the output of this treatment plant: nitrogen extracted from water in the form of ammonia was released into the atmosphere, ashes from incinerated chemical-rich sludges were used for landfill, and contaminants from carbon filters cleaned by heating were dispersed as gases.[42] What has been especially disturbing about this dilemma is that this particular treatment facility is frequently cited as one of of the models for the "best available technology" mandated for 1983.

Federal versus State Regulations

Buiness has to be responsive not only to federal laws, but those passed by state and local governments as well. Environmental protection is one area in which business is likely to find requirement stacked upon requirement as a result of these multiple regulations. In some cases, state laws have been more severe than federal laws, and the consequences for business are apparent. Faced with fragmented and differing rules from state to state, business has turned in self-defense to advocating the concept of "federal preemptive regulations."[43] These would be a single set of national regulatory standards that would preempt state laws. Thus business — so often a critic of federal governmental intrusion — is itself turning in that direction for deliverance from conflicting standards.

Quality of Federal Effort

While some business leaders feel that the federal government must be involved in regulation of the environment, they are not pleased with the manner in which the EPA has approached this responsibility. Two

---

[41]Stahrl Edmunds, "Environmental Impacts: Conflicts and Trade-offs," *California Management Review*, Spring 1977, pp. 5-6.

[42]Alexander, pp. 231-232.

[43]Neil Swan, "Trend to Cut U.S. Regulation Gaining Steam," *Atlanta Journal*, May 2, 1976.

TABLE 6-4
Managerial Response to the Question:
How Would You Characterize the Federal Government's Approach to Environmental Protection in Terms of Realism and Timeliness?

	Realism %	Timeliness %
Highly unrealistic	11.4	
Unrealistic	62.1	
Adequate	20.1	
Realistic	6.4	
Highly realistic	0.0	
Highly premature		8.8
Premature		39.1
Appropriate		39.1
Timely		9.4
Very timely		3.6

SOURCE: Asterios G. Kefalas and Archie B. Carroll, "Perspectives on Environmental Protection: A Survey of the Executive Viewpoint," *Journal of Environmental Systems*, vol. 6, no. 3 (1976-1977), p. 239. Copyright © 1977 Baywood Publishing Company, Inc. Reprinted by permission.

major complaints stand out after several years of EPA experience: (1) the standards set by the EPA were unrealistic because they were derived from insufficient and inaccurate data, and (2) target dates set by the agency were too optimistic. Stated another way, the government acted too quickly and without adequate deliberation.[44]

In an effort to get at the depth and magnitude of these accusations, Kefalas and Carroll in the survey cited earlier asked business executives the following question: How would you characterize the federal government's approach to environmental protection in terms of realism and timeliness? Table 6-4 presents the findings. An overwhelming majority of the 140 executives surveyed, 73.5 percent, considered the federal government's approach unrealistic. In terms of timeliness, 47.9 percent, or almost half, regarded the implementation of environmental plans as premature.[45] Bowman's replication of this question several years later showed only slight changes. The executives he surveyed, though not constituting a national sample, rated the government's efforts as more unrealistic, but not as severely untimely.[46]

[44]Kefalas and Carroll, p. 238.
[45]Ibid., p. 239.
[46]Bowman, p. 42.

Pressure on the EPA to modify its due dates on some environmental standards has had mixed success. The deadline for automobile emission standards, for example, originally established for 1975, was changed to 1978 and may be changed again to as late as 1982.[47] Business has tried to get the 1977 deadline for certain water rules changed to 1982, with the stringent standards of 1983 eliminated entirely.[48] The basic difficulty business faces, thus, stems from a disagreement with the federal government on how much and how fast the government ought to move in the environmental protection arena.

BUSINESS'S RESPONSE TO
THE ENVIRONMENTAL PROBLEM

So far we have considered some of the major dimensions of the environmental problem, and discussed some of the issues that combine to create the complex business-environmental relationship. It is now appropriate to turn our attention briefly to how business is responding to the environmental issue.

To develop a context for our discussion, we suggest three broad avenues for addressing the environmental problem: (1) free market solutions, (2) business altruism (social responsiveness), and (3) governmental approaches. We can dispense with *free market solutions* rather quickly, because it seems that when left to free market forces, business does not effectively address the environmental problem at all. Considering the competitive nature of many of the goods produced in pollution-creating facilities, and the sums of money involved, this is not difficult to understand.

In a similar fashion, because of the high cost of solving environmental problems, *business altruism* is not an extremely attractive avenue of solution either. It is true that some gains can be made in social responsiveness either by business policing itself and applying pressure to other firms in the same industry, or by taking social initiatives in the community. Although we will discuss a few of these efforts shortly, for the most part they have been rather ineffective.

The primary reason for this ineffectiveness can be seen in consumer response to products made by nonpolluting companies. Whether we are considering industrial goods (steel I-beams or industrial chemicals) or consumer goods (automobiles or plastic containers), consumers do not show preference for products that have been produced by a nonpollut-

[47]Edmunds, p. 5.
[48]"The Push to Ease Water Rules," *Business Week,* March 21, 1977, pp. 69-72.

ing process. It is competitively disadvantageous, therefore, for a firm to incur a $35 million expenditure for pollution control to produce a product that would not be especially sought after in the marketplace. The net result of such a decision would simply be that the firm would have to charge a higher price for its product without gaining any market edge or creating a superior product. For this reason, serious initiatives and expenditures of this nature are not common.

Though some firms have been able to rationalize the installation of pollution prevention measures, society at large needs to depend more and more on *governmental approaches* to environmental protection because private, decentralized methods have not been adequate. Jerome Rothenberg has expressed this need clearly:

> Some coordination is clearly needed: to promote recognition of responsibility, to orchestrate separate actions into compatible wholes, to guarantee action on a scale large enough to make real inroads into problems and therefore to promise overall rewards more than commensurate with costs.[49]

Though government has been turned to, there is no assurance that success will follow (we have already discussed some of the difficulties with the EPA's regulatory approach). Yet there are other public policy methods for protecting the environment, some of which include direct government treatment of wastes, public subsidy for private waste treatment, regulation and prohibition, and effluent charges and subsidies.[50] Kefalas and Carroll, in their survey of business executives, sought the business viewpoint on those governmental methods and incentives that are best. Their results are presented in Table 6-5.

We do not plan a lengthy discussion of this public policy issue here, for that is beyond the scope of our present concern. Suffice to say that considerable debate does exist as to how the environmental problem ought to be addressed, and the data in Table 6-5 suggest some desired means.

Specific Business Efforts

Let us take a closer look at specific initiatives that have been undertaken by business in the environmental area. To a certain extent they may seem to contradict the earlier statement that altruism or social responsiveness is not an effective avenue to environmental protection, but that is not really the case. Our earlier focus was on comprehensive

---

[49]Jerome Rothenberg, "The Physical Environment," in James W. McKie (ed.), *Social Responsibility and the Business Predicament* (Washington, D.C.: Brookings Institution, 1974), p. 204.
[50]Ibid., p. 205.

TABLE 6-5
Managerial Response to the Question:
Please Rank Incentives in Terms of Their Effectiveness in Facilitating Environmental Protection
(5 = Most Important; 1 = Least Important)

Incentives	Not Important	Not too Important	Fairly Important	Quite Important	Extremely Important	Rank
Tax credits for pollution control cost	5.0%	12.2%	13.7%	25.9%	43.2%	4
Government grants matching company expenditures	19.4	19.4	26.9	23.1	11.2	1
Government subsidies	24.8	22.6	24.1	16.5	12.0	2
Government-sponsored research and development	7.5	25.4	25.4	21.6	20.1	3
Passing on costs to consumers	7.3	5.8	11.7	24.1	51.1	5

SOURCE: Asterios G. Kefalas and Archie B. Carroll, "Perspectives on Environmental Protection: A Survey of the Executive Viewpoint," *Journal of Environmental Systems*, vol. 6, no. 3 (1976-1977), p. 237. Copyright © 1977 Baywood Publishing Company, Inc. Reprinted by permission.

solutions to the problem, but here we are examining isolated efforts by individual companies. These few examples do hold out hope that social responsiveness may yet be a viable complement to regulatory approaches in the environmental area.

The case of Dow Chemical Company's Midland, Michigan, plant is a particularly good example. Because Dow viewed pollution as a wasted resource, the company felt it could offset completely the cost of its ambitious pollution control effort. Their approach was to eliminate pollution at the source, by altering production methods and converting to recycling. The result of their 1971-72 effort was that they could retrieve chemicals and boost process efficiency, enabling the abatement program to pay its own way.[51] In total, during the first three years of operation, the Midland division was able to save chemicals worth more than $6 million, decrease the amount of waste flowing to its treatment plants by 35 percent, and become one of the first chemical companies to build "zero discharge" plants that recycle waste.

From an organizational standpoint, the company set up a high-level ecology council with twenty-four subcouncils to cover every product line. Their mission was to decentralize pollution control responsibility to the extent of achieving building-to-building accountability. They also established a panel to test new products for environmental hazards, and established the requirement that their researchers assess the environmental impact of their projects while under way.[52]

Other companies, such as Hercules, Inc., U.S. Steel, and Armco Steel, are making efforts in this direction too. Hercules is looking at processes from a different perspective. Repeatedly it claims to be identifying once-hidden payoffs. The company spent $750,000 for a recycling system that reduced pollution by 90 percent and also saved the company $250,000 a year in material and water expenses. U.S. Steel and Armco developed a more efficient, pollution-free process called direct reduction that replaced some dirty coke ovens and blast furnaces.

The approaches taken by Dow and Hercules, in particular, signal the directions cnvironmental solutions will move in the future, particularly in the area of water pollution. The transition in basic thinking seems to be from "Band-aid" solutions using abatement devices for terminal treatment to preventive solutions requiring process changes and the technology of recycling. Though industry is still in the former phase, the emphasis is shifting to designing systems of new plant construction that do not pollute in the first place. This latter kind of thinking depends heavily on processes that emphasize product yield, waste recovery, and closed-loop systems.[53]

[51]"Where Pollution Control Pays Off," *Business Week,* May 20, 1972, p. 97.
[52]Ibid.
[53]*Business Week,* September 9, 1972, p. 97.

The efforts of the 3M Company are also worth examining because of their thoroughness, as claimed by the EPA. The company's 3P program — pollution prevention pays — was begun in 1974. Since that time, their record is impressive. It was an intensive effort to eliminate pollution at the source rather than waiting until stack gases and effluents needed cleaning up.

The company's comprehensive approach was a massive one. Their program included video cassettes, brochures, recognition awards, personal presentations, and a 3P cartoon character. The purpose of this approach was to get all personnel to orient their thinking toward product reformulation, equipment changes, process modifications, and materials recovery.

One feature of the 3P program is that when departments submit proposed pollution control projects, they are examined for environmental benefit, cost savings, individual effort required, and technical accomplishment. In one year alone, the award-winning projects reduced the company's annual pollution output by 500 gallons of waste water, 73,000 tons of air pollutants, and 2,800 tons of sludge. These projects saved 3M roughly $10 million.[54] Every so often 3M's customers save directly too. A case in point occurred when three engineers designed an aerosol product that used compressed carbon dioxide as the propellant rather than fluorocarbons. The result: no harm to the ozone layer due to fluorocarbons, and 20 percent more product in the can without a price increase.[55]

A number of other cases could be cited, but these illustrate the kinds of socially responsive efforts business is undertaking to aid in solving environmental problems. In most cases the programs result in savings or more profits to the company, so they provide a dual benefit. As an increasing number of business managers face up to the inevitabilities of environmental protection, we can expect more of these initiatives in the future. They require, however, a fundamental shift in thinking about the relationship between business and the environment.

SUMMARY

The environmental problem has been brought about by a number of factors. Affluence and the rising standard of living has led to a consumption ethic and a throwaway mentality. Population growth and concentration have exacerbated the problem. Technology, though viewed as a villain by some, is hailed as a possible savior by others.

[54]"3M Gains by Averting Pollution," *Business Week,* November 22, 1976, p. 72.
[55]Ibid.

The major types of pollution are air, water, and solid waste. Other types are present and will increase in importance as the major forms are controlled; they include chemical pesticides, noise, visual, and odor pollution.

In the early 1970s, the EPA was formed by Congress to administer environmental legislation. Perhaps the most visible evidence of the EPA's objectives are manifested in the 1977, 1983, and 1985 goals leading toward zero discharge. The EPA's unrelenting pressure on business to achieve its standards has been the source of continuing controversy between business and the agency.

The issues at stake are very complex. The cost-benefit question is perhaps the one most regularly raised by business. Business also contends that the EPA is attempting to do too much too fast. And evidence is increasing that environmental controls require the use of more energy, hardly a desirable consequence during an energy crisis. Environmental concern also has an impact on innovation, productivity, and profits. Other matters of concern include the impact on inflation and unemployment, the polluting effects of control, federal versus state regulations, and the quality of federal efforts.

Though governmental approaches to environmental protection seem most promising for the larger issues, due to the billions of dollars involved, there are steps business can take voluntarily. Most of these efforts fall under the rubric of corporate social responsiveness. In the final analysis, the complex environmental problem can only be solved by efforts of government and business, with assistance by the consuming public. If cooperation among these three major groups is not achieved, the future will be bleak indeed.

QUESTIONS FOR DISCUSSION

1. What are the primary causes of environmental deterioration? Which is the single most important cause in your opinion? Why?
2. What other factors cause or aggravate the environmental problem?
3. Is technology inherently good or bad? Discuss. Give several examples of "technological determinism."
4. What are the major types of pollution? What are the minor types? Which of these types of pollution do you think society will be most concerned with and least concerned with five years from now? Support your answer with reasons.
5. Comment on the realism, in your judgment, of the EPA's 1977, 1983, and 1985 deadlines. Do research and ascertain where business stands, generally, in achieving these goals.

6. Explain the cost versus benefit issue as it pertains to environmental protection. Draw a graph illustrating the Chattahoochee River case cited in the chapter.

7. Explain the energy versus environment trade-off. Which do you think is more important, energy conservation or environmental protection?

8. Discuss what is meant by federal preemptive regulations. Do you think business is being hypocritical in asking for such additional regulations?

9. Do you agree that free market solutions and business altruism are largely ineffective when compared with governmental approaches to environmental protection? Discuss.

10. What is your overall assessment of 3M's "pollution prevention pays" program? Does it indicate that corporate social responsiveness has merit as a way of dealing with the environment? What other steps could a company take beyond what 3M did?

Cases

The Industrial Waste Exchange Center

The Regional Commerce and Growth Association (RCGA) is an economic development organization based in a large metropolitan area in the Midwest. With the cooperation of a nearby large university, the RCGA began an industrial waste exchange operation. It involved a quarterly publication that listed waste materails available and waste materials wanted. Industry's response was enthusiastic because recycling reduced costs of waste disposal. Costs of raw materials for the waste users were also reduced.

The association charged five dollars for a listing in three consecutive quarterly publications, which covered approximately 115 materials either wanted or offered. Companies offering or seeking material were not identified, but were brought in contact with each other.

Despite the fact that the Environmental Protection Agency dubbed the program a "universally beneficial system," federal regulators from another government agency wanted to confirm suspected pollution violations and filed a petition in a local court in order to gain access to the RCGA's files.

QUESTIONS

1. Do you think the regulators have a right to examine RCGA's files? Why or why not?
2. Would you feel differently if you were told that the regulators merely wanted to investigate a citizens group's claim that one of the firms using the service had spilled chemical waste in the city's major source of drinking water?
3. What impact might regulatory actions such as we see in this case have on cooperative efforts to solve social problems?

The Gossett Paper Company

The Gossett Paper Company was the largest employer in a small town in northeastern North Carolina, employing approximately 16 percent of the working population. For many years the mill had discharged its chemical wastes directly into a small stream that flowed through the town. This was also the typical practice of most pulp wood mills in the area. The state legislature recognized the practice as increasingly dangerous both to the environment and directly to the human population of the region. For these reasons the legislature passed a strict set of regulations for treatment of chemical waste before it could be put into streams. The regulations exceeded those of the EPA.

After reviewing the regulations, Leonard Gossett, the company president, decided that the cost of meeting the requirements prevented the mill from operating profitably, and that the best course of action was to move to South Carolina, where the pollution control laws were not as stringent.

QUESTIONS

1. What social responsiblity does the paper company have in this case? Think in terms of the economic-legal-ethical-discretionary model.
2. Evaluate Mr. Gossett's decision and indicate what you would have done in a similiar situation.
3. Discuss the advantages and disadvantages of a state legislature mandating more rigorous environmental standards than those used by the EPA.

The Grass Is Not Always Greener . . .

Most residents of the small rural borough of Palmerton in eastern Pennsylvania do not know what it's like to mow their lawns during the spring and summer months. They do not have grass on their property to mow. Some people have spent thousands of dollars to get grass to grow on their land, but most have turned to artificial versions of grass, wood chips, gravel, or macadam as ground cover.

At the root of the problem is soil contamination by emissions from the New Jersey Zinc Company, the community's largest taxpayer and employer. Bordered on two sides by the company's zinc smelters, Palmerton has for decades been liberally dusted with zinc and other fallout. Hedges, shrubs, flowers, and trees continue to grow in Palmerton, but the zinc in the soil kills grass.

Removing the zinc altogether may be impossible, but efforts are under way to contain the problem. New Jersey Zinc is spending some $36 million for plant modernization and pollution control to meet terms of a consent agreement with the Pennsylvania Department of Environmental Resources. The 1976 agreement also entailed payment of more than $100,000 in fines. The company claims it has already sharply reduced emissions of zinc dust, zinc oxide, sulfur dioxide, and other contaminants.

In response to residents' anger, the company is now sampling zinc-resistant grasses imported from England and is talking of reseeding parts of Palmerton from an airplane or spray truck if it finds the right seed. The company is also testing various poplar and pine seedlings in several mountainside test plots. Results from one of the test grasses are encouraging, but it is still to early to tell whether it will survive. A decision on the reseeding project has not been made by the company.[1]

QUESTIONS

1. Discuss the social issues that may relate to this case.
2. Is the company meeting its social responsibilities? If yes, how? If not, how can it be more socially responsive?
3. What should the residents realistically expect the company to do? What, realistically, should the company expect to have to do?

---

[1]Based on Daniel Machalaba, "The Grass Is Greener on the Other Side of the Fence? Nope." *The Wall Street Journal*, April 18, 1977, pp. 1, 23. Reprinted by permission of *The Wall Street Journal*, © Dow Jones & Company, Inc., 1977. All rights reserved.

Business and the Community

The history of business's relations with the community in which it resides parallels closely the evolution of the concept of corporate social responsiveness as we have traced it. Over the decades business has recognized the interconnectedness of the health and vitality of the community and that of business. It is not uncommon today, for example, for a company to inquire into the success of such community efforts as the United Fund as an index of the vitality of a community in which it is considering locating. If such funds are growing and are enthusiastically supported by business and the community, this is a good sign of a locale that has recognized and understands the vital partnership between business and the community.

Whole books have been written about the history of the business and community relationship.[1] It is not necessary to read such accounts, however, to gain an appreciation of the relevant issues. What is most important to us today is to understand business's rationale for community involvement, the focus of that involvement in terms of specific issues, the magnitude of that involvement, and the managerial approach that is beginning to characterize business efforts.

So much could be discussed quite legitimately in this chapter, but because some topics are covered elsewhere and because we want to focus on major issues, we will concentrate on a limited number of topics that best represent business and community concerns. Therefore, we intend to cover the following topics in this chapter:

- Community involvement: what and why?
- Business giving — philanthropy
- Business and other community efforts
- Business involvement with local government
- Managing giving and community involvement

[1]Morrell Heald, *The Social Responsibilities of Business: Company and Community, 1900-1960* (Cleveland: Case Western Reserve University Press, 1970).

COMMUNITY INVOLVEMENT: WHAT AND WHY?

When we speak of the community we usually mean the immediate locale — the town, the city, or the state — in which a business resides. In our modern age of instantaneous communication and speedy travel, however, the region, the nation, or even the world can become relevant. This wider community concept also becomes more pertinent as business organizations grow. National business firms thus have a multitude of communities with which they must be concerned. Though this is so, we will be discussing issues in this chapter that, although of concern to larger firms, have a more pointed focus for small to moderate business — the local bank, the retail merchant, and the regional manufacturer.

Whatever the scope of the community, business is now keenly aware that there is an interdependence with most other members of the community in which it resides. Out of this interdependence has grown responsibility and a concern for business citizenship. Business is affected by and affects what goes on in the community, and therefore must treat the community with the same kind of respect and consideration expected of individual citizens. This is not a theoretical matter, but a practical one — it is in business's best interest to do so. Like so many other issues we have examined, the issue here is not whether, but where business should express its concern and to what degree.

Perhaps one of the best ways to explain why business should be interested in its community is to look at the reasoning given by a company executive. Robert Cushman, president of Norton Company in Worcester, Massachusetts, asserts in one of his company's employee manuals:

> Business does not operate in a vacuum, but as a social institution interacting with other social institutions. What business does affects its community; in turn, the people's good will and trust are essential for business to fulfill its primary role, which is to provide goods and services . . .
>
> Therefore, business must — not only for a healthier society, but for its own well being — be willing to give serious consideration to human needs as it does to the needs for production and profits.[2]

Beyond this general statement, Cushman enumerates at least six reasons for business involvement in the community:

1. Business people are efficient problem solvers.

[2]"Community Action Manual" (Worchester, Mass.: Norton Company, April 1978).

2. Employees gain satisfaction and improved morale from involvement in community programs.
3. A positive image in your community helps in hiring.
4. Often, a company gains prestige and greater acceptance in a community when it gets actively involved.
5. Social responsibility in business is the alternative to government regulation.
6. Business helps itself by supporting those institutions that are essential to the continuation of business.[3]

As can be seen in these reasons, there is a note of practicality in business's involvement in the community; it is quite appropriate for business to help itself in the process of helping others. This dual objective of business efforts illustrates clearly that profits and social concerns are not mutually exclusive endeavors. We could go on with other rationales for business involvement in community affairs but it would not add much to what has been said. As we look at business motives for supporting specific community activities, additional insights will be suggested.

What is particularly interesting about business involvement in the community is the range of issues upon which business chooses to utilize its resources. Let us look at one specific comprehensive survey of the types of community programs in which businesses were involved. Since the country's largest corporations are typically more active in sponsoring social programs, the survey by Human Resources Network was sent to 775 of the nation's largest firms. Returns were received from about 56 percent of the firms, detailing involvement in 743 different programs.

As it turned out, only six areas of involvement contained about 46 percent of the total number of projects. These six were as follows:[4]

Education	14.7%
Environment	8.0%
General community affairs	7.1%
Minority enterprise: financial and technical assistance	5.8%
Job training	5.7%
The arts	5.3%

[3]Ibid., pp. 3-4.
[4]From *The Handbook of Corporate Social Responsibility: Profiles of Involvement,* 2nd ed. Copyright 1975 by the authors, Human Resources Network. Reprinted with the permission of the publisher, Chilton Book Company, Radnor, PA.

Other programs named — that might include community involvement emphasis — were:[5]

Employment	4.7%
Youth	4.2%
Volunteerism	3.8%
Urban development	3.1%
Summer jobs for youth	3.0%
Health	2.2%
Housing	2.0%
Drug and alcohol abuse	2.0%
Nutrition	1.9%
Prisoner rehabilitation	1.5%

This survey obviously has limitations and may not be representative of all businesses, but it does provide some interesting insight into where large businesses are exerting community efforts. When an analysis is made of what types of companies participate most in what types of programs, it is apparent that companies in similar fields tend to support similar social programs. Industrial companies, for example, show a pattern of emphasizing environmental projects, retailers emphasize consumerism, and the arts are of great interest to banks.[6] This, of course, makes sense from a managerial point of view, as companies seek a match between their social efforts and their economic endeavors.

Community social involvement, for the most part, is not a legal responsibility of business. Thus business finds its best rationale for participating in community affairs in the ethical and, most particularly, the discretionary categories of our four-part model. Economic overtones are present, of course, as they frequently are.

Let us now turn to an examination of business philanthropy, with special emphasis on giving to education and the arts, Later, we will direct our attention to other types of community programs in which outright donations of money are not the primary focus.

BUSINESS GIVING — PHILANTHROPY

Though the dictionary defines *philanthropy* as "a desire to help mankind as indicated by acts of charity, etc.; love of mankind,"[7] one contemporary usage of the word is "business giving." One problem with the dic-

[5]Ibid.
[6]Ibid., p. 12.
[7]*Webster's New World Dictionary* (Cleveland: World Publishing Company, 1964), p. 1098.

tionary definition is that the motive is characterized as charitable, benevolent, or generous, but it is difficult in practice to assess the true motives that go into businesses' — or anyone's — giving of themselves and their financial resources.

Business philanthropy of one kind or another can be traced back many years. It was in the 1920s that the most significant effort to "translate the new social consciousness of management into action" emerged in the form of organized corporate philanthropy.[8] Before World War I steps had been taken toward establishing systematic, federated fund raising for community services. The early success of the YMCA and the wartime chests, welfare federations, Community Chests, colleges and universities, and hospitals provided impetus for these groups to organize their solicitations. The business response to the opportunity for giving contributions to help community needs was varied. At one extreme, large enterprises such as the Bell Telephone system, with branches, offices, and subsidiaries in thousands of communities, contributed to literally thousands of civic and social organizations. Smaller firms, such as the companies in small mill towns of North Carolina, supported schools, housing, religious activities, and community welfare with a degree of enthusiasm that exceeded most nineteenth-century paternalism.[9]

Corporate giving in the period 1918-1929 was dominated by the Community Chest movement. In the period 1929-1935 there was an attempt to allow business to deduct up to five percent of its pretax net income for its community donations. The years 1935-1945 were marked by the Depression and World War II, and did not show expansion of business giving. The period 1945-1960 saw new horizons of corporate responsibility, and the period since about 1960 can truly be called a period in which social responsibility flourished and went beyond simple corporate giving. But because we are focusing on business giving — corporate contributions to the community — we will exclude those broader endeavors that began in the 1960s. Debate is still going on and probably will continue about whether businesses should give away money. The evidence shows that they are doing so, and they probably will continue to do so in the future.

Philanthropist John D. Rockefeller III has argued that business giving is necessary to support what he calls the third sector: the nonprofit sector. The first two sectors — business and government — have support through profits and taxes, but the third sector (which includes hundreds of thousands of churches, museums, hospitals, libraries, private colleges and universities, and performing groups) depends on phi-

[8]Heald, p. 112.
[9]Ibid.

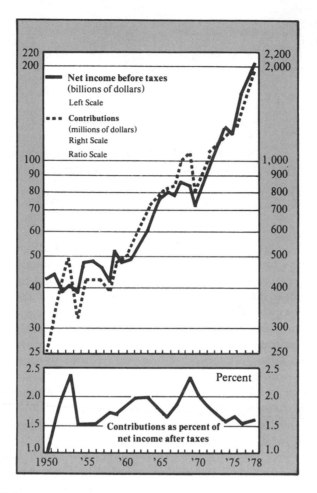

FIGURE 7-1
Corporate Contributions and Income Before Taxes

SOURCE: "Economic Road Maps, U.S. Philanthropy," Nos. 1870-1871 (New York: The Conference Board, January 1980), p. 3. Reprinted by permission.

lanthropy for support. Philanthropy gives these institutions the crucial margin that assures them of their most precious asset: their independence.[10]

It is difficult to say exactly how charitable business firms are supposed to be. Though under federal tax law, for-profit corporations are allowed

[10]John D. Rockefeller III, "In Defense of Philanthropy," *Business and Society Review,* Spring 1978, pp. 26-29.

TABLE 7-1
Contributions as a Percent of Pretax Net Income, 1976 —
Companies Grouped by Rate of Giving[a]

Contributions as Percent of Pretax Net Income	Domestic Pretax Income: Number of Companies[b]	Worldwide Pretax Income: Number of Companies[c]
0 - 0.24%	47	72
0.25 - 0.49%	101	156
0.50 - 0.74%	68	115
0.75 - 0.99%	56	82
1.0 - 1.49%	54	69
1.5 - 1.99%	46	48
2.0 - 2.99%	38	40
3.0 - 3.99%	14	14
4.0 - 7.49%	7	10
7.5 - 9.99%	1	0
Over 10%	3	1
Total	435	607

[a]Insurance companies excluded.
[b]15 net loss companies excluded.
[c]18 net loss companies excluded.
SOURCE: Anne Klepper and Kathryn Troy, *Annual Survey of Corporate Contributions, 1976* (New York: The Conference Board, 1978), p. 5. Reprinted by permission.

to deduct up to five percent of their net profits for charitable contributions, historically they have given only about one percent of their pretax dollars.[11] Data from The Conference Board, which seems to have the most reliable figures over time, indicate the pattern of corporate giving. Figure 7-1 shows corporate contributions from 1950 to 1978 as a percentage of net income before taxes.

Table 7-1 provides some additional interesting data — contributions as a percentage of pretax net income for the year 1976, with companies grouped according to the rate of giving. It can be seen that the 0.25-0.49 percent category contains the largest number of contributors.

These tables document the magnitude of corporate giving historically, but they do not indicate whether the amounts given were considerable or slight. When these determinations are made, they are based on a number of personal or organizational considerations — philosophy, past giving, capacity to give, and so on.

[11]"How Charitable Should American Corporations Be?" *The Chronicle of Higher Education,* October 31, 1977, p. 12.

Why Do Companies Give?

Perhaps it would be more worthwhile to know why companies give to charitable causes rather than the amounts they give. Most of the executives present at a recent conference on corporate giving tended to agree with Secretary of Commerce Juanita M. Kreps that, in the long run, giving is good for business.[12] For more specific reasons, however, we must turn to a survey conducted by The Conference Board when pursuing

TABLE 7-2
Reasons for Undertaking Contributions Activities
(Responses of 417 Chairmen and Presidents)

Possible Reasons for Undertaking Contribution Activities	SPECIFIC ACTIVITIES*		
	United Funds	Higher Education	The Arts
Corporate citizenship: practice good corporate citizenship	74%	49%	48%
Business environment: protect and improve environment in which to live, work and do business	68%	46%	43%
Employee benefits: realize benefits for company employees (normally in areas where company operates)	47%	31%	31%
Public relations: realize good public relations value	34%	20%	32%
Pluralism: preserve a pluralistic society by maintaining choices between government and private-sector alternatives	28%	40%	10%
Commitment: of directors or senior officers to particular causes, involvement	23%	31%	28%
Pressure: from business peers, customers, and/or suppliers	12%	8%	17%
Altruism: practice altruism with little or no direct or indirect company self-interest	10%	8%	16%
Manpower supply: increase the pool of trained manpower or untrained manpower or access to minority recruiting	5%	63%	2%
No contributions or activities in this area	2%	2%	7%

*Adds to more than 100% because multiple responses were requested.

SOURCE: James F. Harris and Anne Klepper, *Corporate Philanthropic Public Service Activities* (New York: The Conference Board, 1976), p. 16. Reprinted by permission.

[12]Ibid.

this question. In a study of *Fortune* 500 companies, with 417 chairmen and presidents responding, Table 7-2 shows the reasons why companies contribute to United Funds, higher education, and the arts.[13] Interestingly, except for the category of higher education, where the manpower supply was the prime motive, the primary reason reported was a rather benevolent or altruistic one: corporate citizenship.

In a study that raises a few questions about the validity of the above data, J. R. Block and Norman Goodman also attempted to ascertain why companies give. They designed two fund-gathering strategies, one aimed at the motive of giving for the less fortunate in the community (altruism) and the other aimed at self-interest. Though their research effort had some self-admitted flaws, their conclusion was that the approach that appeals to the self-interest of the givers is more effective in motivating giving than is the approach that emphasizes others.[14]

To Whom Do Companies Give?

During the course of any budget year, companies receive numerous requests from a wide variety of applicants for contributions. Companies must then weigh and balance both quantitative and qualitative factors to arrive at a decision regarding recipients of their gifts. By looking at the beneficiaries of corporate contributions, we can estimate the value business has placed on various societal groups and endeavors.

Figure 7-2 reports where corporate contributions went for the years 1968 and 1978 (the latest data available).[15] Changes in the giving categories were minor over that time, so we can assume the 1978 data summarize where business currently spends its money. A brief discussion of each of the five categories included in Figure 7-2 will help explain the nature of business's involvement in philanthropy.

Education. Most of the corporate contributions in this category went to higher education — colleges and universities. The major educational recipients were capital grants (including endowments), unrestricted operating grants, departmental and research grants, scholarships and fellowships, and employee matching gifts. Also included in this category would be educational groups (e.g., United Negro College Fund, the Council for Financial Aid to Education) and primary and secondary schools.

[13]James F. Harris and Anne Klepper, *Corporate Philanthropic Public Service Activities* (New York: The Conference Board, 1976).

[14]J. R. Block and Norman Goodman, "Why Companies Give," *Journal of Advertising Research,* October 1976, pp. 59-63.

[15]"Economic Road Maps, U.S. Philanthropy," Nos. 1870-1871 (New York: The Conference Board, January 1980), p. 3.

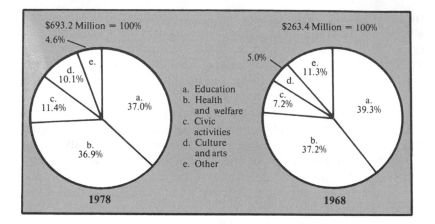

FIGURE 7-2
Distribution of Contributions *

*Based on Conference Board survey of 401 companies in 1968 and 759 companies in 1978.

SOURCE: "Economic Road Maps, U.S. Philanthropy," Nos. 1870-1971 (New York: The Conference Board, January 1980), p. 3. Reprinted by permission.

As we saw earlier, business's most frequently reported reason for supporting higher education was to increase the pool of trained personnel. This has obvious credibility as higher education institutions do, indeed, form the resource base from which business fills its managerial and professional positions.

Though contributions to educational institutions rank high in business giving (37 percent of all business contributions in 1978), companies do not always blindly give expecting nothing in return. Indeed, in the last several years there has been some controversy about whether business should give to educational institutions that do not support the free enterprise values so important to business. The basic issue is support of education "with strings attached" or "without strings attached."

Those who argue that business should give to education without strings attached feel that attempts to dictate to educational institutions will create conflict between the institutions and industry. Louis W. Cabot, chairman of the board of Cabot Corporation, argues that it is neither wise nor advantageous for business to limit its gifts to institutions that support free enterprise.[16] His belief is that the corporate self-interest criterion is both illusory and dangerous. It is illusory in that it

[16]Louis W. Cabot, "Corporate Support of Education: No Strings Attached," *Harvard Business Review,* July-August 1978, pp. 139-144.

calls for sweeping generalizations about faculty members, and dangerous because it tends to discourage all educational giving. He feels, in addition, that if a company genuinely wants to help education function with maximum effectiveness, it should support schools as a whole rather than try to control the use of its funds. Cabot summarizes his view as follows:

> It is in the corporate community's self-interest to step up its level of financial support. At the same time, it is *not* in the corporate interest to dilute this effort by burdening it with uncalled-for constraints.[17]

On the other side of the issue are those who feel business ought to be more selective in its giving. Robert H. Malott, chairman of the board of FMC Corporation, argues that corporate self-interest ought to serve as a guide for business giving to education. Malott is especially concerned about corporations giving financial support to schools and colleges that favor in their teachings the views of "radical" economists and others who want government to grow at the expense of free enterprise.[18]

Irving Kristol also argues forcefully that business has a responsibility to be discerning in its corporate contributions. He maintains that though universities feel they have a *right* to business's money, "they have no such right."[19] His position is that if educational institutions want money from a particular segment of the population, they must earn the good opinion of that segment. If educational institutions are indifferent to that good opinion, they will just have to learn to be indifferent to the money also. Kristol argues against giving business money to support educational organizations whose views are "inimical to corporate survival." He summarizes his feelings well:

> . . . your philanthropy must serve the longer-term interests of the corporation. Corporate philanthropy should not be, cannot be disinterested.[20]

Unfortunately, there are no data to tell us which of these extreme positions is the most effective; they represent opposite philosophical postures. A somewhat tempered version of the discretionary philosophy would be consistent, however, with the belief that managers should exercise some control over their corporate giving to education and should strive to achieve a policy of giving with the company's self-interest at least kept in mind. This approach to giving would attempt to achieve economic and social goals simultaneously.

[17]Ibid., p. 144.
[18]Robert H. Malott, "Corporate Support of Education: Some Strings Attached," *Harvard Business Review,* July-August 1978, pp. 133-138.
[19]Irving Kristol, "On Corporate Philanthropy," *Wall Street Journal,* March 21, 1977, p. 18.
[20]Ibid.

Health and Welfare. The major reason health and welfare is one of the largest categories of business giving is the huge amount donated to such federated drives as the United Way. Dating back to the Community Chest movement cited earlier, business has traditionally cooperated with federated giving mechanisms. Money given to federated drives usually goes directly to assist various agencies in a local community. Great public pressure is placed on businesses to actively support such federated campaigns, so it is not surprising that this category is one of the largest beneficiaries. Business hopes, just as the community does, that such consolidated efforts will lend some order to the requests of major recipients in the community that business has chosen to support.

In addition to federated drives, other major recipients in this category are hospitals, youth agencies, and other local health and welfare agencies. Hospitals represent an obviously important need in most communities; they receive financial support for capital investments (new buildings and equipment), operating funds, and matching employee gifts. Youth agencies include such groups as the YMCA, Boy Scouts, Girl Scouts, and Boys Clubs. Since a great part of the country's turmoil of the late 1960s and early 1970s had its source in the dissatisfaction of young people, many of whom were antagonistic toward large corporations, it is quite logical for business to include youth as a prominent part of its health and welfare contributions.[21]

Civic Activities. This category of business giving represents a wide variety of philanthropic activities in the community. Dominant among these are support for community improvement activities, environment and ecology, research organizations other than academic (e.g., Brookings, Committee for Economic Development, Urban League), and neighborhood renewal. Because community improvement receives the largest share of this category, perhaps several examples would help illustrate the wide variety of ways in which business is involved in community endeavors.

One interesting example is the Community Relations Committee of Salem, New Jersey, established by the Anchor Hocking Corporation. Started in 1967, the purpose of the program was to relieve racial tensions and to involve a large number of citizens in identifying and solving community problems. Representatives of city government; civic, social, and other organizations; and citizens at large met and first identified positive factors affecting community life. Negative factors were identified later, followed by group problem-solving sessions and assignment of project groups for in-depth investigation and implementation of solutions. Future plans call for training more citizens in techniques of

---

[21] *The Handbook of Corporate Social Responsibility,* p. 39.

leading groups in problem solving, in an effort to transfer leadership to private citizens and community groups rather than rely so heavily on business leadership.

The company has identified a number of indices of success, including the fact that there have been no riots or civil disturbances in this community of 10,000, although rioting has taken place in communities within twenty miles. Also, the first community swimming pool has been built, a day care center has been expanded and improved, and playground and recreational facilities have been created.[22]

Another interesting example of a business involved in community improvement is the "Spring Cleaning" program of the Citizens and Southern National Bank of Georgia. The purpose of this program was to spruce up the approaches to Savannah, Georgia, so tourists would stop and stay in Savannah rather than go on to Florida. In conjunction with the Savannah Visitors Center and other banks in the community, Citizens and Southern sponsored a big "work day" to show the community that business was supporting efforts to help develop tourist trade.[23]

The example of Eli Lilly and Company's "Big Brother and Big Sister" programs exemplifies civic involvement where youth was the focus. In attempting to establish a "Big Brother" program at a nearby inner-city high school in Indianapolis, Indiana, thirty-seven male employees from the company volunteered to work with a group of disadvantaged students. They tried to discover something they had in common with the students that would encourage further communication, thereby providing each student with a mature friend and sounding board. The volunteers entertained the students at professional sporting events, vocational field trips, and family outings. The "Big Sister" program was very similar, aimed at economically underprivileged female students. Women employees of Eli Lilly exposed the young persons to cultural, educational, vocational, and entertainment activities.[24]

Culture and Arts. Support for culture and the arts has been a favorite and prestigious outlet for business philanthropy for some time. Indeed, in 1967 Richard Eells wrote an entire book entitled *The Corporation and the Arts*.[25] Business's support of the arts is somewhat interesting because there has never been any pressure on it from government to do so; its efforts have been purely voluntary.

Of the various cultural beneficiaries of business support, museums tend to be the most frequent, followed in order by radio and television (especially public broadcasting), music (for example, symphony or-

---

[22] *The Handbook of Corporate Social Responsibility,* pp. 110-111.
[23] Ibid., pp. 143-144.
[24] Ibid., p. 223.
[25] Richard Eells, *The Corporation and the Arts* (New York: Macmillan, 1967).

chestras), arts funds or councils, and theaters. But as our data show, culture and the arts ranked a distant third behind health and welfare and education in total business giving.

Perhaps the most prominent organized effort on the part of business to give to the arts is the Business Committee for the Arts (BCA). Formed in the mid-1960s, the BCA is a private nationwide group formed to "unite corporate money with artistic need."[26] According to BCA data, when the group was formed corporate giving to the arts was about $22 million. This grew to $90 million in 1968 and $110 million in 1970.[27] The amount was probably about $150 million in 1976. Business also takes pride in pointing out that it gives about the same amount to the arts as does government, but that none of its money goes for administration.[28]

It is interesting to consider why business gives to the arts. There seems to be no direct benefit to business, as is the case with donations to education. As with other philanthropic categories, businesses claim various motives for their giving. There are those who argue altruistically that the reason for business's largesse is because business recognizes that art contributes to the kind of vitality and creativity that is important to society. The object of the BCA awards, given each year to companies that support the arts, is to "stimulate and encourage independent assistance of the arts" by businessmen.[29]

On the other hand, there are business executives who say openly that their support for the arts is at least in part a reflection of self-interest. Paul H. Eliker, president of SCM Corporation, argues for giving to the arts to gain recognition or visibility, and for general image building.[30] He claims this is no different than the reasons the great patrons of the Renaissance — the Medicis and Pope Julius II — supported culture and the arts, to associate themselves with the grandeur of the times.

Eliker tells the story of a reporter who once asked George Weissman, vice-chairman of Phillip Morris, why his company supported such exhibitions as American Folk Art. Mr. Weissman is reported to have responded, "It's a lot cheaper than taking out ads saying how great we think we are."[31]

Though one cannot climb into an executive's mind to find out why business really gives to the arts, at least one sociologist suggests that

[26]John B. Forbes, "Corporate America Giving More to the Arts," *New York Times,* May 15, 1977, p. F-19.
[27]Ibid.
[28]"Where Art and Business Meet," *Forbes,* February 1, 1977, p. 6.
[29]Ibid.
[30]Paul H. Eliker, "Why Corporations Give Money to the Arts," *Wall Street Journal,* March 31, 1978, p. 15.
[31]Ibid.

although business claims altruism and social responsibility are what motivate them, it is really self-interest. This many not sound too startling, given the public admission of some executives that this is so, but M. David Ermann sees the giving efforts as part of an extremely selfish scenario. Citing gifts from major corporations totaling $12 million per year to the Public Broadcasting System (PBS), Ermann argues that such contributions are intended to create a less hostile social climate and thus mute criticism of business. In his words, the purpose of the corporate charity was to favorably "influence the social milieu . . . to ensure rewards and reduce penalties and uncertainty for the company."[32]

Recipients of business donations to the arts are not likely to turn down such contributions because the giver's motives may not be pure. Business giving, whatever the intent, does benefit the giver and the receiver, as well as the general public. Though Paul Eliker's earlier comments suggested an economic motive, he fully recognizes that his company is not the sole beneficiary. He concludes:

> We do it because it's good for the arts, it's good for the millions of people who get pleasure viewing great works of art, and — not least — it's good for SCM Corporation.[33]

Other Activities. In addition to civic activities, culture and the arts, education, and health and welfare, Figure 7-2 shows that of the 759 companies reporting in 1978, 4.6 percent of their donations went to "other activities." It is not clear what all these other activities were, but some of them were identified as groups devoted to economic education (e.g., Joint Council on Economic Education, Junior Achievement), groups whose purpose is to aid other countries, and groups engaged in religious activities.

BUSINESS AND OTHER COMMUNITY EFFORTS

We would now like to discuss briefly four other significant areas of relationship between business and community that are not always evident in surveys of business donations. These areas, which include urban development, minority enterprise, job training, and volunteerism are interdependent as far as the community is concerned.

---

[32]Robert Toth, "PBS Corporate Gifts Selfish?" *Atlanta Journal,* September 11, 1977, p. F-7.
[33]Eliker, p. 15.

Urban Development

Corporate efforts in urban development represent attempts by companies to deal with those problems, especially in the inner city, that are having adverse effects on business and the people living in those areas. Important aspects of these efforts include housing, urban beautification, recreational areas, jobs, neighborhood cohesiveness, and delivery of social services. The rationale for business's concern is that the community where one does business must also be a reasonable place in which to live.[34] Business has a stake in seeing that neighborhoods do not deteriorate and that the larger physical community does not decay.

Urban development and planning thus presents business with an opportunity to simultaneously reflect a social concern while being assured that the community remains a good place in which to live and work.

Minority Enterprise

Closely related to the concern for urban development is the belief that support of businesses owned or operated by minorities is crucial to the survival of the community, particularly in the inner cities. One of the most significant ways to bring minorities into the mainstream is to facilitate establishment and operation of their own businesses, an idea that, since 1970, has been receiving increasing federal support. Between 1970 and 1975 federal aid to minority businesses increased 265 percent.[35] Ever since the urban riots of 1966-1969, business's support of minority enterprise has increased too, as manifested in three major ways. First, business has offered vendor purchasing programs, in which companies purchase goods and services from minority-owned enterprises. Second, business has provided financial and technical assistance in such forms as special bank loans and loaned executives. Third, business has initiated bank deposit programs, in which it deposits its money in minority-owned banks.

Two programs offer interesting illustrations of how business supports minority enterprise. One is Chase Manhattan Bank of New York's minority lending and purchasing effort, designed to increase participation of minorities in the overall economic structure of New York City. Its purchasing department operates a bank-wide program to generate minority business. The bank has also loaned millions of dollars to minority businesses that do not meet conventional criteria for such loans, but that have high potential for success.

[34] *Handbook of Corporate Social Responsibility,* p. 29.
[35] Ibid., p. 66.

The second program, offered by Cummins Engine Company of Columbus, Indiana, is one of technical assistance. It commits full- and part-time advisors to minority economic development organizations. These advisors are Cummins' employees, whose expenses and salaries are paid by the company while they are on assignment.[36] There are hundreds of other business firms offering programs of minority assistance similar to the two described above.

Job Training

Employment and job training are vital community concerns that are supported by business for both social and economic motives. Early efforts by the National Alliance of Business and its JOBS Corps of the 1960s have been supplanted by programs run by individual companies. In some of the large job-training programs of the past, however, trainees were thrust into new job situations with very little knowledge of the working world. To overcome this problem, it is now recognized that a total cultural transition has to be included as part of any job-training effort.

Volunteerism

Volunteerism encompasses a broad spectrum of business and individual contributions to the community. The basic idea behind volunteerism is to give employees time off to work on social programs while still being paid full or partial salary by the company. This enables the employees to apply their managerial skills or technical expertise to social service projects without loss of income or seniority. These kinds of programs are sometimes obscured in aggregate data on business's support of the community, but they are obviously of great importance.

Though there are numerous examples of volunteerism at work, the cases of Xerox and IBM are especially interesting. Xerox's program, started in 1971, is called the Social Service Leave Program (SSLP). Under the SSLP, employees with three or more years of service were eligible to apply for up to one year's leave with full pay to work with a social service agency of their own choosing. The determination of who was granted leave was made by an evaluation committee of employees. When the employees went on leave, they were guaranteed the same or equivalent jobs upon returning.[37]

IBM's program, begun in the 1960s, is very similar. Social service projects that IBM employees have been given leave to be involved in

[36]Ibid., pp. 536, 540.
[37]Ibid., p. 229.

include work with the Legal Aid Society, aid to a Beirut orphanage, assistance to minorities in getting into college, and teaching ghetto youngsters.[38]

What is especially notable about these other community efforts by business is that they indicate business understands that using a company's human resources is as important as using its financial resources. There are some business and community projects that simply cannot be handled with financial commitments alone.

BUSINESS INVOLVEMENT WITH LOCAL GOVERNMENT

In addition to the kinds of contributions discussed so far, business is also involved on a cooperative basis with local governments. The purpose of this involvement is to improve the community in which a business resides. The cooperation between business and government reflects, if only on a small scale, the kind of business-government partnership that we have already discussed in Chapter 4.

To provide as factual a basis as possible for our discussion, we will report on data gathered recently by The Conference Board, which surveyed 2,200 companies on their involvement with local government. Of the more than 1,100 responses to the survey, about 700 companies indicated no direct involvement with local government, though most indicated they cooperated in other community affairs. The other 400 firms reported involvement of various kinds.[39] Multiple involvements were common, particularly in smaller communities where fewer businesses were available to address community needs.

Of the various types of businesses, banks and utilities were the ones most deeply involved, accounting for about one-fourth of all involvement programs reported. This is probably not surprising given their function in and identification with particular cities.[40] The type of involvement by companies was quite varied, with economic development programs being more prevalent in smaller and medium-sized cities, and executive exchange or assistance programs more frequent in larger cities. Table 7-3 shows data from companies reporting involvement in selected programs in several metropolitan areas.

Involvement in each of the metropolitan areas included in Table 7-3 partially reflects an assessment of the needs of that area. In Min-

---

[38]"Doing Good Works on Company Time," *Business Week,* May 13, 1972, pp. 166-167.

[39]Leonard Lund, "Business Involvement with Local Government," *Information Bulletin No. 30* (New York: The Conference Board, October 1977), pp. 1-6.

[40]Ibid., p. 2.

TABLE 7-3
Companies Reporting Involvement in Selected Programs in Some Metropolitan Areas

Programs	Number of Companies Located in						
	New York	*Chicago*	*Los Angeles*	*Philadelphia*	*Detroit*	*Boston*	*Minneapolis*
Loaned executive	12	7	2	7	8	4	8
Management advisor	9	10	3	7	9	6	5
Economic development	7	7	5	6	8	4	12
Community goal setting	5	11	5	4	9	2	9
Financial management	7	4	3	9	5	6	2
Loan of facilities	7	8	2	12	7	5	3

SOURCE: Leonard Lund, "Business Involvement with Local Government," *Information Bulletin No. 30* (New York: The Conference Board, October 1977), p. 3. Reprinted by permission.

neapolis, for example, local efforts tend to focus on economic development. In New York City, the loaned executive program is important because of the need to improve the city's management approaches and systems. In Detroit, there is concern for the automotive industry, environment, and zoning.[41]

A question that is always raised in such endeavors is whether they were or are worth the effort. The respondents to The Conference Board survey were asked to evaluate their efforts, and Table 7-4 presents summary data of each firms' self-assessment. Seventy-five percent of the 2,384 programs evaluated were deemed successful, with only 2 percent considered failures. If one were to predict business's future involvement with local government based on these data, the future looks optimistic.

Business's involvement with local government is just as carefully considered as are other community projects. As Table 7-4 indicates, business-government cooperation as one option for business involvement in the local community is a viable and reasonably successful effort. Such successes lay the foundation for new dimensions of business involvement in communities in the future.

[41]Ibid., p. 3.

TABLE 7-4
Evaluation of Involvement in Selected Programs

Program	Number of Cases	Percentage Evaluated as		
		Success	Failure	Indefinite
Loaned executive	180	86.3	0.5	13.2
Management consultation	251	70.9	2.9	26.2
Economic development	321	66.4	2.2	31.4
All programs	2,384	75.3	2.2	22.5

SOURCE: Leonard Lund, "Business Involvement with Local Government," *Information Bulletin No. 30* (New York: The Conference Board, October 1977), p. 4. Reprinted by permission.

MANAGING GIVING AND COMMUNITY INVOLVEMENT

Business should approach its giving programs and community involvement just as carefully as it does its production and distribution functions, with objectives, plans, and a rationale. To achieve this goal, we will consider how business should systematically manage its giving programs and community involvement. In later chapters we will develop in more detail the entire spectrum of managerial approaches to social issues; here, however, we will address some concerns that deal particularly with involvement in the community.

The starting point of a rational approach to managing giving and community involvement is the setting of objectives. Proper planning requires that managers delineate the ends sought in any endeavor. In Chapter 12 on planning, we will present a detailed approach to setting such objectives; here we will assume that a clear concept of what a firm is attempting to achieve in the social realm has already been determined.

Four steps in developing a community action program, as articulated by the Norton Company, provide a framework for thinking about community involvement. These four steps are: (1) knowing the community, (2) knowing the range of company resources available, (3) selecting a project, and (4) monitoring the project.[42] Each of these steps will be discussed briefly.

[42]"Community Action Manual," pp. 11-21.

Knowing the Community

A key to developing worthwhile community involvement programs is knowing the community in which the business resides. This is a research step that requires management to assess the characteristics of the local area. Every locale has certain particular characteristics that can help shape social programs of involvement. Who lives in the community? What is the ethnic composition? What is the unemployment level? Are there inner-city problems or pockets of poverty? What are other organizations doing? What are the really pressing social needs of the area? What is the community's morale?

Knowing the leadership in the community is another factor. Is the leadership progressive? Is leadership cohesive and unified, or is it fragmented? If it is fragmented, the company may have to make difficult choices of which groups with which to work. If the community's present approach to social issues is well led, all that may be necessary is "jumping on the bandwagon." If the community's leadership is not well organized, the company may want to provide an impetus and an agenda for restructuring or revitalizing the leadership.

Knowing the Company's Resources

To effectively address various community needs, an inventory and assessment of the company's resources and competences are needed. What is the variety, mix, and range of resources — manpower, money, meeting space, equipment, and supplies? Many companies are willing to give employees some released time to engage in and support community projects. This may be in the form of managerial assistance, technical assistance, or just sheer manpower. A wide spectrum of abilities, skills, interests, potentials, and experience exist in most organizations. To put any of these resources to work, however, it is necessary to know what is available, to what extent it is available, on what terms it is available, and during what times it is available.

Selecting Projects

The selection of community projects for the company to be involved in grows out of the matching of community needs with company resources. Frequently, because there are a number of such good matches, the company must be quite selective in deciding among them. Sometimes companies develop and refine policies or guidelines to help make decisions in the selection process. These policies are extremely useful because they further delineate areas in which the company may be involved, and provide perspective for channeling the organization's energies.

George Steiner has identified several social policies that could be extremely useful to management in its attempts to inject rationality into its selection of community projects. These policies are illustrative of those that an organization might develop.

1. It is the policy of this company "to concentrate action programs on areas strategically related to the present and prospective economic functions of the business."
2. It is the policy of this company "to begin action programs close at home before spreading out in far distant regions."
3. It is the policy of this company "to facilitate employee actions which can be taken as individuals rather than as representatives of the company."[43]

In addition to these useful policies, guidelines for developing a strategy for corporate giving and community involvement have been spelled out by Frank Koch, vice-president of Syntex Corporation in Palo Alto, California.[44] The following list summarizes some of these guidelines:

1. Contributions and community involvement must be planned and organized with the same care and energy devoted to other parts of the business.
2. Corporate contributions must meet the same measure of cost effectiveness that is expected from money invested in research, marketing, production, or administration.
3. The corporation should capitalize on its talents and resources. Those responsible should get involved in things they understand. The company should look at social problems that impact on its realm of operations.
4. Employees should be involved in contributions. The contributions program should focus on some of the things that affect and interest employees.
5. The corporation should get involved in the communities it knows, with the people it knows best, and with the needs that have the best chance of being fulfilled and are important goals of the community.
6. All action should not originate in company headquarters. Effective corporate giving should occur wherever business is done.

[43]George A. Steiner, "Social Policies for Business," *California Management Review,* Winter 1972, pp. 22-23.
[44]Frank Koch, "A Strategy for Corporate Giving and Community Involvement," *Management Review,* December 1977, pp. 7-13.

7. Corporate policy should allow continuing support to established causes while finding some new initiatives.
8. The best kind of support is that which helps others to help themselves.

Policies and guidelines such as those above go a long way toward rationalizing and systematizing business involvement with the community. Such policy statements should be developed and articulated throughout the organization to help provide a unified focus for company efforts.

Monitoring Projects

As action programs evolve, mature, and are implemented, the problem of monitoring them arises. The quality of the company's efforts can be enhanced by careful monitoring, which makes it a vital part of the overall attempt to systematize the approach to managing community involvement. The monitoring of company projects involves review and control. Follow-up is necessary to ensure that projects are being executed according to plans and on schedule. Feedback from the various steps in the process provides information management needs to monitor progress.

In later chapters we will develop more fully the managerial approach to dealing with various social issues. The above, however, provides some insights into the development of a strategy or posture for the working of business-community relationships. As we stated earlier, community involvement is a discretionary activity in our corporate social performance model; however, it is an extremely costly area of endeavor. Our stance is that it should be carefully managed, just as other business functions are, so that rationality and effectiveness can be maintained in what otherwise might become just an expensive arena of corporate "do-goodism."

SUMMARY

Just as the community expects private individuals to assume a social role in its affairs, business, too, is expected to be a part of community activities. Nowhere else is business's role as a citizen more clearly seen than in its relationships with the local community.

Business, in general, accepts this responsibility; as one corporate executive recently stated, it is "sound business."[45] Business understands that it is highly interdependent with most other members of the community, and that this interdependence results in a need for business citizenship.

Business giving — or philanthropy — is one of the primary ways in which business has manifested its concern for the community. This giving has been primarily directed to such areas as health and welfare, education, civic activities, and culture and the arts. Other efforts by businesses to be responsible community citizens have resulted in support for urban development, minority enterprise, job training, and volunteerism.

Business is also involved on a cooperative basis with local governments. The purpose of this involvement is to improve the community in which business resides.

It is important that business manage its giving and community involvement for maximum effect. The assumption is that just as business has objectives, plans, and a rationale for its production and distribution functions, it should approach its community relationships as carefully. Four important steps in any community action program require that business (1) know the community, (2) know the range of available company resources (financial and human), (3) carefully select projects, and (4) carefully monitor the projects. In addition, there are a number of useful policies and guidelines that can be developed for business giving and community involvement.

QUESTIONS FOR DISCUSSION

1. What is meant by the term community as used in this chapter? Discuss.
2. What is business's rationale for community involvement?
3. What are the major issues that business is concerned with in its community relations programs?
4. Define business philanthropy. Why do companies give?
5. Discuss the pros and cons of corporate support of education. Where corporate support is given, is it right that there be strings attached? Discuss.
6. Why has support for culture and the arts been such a favorite and prestigious outlet for business philanthropy?

[45] Jerry Schwartz, "Atlanta Corporations Find Giving to Arts Sound Business," *Atlanta Journal and Constitution,* January 5, 1980, p. A-4.

7. Outline and discuss some of the community efforts business has been involved in over the years.

8. Discuss business involvement with local government. What are some of the kinds of involvement business engages in with respect to local government? Which kinds of programs seem to be most successful?

9. What are the essential steps in developing a community action program? Discuss these steps.

10. Enumerate and discuss guidelines for developing a strategy for corporate giving and community involvement.

Cases

Jonestown Savings and Loan Association

Jonestown Savings and Loan, founded more than fifty years ago and located in a town of about 65,000 in population, had long had the philosophy of being a good community citizen. For the past several decades Jonestown Savings and Loan provided capable managers and other employees the opportunity to be involved in various joint business and community projects. In addition to employees participating on their own behalf in such community activities as education, civic groups, Boy Scouts, recreation, and county government, the association made its top floor (known as the penthouse) available as meeting space for worthy civic programs. On more than one occasion the association had helped community leaders to achieve financial goals when fund-raising efforts fell short. As a consequence, Jonestown had a good community-minded image.

Ted Anthony and several others of the top management group at Jonestown Savings and Loan were very pleased with the social status they had achieved as a result of their benevolent efforts, but were somewhat concerned that local civic leaders were becoming overly dependent on the association to provide financial support and leadership. Anthony felt that the community was becoming so accustomed to the association rescuing its various fund drives that leaders were not trying as hard as they should to get "fair share" contributions from other businesses in the community.

Because of this concern Anthony instructed Judy Benson, a graduate business student who was working with the association that summer, to put together a report on the association's past monetary contributions.

Excerpts from Judy's report confirmed what Anthony suspected was their level of contribution for the last six years.

Year	Amount Contributed
1975	$38,321
1976	41,025
1977	47,115
1978	52,190
1979	60,435
1980	71,289

As the report disclosed, approximately 75 percent of the money the association contributed went to the local United Fund, and management felt that they had to draw the line before they themselves became recipients of the fund. The straw that seemed to break the camel's back, however, was a request Anthony received from the 1981 chairman of the United Fund that he be permitted to budget $80,000 as a contribution from Jonestown Savings and Loan for that year. It was Anthony's understanding that this amount was to be over and above any contributions received from the association's 81 employees.

Because of Anthony's concern about this request, he called a special top management meeting to discuss (1) the association's "social responsibilities" in general, and (2) the United Fund's request, in particular, to contribute $80,000 during the forthcoming fund drive in Jonestown.

QUESTIONS

1. What are the "social responsibilities" of Jonestown Savings and Loan in the case?
2. Assume Mr. Anthony has asked you to prepare a set of "policies" or "guidelines" to help rationalize the association's giving program. What would you recommend? Be sure they are written in policy or guideline form.

GM Spruces Up Detroit

General Motors, the nation's largest manufacturing corporation, is commiting itself to help clean up one of the country's most troubled cities — Detroit. Specifically, it is joining what has been called Detroit's "urban renaissance" by refurbishing the aging residential neighborhood around its main office.

During 1978, GM quietly acquired title to over 100 rundown houses —

nearly 70 percent of all the houses in a square-mile radius adjacent to the GM headquarters. The company's goal was to turn the physically deteriorated, lower-middle-class neighborhood around its headquarters into a suburban-style neighborhood where families with children — including GM's own employees — would be comfortable living.

There was one major problem, however. A storm of protest followed from current residents in the neighborhood who said the renovated area would be too expensive for them to live in and would disrupt their lives. A government-paid relocation plan quieted some of the protests and the project moved ahead.

This experience came as a fresh reminder of just how complicated the issue of urban renewal is — not only for the notoriously inefficient government bureaucracy, but even for one of the nation's largest and most efficiently managed corporations. GM discovered that there is no consensus on what it takes to help a deteriorating inner-city neighborhood. Though the large corporation may bring a wealth of financial and managerial expertise, it has no guarantee of success.

Many of the 1,000 or so affected residents reacted strongly. They felt GM had no business doing this without consulting them. When the protest started, GM found itself having to meet with the angry residents. GM formed a committee, comprised mostly of local businesses and church leaders, to deal with the complaints. One result was a series of offers by GM, all rejected by the residents: to move the residents from one unrenovated building to another while construction progresses, to offer local residents first chance to buy the renovated houses and to rent the renovated apartments, and to offer rent rebates.

GM finally conceded a number of things. Among them were agreements to accept job applications from unemployed residents to work on the project and to include some additional low-cost housing in the plan.

At one point GM chairman Thomas Murphy was quoted as saying, "Frankly, I'm a bit frustrated. After all, we're trying to help these people."[1]

QUESTIONS

1. What are the social issues in this case?
2. Critique GM's approach to helping the community in this way. How should they have gone about it differently?
3. What are the advantages and disadvantages, as you see them, of the proposed project? Do you anticipate it would be a success? Discuss.

[1]From Amanda Bennett, "Houses by General Motors," *The Wall Street Journal*, June 12, 1979, p. 26. Reprinted by permission of *The Wall Street Journal*, © Dow Jones & Company, Inc., 1979. All rights reserved.

Should Companies Give Advance Notice?

One very heated question in business-community relationships is whether companies should give advance notice when they plan to close down their operations in a community. Some political pressures are mounting for a law that would require firms to give such notice.

Recently the United Auto Workers, the United Steel Workers, and the International Association of Machinists jointly published a study commenting positively on advance notice requirements in West Germany, Sweden, and Great Britain. Legislation has been introduced in several states that would require anywhere from one to two years' notice. Ralph Nader also advocated a 24-month notice provision in the Corporate Democracy Act of 1980 that he was hoping to get passed.

Though some companies already provide advance warnings to communities in accordance with labor agreements, in a large number of instances little or no notice is given before layoffs and plant closings.

Business thinks some of the major results of advance notice would be increased employee absenteeism as employees begin seeking new jobs, diminished morale, reduced pride in work and productivity, and possibly vandalism. Also, business thinks that once the word is out that a plant is closing bankers may refuse to grant credit, and customers who worry about the flow of spare parts may stop placing new orders.

The major benefit of advance notice is that it would be easier for displaced employees to find new jobs. Some research has shown that workers have a better chance of finding another job while they still carry the "employed" label.[2]

QUESTIONS

1. What social responsibility does business have with respect to leaving a community?
2. What is your evaluation of the proposals to mandate an advance notice law? Look at this from the standpoint of business, the employees, and the community.
3. What does business gain in advance notice arrangements? Discuss.

[2]From Robert B. McKersie, "Advance Notice," *The Wall Street Journal*, February 25, 1980, p. 20. Reprinted by permission of *The Wall Street Journal*, © Dow Jones & Company, Inc., 1980. All rights reserved.

Part III:
Internal Publics
and Issues

Basic Question What are the specific issues concerning internal publics?

Objectives of Part III To demonstrate that pressures toward change come from employees and owners as well as from external sources

To examine the question of business legitimacy and various proposals for reformulating corporate governance

Chapters in Part III

INTRODUCTION TO PART III

Historically, most of the social pressure on business has been from external groups and publics, but this is changing somewhat. External issues have not lessened, rather, social issues emanating from internal publics (e.g., employees and shareholders) have intensified. Business's internal social responsibilities have the potential to be even more pressing during the 1980s. In Chapter 8 we discuss business, employees, and the individual — the concern of employees that they be afforded certain job rights and treated as individuals. Related to Chapter 8 is the subject of Chapter 9 — business and discrimination — in which the chief issue is discrimination against minorities, women, and others. Then, because in recent years much has been made of the rights of shareholders, we will discuss in Chapter 10 the issues that have emerged as shareholders have demanded more rights.

After our study of internal publics and issues, we will turn to the question of managing the business and society relationship, as management deals with issues arising both from without and from within the organization.

Business, Employees, and the Individual

8

Society's changing values are probably having no greater impact than on the workplace. Though the environment, consumerism, government, and business's role in the community continue to be major issues in business's concern for the social environment, considerable attention is now being given to employees in the workplace — their status, their satisfaction, and their rights.

This should come as no surprise when one considers that most adult Americans spend the bulk of their hours during the day at work. It was only a matter of time until people would express the same kind of concern for their work life as they have expressed for external, more remote social issues.

Though we cannot give a complete historical account of this development, it is reasonably safe to say that it has been a direct outgrowth of the kinds of social changes that have brought other societal issues into focus. The history of work has been one of steady improvement for labor, but in recent years issues have emerged that are quite unlike the old bread-and-butter ones advocated by early labor unions — more pay, shorter hours, more job security, and better working conditions. These desires still exist, but they have given way to more complex expectations.

In this chapter we will discuss some of the major new demands by employees and how these demands have become, in the eyes of many, social responsibilities of business. After discussing the changing nature of work, we will look at the subject of employees' rights, which include (1) job satisfaction, (2) the right to speak out in the workplace without fear of reprisal, (3) the right to due process, (4) the right to privacy, and (5) the right to safety while working.

In summary, our chapter outline is as follows:

- Changing nature of work
- Employee rights
- Job satisfaction

- Freedom of speech
- Right of due process
- Privacy
- Safety

Because the subject of employment discrimination has assumed such magnitude and scope over the last twenty years, this topic will be covered separately in Chapter 9.

CHANGING NATURE OF WORK

Work is viewed, perceived, and regarded differently today than in the past. There have also been changes in management's perceptions of and regard for the employees who do the work — the treatment they receive, the respect they are afforded, and the role they are allowed to assume in decision making.

Figure 8-1 illustrates one view of the changing meaning of work, as presented by Barry Posner, Alan Randolph, and Max Wortman.[1] As Figure 8-1 indicates, work has assumed significantly different roles in various civilizations. In primitive cultures it was viewed as being "as natural as play," and the authors see its future role as being once again "as natural as play." This is only one possible interpretation of work's evolution, but it is an interesting one in that it shows different stages based on whether the distinction between work and nonwork was high or low.

It should be noted that work in this illustration is related to the views of early Christianity. The work ethic, sometimes referred to as the Protestant ethic, had its beginning in biblical times. Ever since Adam, religious sanctions have existed for hard work and labor. The Scripture tells us that God placed Adam in the Garden of Eden and instructed him "to till it and keep it." After Adam's fall, conditions became worse; God cursed the ground and made it bring forth thistles and thorns, and man was thereafter condemned to make a living by the "sweat of his brow."

With the exception of several early races, mankind has bestowed an aura of dignity and worth on work. Christianity was a dominant force in this trend. St. Paul stated, "If any one will not work, let him not eat." The perspective of the medieval monks was that work was a glorification of God. St. Benedict and his followers pursued the same theme

[1]Barry Z. Posner, W. Alan Randolph, and Max S. Wortman, Jr., "A New Ethic for Work? The Worth Ethic," *Human Resource Management,* Fall 1975, pp. 15-20.

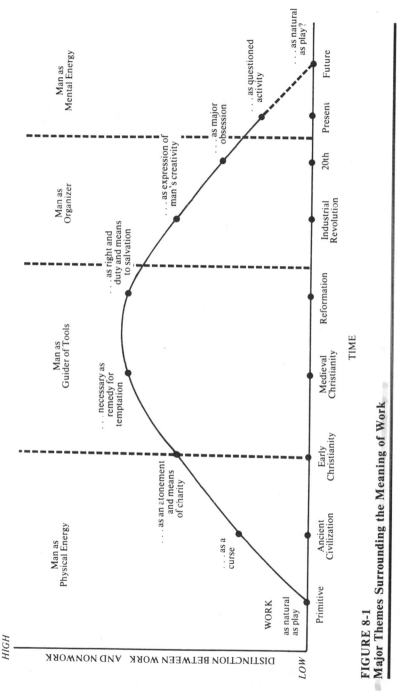

FIGURE 8-1
Major Themes Surrounding the Meaning of Work

SOURCE: Barry Z. Posner, W. Alan Randolph, and Max S. Wortman, Jr., "A New Ethic for Work? The Worth Ethic," *Human Resource Management,* Fall 1975, p. 16. Reprinted by permission of the Graduate School of Business, University of Michigan, Ann Arbor, Michigan.

with the philosophy, *Laborare est orare*— "to work is to pray." At a later time the stern Protestantism of Luther and Calvin provided additional religious sanctions for work.[2]

The work ethic most likely was brought to America by the Puritans, who were followers of Calvin. They abhorred idleness and punished those who indulged in it. They preached to their youth that "the devil finds uses for idle hands" and that "God helps those who help themselves." A number of corollaries with religious overtones emerged to support the basic work ethic — for example, "waste of time is the deadliest of sins," and because consumption beyond basic needs is wasteful and therefore sinful, "Waste not, want not."

The work ethic prospered during the great depression of the 1930s because workers had to work in order to survive. As a direct outgrowth of the Depression, having a job became a major obsession. Then, during World War II the work ethic flourished under the rationalization of patriotism and dedication to country. Thus, more and more as time passed during the twentieth century, the concept of work was separated from religious doctrine.

There is some question today as to whether the work ethic is alive and well. Many observers have talked about the demise of the work ethic as questions are being raised about why people work at all and how people view their work. Research evidence confirms time and again that workers today do not view work only in functional terms — to provide income for purchases — but to help affirm the dignity and worth of the individual. Surveys show that modern workers want interesting work, enough authority to get the job done, opportunity to develop special abilities, and the opportunity to see the results of their work.[3] Young workers today also express a desire for such intrinsic rewards as the opportunity to make a contribution, job challenge, and the chance for self-expression.[4] It might be added that a comparison of attitudes between younger and older workers fails to indicate that young people do not endorse the necessity and importance of work and the realization of rewards based on that work.[5]

Thus there appears to be growing dissatisfaction among workers today because the nature of *work* has not changed at the same pace as the nature of *workers*. All the efforts by management in recent years to

[2]Archie B. Carroll, "Youth's Work Ethic— An Expectations Gap," *The Personnel Administrator,* September-October 1973, pp. 11-14.

[3]Special Task Force to the Secretary of Health, Education, and Welfare, *Work in America* (Cambridge, Mass.: MIT Press, 1972), p. 13.

[4]Ibid., p. 45.

[5]Robert D. Gatewood and Archie B. Carroll, "The Interaction of the Social Environment and Task Specialization on Worker Attitudes," in Richard C. Huseman and Archie B. Carroll (eds.), *Readings in Organizational Behavior: Dimensions of Management Actions* (Boston: Allyn and Bacon, 1979), pp. 187-191.

make work more challenging and meaningful apparently have not been enough. Employees are discontented; they continue to want and expect more from their jobs now than they have in the past. A 1979 study of 175,000 employees in 159 companies for which Opinion Research Corporation has conducted employee attitude surveys since 1950 shows this trend to be continuing.[6]

EMPLOYEE RIGHTS

Just as employees' values and concepts regarding work have changed, modern workers are increasingly more demanding in the area of civil liberties in the workplace. Alan F. Westin, editor of the *Civil Liberties Review,* has gone so far as to say:

> Apart from direct economic issues, I think the most important issue in the corporate world of the 1980s will be employee rights.[7]

To appreciate the background of the employee rights issue (especially the rights of freedom of speech and due process), it is useful to consider the underyling public sector-private sector dichotomy society faces. The public sector is subject to constitutional control of its power. The private sector generally is *not* subject to constitutional control because of the concept of private property. The *private property* notion holds that individuals and private organizations are free to use their property as they desire. As a result, private corporations traditionally have not had to recognize employee rights because society honored the corporation's private property rights. The underlying issues then become why and to what extent the private property rights of business should be diluted.

Though Americans have enjoyed civil liberties for nearly two centuries (freedom of the press, speech, assembly, due process, privacy, freedom of conscience, and other important rights), these same rights have not been afforded in most companies, government agencies, and other organizations where Americans work. David W. Ewing states the matter quite strongly:

> Once a U.S. citizen steps through the plant or office door at 9 A.M., he or she is nearly rightless until 5 P.M., Monday through Friday. The employee continues to have political freedoms, of course, but these are not the significant ones now. While at work, the important relationships are with bosses, associates, and subordinates. Inequalities in dealing with these people are what really count for an employee.[8]

---

[6]M. R. Cooper, B. S. Morgan, P. M. Foley, and L. B. Kaplan, "Changing Employee Values: Deepening Discontent?" *Harvard Business Review,* January-February 1979, pp. 117-125.

[7]"Employee Rights and Civil Wrongs," *Forbes,* April 2, 1979, p. 110.

[8]David W. Ewing, *Freedom Inside the Organization: Bringing Civil Liberties to the Workplace* (New York: McGraw-Hill Book Company, 1977), p. 3.

Although there are exceptions to Ewing's rather strong statement, it does call attention to the importance of the issue. Ewing goes on to state:

> The employee sector of our civil liberties universe is more like a black hole, with rights so compacted, so imploded by the gravitational forces of legal tradition, that, like the giant black stars in the physical universe, light can scarcely escape.[9]

A brief comment on the role of labor unions might be appropriate here, for it has been out of some of the job rights that unions have won over the years that other rights have begun to grow. In general, though labor unions have been quite successful in improving the material conditions of work life — pay, fringe benefits, and working conditions — they have not been as interested in pursuing civil liberties or rights. Unions must be given credit, however, for the gains they have made in converting what were typically regarded as management's rights or prerogatives into issues in which labor could participate. For nonunion workers, however, rightlessness continues to be a prevailing condition.

Many managers find the movement toward employees' rights disturbing. Management prerogatives are being challenged at an unprecedented rate, and the traditional model of employee loyalty and conformity to the wishes of management is rapidly fading from the scene. It seems to be disappearing as a concept more than as a reality, however. Though managers indicate strong support for wider employee rights when responding to questionnaires, practice does not show widespread employee rights prevailing in business today. Indeed, though managers support the concept in principle, they sometimes express an ambivalence about employee rights and their costs. A recent survey of managers showed a higher concern for social instability in our society (confusion about sexual standards, attitudes towards drugs, treatment of criminals, respect for the family and authority, breakdown of law and order, and disintegration of the work ethic) than for obstacles to individuality in the workplace.[10] Thus, while managers sympathize with the need for privacy, due process, and free speech in the workplace, they are more concerned with general social trends and their impact.

Lest we dwell too much on such civil liberties as freedom of speech and due process in organizations, we should make it clear that basic job satisfaction remains a central concern, along with the significant obsession with workplace safety. Thus, there exists an array of issues that might be grouped together as business's internal social responsibilities,

[9]Ibid., p. 5.
[10]David W. Ewing, "What Business Thinks About Employee Rights," *Harvard Business Review,* September-October 1977, pp. 81-94.

and that must be understood and addressed if business is to satisfy its employees. The ones we shall look at in greater detail in this chapter are, in the author's opinion, the most pressing ones business faces today. (Keep in mind that the issue of discrimination also ranks high, but we will discuss that in the next chapter.)

JOB SATISFACTION AS A SOCIAL CONCERN

We will not dwell extensively on this topic; nevertheless, job satisfaction must be considered as a major concern underlying most other worker expectations today. Since the *job itself* has been shown to be of such fundamental importance in fulfilling the worker's higher-order needs, job satisfaction is crucial to a harmonious relationship between business and the worker.

We discussed earlier how worker needs and interests today tend toward self-fulfillment, personal growth, self-expression and similar aims, as many research studies have indicated.[11] The list is long of the kinds of experiences workers want. Behavioral scientists have found, however, that there are three basic "psychological states" that are critical in determining a person's motivation and satisfaction on the job:

1. Experienced meaningfulness: work must be perceived as worthwhile or important by some system of values the worker accepts.
2. Experienced accountability: the worker must perceive personal accountability for the effort's outcomes.
3. Knowledge of results: the worker must be able to determine on some fairly regular basis whether or not work outcomes are satisfactory.[12]

When these three conditions are present, a person tends to feel good when performing well. Those good feelings will prompt the worker to try to continue to do well so future positive feelings can be earned. This is what is meant by "internal motivation."

Management's motivational task is to ensure that both job satisfaction and job productivity (performance) remain high. To that end, we have seen a continuing stream of experimentation with management approaches and techniques in recent years — job redesign, job enrichment, management by objectives, and so on.

---

[11]See, for example, David G. Bowers and Jerome L. Franklin, "American Work Values and Preferences," *Michigan Business Review,* March 1977, pp. 14-22.

[12]J. Richard Hackman, Greg Oldham, Robert Hanson, and Kenneth Purdy, "A New Strategy for Job Enrichment," *California Management Review,* volume XVII, no. 4, pp. 57-72.

No longer are these techniques used just for improving satisfaction, which will then perhaps improve productivity. Workers today have a high expectation of job satisfaction and, indeed, often feel it is their right. They view it as one of business's responsibilities to provide them with meaningful, challenging work. As this idea has spread, business has suddenly realized that job satisfaction is not just a motivation-productivity issue, but one that transcends previous purposes. Thus, in order merely to survive, business must respond to the growing belief by many employees that job satisfaction is owed them.

FREEDOM OF SPEECH

In letters written by a chemical researcher and published in newspapers, he stated that the cosmetics industry (of which his employer was a member) was charging unconscionably high prices caused by exorbitant advertising expenses. After he was fired he sued his employer, alleging that his right to free speech had been infringed and that he was due damages. The court affirmed his right to free speech but not to a job in private industry. The company did not need a reason for firing him so long as they did not violate employment laws regarding sex and race.[13]

Another case had different results, though it is not clear why. An engineer in a California company alleged that a new computer console developed by the company failed to meet the state safety codes. He voiced his objections to management, even though management did not want to hear them. He was fired, he went to court, and was awarded damages by the Superior Court in Santa Clara.[14]

Unfortunately for employees who feel they have a legitimate right to speak out against a company that is engaging in an illegal or unethical practice, the resolution of the first case above is more common than that of the second. Nevertheless, the willingness to challenge management is typical of a growing number of employees today.

The current generation of employees has a different concept of loyalty and acceptance of authority than do those of years past. The result is an unprecedented number of cases of employees "blowing the whistle" on their employers. A whistle blower has been called a "muck raker from within, who exposes what he considers the unconscionable practices of his own organization."[15]

What is at stake is the employee's right to speak out in cases where he or she thinks the company or management is engaging in an unaccepta-

[13]David W. Ewing, "Multiple Loyalites, *Wall Street Journal,* May 1, 1978, p. 16.
[14]Ibid.
[15]Charles Peters and Taylor Branch, *Blowing the Whistle: Dissent in the Public Interest* (New York: Praeger Publishers, 1972), p. 4.

ble practice. This speaking out flies in the face of the longstanding tradition in our culture that one's superiors' decisions and acts are not to be questioned — and most certainly not to be challenged in public.

Perhaps the primary reason we have witnessed so many cases of whistle blowing in the last decade lies with the growing numbers of professional employees who carry with them into the workplace an allegiance to their profession and its ethics. Though numbers alone do not reveal everything, they do suggest the direction and speed of the change. Between 1950 and 1975 the number of managers and administrators in the United States increased by about one-third, the number of salesworkers increased by one-half, and the number of clerical workers doubled. But the number of professional and technical employees almost *tripled* during that same period.[16]

It is characteristic of professionals that they bring multiple loyalties into the workplace. These multiple loyalties challenge the tradition in which management has demanded and received almost exclusive allegiance from employees. The professional shares his loyalty to the company with loyalty to society and to his profession. As an illustration, the code of the National Society of Professional Engineers states that the engineer "will use his knowledge and skill for the advancement of human welfare." When this duty brings the engineer into conflict with employer expectations, the code directs him to "regard his duty to the public welfare as paramount."[17]

As laudatory as it may seem for professionals and other employees to put the public interest above the immediate profitablity of their organization, whistle blowers have paid dearly for their lack of loyalty to the firm.[18] In one study of forty-four cases of whistle blowing, for example, the following employment problems and results were identified:[19]

Problem	Result
Resigned prior to blowing whistle	8
Resigned under pressure	4
Fired subsequent to whistle blowing	9
Discharged through reduction in force	2
Either transferred or jobs/funds reduced	5
In different organization when acted	10
Remained on the job	6

[16]Ewing, *Wall Street Journal,* May 1, 1978, p. 16.
[17]Ibid.
[18]See, for example, what happens to many whistle blowers in Robert L. Heilbroner, *In the Name of Profit* (New York: Warner Paperback Library, 1972).
[19]Ralph Nader, Peter Petkas, and Kate Blackwell (eds.), *Whistle Blowing: The Report of the Conference on Professional Responsibility* (New York: Grossman Publishers, 1972).

The status of the law protecting whistle blowers is presently not clear. Those who advocate an employee's right to speak out against a company are, of course, continuing their push to develop laws that will ensure employee freedom of speech. Even among executives, a survey revealed, nearly 60 percent believe that whistle blowers, if sincerely motivated, should be protected and not penalized for attempting to reveal the truth.[20] But the motivation of the whistle blower continues to be at the heart of the debate over whether such actions constitute disloyalty or legitimate dissent. The courts have looked increasingly at the employee's motive for blowing the whistle in determining whether or not freedom of speech should be protected.[21] Another recent survey of executives revealed, moreover, that over half felt that whistle blowing "is done for personal gain, glory seeking, or possibly revenge."[22] It should be kept in mind that these are just managers' opinions, but they do form the basis for much of the legitimate opposition managers today hold for such revelations.

Though we see more and more cases of employees wanting the right to question management and to speak out, David Ewing argues that there are some kinds of speech that should be protected:[23]

1. Employees should not have the right to divulge information about legal and ethical plans, practices, operations, inventions, and other matters that must be kept confidential if the organization is to do its job in an efficient manner.

2. Employees should not have the right to make personal accusations or slurs that are irrelevant to questions about policies and actions that seem illegal or irresponsible.

3. Employees should not be entitled to disrupt an organization or damage its morale by making accusations that do not reflect a conviction that wrong is being done.

4. Employees should not be entitled to rail against the competence of a manager to make everyday work decisions that have nothing to do with the legality, morality, or responsibility of management actions.

5. Employees should not be entitled to object to discharge, transfer, or demotion, no matter what they have said about the organization or

---

[20]Ewing, *Harvard Business Review,* September-October 1977, pp. 92-93.
[21]See Kenneth D. Walters, "Your Employees' Right to Blow the Whistle," *Harvard Business Review,* July-August 1975, pp. 26-34, 161-162, for a discussion of this.
[22]Ewing, *Harvard Business Review,* September-October 1977, p. 93.
[23]Ewing, *Freedom Inside the Organization,* pp. 109-110.

how they said it, if management can demonstrate that unsatisfactory performance or violation of a code of conduct was the reason for its actions.[24]

In the final analysis, an employee should have a right to dissent, but this right may be constrained or limited by the above kinds of reasons.

A legitimate question, from the standpoint of efforts to manage social responsibility, might be: "How can an organization work with its employees to reduce their need to blow the whistle?" Kenneth Walters has suggested five procedures that might be kept in mind.[25]

1. The company should assure employees that the organization will not interfere with basic political freedoms.

2. The organization's grievance procedures should be streamlined so that employees can obtain a direct and sympathetic hearing for issues on which they are likely to blow the whistle if their complaints are not heard quickly and fairly.

3. The organization's concept of social responsibility should be reviewed to make sure it is not being construed as merely corporate giving to charity.

4. Organizations should formally recognize and communicate a respect for the individual consciences of employees.

5. The organization should realize that dealing harshly with a whistle-blowing employee could result in needless adverse public reaction.

To summarize, modern employees are different. They possess a new concept of loyalty and they accept the authority of management in a narrower scope than in the past. One result is that they view the right to speak out as one of their fundamental entitlements. Though the law is not yet clear on the status of whistle blowing, an increasing number of organizations are likely to face such acts. This being the case, management should carefully assess where it stands on this vital issue. It may very well be that respecting an employee's right to differ with management — though the law does not currently require it — serves best the long-term interests of the organization.[26]

[24]Ibid.
[25]Walters, pp. 33, 161.
[26]Ibid., p. 162.

RIGHT OF DUE PROCESS

One of the employee rights issues most frequently discussed in the last ten years has been the right to due process within organizations. Basically, *due process* is the right to receive an impartial review of one's complaints and to be dealt with fairly.

What are the job issues over which employees might be concerned in connection with their right to due process? Most experts who have worked in this area include promotions, transfers, performance appraisals, wage inequities, discrimination, and discharges. Sometimes the employee is treated unfairly in such a subtle way that it is difficult to know that unfair treatment has taken place. What do you do, for example, if your supervisor thinks you are so good that he refuses to recommend you for promotion or permit you to transfer, because he does not want to lose you? How do you prove that a manager has given you a low performance appraisal because you resisted sexual advances? The issues over which due process questions can arise can be quite difficult.

It has been only since the early 1970s that some leading companies have given special consideration to employees' rights to due process. Historically, management has had almost unlimited freedom to deal with employees as they wished. In many cases unfair treatment was not intentional but the result of inept or distracted supervisors inflicting needless harm on subordinates.[27]

David Ewing, an authority on the question of employee civil liberties, has argued that employee due process should be regarded as but one part of employee constitutionalism. He suggests that *employee constitutionalism* "consists of a set of clearly defined rights, and a means of protecting employees from discharge, demotion, or other penalties imposed when they assert their rights."[28] He goes on to list the main requirements of a due process system in an organization:

1. It must be a procedure; it must follow rules. It must not be arbitrary.
2. It must be visible and well-known enough that potential violators of employee rights and victims of abuse know about it.
3. It must be predictably effective.
4. It must be "institutionalized" — a relatively permanent fixture in the organization.
5. It must be perceived as equitable.
6. It must be easy to use.
7. It must apply to all employees.

[27]Ewing, *Freedom Inside the Organization,* p. 10.
[28]Ibid., p. 11.

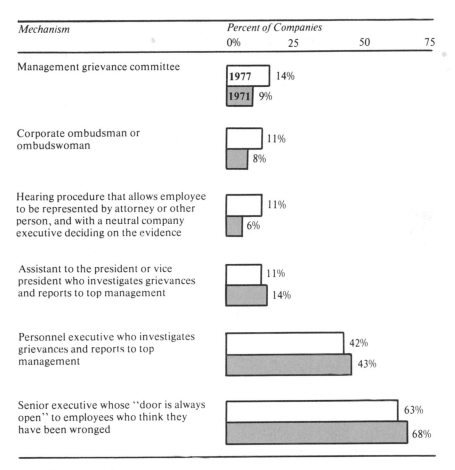

Mechanism	Percent of Companies			
	0%	25	50	75
Management grievance committee	1977 14%			
	1971 9%			
Corporate ombudsman or ombudswoman	11%			
	8%			
Hearing procedure that allows employee to be represented by attorney or other person, and with a neutral company executive deciding on the evidence	11%			
	6%			
Assistant to the president or vice president who investigates grievances and reports to top management	11%			
	14%			
Personnel executive who investigates grievances and reports to top management			42%	
			43%	
Senior executive whose "door is always open" to employees who think they have been wronged				63%
				68%

FIGURE 8-2
Due Process Mechanisms in Use 1971-1977

SOURCE: Reprinted by permission of the *Harvard Business Review.* From "What Business Thinks About Employee Rights," by David W. Ewing (September-October 1977). Copyright © 1977 by the President and Fellows of Harvard College; all rights reserved.

There are many different ways a company can devise a procedure to ensure such due process. Different methods have been experimented with, mostly in the past decade. Figure 8-2 summarizes recent research data indicating the percentage of companies surveyed that used various due process mechanisms in the period 1971-1977. As can be seen in Figure 8-2, due process mechanisms have ranged from senior executives using an open-door policy to formal hearing procedures that allow the employee to be represented by an attorney or other person.

Of particular interest among the various approaches reported is that of the corporate ombudsman or ombudswoman. *Ombudsman* is a Swedish word which refers to one who investigates reported complaints and helps to achieve equitable settlements. The ombudsman approach has been used in Sweden to curb abuses by government against individuals since 1809. The corporate version of the ombudsman was first experimented with in 1972, when the Xerox Corporation named one for its largest division. General Electric and the Boeing Vertol division of Boeing were quick to follow.[29] As the survey data in Figure 8-2 indicate, however, only 11 percent of the companies questioned in 1977 used the technique.

The operation of the ombudsman program at Xerox to help ensure employee due process is representative of these programs generally. The ombudsman began as "employee relations manager" on the organization chart in Xerox's Information Technology Group (ITG), but everyone soon knew his function was to ensure fair treatment of employees. He reported directly to the ITG president, who was the only one who could reverse the ombudsman's decisions. During the early years of the program, none of the ombudsman's decisions were overturned — a point significant to the power and effectiveness of the one holding the job.

Under the Xerox due process system the employee was expected to try to solve his or her problem through an immediate supervisor or the personnel department before submitting a complaint to the ombudsman. At this point, the ombudsman studied the complaint and the company file on the case, and discussed both with a personnel department representative and then with the employee. Subsequently, his recommended solution was passed on to the personnel department, which presented it as its own idea to the manager involved. Only if the manager declined to go along did the ombudsman reveal his identity and put his authority behind the recommendation.[30]

The ombudsman approach to ensuring due process is not without its problems. Managers may feel threatened when employees go to the ombudsman, who must be willing to anger executives in order to get the job done. There is also the fear that employees might experience retribution for going to the ombudsman in the first place. Despite these potential problems, the system has worked once in place and understood. One positive and unexpected result of the Xerox experience is that even supervisors now go to the ombudsman for advice on personnel problems. Thus, issues are referred to him even before managerial decisions are made in some cases.[31]

[29]"Where Ombudsmen Work Out," *Business Week,* May 3, 1976, pp. 114-116.
[30]"How the Xerox Ombudsman Helps Xerox," *Business Week,* May 12, 1973, pp. 188-190.
[31]Ibid., p. 190.

Whether it is the ombudsman approach to providing due process or some other technique, many enlightened companies today are attempting to make due process a reality. As Ewing has indicated, "Due process is a way of fighting institutionalized indifference to the individual — the indifference that says that productivity and efficiency are the goals of the organization, and any person who stands in the way must be sacrificed."[32] Increasingly, companies are acknowledging due process to be not only an employee right but also a sound management practice, in keeping with the wishes and expectations of employees.

EMPLOYEE RIGHT TO PRIVACY

A review of the titles of recent articles in newspapers and magazines illustrates the importance of the employee privacy issue:

* "Invasion of Privacy Increasingly Worries U.S. Public, Poll Says"
* "New Push for Employee Privacy"
* "The Problem of Employee Privacy Still Troubles Management"

A recent public opinion poll by Louis Harris and Associates has clearly revealed the growing public awareness of and concern about invasion of privacy by organizations.[33] The poll revealed, for example, that 62 percent of the public and 65 percent of employees want Congress to pass legislation regulating and defining information that private employers can collect about individuals. Even more people favor laws giving employees access to their personnel files and forbidding employers from using lie detectors in hiring, watching worker efficiency on closed-circuit television, or monitoring employee conversations for personnel supervision.[34]

Champions of employee privacy have long pointed to such practices as the use of lie detectors for pre-employment screening, questioning of applicants about whether they have had psychological or psychiatric treatment, the use of personality tests by employers, and collection of sensitive health information as illustrations of possible invasions of privacy.

Many corporate leaders express astonishment that such claims are being made, because so many companies are moving toward policies of

[32]Ewing, *Freedom Inside the Organization,* pp. 172-173.
[33]"Invasion of Privacy Increasingly Worries U.S. Public, Poll Says," *Wall Street Journal,* May 4, 1979, p. 13.
[34]Alan F. Westin, "The Problem of Employee Privacy Still Troubles Management," *Fortune,* June 4, 1979, pp. 120-126.

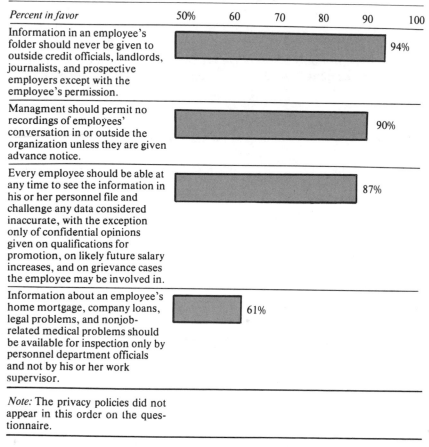

*During recent years the subject of employee privacy, especially with regard to personal informa-
tion, has been discussed by many businessmen and attorneys. We are interested in your opinion
on the following policies. Please check as many as you wish that you agree with; assume you are
answering for your current or most recent employer company.*

| *Percent in favor* | 50% | 60 | 70 | 80 | 90 | 100 |

Information in an employee's folder should never be given to outside credit officials, landlords, journalists, and prospective employers except with the employee's permission. — 94%

Managment should permit no recordings of employees' conversation in or outside the organization unless they are given advance notice. — 90%

Every employee should be able at any time to see the information in his or her personnel file and challenge any data considered inaccurate, with the exception only of confidential opinions given on qualifications for promotion, on likely future salary increases, and on grievance cases the employee may be involved in. — 87%

Information about an employee's home mortgage, company loans, legal problems, and nonjob-related medical problems should be available for inspection only by personnel department officials and not by his or her work supervisor. — 61%

Note: The privacy policies did not appear in this order on the questionnaire.

**FIGURE 8-3
Executive Support for Privacy**

SOURCE: Reprinted by permission of the *Harvard Business Review.* From "What Business Thinks About Employee Rights," by David W. Ewing (September-October 1977). Copyright © 1977 by the President and Fellows of Harvard College; all rights reserved.

ensuring privacy protection. Figure 8-3 indicates the extent to which a large number of business executives favor employee privacy in specific cases.

Nevertheless, advocates continue to push for complete employee privacy. Their main claims are that confidential information gathered by

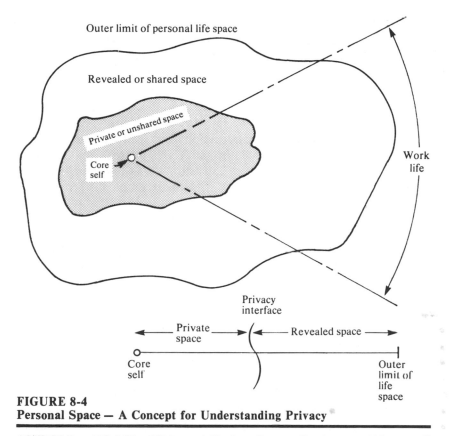

FIGURE 8-4
Personal Space — A Concept for Understanding Privacy

SOURCE: Donald B. Miller, "Privacy: A Key Issue Between Employees and Managers," *University of Michigan Business Review,* January 1976, p. 8. Reprinted by permission.

companies either has no bearing or should have no bearing on employment decisions, and that it can possibly be abused if used in the wrong fashion or revealed to the wrong people.

Most of the privacy advocates would probably agree with Donald Miller, who has aruged that work life is in a realm of the individual's personal privacy space which is at the outer limits of that which should be revealed to others.[35] In other words, as we see in Figure 8-4, the individual has at least three levels of personal space, and work life falls into that category which is farthest from the core self — the most private or exclusive of the three domains. Privacy advocates are arguing primarily that business should be more sensitive to protecting an employee's private or unshared space, and should be more careful as to where the privacy interface that we see in Figure 8-4 is drawn. They

[35]Donald B. Miller, "Privacy: A Key Issue Between Employees and Managers," *University of Michigan Business Review,* January 1976, pp. 7-12.

would probably argue, too, that many of business's actions in the past represented a violation of the individual's private space. Obviously, where the privacy interface is drawn is subject to some discussion, but privacy advocates would argue that it should be done so that more, rather than less, private space is protected.

A brief look at the history of concern for employee privacy shows that it is largely a phenomenon of the late 1960s and early 1970s. In the 1950s and early 1960s, most corporations engaged in practices that would be viewed as unacceptable by today's standards. For the most part, too, these early practices were consistent with the general public's view of what employees were entitled to. In sum, employee privacy was practically an unknown concept.[36]

In the late 1960s and early 1970s a number of socially sensitive firms began pioneering employee privacy programs. Among these companies were IBM, Bank of America, Prudential Insurance, and Atlantic Richfield.[37] Today, these companies and such others as General Motors, Exxon, Aetna Life and Casualty, and Cummins Engine are working on privacy programs.[38]

✲ Though many companies have taken the lead in initiating employee privacy protection plans, some of the impetus for the efforts came from passage of the Privacy Act of 1974 and the Privacy Protection Study Commission's 1977 recommendations. The commission was created by the Privacy Act; one of its goals was to take a careful look at what was happening to the rights of employees of state and local governments and corporations. To many business people's satisfaction, the commission made thirty-four recommendations and advocated that most of its suggestions be adopted "by voluntary action." The major exception to the commission's voluntary suggestion came with the recommendation that Congress consider a federal law governing the use of polygraphs (lie detectors) and arrest-record inquiries in preemployment investigations.

✲ Not much federal legislation has yet been passed; on the state level, however, there has been more activity. In 1978, for example, the state of Michigan enacted a broad "Employee Right to Know" law, which granted employees the privilege of seeing any information in their personnel file (with a few exceptions) used "in determining employment, promotion, transfer, additional compensation, or disciplinary action."[39]

Besides movement, or lack of it, on the legal front, employee privacy

[36]Westin, p. 121.
[37]Ibid.
[38]John Perham, "New Push for Employee Privacy," *Dun's Review,* March 1979, pp. 112-114.
[39]Westin, p. 122.

has become quite an issue at the corporate level. Some of the companies mentioned earlier were among those that exchanged ideas at the First National Seminar on Individual Rights in the Corporation, held in 1978. Rather than deciding that such programs hamper effective personnel management, the seminar participants came to four conclusions:

1. Fair information practices necessitate an open process in which employees share the facts on just how decisions about people are made.
2. Management's credibility demands a clear definition of merit and demonstration of equitable treatment.
3. Organizations must provide clear mechanisms for fair procedure, making it clear what information is used in decisions.
4. All company policies must take into account every employee's need for self-expression and individual dignity.[40]

These conclusions, too, transcend our employee privacy discussion and get at the heart of the whole issue of employee rights.

Our discussion could also include some of the specific steps companies are taking to protect employee privacy.[41] Rather than attempting to catalog them, however, let us refer to two sets of guidelines that have emerged as illustrations of the kinds of things companies are now undertaking. First, Exhibit 8-1 shows four principles of privacy that IBM has developed and widely disseminated. These guidelines seem self-explanatory and the reader is encouraged to study them carefully.

Second, according to four corporate policy guidelines suggested by Robert Goldstein and Richard Nolan, organizations should:

1. Prepare a "privacy impact statement." This would analyze the potential privacy implications that all systems (especially computerized ones) should be subjected to.
2. Construct a comprehensive privacy plan. The purpose of such planning would be to make sure that the necessary privacy controls are integrated into the design of a system at its very beginning.
3. Train employees who handle personal information. Be sure they are aware of the importance of protecting privacy and the specific procedures and policies to be followed.
4. Make privacy a part of social responsibility programs. Companies need to acknowledge that they have an internal social responsibility

---

[40]Westin, p. 126.

[41]See, for example, Frank T. Cary, "IBM's Guidelines to Employee Privacy," *Harvard Business Review*, September-October 1976, pp. 82-90.

EXHIBIT 8-1

IBM Reports

Four principles of privacy

For some time now, there has been a growing effort in this country to preserve the individual's right to privacy in the face of expanding requirements for information by business, government and other organizations.

In searching for appropriate guidelines, private and governmental groups have explored many avenues and considered many aspects of the privacy question.

As a company with a vital interest in information and information handling, IBM endorses in their basic purpose four principles of privacy which have emerged from various studies, and which appear to be the cornerstones of sound public policy on this sensitive issue.

1. Individuals should have access to information about themselves in record-keeping systems. And there should be some procedure for individuals to find out how this information is being used.

2. There should be some way for an individual to correct or amend an inaccurate record.

3. An individual should be able to prevent information from being improperly disclosed or used for other than authorized purposes without his or her consent, unless required by law.

4. The custodian of data files containing sensitive information should take reasonable precautions to be sure that the data are reliable and not misused.

Translating such broad principles into specific and uniform guidelines will, of course, not be easy. They must be thoughtfully interpreted in terms of the widely varying purposes of information systems generally.

In particular, the proper balance must be found between limiting access to information for the protection of privacy on one hand, and allowing freedom of information to fulfill the needs of society on the other.

But solutions must be found. And they will call for the patient understanding and best efforts of everyone concerned. In this search, IBM pledges its full and whole-hearted cooperation.

Reprinted by permission.

to employees, and not fail to consider this when designing and implementing corporate social efforts.[42]

The employee privacy issue seems to be growing in importance. Some action is taking place on the legislative front, but the issue is so complex that it will require individual company efforts to bring about any measurable improvements. Those initial efforts already made by large companies are likely to continue, with smaller companies following later, but whether business moves fast enough and in the right direction will be up to the people to decide.

SAFETY IN THE WORKPLACE

The late 1960s saw the federal government becoming increasingly concerned with the safety of the individual worker in the workplace. It was a noble concern and one which business itself had perhaps not stressed enough. In 1970 Congress passed the Occupational Safety and Health Act, which has since become to business groups the leading symbol of the federal regulatory presence. The Occupational Safety and Health Administration (OSHA), created by the act, is without question one of the most controversial and troubled of the many federal regulatory agencies.

The controversy has arisen despite the fact that, with increasing emphasis on the quality of life, workplace health and safety has been and continues to be a very legitimate concern of employees. OSHA's goals seemed quite appropriate: inspections in the workplace; development of safety standards — especially relating to health; training of employers and employees to develop self-inspection programs; approval of state plans to provide job safety and health; and administration of programs for federal employees.[43]

The time was right for such an effort, but the effort that followed was not exactly what OSHA or its designers had in mind. OSHA was troubled from the very beginning by the sheer size of its task — to monitor workplace safety and health in millions of workplaces with only several thousand inspectors to cover them all.[44]

In addition to the shortage of staff and funds, OSHA added to its own troubles by promulgating rules and standards that seemed quite trivial

---

[42]Robert C. Goldstein and Richard L. Nolan, "Personal Privacy Versus the Corporate Computer," *Harvard Business Review,* March-April 1975, pp. 62-70.

[43]John L. Paluszek, *Will the Corporation Survive?* (Reston, Va.: Reston Publishing Company, 1977), p. 120.

[44]"Now OSHA Must Justify Its Inspection Targets," *Business Week,* April 9, 1979, p. 64.

when compared to the larger issues of health and safety. It was not until 1978 that OSHA decided to purge itself of some of these nitpicking rules. A few illustrations will make the point. Some of its standards were quite silly, like the one that said, "Piping located inside or outside of buildings may be placed above or below the ground." That of course, covered just about every possibility. Or consider one that went too far in specifying product design: "Every water closet (toilet) should have a hinged seat made of substantial material, having a nonabsorbent finish. Seats installed or replaced shall be of the open front type."[45] Another: The telephone company was instructed that it could only provide linemen "belts that have pocket tabs that extend at least 1½ inches down and 3 inches back of the inside of the circle of each D-ring for riveting on plier or tool pockets. . .There may be no more than 4 tool loops on any belt."[46]

Such nuisance rules and standards have created serious credibility problems for OSHA and, though at least 928 such rules were rescinded in 1978, many times this number are still on the books.

→ Court decisions of the last several years have ruled that OSHA must consider economic feasibility in its regulatory activities. This decision was a victory for business, which has long argued that many of OSHA's rules would not exist if a cost-benefit analysis were done.[47] In a recent decision, OSHA began backing away from a proposed 85-decibel noise standard for workplaces because of the high cost involved in meeting such a standard.[48]

As hard as OSHA has tried to have an impact on health and injury statistics, evidence of the last several years does not show any notable results. After a three-year decline from 1973 to 1976 in workplace fatalities, 1977 data showed a 20 percent rise. In addition, the injury rate increased for the third year in a row after a decline in the early 1970s. Though these statistics should not be considered an indictment of OSHA, they did cast an atmosphere of gloom over the organization.[49]

Many observers have long argued that accident rates mostly reflect demographic factors — such as the young, inexperienced work force in the boom years of the late 1960s. Increases in employment have also increased the accident figures. A recent report by a presidentially appointed task force on workplace safety and health estimated that only 25 percent of accidents could be prevented through compliance with

[45]"OSHA's Nitpicking Rules Die," *Athens Banner Herald,* November 24, 1978, p. 5.
[46]Ibid.
[47]"A Court Orders OSHA to Consider Economics," *Business Week,* October 3, 1977, pp. 46-47.
[48]"Osha's Deaf Ear to Tighter Noise Control," *Business Week,* March 26, 1979, p. 30.
[49]"Accident Statistics that Jolted OSHA," *Business Week,* December 11, 1978, pp. 62, 66.

OSHA rules. Safety experts stress that the causes of accidents are complex and sometimes transitory in nature. Oil spilled on the floor, for example, is a condition that violates an OSHA good housekeeping standard but not one that an OSHA inspection visit is likely to prevent.[50]

We have not stressed the individual worker's right to safety in the workplace, as that seems to be acknowledged by business and government alike. More than any other issue treated in this chapter, however, government has institutionalized a method by which safety and health can be addressed. OSHA's efforts, for various reasons, have not been effective. Business is not relieved of the responsibility for worker health and safety just because a federal regulatory body exists to monitor compliance with its standards. Like the issues that have been discussed earlier, safety in the workplace is a very reasonable internal social responsibility of business. Only time will tell whether business or government turns out to assume the larger role in meeting it. Like most other initiatives, it will most likely require joint effort.

SUMMARY

In addition to social responsibilities outside the firm, business also has internal social responsibilities. In particular, expectations of employees that they be granted certain rights have been the focus of recent attention. Though business's concerns for employees as individuals have taken on a number of different forms, five employee rights in particular have been emphasized in recent years: (1) job satisfaction in work, (2) freedom of speech, (3) due process, (4) privacy, and (5) safety in the workplace.

Initiatives have been made by some organizations in these areas. Companies are beginning to recognize that these worker expectations are not unreasonable and have begun experimenting with programs to assure these rights. The federal government, too, has become involved in the areas of privacy and safety. With the combined efforts of business and government, the workplace of the future will be more acceptable to individuals. This trend is just a continuation of the quality-of-life initiatives that have been taken in the areas of the environment and consumerism.

[50]Ibid., p. 66.

QUESTIONS FOR DISCUSSION

1. Discuss the ways in which the nature of work has changed. What has changed more — the work or workers?
2. What is meant by the work ethic? Discuss its origin and comment on its modern status. Do you think the work ethic is dead? Justify your answer.
3. What is meant by "employee rights"? How does the concept of "employee constitutionalism" relate to this issue?
4. In what sense is job satisfaction a social concern?
5. What type of freedom of speech do employees want? Is the whistle-blowing variety the only kind? Should whistle blowers have a mechanism for protecting their rights? Discuss what such a mechanism might be.
6. Discuss what is meant by employees' "right of due process." What are some techniques or mechanisms that companies employ to ensure due process? Discuss the usefulness, in your view, of an employee ombudsman.
7. What are the major concerns that employees have regarding their right to privacy? Discuss basic principles or guidelines that companies could follow to help protect employee privacy.
8. What is the future for OSHA and the whole issue of safety in the workplace? Will safety and health become more important than privacy, freedom of speech, and due process?

Cases

Phil Stallings

Phil Stallings is a spot welder on an automobile assembly line, working the third shift: 3:30 p.m. to midnight. He is twenty-seven and just recently married. When interviewed about his job, he made the following comments:

> I stand in one spot, about a two- or three-foot area, all night. The only time a person stops is when the line stops. We do about thirty-two jobs per car, per unit. Forty-eight units an hour, eight hours a day. Thirty-two times forty-eight times eight. Figure it out. That's how many times I push that button.
>
> Repetition is such that if you were to think about the job itself, you'd slowly go out of your mind.

Because you're nothing better than a machine when you hit this type of thing. They give better care to that machine than they will to you. They'll have more respect, give more attention to that machine. And you know this. Somehow you get the feeling that the machine is better than you are.

You really begin to wonder. What price do they put on me? Look at the price they put on the machine. If that machine breaks down, there's somebody out there to fix it right away. If I break down, I'm just pushed over to the other side till another man takes my place. The only thing they have on their mind is to keep that line running.

I know I could find better places to work. But where could I get the money I'm making? Let's face it, $4.32 an hour. That's real good money now.

Proud of my work? How can I feel pride in a job where I call a foreman's attention to a mistake, a bad piece of equipment, and he'll ignore it. Pretty soon you get the idea they don't care. You keep doing this and finally you're titled a troublemaker. So you just go about your work. You *have* to have pride. So you throw it off to something else. And that's my stamp collection.[1]

QUESTIONS

1. Within the context of the above comments, discuss what social responsibility, if any, companies have to provide meaningful work and job satisfaction. Is this a legitimate "employee right"?

2. Does the good pay that spot welders receive make up for the highly repetitive jobs they perform?

3. What could the company do that would make Phil Stallings feel better about himself and the company?

4. Is this type of situation something we just have to "learn to live with" in a highly automated, industrial society?

A Little Larceny Can Do a Lot for Employee Morale

Dr. Lawrence R. Zeitlin, an industrial psychologist, says that employees in American business steal between 8.5 and 10 billion dollars a year from their employers. About four billion of this total is theft in cash and merchandise from retail establishments. Thefts of merchandise alone amount to approximately 5 percent of the yearly sales of American retail stores, and the stores' own employees steal three times as much as do shoplifters. Well over 75 percent of all employees participate to some

---

[1]Studs Terkel, *Working: People Talk About What They Do All Day and How They Feel About What They Do*, pp. 159-162. Copyright © 1972, 1974 by Studs Terkel. Reprinted by permission of Pantheon Books, A Division of Random House, Inc.

extent in "merchandise shrinkage." The amount stolen per person is about $300 a year, or about $1.50 each working day. The amount of internal theft in retail establishments averages out to between 5 and 8 percent of the typical employee's salary.

Business is aware of employee dishonesty, and most retail establishments have some form of internal security system to discourage dishonest employees. Despite the precautions taken to minimize "shrinkage," employees concoct elaborate schemes to steal, and in most cases they get away with it.

In spite of these statistics — which may be alarming to some — Zeitlin suggests employee theft can have some benefits for the employer. In fact, "Properly utilized, controlled employee theft can be used as another implement in management's motivational toolbox." Other, more traditional motivational tools include job enrichment and increasing worker pay and benefits. Job enrichment provides an increased variety of work, opportunity for advancement, and opportunities for individuals to assume responsibility. By enriching the job, management can increase worker pay and benefits without improving low-quality jobs, and still keep many employees.

Zeitlin suggests "supervised" employee theft can be used by the employer instead of one of the more traditional motivational tools. "By permitting a controlled amount of theft, management can avoid reorganizing jobs and raising wages." The dishonest worker is enriching his job in a manner which — Zeitlin claims studies show — is very satisfying to him. This enrichment is only costing management $1.50 per day. Management still keeps most business decision-making functions in its own hands and retains workers without increasing salaries and benefits.

Before deciding to minimize or eliminate employee theft, Zeitlin says management should ask itself four questions:

1. How much is employee theft actually costing us? How much would enforcing employee honesty cost us?
2. What increase in employee dissatisfaction could we expect if we controlled theft?
3. What increase in employee turnover could we expect?
4. What would it cost to build employee motivation up to a desirable level by conventional means of job enrichment or through higher salaries?

If employee theft is chosen by management as its motivational tool, an "allowable amount of theft should be determined." This level should then be enforced (employee theft controlled) through the use of an informal signaling system. A figurehead security system is also recommended by

Zeitlin, because the employee "gets his kicks" from the "challenge of beating the system," and there has got to be a system there for the employee to beat.

In closing, Zeitlin does not advocate complete abandonment of the traditional motivational techniques, but does suggest that management recognize the benefits that can be obtained by using employee theft as a motivational tool.[2]

QUESTIONS

1. What employer-employee issues are seen in this case?
2. Does management's internal social responsibility preclude using employee theft as a motivational tool?
3. What, if any, ethical problems do you see resulting from allowing — if not encouraging — employee theft?
4. In general, how would you evaluate a company management that permitted employee theft in an effort to keep jobs interesting?

Using the Lie Detector in Business

Use of the lie detector in business has been controversial for many years. The controversy stems from its less than perfect accuracy, tester variability, and the allegations that it invades an indivdual's right to privacy and that the Fifth Amendment to the United States Constitution guarantees the right to avoid self-incrimination. Many legal and ethical questions concerning its use have been raised.

There are basically two types of lie detectors in use today. One is the polygraph, which simultaneously measures several physiological activities, such as galvanic skin response, blood pressure, and breathing rates. The second kind is a relatively new device called the Psychological Stress Evaluator (PSE). The PSE has an advantage over the polygraph in that it need not be directly hooked up to an individual. The PSE measures only the person's voice and can be used to evaluate tape-recorded material. While the polygraph has been found to be accurate about 85 percent of the time, the PSE is accurate only in about 35 percent of cases.

About one-fifth of all major firms in the United States use the polygraph today. The American Polygraph Association has suggested three

[2]From Lawrence R. Zeitlin, "A Little Larceny Can Do a Lot for Employee Morale," *Psychology Today*, June 1971, pp. 24-26 and 84. Reprinted by permission from *Psychology Today* Magazine. Copyright © 1971 Ziff-Davis Publishing Company.

possible employment uses for the device: (1) to verify employee applications, (2) to periodically assess employees' honesty and loyalty, and (3) to help investigate specific thefts.[3]

QUESTIONS

1. What issues arise in your mind concerning these devices?
2. Do you think the lie detector is something business has a right to use in the above kinds of situations? Is it appropriate for some situations and not others?
3. What alternatives to lie detectors could management use?
4. Predict the future use of lie detectors in business.

Does Whistle Blowing Pay?

Honesty doesn't always pay. Ask three whistle blowers — individuals who uncovered and publicly revealed fraudulent, harmful, or wasteful acts on the part of their employers. After their revelations, their lives took a decided turn for the worse. One was forced to give up a promising career; another's marriage broke up; a third received threats on his life.

When one looks at the price these persons paid for their disclosures, it suggests that despite business's professed high ethical standards, loyalty is still frequently valued more highly than conscience. The president of a middle-sized company gave one business viewpoint: "In our culture we have a negative attitude about people who inform. The emphasis in our culture is on loyalty." He adds that he thinks whistle blowing is a good idea, but only if the employee has uncovered some criminal activity and is not simply voicing unsubstantiated allegations.

The range of issues whistle blowers have revealed is wide. In several cases evidence of safety defects in airplane brakes, trucks, and automobiles have been disclosed. Improper disposal of radioactive waste also has been revealed. A drug company's falsified test data and a firm's illegal campaign contributions are other issues brought to light.[4]

Though whistle blowers risk serious reprisals, in one notable instance it turned out quite well when all was said and done. This was the case of Ray Dirks, the now well-known securities analyst who blew the whistle that broke open the Equity Funding scandal. Though Dirks did lose his

[3]From Phillip G. Benson and Paul S. Krois, "The Polygraph in Employment: Some Unresolved Issues," *Personnel Journal*, September 1979, pp. 67-72. Reprinted with permission of *Personnel Journal*. Copyright September 1979.

[4]From Joan Lublin, "Spilling the Beans: Disclosing Misdeeds of Corporations Can Backfire on Tattlers," *The Wall Street Journal*, May 21, 1976. Reprinted by permission of *The Wall Street Journal*, © Dow Jones & Company, Inc., 1976. All rights reserved.

job and earned the enmity of many people on Wall Street, he authored a book on the subject, *The Great Wall Street Scandal*, and has formed a movie company to turn the book into a movie. As a result, Mr. Dirks is getting quite rich.[5]

QUESTIONS

1. Does whistle blowing pay? Discuss all ramifications of this question.
2. What would you do if faced with an issue in which whistle blowing seemed the thing to do?
3. What mechanisms could exist in companies that would ensure whistle blowers due process?

[5]From Priscilla Meyer, "Blowing the Whistle Ends in Book, Movie and $500,000 a Year," *The Wall Street Journal*, February, 15, 1978, pp. 1, 31. Reprinted by permission of *The Wall Street Journal*, © Dow Jones & Company, Inc., 1978. All rights reserved.

Business and Employment Discrimination

No issue better exemplifies current concern over employment discrimination than the American Telephone and Telegraph (AT&T) settlement case, which spanned the entire decade of the 1970s.

The origins of the AT&T case go back to an attack on the company in 1970-71, a time, ironically, when AT&T was viewed by the Equal Employment Opportunity Commission (EEOC) as a leader in the employment and training of minorities.[1] The government's interpretation of discrimination laws — especially in regard to sex discrimination — was changing during this period, and the EEOC found at AT&T a situation that became symbolic of all that the government was beginning to protest. Specifically, the EEOC had identified systemic patterns of discrimination at AT&T, especially among women. They found a concentration of women in the traffic department employed as telephone operators. These women had no upward mobility. They also found an underutilization of women in craft employment. These skilled jobs were dominated by men.

In 1973 AT&T signed a consent decree which, in 1979, it was finally about to fulfill. The decree required AT&T to overhaul its hiring and promotion practices, even to the point of sometimes having to hire and promote people other than those best qualified to do a job. The decree broke new ground in that it ordered the company to make compensatory payments to women and minority men who had "possibly" been discriminated against. The company paid off — about $18 million — mostly to 20,000 presumed victims of unequal pay practices, with many getting as much as two years' back pay.[2] A commitment was made by the company to permanently wipe out equal-pay problems; this produced pay increases for 72,000 employees at an annual cost estimated to

[1]Carol J. Loomis, "AT&T in the Throes of 'Equal Employment,' " *Fortune,* January 15, 1979, pp. 45-57. See also Phyllis A. Wallace, *Equal Employment Opportunity and the AT&T Case* (Cambridge, Mass.: MIT Press, 1976).
[2]Ibid., pp. 46-47.

have been approximately $53 million. Other accommodations agreed to by AT&T included the complete overhaul of its employment and promotion practices. Six years later (in 1979) the firm's executives were unsure whether the government was able to tell the federal court overseeing the case that the company had fulfilled the terms of the agreement.

The controversial experience of the nation's largest private employer makes an intricate and fascinating case study in modern business discrimination. Though the AT&T case was singled out here for our introduction, it is by no means an isolated instance. The same can happen to any business that is suspected of employment discrimination. To fully appreciate the situation business finds itself in today with respect to employment discrimination, we will trace some of its history. After that we will discuss some of the problems business faces in attempting to carry out society's will, as expressed in contemporary discrimination legislation.

We mentioned in the last chapter that discrimination is at the heart of one of the employee rights issues of today — equal employment opportunity. Thus one can think of this chapter as an extension of the last one.

In this chapter, then, we will cover the following:

- A brief history of employment discrimination
- Laws prohibiting discrimination
- The meaning of discrimination
- Achieving equal opportunity — some problems
- Other disadvantaged persons
- Minority-owned businesses: wave of the future?

A BRIEF HISTORY OF EMPLOYMENT DISCRIMINATION

It would take volumes to trace the history that led ultimately to passage of the first significant piece of civil rights legislation — the Civil Rights Act of 1964. A brief analysis of these events, however, is provided by William Glueck and James Ledvinka. They have argued that the act grew out of a conflict which had been apparent for years but which erupted in the 1950s and 1960s in the form of protests and boycotts.[3]

---

[3]William F. Glueck and James Ledvinka, "Equal Employment Opportunity Programs," in William F. Glueck, *Personnel: A Diagnostic Approach,* Revised edition (Dallas, Texas: Business Publications, 1978), pp. 593-633.

Behind the American dream has historically been the belief that merit rather than privilege is the means of getting ahead. Equal opportunity, in other words, was everyone's birthright. Blacks and other minorities, however, have not shared fully in this American dream. In the 1950s and 1960s the disparity between American ideals and American realities became quite pronounced in the case of minorities. Americans became aware of it not because they suddenly awoke to the realization that equal opportunity was not available to everyone, but because of individuals who had the courage to stand up for what they believed were their rights.

It began, Glueck and Ledvinka recount, on December 1, 1955, when Mrs. Rosa Parks, a black department store worker, was arrested for refusing to yield her seat on a bus to a white man. Out of that previously unthinkable act grew yet another — a bus boycott by blacks. One of the leaders of the boycott was a young minister, Dr. Martin Luther King, Jr.[4]

After the bus boycott came years of demonstrations, marches, and battles with police. Television coverage included scenes of civil rights demonstrators being attacked by officials with cattle prods, dogs, and fire hoses.[5] Along with the violence that grew out of confrontations between protestors and authorities came the awareness of the economic inequality that existed in the United States at that time.

In the voluminous data gathered by the Bureau of the Census, a few notable statistics illustrate the point quite well. Unemployment figures for blacks were double those for whites, and higher still among nonwhite youth. Blacks accounted for only 10 percent of the labor force but represented 20 percent of total unemployed and nearly 30 percent of long-term unemployed. In 1961, only about one-half of black men worked steadily at full-time jobs whereas nearly two-thirds of white men did so.

Tracing the statistics into the 1970s, we see some improvements among blacks and other minorities, but for the period prior to the passage of the Civil Rights Act, the numbers were clearly unfavorable to minorities. Figure 9-1 presents statistics for the period of 1967-1979 which illustrate the mixed results blacks experienced. Figure 9-2 presents data showing the scant progress made by women during the same period. Against this backdrop of blacks and other minorities being denied access to the American ideal of equal opportunity in employment, it should have been no surprise that Congress finally acted in 1964 in a dramatic way.

[4]Ibid., pp. 597-598.
[5]Ibid., p. 599.

BLACK PROGRESS: MIXED RESULTS

Until the 1973-75 recession, nonwhites were making strong gains in employment and earnings.
Since that time, progress has stalled while many suffer poverty and unemployment.

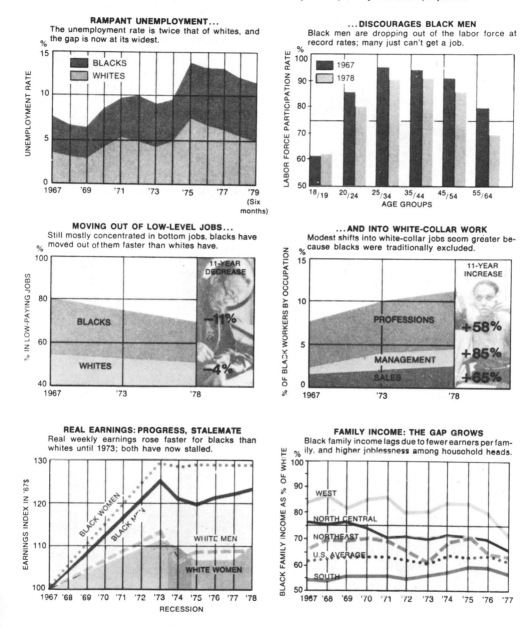

RAMPANT UNEMPLOYMENT...
The unemployment rate is twice that of whites, and the gap is now at its widest.

BLACKS
WHITES

UNEMPLOYMENT RATE (%)
1967 '69 '71 '73 '75 '77 '79 (Six months)

...DISCOURAGES BLACK MEN
Black men are dropping out of the labor force at record rates; many just can't get a job.

LABOR FORCE PARTICIPATION RATE (%)
1967
1978
18/19 20/24 25/34 35/44 45/54 55/64
AGE GROUPS

MOVING OUT OF LOW-LEVEL JOBS...
Still mostly concentrated in bottom jobs, blacks have moved out of them faster than whites have.

% IN LOW-PAYING JOBS
11-YEAR DECREASE
BLACKS −11%
WHITES −4%
1967 '73 '78

...AND INTO WHITE-COLLAR WORK
Modest shifts into white-collar jobs seem greater because blacks were traditionally excluded.

% OF BLACK WORKERS BY OCCUPATION
11-YEAR INCREASE
PROFESSIONS +58%
MANAGEMENT +85%
SALES +65%
1967 '73 '78

REAL EARNINGS: PROGRESS, STALEMATE
Real weekly earnings rose faster for blacks than whites until 1973; both have now stalled.

EARNINGS INDEX IN '67$
BLACK WOMEN
BLACK MEN
WHITE MEN
WHITE WOMEN
1967 '68 '69 '70 '71 '72 '73 '74 '75 '76 '77 '78
RECESSION

FAMILY INCOME: THE GAP GROWS
Black family income lags due to fewer earners per family, and higher joblessness among household heads.

BLACK FAMILY INCOME AS % OF WHITE
WEST
NORTH CENTRAL
NORTHEAST
U.S. AVERAGE
SOUTH
1967 '68 '69 '70 '71 '72 '73 '74 '75 '76 '77

Sources: Bureau of the Census (data includes all non-white minorities), Bureau of Labor Statistics

FIGURE 9-1

SOURCE: "Equal Opportunity: A Scorecard," p. 107. Reprinted with special permission of *Dun's Review,* November 1979, Copyright 1979, Dun & Bradstreet Publications Corporation.

FEMALE PROGRESS: HARDLY ANY

Women flooding the job market have sought refuge in traditionally low-paying
"women's jobs." Consequently, unemployment still remains high and earnings are low.

UNEMPLOYMENT: STEADY GAP...
The female unemployment rate remains one-and-a-
half times that of males, down a bit from the 1960s.

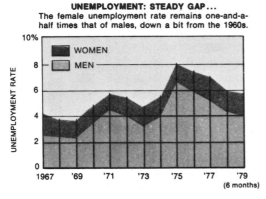

...DESPITE HUGE LABOR FORCE HIKES
Average labor participation rates for white women
are up ten points; the young gain more.

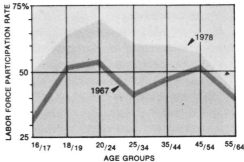

WOMEN IN LOW-PAYING JOBS...
Women have hardly moved out of low-income jobs;
men continue their slightly faster exodus.

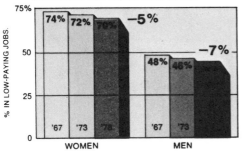

...REINFORCE JOB SEGREGATION
Over half of all women are still in "women's jobs"—
those with low pay, poorer prospects.

FEMALE % OF JOB HOLDERS

SOME UPWARD MOBILITY...
Slight gains have been made in higher paying managerial and craft jobs, but progress is still slow.

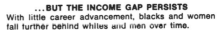

...BUT THE INCOME GAP PERSISTS
With little career advancement, blacks and women
fall further behind whites and men over time.

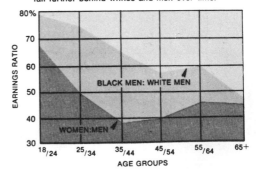

Sources: Bureau of the Census (data includes all non-white minorities), Bureau of Labor Statistics

FIGURE 9-2

SOURCE: "Equal Opportunity: A Scorecard," p. 108. Reprinted with special permission
of *Dun's Review,* November 1979, Copyright 1979, Dun & Bradstreet Publications Corporation.

LAWS PROHIBITING DISCRIMINATION

✷*Title VII* of the *Civil Rights Act of 1964* forms the backbone of laws prohibiting discrimination in employment. The law mandated that discrimination based on race, color, religion, sex, or national origin be prohibited. Title VII prohibits discrimination with regard to any employment condition, including hiring, firing, promotion, transfer, compensation, and admission to training programs.

✷ The *Equal Employment Opportunity Act of 1972* amended Title VII by providing for stronger enforcement and expanding its coverage so that it includes employees of state and local governments and educational institutions as well as private employers of more than fifteen persons.[6] We will discuss later some of the activities of the Equal Employment Opportunity Commission (EEOC), which enforces these laws.

✗ Another significant law is *Executive Order No. 11246*, which was signed by President Lyndon Johnson in 1965. This law prohibits employment discrimination by federal government contractors, subcontractors, and federally assisted construction contractors. Under the law, federal contractors are required to develop written affirmative action plans and establish goals and timetables to achieve equal opportunity.[7]

Though Title VII and Executive Order 11246 embody most clearly current legislative thinking regarding employment discrimination, it should be noted that there are other antidiscrimination laws and orders as well. A select few of these are listed in Table 9-1.

We have discussed some of the legislation that is behind current enforcement of equal employment opportunity, but a closer look at what is really meant by discrimination will make it clear why, as business continues to wrestle with this social issue, it often finds itself out of compliance with one law or another. A brief look at the evolution of the meaning of discrimination shows how it has changed and become more complex over time.

THE MEANING OF DISCRIMINATION

According to Jain and Ledvinka, employment discrimination laws were designed by Congress to reduce job barriers that contributed to *economic inequality*. In that pursuit, the courts developed increasingly strict

---

[6]See *EEOC at a Glance* (Washington, D.C.: U.S. Equal Employment Opportunity Commission, September 1974).

[7]Harish C. Jain and James Ledvinka, "Economic Inequality and the Concept of Employment Discrimination," *Labor Law Journal,* September 1975, pp. 579-584.

TABLE 9-1
✗Other Antidiscrimination Laws and Orders

Law	Coverage
Equal Pay Act of 1963	Prohibits sex differences in pay for equal work
Executive Order 11141 of 1964	Prohibits age discrimination among federal contractors and subcontractors
Age Discrimination in Employment Act of 1967	Prohibits age discrimination against those between ages 40 and 60
Executive Order 11478 of 1969	Prohibits discrimination in the federal government based on race, color, religion, sex, national origin, political affiliation, marital status, or physical handicap
Rehabilitation Act of 1973 and Executive Order 11914 of 1974	Prohibits discrimination based on physical or mental handicap and requires affirmative action; applies to federal government and federal contractors

meanings of discrimination, and at least three different views or definitions of discrimination have evolved.[8]

Back in the 1940s, discrimination was defined as *prejudiced treatment.* This referred to harmful actions motivated by personal animosity toward the group of which the target person was a member.[9] That is, prejudice against a person just because, for example, he or she was black, or Jewish, or fat. This definition did not solve the economic inequality problem because it was almost impossible to prove motives. Thus, this definition was largely ineffective.

The courts later defined discrimination to mean *unequal treatment.* Under this definition, a practice was illegal if it applied different *standards* or different *treatment* to different groups of employees or applicants. This definition made it unlawful to keep minorities in different departments (different treatment), or to reject, for example, women job applicants with children under five years old (different standards). The employer was allowed to impose any criteria so long as they were imposed on *all groups alike.*[10]

---

[8]Alfred Blumrosen, "Strangers in Paradise: Griggs v. Duke Power Co. and the Concept of Employment Discrimination," *Michigan Law Review,* November 1972, pp. 59-110.
[9]Glueck and Ledvinka, p. 604.
[10]Ibid.

The problem with this definition was that even though an organization may have imposed criteria on all groups equally, they could have an adverse effect on blacks. Blacks were usually less able to meet educational requirements or to attain a predetermined score on employment tests. The definition, then, allowed employers to impose standards that minorities were *less likely to meet* than whites, and that possibly may have had no relationship at all to the job in question. This interpretation of discrimination threatened to leave blacks and other minorites in the same disadvantaged position that prevailed prior to Title VII.[11]

So that the objective of economic equality could be better achieved, the United States Supreme Court arrived at yet a third definition of discrimination — *unequal impact.* This definition was established as a result of the landmark *Griggs v. Duke Power Company* case.[12] The court said ✳ that it was the *consequences* of an employer's actions, not the employer's intention, that determined whether discrimination had taken place. If any practice or test had an adverse or a differential effect on minorities, then this was a discriminatory practice. An unequal impact — or adverse effect — simply meant that fewer minorities were included in the outcome of the test or the hiring or promotion practice than would be expected by their numerical proportion. The employer must be able to demonstrate a "business necessity" for such an adverse impact — that is, the differential effect must be clearly justified by the need for satisfactory performance on the job. In the Duke Power case, for example, a high school diploma and good scores on a general intelligence test were *not* shown to have a clearly demonstrable relationship to successful performance on the job.[13]

The unequal impact definition is quite significant because it runs counter to so many traditional employment practices. There are many other examples. The minimum height and weight requirements of some police departments have unequal impact and have been struck down by courts because they tend to disproportionately screen out women, Orientals, and Hispanics.[14] The practice of discharging employees who have had their wages garnished to pay off debts has also been struck down because it falls heavily on minorities.[15]

With at least three different ways in which to define discrimination, managers have to be extremely careful, because practically anything they do may have possible discriminatory effects. The net result is that

[11]Ibid.

[12]*Griggs v. Duke Power Co.,* 401 U.S. 424, 1971.

[13]Theodore Purcell, "Minorities, Management of and Equal Employment Opportunity," in L. R. Bittel (ed.), *Encyclopedia of Professional Management* (New York: McGraw-Hill Book Company, 1978), pp. 744-745.

[14]*Smith v. City of East Cleveland,* 502 F.2d 492, 1975.   ✳

[15]*Wallace v. Debron Corp.,* 494, F.2d 674, 8th Cir., 1974.

business must take precautions at every turn to make sure that it is in compliance with the law. Thus, discrimination laws, along with their attendant problems, probably consume as much of business's time as any other internal social issue. As we examine the EEOC and the current issues of affirmative action and reverse discrimination in more detail, we will see the technical, complex bureaucratic morass that characterizes the state of employment practices today.

ACHIEVING EQUAL OPPORTUNITY — SOME PROBLEMS

In addition to the difficulty of defining discrimination, a number of other serious problems have hampered the achievement of equal opportunity in the workplace. We will discuss the difficulties the EEOC, the organizational body assigned to enforce the discrimination laws, has had with these complex laws because they lack the power and staff to administer them effectively. We will also discuss the policy and requirement of *affirmative action*, which grew out of Executive Order 11246 mentioned earlier. Finally, we will discuss the problem of *reverse discrimination*, one of the direct consequences of efforts to move minorities and women into jobs at a quicker pace. These issues do not touch upon every problem that has arisen with regard to achieving economic equality among all persons, but they do represent the basis of most of the other difficulties.

The EEOC: A Closer Look

There are actually several dozen different federal agencies charged with enforcing some aspect of the half dozen or so discrimination laws and executive orders. The EEOC, however, is probably the major one; and if current reorganization plans materialize, it will have consolidated responsibility for administering most if not all of the job-bias laws. The EEOC is part of what has been criticized as a largely ineffective effort by the federal government. Report after report in recent years — whether issued by Congress, business, labor, or civil rights advocates — has concluded that the entire federal antidiscrimination effort is a shambles.[16]

In fairness to the EEOC, it should be understood that during the past decade or so it has been but one of the many federal agencies administering the law and thus has received some criticism that should have

[16]Walter S. Mossberg, "Besieged by Criticism, Job-Bias Agencies Seek to Bolster Programs," *Wall Street Journal,* August 26, 1977, pp. 1, 16.

been shared. The centralization of the federal antidiscrimination effort under the Carter administration into only two agencies, the EEOC and the Office of Federal Contract Compliance Programs (OFCCP), should help remove one major complaint of business — the confusing array of government agencies, each with distinct equality requirements.[17]

The EEOC has been troubled since it opened its doors in 1965. The commission has had seven chairmen, three in the period 1975-77. Mismanagement apparently was so rampant that in 1975 the agency overspent its budget by $800,000. A special internal audit turned up widespread malfeasance and corruption in the EEOC's thirty-two field offices.[18] When Eleanor Holmes Norton finally took over as EEOC chairman in 1977, she faced a bewildering situation.

Charges against the EEOC included massive backlogs, ineptness, and inefficiency. In 1977 there was a backlog of 130,000 cases, and it was taking the agency about two years to settle an average complaint. When awards were finally made, they came after interminable delays.[19]

One of the primary reasons so many cases were caught in a backlog was that in the EEOC's earlier years casual complaints often were accepted as formal charges, and then the onus immediately fell on business to prove its innocence. Some business people felt it was a "guilty until proven innocent" situation for them. One streamlining device initiated by Norton is investigating complaints and eliminating those that are shown to have no merit after a few simple facts are ascertained.

One big decision EEOC faces is whether to continue to focus on individual complaints that are brought to it, or to search out and eliminate patterns of discrimination, using all the tools it has available: lawsuits, back-pay awards, and loss of government contracts. Mrs. Norton seems to be opting for the latter approach. She has stated, "Beginning in 1979 a very substantial part of this staff will put an unprecedented amount of its work into class action suits against companies."[20] She is also trying to persuade Congess to give the EEOC authority to issue cease-and-desist orders, thereby enabling the agency to halt immediately what it judges to be abuse. She also wants to convert EEOC from a forum for petty disputes to a quasi-judicial body which would gain the respect of Congress and the public.[21]

Despite the recent gains EEOC has made, it is still having trouble es-

[17]Jerry Flint, "Affirmative Action Programs Face New Test in '79," *Atlanta Journal and Constitution,* January 1, 1979, p. C-14.

[18]Mossberg, p. 16.

[19]"The Troubled Drive for Efficiency at the EEOC," *Business Week,* December 19, 1977, pp. 90, 91, 94.

[20]Flint, p. C-14.

[21]"An Eager New Team Tackles Job Discrimination," *Business Week,* July 25, 1977, p. 116.

caping the reputation it established before 1977. Business has perceived the atmosphere as one in which the government and activist groups are like prosecuting attorneys perpetuating the "guilty until proven innocent" treatment. One major consequence of this has been that thousands of employees have used equal-employment procedures to settle old grudges or just to cause trouble for companies. Three unreasonable cases show how the situation has gotten out of hand:

- A white female office worker, fired after she was caught fornicating on business premises during working hours, filed a charge against the employer, contending that she had been dismissed only because her sexual partner was black.[22]

- A young man fascinated by an expensive dress in a boutique window complained of discrimination because the shopkeeper would not let him try it on.[23]

- A Caribbean-born stewardess alleged that her airline discriminated against her by asking that she desist from flaunting her voodoo equipment on the job.[24]

These cases did not turn out successfully for the individuals filing suit, but they do illustrate the sometimes absurd lengths to which some people will go in today's climate.

Another impression that business has of equal opportunity efforts is captured in the article title, "Is Equal Opportunity Turning into a Witch Hunt?" The feeling here is that in enforcing equal employment opportunity laws, the government and activists seem more interested in punishing business for past wrongs than in promoting progress toward genuine equality of opportunity. Business finds this ironic because they believe they have made more progress in EEO than any other sector, including the federal and state government, educational institutions, and unions.[25] And they are probably right.

Most of this discussion has been anti-EEOC because it is very hard to find authorities who think EEOC has done an admirable job. Critics insist the progress that has been made is minuscule and unimpressive. When one considers the magnitude of the task, however, some ineffectiveness is understandable. The inconsistency of court rulings and the

[22]Frank Trippert, "The Sensible Limits of Non-Discrimination," *Time,* July 25, 1977, pp. 52-53. Reprinted by permission from *Time,* The Weekly Newsmagazine; Copyright Time Inc., 1977.
[23]Ibid.
[24]Ibid.
[25]Bob Tamarkin, "Is Equal Opportunity Turning into a Witch Hunt?" *Forbes,* May 29, 1978, pp. 29-31.

uncertainty surrounding such issues as affirmative action and reverse discrimination cause problems for everyone.

Affirmative Action

Affirmative Action basically means the taking of positive steps to hire and promote persons from groups previously discriminated against.[26] The concept of affirmative action was formally introduced to the business world by the Department of Labor's Office of Federal Contract Compliance Programs (OFCCP) in its regulation commonly known as Revised Order No. 4. The OFCCP was originally established to enforce Executive Order 11246, referred to earlier, the purpose of which was to require affirmative action plans for all companies doing business with the government. Most companies today have such plans.

The idea of taking positive steps to hire and promote persons who as a group have been previously discriminated against has a certain natural appeal. As an operational policy, however, its intuitive simplicity turns into a complex philosophical issue. Daniel Seligman, for example, pondering on what affirmative action really meant, wrote an article he entitled "How 'Equal Opportunity' Turned into Employment Quotas."[27] Seligman identified four postures that could be taken by companies concerning affirmative action.

1. Passive Nondiscrimination. This involves a willingness in hiring, promotion, and pay decisions to treat the races and the sexes alike. This posture fails to recognize that past discrimination leaves many prospective employees unaware of or unprepared for present opportunities.

2. Pure Affirmative Action. This posture involves a *concerted effort* to enlarge the pool of applicants so that no one is excluded because of past or present discrimination. At the point of decision to hire or promote, however, the company selects the most qualified applicant without regard to sex or race.

3. Affirmative Action with Preferential Hiring. Here, the company not only ensures the maximum labor pool but systematically favors minorities and women in the actual decisions. This could be thought of as a "soft" quota system.

4. Hard Quotas. In this posture, the company specifies numbers or proportions of minority group members that must be hired.[28]

[26]Tom L. Beauchamp and Norman E. Bowie (eds.), *Ethical Theory and Business* (Englewood Cliffs, N.J.: Prentice-Hall, 1979), p. 585.

[27]Daniel Seligman, "How 'Equal Opportunity' Turned into Employment Quotas," *Fortune*, March 1973, pp. 160-168.

[28]Ibid., pp. 160-162.

Much of the confusion surrounding the affirmative action concept has resulted from the government's failure to indicate which posture it is most interested in. Officials deny strongly that they are trying to push for No. 4, though some business people would swear that is what the government's basic objective is. The real issue, Seligman argues, is No. 3 — preferential hiring — though some governmental officials talk as though the objective is No. 2. Most current writers seem to assume No. 3 as they talk about present affirmative action programs. Some companies operate primarily on the basis of posture No. 2.

The underlying rationale for preferential treatment is similar to the *principle of compensatory justice.* This holds that whenever an injustice is done, just compensation or reparation is owed to the injured parties.[29] It is a view held by many that groups discriminated against in the past (women, blacks, North American Indians, and Mexican-Americans) should be recompensed for these injustices by positive affirmative action. Over the years deliberate barriers were placed on opportunities for minorities — especially blacks. These groups were prevented from participating in universities, business, law, and other desirable institutions. Additionally, when official barriers were finally dropped, matters frequently did not improve. Inequalities were built into the system; and though mechanisms for screening and promotion did not intentionally discriminate *against* certain groups, they did *favor* other groups. Thus, the view that we can and should restore the balance of justice by showing preferential treatment became established as a viable option for moving more quickly toward economic equality in our society.[30]

There are those who claim that such compensatory measures are unjust; they assert that no criteria exist for measuring compensation, that the extent of present discrimination is minor, and that none of those actually harmed in the past are available now to be compensated. They further argue that attempting reparations for *all* oppressed groups (women and blacks being just two among many) would compound initial injustices with a vastly complex system of further injustices.[31]

What, then, does the OFCCP expect in the way of affirmative action? ✶Revised Order No. 4 calls on the employer first to survey the labor market to determine the availability of women and minority group members as potential employees. Second, the employer is expected to identify the jobs in which these persons are underrepresented in the organization. Third, the employer is expected to set numerical integra-

[29]Beauchamp and Bowie, p. 586.
[30]Ibid., pp. 586-587.
[31]See, for example, Robert Simon, "Preferential Hiring," and Tom Beauchamp, "The Justification of Reverse Discrimination in Hiring," in Beauchamp and Bowie (eds.), pp. 622-624 and 625-635.

tion goals and timetables for removing that underrepresentation, and, finally, to indicate how employment practices are to be altered to achieve those goals.[32]

The numerous problems associated with complying with Revised Order No. 4 reduce some affirmative action plans to mere guides for helping management bring about equality of opportunity in the workplace. Thus, some plans turn out to be documents prepared in a perfunctory manner just to satisfy agency officials. In other organizations, however, affirmative action plans are seriously implemented; when this is done a certain amount of preferential treatment invariably occurs, as well as other side effects.

Because considerable good has come from affirmative action efforts, executives, in general, tend to favor such efforts.[33] It would be fair to say, too, that there has been considerable backlash created as a direct result of such efforts, requiring the attention of company management and personnel officers.

Affirmative action programs have created unanticipated and potentially serious problems for employers. They have also altered the way personnel decision making is done. The most serious difficulty is the feeling on the part of nonminorities in companies that affirmative action is taking place at their expense. One personnel officer in a major company stated, "Suddenly it seems as though everybody in this company thinks he — or she — has been deprived of equal opportunity."[34] As employees learn of special efforts undertaken by their employers to recruit, train, and offer advancement opportunities to women, blacks, and other groups, they feel unjustly treated — discriminated against.

The justice these individuals care about is justice for themselves. They fear compensatory discrimination — compensatory to currently preferred groups but harmful to them. These nonminorities may very well support their employer's efforts to stop inequitable practices of the past, but are understandably unwilling to be penalized themselves so that others can benefit.[35]

The AT&T case cited at the beginning of this chapter contained some sizable commitments to affirmative action which are still considered controversial because of their implications for employees who might have been passed over because they were not women or minorities.

Several other effects of affirmative action can be mentioned. There is

---

[32]Glueck and Ledvinka, p. 609.

[33]"Affirmative Action Is Accepted by Most Corporate Chiefs," *Wall Street Journal,* April 3, 1979, p. 1.

[34]Jules Cohn, "Coping with Affirmative Action Backlash," *Business and Society Review/Innovation,* Winter 1973-1974, pp. 32-36.

[35]Ibid.

the real possibility that morale can be so adversely affected that productivity declines. As perceptions of equity and fair treatment change, personnel officers must be prepared to cope with grievances from white males who feel they are being passed over in favor of someone less qualified. Companies that originally established an ombudsman position for minorities and women may now need these posts for the "new minorities."

Added burdens of record-keeping are another effect of affirmative action. New kinds of files have to be kept. Reports must be prepared. Data systems must be designed and kept up to date. Extra time and manpower must be budgeted. The corporate personnel function has become more important, and this has repercussions throughout the organization.[36]

One of the most publicized examples of affirmative action backlash came at the corporate level. It took the form of a lawsuit filed by Sears, Roebuck and Company, the nation's largest retailer.[37] In January 1979 Sears filed a class action suit against ten federal agencies charging the United States government with responsibility for the confusion over affirmative action hiring.[38]

Sears' basic position was that by issuing conflicting laws and regulations, the government ensured that the laws could not be obeyed. The 33-page suit accused the government of holding employers like Sears liable for the composition of a work force that was created largely by the government itself. Though Sears does not challenge the government's right to require affirmative action in hiring, it charges that contradictory policies have made it impossible for employers to follow all the guidelines. Sears said, for example, that the government forced employers to favor white males through veteran's-preference laws; now it is accusing employers of discriminating against women and minorities.[39] Sears also charged that the government's own failures in such areas as integrated housing and education have hindered the development of a qualified minority work force.

Sears did not win the suit, but it won tremendous applause from the business community. The suit was a manifestation of the same frustration thousands of businesses have felt as they attempted to comply with the government's often conflicting mandates. The Sears suit may be just the first in a series of clashes between big government and big business over affirmative action and equal employment opportunity.

[36]Ibid.

[37]"Sears Turns the Tables," *Newsweek,* February 5, 1979, pp. 86-87.

[38]"Sears Strikes Back," *Wall Street Journal,* January 26, 1979, p. 14.

[39]Lawrence Ingrassion, "Sears Suit Challenging U.S. Enforcement of Antibias Laws Raises Some Key Issues," *Wall Street Journal,* March 7, 1979, p. 41.

In sum, though affirmative action appeared quite attractive, it has had mixed consequences. It has moved some minorities and women more speedily into entry-level jobs and positions with higher responsibility, but charges of reverse discrimination loom on the horizon as a potential deterrent to these efforts.

Reverse Discrimination

As already mentioned, there can be an inherent conflict in affirmative action programs. The problem is that when some sort of preference is given to minorities or women, discrimination may occur against those in the majority — for example, white males. Increasingly, white males are filing charges of reverse discrimination — and they are making some of the charges stick. Their interpretation is that Title VII prohibits discrimination based on race and sex, and that includes discrimination against white males as well.[40]

The country hoped for a definitive opinion regarding the legality of affirmative action that may lead to reverse discrimination in the celebrated Bakke case (*Regents of the University of California v. Bakke*). ✳ Bakke, a white male, had been denied admission to medical school while a special admissions program for minorities was in effect. He charged that because the admissions programs gave preference to less qualified minorities this constituted discrimination against him. The United States Supreme Court, in a less than definitive decision, ruled that Bakke should be admitted, that strict racial quotas were illegal, but that race could continue to be "taken into consideration" in admissions.[41]

After the Bakke decision straddled the issue of the acceptability of affirmative action, the EEOC issued a new set of guidelines that said, in effect, the agency would not support charges that companies are violating the civil rights of white men in cases where "reasonable" affirmative action programs favor minorities or women. They interpreted "reasonable" to mean that some attention to race or sex was permissible even if hard quotas were not.

A somewhat more definitive decision — that of *Kaiser Aluminum and* ✳ *Chemical Corporation v. Weber* — has had the effect of smoothing the way for affirmative action programs. Brian Weber, a white man, charged that he was illegally discriminated against by being denied a position in a quota-based training program at Kaiser Aluminum. His case was upheld by the lower courts. If Weber's charge of reverse discrimination had

---

[40]For further information on the Weber case, see *United Steelworkers of America, AFL-CIO-CLC v. Weber et al*, 443 U.S. 193.

[41]"Bakke Wins, Quotas Lose," *Time*, July 10, 1978, pp. 8-20.

been upheld by the Supreme Court, it would have represented a major setback to the concept of affirmative action.

As it turned out, however, the Supreme Court in 1979 overturned the lower courts and ruled that employers could give preference to minorities and women in hiring and promotion for "traditionally segregated job categories." The majority opinion, written by Justice William Brennan, relied on what he determined was the "spirit" of the job-bias provisions of the 1964 Civil Rights Act. He argued:

> It would be ironic indeed if a law triggered by a nation's concern over centuries of racial injustice and intended to improve the lot of those who had been victims of discrimination constituted the first legislative prohibition of all voluntary, private race-conscious efforts to abolish traditional patterns of racial segregation and hierarchy.[42]

The majority opinion made it clear that a racial preference in private employment is permissible whenever there are manifest racial imbalances in traditionally segregated job categories.

The Weber decision, in essence, gave the green light to employers who have wanted to set up affirmative action programs but who have feared to do so because of possible reverse discrimination suits by white males. Though charges of reverse discrimination are not likely to disappear because of the Weber decision, companies should have an easier time in justifying their affirmative action efforts in the future.

OTHER DISADVANTAGED PERSONS

Thus far we have discussed employment discrimination as though blacks, other ethnic minorities, and women were the only groups disadvantaged in employment. They certainly are not. They *are* the "majority minority" groups, however, and thus far constitute the bulk of employment discrimination cases. Charges have come from other groups in recent years, most notably on the basis of handicap, age, and religious preference.

The Handicapped

The legal basis for charges of discrimination against the physically and mentally handicapped is the Vocational Rehabilitation Act of 1973, which is enforced by the OFCCP. It requires employers doing business

---

[42]Urban C. Lehner and Carol H. Falk, "Beyond Bakke: High Court Approves Affirmative Action in Hiring, Promotion," *Wall Street Journal*, June 28, 1979, pp. 1, 30.

with the government to set up affirmative action programs. These programs do not presently require numerical goals, but they do ask for special efforts in recruiting handicapped persons, which can include: (1) outreach programs, (2) communication of their obligation to hire and promote the handicapped, (3) development of procedures to find and promote handicapped persons already on the payroll, and (4) making physical changes in buildings, such as the addition of ramps, to allow the handicapped to move about more easily.[43]

Companies that really desire to be responsive to the needs of the handicapped have set up training programs and even partially redesigned jobs so that handicapped persons can hold them and perform effectively.[44]

Some experts have argued that the major problems handicapped people face are the negative attitudes and myths that prevail about their abilities and their disabilities. It has been shown that affirmative action programs may give the handicapped the chance they need to prove themselves.[45]

Older People

The following suicide note was left by a man who had filed a complaint about age discrimination:

> To Whom It May Concern:
>
> January 23, 1974. Too depressed to go on any longer haven't worked since March 23. Worked five nights for [grocery store] and they told me what I was worth — they laid me off for being too old (48). Company policy on that job is 30. I should have killed myself 18 years ago. If I'm too old to stack shelves what am I good for. I can't let my family starve. Let [grocery store] provide for them — I can't.[46]

The singular experience dramatized by this note tells us much about the feelings of those discriminated against because of age. In the 1970s, in particular, groups have begun protesting the treatment some employees or potential employees receive because of age. The legal bases for their charges are the Age Discrimination in Employment Act of 1967, which prevents discrimination of those between the ages of 40

---

[43]Louis Decker and Daniel Peed, "Affirmative Action for the Handicapped," *Personnel,* May-June, 1976, pp. 64-69.

[44]Joan Lublin, "Lowering Barriers: Pressured Companies Decide the Disabled Can Handle More Jobs," *Wall Street Journal,* January 27, 1976.

[45]Glueck and Ledvinka, pp. 621-622. See also Sandra Kalenik, "Myths About Hiring the Physically Handicapped," *Job Safety and Health* vol. 2, no. 9 (1974), pp. 9-12.

[46]Richard Peres, *Dealing with Employment Discrimination* (New York: McGraw-Hill Book Company, 1978), pp. 36-37.

and 65 in private employment, and the Age Discrimination Act of 1975, which prohibits age discrimination among employers receiving federal financial assistance.

Older persons are increasing in numbers and proportion as the average age in the United States has increased. Increasingly, older persons are demanding their rights and insisting that they not be taken advantage of or ignored. The recently passed law raising the mandatory retirement age to 70 from 65 will make this kind of discrimination an even more common issue in the future.

Religious Preference

In recent years there have been only a few cases in which religion was charged as the basis of ;job discrimination, and most of those cases have usually been concerned with the degree to which employers would accommodate the observance of religious practices. A section added to the 1972 amendments to Title VII held that employers are expected to interpret "religion" to "include all aspects of religious observance and practice. . .unless an employer demonstrates that he is unable to reasonably accommodate to an employee's. . .religious observance or practice without undue hardship on the conduct of the employer's business."[47]

Observance of the Sabbath is one religious practice that has become an issue. For some religious groups, such as Orthodox Jews and Seventh Day Adventists, the Sabbath is Saturday. Because some members of these groups believe it is wrong to work on the Sabbath, they are in direct conflict with employers who insist employees work on Saturday.

In general, the courts have held that employers must respect an employee's wishes not to work on his or her Sabbath. Companies are restrained and strictly limited in the situations in which they can fire such employees. Exhibit 9-1 summarizes when an employer can fire an employee who will not work on the Sabbath.

MINORITY-OWNED BUSINESSES:
WAVE OF THE FUTURE?

There is a growing feeling that for minorities to succeed in the business world, they must own and operate their own firms. This trend, which might be termed minority entrepreneurship, is increasing in importance.

[47]Ibid., p. 37.

EXHIBIT 9-1
Can You Fire an Employee Who Won't Work on the Sabbath?

YES, if . . .   No other employee has the skills to substitute for him.
              The job requires availability around the clock.
              The extra costs involved would hurt competitively.
              Employee discontent reaches "chaotic" proportions.
              His absence makes it unsafe for others.

NO, if . . .   His absence is merely an inconvenience.
              A replacement would demand premium wages.
              Other employees would merely be resentful.
              Others would want the same time-off privilege.
              Union provisions require the assignment.

SOURCE: Reprinted from "The Employer's New Worry: Saturday Work," in the March 15, 1976, issue of *Business Week* by special permission. © 1976 by McGraw-Hill, Inc. All rights reserved.

Part of the impetus behind business and government assistance to minority-owned companies is coming from such groups as the National Urban League, which contends that government action is necessary to bring about a better economic future for blacks and other minorities.[48] The groups argue that because of historic exclusion from the business world, black and minority business should be encouraged with specific commitments from government and companies to do more of their business with minority-owned firms.

According to most government estimates, the nation's 17 percent minority population controls only 4 percent of its businesses, and these firms account for less than 1 percent of total business receipts.[49] The data support what we already know: minority-owned businesses are few in number, and they certainly do not equal the proportion of minority citizens in the country. In recent years, however, both government and businessiness have taken affirmative steps to encourage minority-owned businesses.

Government Efforts

President Jimmy Carter set a goal of $3 billion to be spent in 1980 for federal contracting and subcontracting with minority vendors,[50] tripling

[48]"What Black Leaders Want from Business," *Business Week,* October 10, 1977, pp. 85-92.
[49]David Gumpert, "Minority-Group Firms Get More Subcontracts Under Federal Programs," *Wall Street Journal,* September 14, 1978, pp. 1, 35.
[50]"More of the Action for Minority Vendors," *Business Week,* March 26, 1979, pp. 106, 108.

the fiscal 1979 expenditures for such purposes. Thus, the federal government has clearly taken the lead in committing funds to minority businesses. To illustrate: the Department of Transportation stipulated that 15 percent or more of its money to be spent on large projects be directed to companies owned by blacks, Hispanics, or other racial minorities; the Commerce Department included a stipulation that at least 10 percent of its contracts go to minority firms; and the Department of the Interior is contemplating a goal that 20 percent of its spending be with minority firms. In each of these cases millions of dollars are involved.

In addition to these efforts, a proposal sent to Congress would strengthen the government's ability to encourage minority-business subcontracting on federal projects by requiring winners of contracts exceeding $1 million for construction and $500,000 for other purposes to work out a plan for such subcontracting before a contract is awarded. Current law merely requires that federal contractors show, after contracts are completed, that they did their best to find minority contractors.[51]

Business Efforts

Some business efforts in this realm have been made as a result of pressure from government, and some have been voluntarily undertaken as part of social responsibility programs.

The National Minority Purchasing Council (NMPC), a federally funded group of businesses that includes such members as GM, IBM, IT&T, Mobil, DuPont, and Shell Oil, set for itself a goal of $3 billion (similar to President Carter's) as the value of business purchases from minority sources in 1980. The NMPC's 120 members spent $1.8 billion in 1978 and were expected to spend $2.3 billion in 1979.[52]

As a group, NMPC members agree on what determines the success of an effective minority vendor program — top management involvement. Some companies have reinforced this point by establishing a policy that merit raises for buyers depend in part on how much the buyers increase their minority purchasing.[53] Buyers for many companies insist that they go to great lengths to find and assist minority vendors. Some corporations also help minority vendors prepare bids, help them organize their office procedures, provide technical assistance

[51] *Wall Street Journal,* September 14, 1978, pp. 1, 35.
[52] *Business Week,* March 26, 1979, p. 106.
[53] Ibid.

with their products, and furnish payments for work in progress to help safeguard their cash flow.

To simplify the search for reliable minority vendors, regional and national minority purchasing councils compile vendor lists that are updated quarterly. The NMPC, for example, maintains a computerized list of more than 10,000 vendors. Members of such councils agree on an ultimate goal: to go out of business because minority vendors no longer need their help. As one manager put it: "We want to convert minority vendors into just vendors."[54]

At the present time, enterprises owned by women do not qualify as minority vendors, but that situation is likely to change. A government committee is planning an executive order on women-owned businesses comparable to the order that launched the minority vending programs. It should only be a short time before business follows.

SUMMARY

Discrimination against minorities, women, and other disadvantaged groups is not likely to be eradicated completely any time soon. Great strides have been made, however, through legislation and business efforts. But the problem persists because it is so complex. The great complexity arises out of society's desire to eliminate discrimination and to achieve economic equality on the one hand, but to do so with no negative effects on any majority group on the other. Thus, affirmative action programs were initiated, but they created a new problem, one called "reverse discrimination."

Another effort by government and corporations has emphasized channeling business to minority-owned enterprises. Begun in the late 1960s, this idea of encouraging and supporting minority entrepreneurship continues to flourish.

The issue of discrimination in business is more than just an extension of employees' concern for their rights in the workplace. It strikes at the very heart of recent social trends and is thus a part of the growing alarm over the disadvantageous position of blacks, women, and other minorities in business. Not only are jobs and stature in business at stake, but minorities want better housing, better medical care, better educational opportunities — in short, full economic and social parity.

[54]Ibid., p. 108.

QUESTIONS FOR DISCUSSION

1. Discuss the events leading up to the passage of the Civil Rights Act of 1964.
2. Outline the essential features of Title VII and Executive Order No. 11246. After studying the chapter, can you see why these are the two most significant antidiscrimination laws? Discuss.
3. Identify the three ways in which discrimination has been defined. Give an example of each.
4. What was the specific contribution of the Griggs v. Duke Power case? Why is it considered a landmark?
5. What are some of the problems with the EEOC? In what directions will its activities in the future probably evolve?
6. Define affirmative action. Outline the four postures that could be taken by companies concerning the issue. Which posture do you think is most reasonable? Discuss the reasons why.
7. Define the principle of compensatory justice. Explain its ramifications for affirmative action.
8. What is meant by affirmative action backlash? Discuss the specifics of this backlash.
9. What is your opinion of the Sears suit? Did it seem reasonable to you? Do you think the company should have won its case?
10. Explain what is meant by reverse discrimination. Explain its relationship, if any, to affirmative action.
11. Who are some of the other disadvantaged groups that sometimes claim discrimination? Are their claims any less legitimate than those made by minorities and women? Discuss.
12. Discuss what the government and business are doing do assist minority-owned enterprises. What is your appraisal of thse efforts? Do you think they could have some possible negative consequences? Discuss.

Cases

The Ineffective Memo

The president of a large manufacturing firm had a special interest in hiring and promoting minorities and women. He circulated a memo to all upper-level managers stating that it was the policy of the company to "hire, promote and generally encourage the personal development of women and minorities." The memo also expressed a desire to increase the number of minority and female managers "significantly." The president did not specify any quantitative goal in this regard, as he felt it would restrict his managers too severely. A little over a year after the memo was issued, the president asked the personnel department for comparative data in this area. The data showed that minority managers had increased by 3 percent and women managers by only 2 percent. The president was very unhappy with these results and wondered what steps he should take next.

QUESTIONS

1. Why do you suppose this effort to improve the status of women and minorities failed?
2. Outline the characteristics of an approach that would have gotten better results, yet would not have left the company open to charges of reverse discrimination.

Has Discrimination Occured?

Presented below are a number of employment situations. Read and analyze each, then determine whether *prejudiced treatment, unequal treatment,* or *unequal impact* has occured; or if you think no discrimination has occured.[1]

Situation 1

A department head refuses to hire a female applicant for a supervisory position because he does not believe that it is the place of females to supervise male workers.

Situation 2

It is department policy not to hire women with preschool children, because child care responsibilities often compete with job responsibilities.

Situation 3

A supervisor who resisted the initial integration of his work group is harsher in disciplining a black worker than he has been in disciplining white workers in comparable situations.

[1]The situations for this case were supplied by James Ledvinka of the University of Georgia.

Situation 4

A high school diploma is required of applicants for supervisory positions.

Situation 5

A police department requires patrol officers to be at least 5′10″ tall.

Situation 6

Becasue of customer complaints, black salespeople are no longer hired.

Situation 7

Because of customer preferences, an airline refuses to hire men as cabin flight attendants. ("I'm George, fly me.")

Situation 8

A black applicant for a file clerk position is rejected because he had been convicted of the felony of refusing to accept military induction.

Situation 9

Because women live longer than men, a company requires them to contribute more each month to the pension fund.

Situation 10

A female employee complains that her boss has been pressuring her for sexual favors.

Situation 11

Two white employees and one black employee were caught stealing antifreeze from the company's warehouse. The company discharged the whites, but the black employee was let off with a warning.

Barrier Free

The term *barrier free* has recently become a crusading cry, cheered by thousands of handicapped Americans. The government has reacted to this effort and has urged legislation that would require all newly constructed buildings to be barrier free, thus allowing wheelchair access to all who require it.

The Greyhound Corporation has attempted to lead the business sector by innovating changes in many of its terminals throughout the

United States. Greyhound has specially constructed ramps, restrooms, handrails, water fountains, and telephone booths, all accessible to persons in wheelchairs. Greyhound has also instituted a "Helping Hand Service." Essentially, this service allows an individual to ride free as a companion to a handicapped person. All the company requires is a written statement from the handicapped individual's physician acknowledging the fact that assistance is needed while traveling. Upon receipt of this verification, Greyhound promptly grants free fare to the companion.

QUESTIONS

1. Would you consider Greyhound's efforts socially responsible?
2. Considering this case, discuss the concept "the business of business is business."
3. Do you think the company has gone overboard in attempting to accommodate handicapped people?
4. Would you think any less of the company if you learned that it makes no special efforts to hire the handicapped?

Business, Ownership, and Corporate Governance

10

As if it were not enough that business today must contend with the rising disenchantment of consumerists, environmentalists, civil rights activists, and other vocal critics, it also faces burgeoning criticism and questioning about how the corporate system is structured, business's legitimacy as a social institution, and the respective roles of shareholders, boards of directors, management, and employees in decision making and governance.

Much of the dissension about modern corporations has been generated by shareholders — those who own and, ostensibly, control business. The problem is that, though shareholders own businesses in a technical sense, they do not really own and control a business as an individual owns and controls his or her personal property — a house, a car, or a boat.

Because large corporations have thousands of shareholders, many of whom own only a few shares of stock and are widely separated geographically, the shareholders have no mechanism for becoming an organized source of power over corporate actions. As a consequence, ownership (represented by numerous and widely dispersed shareholders) is separated from control (represented by on-the-scene, daily management).

Since much of the concern about business's internal structure — its ownership, control, accountability, and management — has emanated from the shareholders and employees, we have decided to place this chapter among those dealing with internal publics and issues. To be sure, just as with the issues covered in the last two chapters, this issue transcends corporate walls and is, indeed, a topic of great importance to society at large.

What seems to be at stake is the issue of *corporate governance*. A more specific definition will follow later, but suffice it to say here that corporate governance involves the general question of business's legitimacy, responsibilities, mode of structure, method of operating, and ultimate accountability. Indeed, the very existence and future of the current system of corporate-based capitalism in America are at stake.

In an effort to address this wide range of issues in a coherent fashion, we will discuss the following topics:

- The major elements in corporate organization
- Legitimacy: the basic issue
- Corporate governance: the broad issue
- Federal chartering of corporations
- Restructuring the board of directors
- Role of shareholders
- Role of employees

THE MAJOR ELEMENTS IN CORPORATE ORGANIZATION

The corporate form of business organization is recognized as the dominant one in power and influence. As such, we will consider the main elements or essential parties that comprise it in order to see how major groups and issues enter into the corporate governance question. We hope to show, too, the social questions that are being raised in the context of the modern corporation.

There are at least four major groups we need to mention in setting the stage for our later discussion: shareholders, the board of directors, management, and employees. On top of these, there is the charter issued by the state giving the corporation the right to exist and laying down the basic terms of its existence. Figure 10-1 presents these four groups, along with the state charter, in a hierarchy of authority.

We will discuss each of these groups and the roles each is intended to assume. Let us begin with the *shareholders*. Under American corporate law, shareholders are the owners of the business. As owners, they should have ultimate control over the corporation. This control is manifested primarily in the right to select the directors of the company. The degree of each shareholder's right is determined by the number of shares of stock owned. The individual who owns one hundred shares of Mattel Toy Company, for example, has one hundred "votes" when election time comes for the board of directors.

Since large organizations have thousands of shareholders, they elect a smaller group — known as the *board of directors*— to govern and oversee the management of the business. Traditionally, the board has been comprised of individuals from outside the management ranks. These have been people whose principal employment was with some other

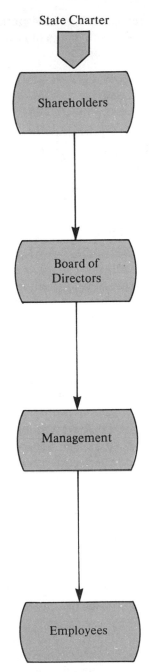

FIGURE 10-1
The Corporation's Hierarchy of Authority

company. In the twentieth century, however, the practice of appointing inside directors — individuals serving as directors of the very companies that employ them — has become prevalent.[1]

The third major group in the authority hierarchy is *management*, that group of individuals who have been hired by the board to run the company and manage it on a daily basis. Along with the board, top management establishes overall policy. Middle and lower managers carry this policy out and conduct the daily supervision of the employees. *Employees*, of course, are those hired by the company to perform the actual work. Managers are employees too, but here we are referring to non-managerial employees.

Perhaps all this description is not needed; but it does indicate the major constituent groups that comprise the interal structure of modern business corporations. The major social issues that have evolved in recent years have involved the theoretical versus actual roles, rights, and responsibilities of these four major groups. Corporations have not been run the way they were designed to run, and this is the basis for the current debate over corporate governance.

Questions that have been raised include: Should federal rather than state charters be required for business? What are the shareholders' actual rights? What can shareholders do if they are displeased with how the firm is being run but do not own enough shares of stock to bring about change? Can shareholders sue managers and board members? Can shareholders speak out at annual meetings? How should boards be structured? What is their authority and responsibility? Are they really effectively overseeing management practices and ethics? Should special "public interest" directors be placed on the board to ensure all constituent groups of representation? Who are management and the board accountable to? Do they view the shareholders as a constituency? Is management a self-perpetuating power elite? Should employees have some say in the governance of the corporation? Figure 10-2 summarizes these questions.

These are just a sample of the questions being asked, but they do provide the flavor of the kind of issues that are part and parcel of the emerging debate over business ownership and corporate governance. Underlying these concerns is the fundamental question of business's legitimacy today, a discussion of which will help us appreciate what is at stake here.

---

[1]Jeremy Bacon, *Corporate Directorship Practices: Membership and Committees of the Board* (New York: The Conference Board and the American Society of Corporate Secretaries, 1973).

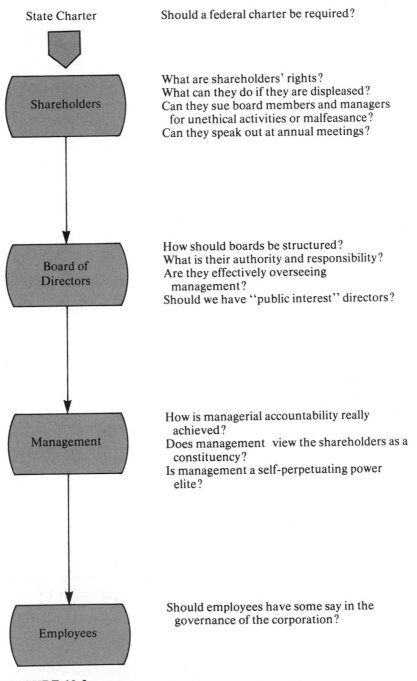

State Charter   Should a federal charter be required?

Shareholders

What are shareholders' rights?
What can they do if they are displeased?
Can they sue board members and managers
   for unethical activities or malfeasance?
Can they speak out at annual meetings?

Board of Directors

How should boards be structured?
What is their authority and responsibility?
Are they effectively overseeing
   management?
Should we have "public interest" directors?

Management

How is managerial accountability really
   achieved?
Does management view the shareholders as a
   constituency?
Is management a self-perpetuating power
   elite?

Employees

Should employees have some say in the
governance of the corporation?

FIGURE 10-2
The Major Corporate Groups and Questions that Are Being Asked

LEGITIMACY: THE BASIC ISSUE

Legitimacy is a somewhat abstract concept, but is important insofar as it helps explain the relative roles of a corporation's charter, shareholders, board of directors, management, and employees. Thus, legitimacy must be understood as a somewhat abstract notion before corporate governance can be intelligently studied as a practical problem.

Let us start, as others have, with a slightly modified version of Talcott Parsons' definition:

> Organizations are legitimate to the extent that their activities are congruent with the goals and values of the social system within which they function.[2]

From this we see legitimacy as a *condition* that prevails when there is a congruence between the organization's activities and society's expectations. Thus, while legitimacy is a condition, legitimation is a *dynamic process* by which business seeks to perpetuate its acceptance. The dynamic process aspect should be emphasized because society's norms and values change, hence business must change if legitimacy is to be continued.

It is useful to consider legitimacy at both the micro, or company level, and the macro, or business institution level.

Legitimacy: The Micro View

At this level we are referring to individual business firms maintaining legitimacy by remaining in conformance with societal expectations. Companies seek legitimacy, Epstein and Votaw tell us, in several ways. First, a company may adapt its methods of operating to conform to what it perceives to be the prevailing standard. For example, a company may discontinue door-to-door selling if that marketing approach comes to be viewed in the public mind as a shoddy sales technique.[3] Or a pharmaceutical company may discontinue offering free drug samples to medical students if this practice begins to take on the aura of a bribe.

Second, a company may try to change the public's values and norms to conform to its own activities by advertising and other techniques. Avon, for example, was successful at this with its door-to-door marketing of cosmetics.

Finally, an organization may seek to enhance its legitimacy by iden-

---

[2]Cited in Edwin M. Epstein and Dow Votaw (eds.), *Rationality, Legitimacy, Responsibility: Search for New Directions in Business and Society* (Santa Monica, Calif.: Goodyear Publishing Co., 1978), p. 72.

[3]Ibid., p. 73.

tifying itself with other organizations, persons, values, or symbols that have a powerful legitimate base in society.[4] This occurs at several levels. At the national level, companies proudly announce appointment of celebrities, former politicians, or famous persons to managerial positions or the board of directors. At the community level, the winning local football coach may be asked to endorse a company by sitting on its board or promoting its products.

Legitimacy: The Macro View

This is the level with which we are most concerned in the present chapter. Here were are referring to the corporate system — the totality of business enterprises. It is difficult to talk about the legitimacy of business in pragmatic terms at this level. American business is such a potpourri of institutions, such a collection of miscellaneous shapes, sizes, and industries, that saying anything definite about it is difficult.

Yet this is precisely the level at which business needs to be concerned about its legitimacy. What is at stake is the existence and form of business as an institution in our society. William Dill has suggested that business's social (or societal) legitimacy is a fragile thing in his statement:

> Business has evolved by initiative and experiment. *It never had an overwhelmingly clear endorsement as a social institution* (emphasis added). The idea of allowing individuals to joust with one another in pursuit of personal profit was an exciting and romantic one when it was first proposed as a way of correcting other problems in society; but over time, its ugly side and potential for abuse became apparent.[5]

Quite a bit of the excitement and romanticism has long since worn off; business must face up to its fragile mandate. It must realize that its legitimacy is constantly subject to ratification. And it must realize that it has no inherent right to exist — it exists as it does solely because society has given it that right.

In comparing the micro view of legitimacy with the macro view, one is led to observe that while specific business organizations can be found scurrying about trying to perpetuate their own legitimacy, the corporate or business system as a whole rarely addresses the issue at all. This is unfortunate because the spectrum of powerful issues regarding business conduct clearly indicates that such institutional introspection is needed if business as we know it is to survive. If business is to continue

---

[4]Ibid.

[5]William R. Dill (ed.), *Running the American Corporation* (Englewood Cliffs, N.J.: Prentice-Hall, 1978), p. 11.

to justify to society its right to exist, then the question of legitimacy and its operational ramifications cannot be ignored.

CORPORATE GOVERNANCE: THE BROAD ISSUE

Corporate governance as an issue is a direct outgrowth of the question of legitimacy. For business to be legitimate and to maintain its legitimacy in the eyes of the public, its governance must correspond to the will of the people.

Not since the early days of the New Deal has the field of corporation law been so astir with proposals to reform the corporation.[6] Indeed, the subject has become a favorite preoccupation of congressmen, SEC commissioners, legal scholars, and Naderites.[7]

The issue has not arisen out of a vacuum. Questions about how corporations govern themselves and to whom they are accountable are a direct consequence of their failure to perform in the social arena to society's satisfaction — or at least to the satisfaction of many of society's most vocal social activists and opinion leaders.

Business corporations have grown large and powerful. The people who manage them have become powerful. We do not argue that their power is irreparably socially destructive. Yet despite the many economic and financial successes of modern business, a number of incidents have raised questions about management's performance in non-economic spheres. Because many corporate giants have been tarnished by charges of malfeasance, there are more demands for closer scrutiny of large corporations and more accountability for their actions. As the public has learned of corporate directors who claim to have no knowledge of admitted bribes, unlawful political contributions, and other chicanery, the question being raised time and again is: "Who governs the corporation?" The issue is stated by some in this way: "Is corporate management really responsible to anyone except itself?"[8]

As company executives have become insulated from effective control by directors and shareholders, to whom they are legally responsible (as we saw in Figure 10-2), they become even further removed from the influence of customers, employees, community groups, and others who have an interest in how the company performs.[9]

[6]Sumner Marcus and Kenneth Walters, "Assault on Managerial Autonomy," *Harvard Business Review,* January-February 1978, pp. 57-66.
[7]Victor H. Palmieri, "Officers of the Board?" *Wall Street Journal,* August 14, 1978.
[8]"Corporate Governance — New Heat on Outside Directors?" *Forbes,* October 1, 1977, p. 33.
[9]Dill, p. 2.

The corporate governance issue, then, comes back to the question, "Who governs the giant corporation, and for whom is it governed? The shareholders? The management? The directors? The government?[10]

Some proposals for reform of corporate governance would bring corporate operations back into line with the chain of responsibility we saw in Figure 10-1. Alternative proposals, however, might change this chain of responsibility so that other orderings of authority become the accepted norm.

Though it is difficult to describe all the proposed solutions to corporate governance questions, four possibilities stand out as representative of the kinds of solutions being discussed. These are (1) the federal chartering of corporations, (2) restructuring the board of directors, (3) strengthening the role of shareholders, and (4) strengthening the role of employees. Each of these merits closer examination.

FEDERAL CHARTERING OF CORPORATIONS

Many experts have said that corporate governance is loose, ambiguous, and unaccountable because current corporate laws are too permissive. A corporation must get its charter — its right to exist — from a state. In practice, though corporations do business in many states and often in foreign countries, all they need to secure is one charter from one state to do business anywhere in the world.

The trouble with such charters, many argue, is that the states are either unable or unwilling to place strictures on corporations for fear they will cease to attract them, or cause confusion by enacting tougher standards than other states. Indeed, Bayless Manning, former dean of Stanford Law School, said that current state corporate statutes are "towering skyscrapers, internally welded together and containing nothing but wind."[11]

William L. Cary, a former chairman of the SEC and now a professor, has worked in recent years to develop federal standards for corporation law. Suggestions for reform range from federal chartering of corporations at one extreme — a position advocated most strongly by Ralph Nader — to a "minimal standards act," which would merely create "corporate accountability," at the other extreme.

One reason the federal chartering proposal is so attractive is that it would most effectively eliminate the leniency of the state statutes. Cary has been quoted as saying that the problem with existing corporation

[10]Tom Goldstein, "Who Governs Corporations?" *New York Times,* December 22, 1978, p. D-4.
[11]"New Fire in the Drive to Reform Corporation Law," *Business Week,* November 21, 1977, p. 98.

law is, in a word, Delaware. He argues that the state of Delaware "has a laissez-faire attitude toward the fiduciary role and responsibility of management to its shareholders." He goes on to say that most state legislatures have engaged in a competitive race, recklessly outbidding each other in efforts to offer management "maximum freedom from restrictions."[12] Most states have followed Delaware's lead in a nation-wide surge toward permissiveness, tending to create a Gresham's Law effect — bad corporation law drives out the good. It should come as no surprise, therefore, that more than half of the top 500 industrial corporations have incorporated in the state of Delaware.[13] Donald Schwartz has tempered the attack somewhat by pointing out that the issue is not Delaware but state law. He has stated that "state courts do not seem capable of achieving a balanced corporation law."[14]

One way to appreciate all that is typically involved in proposals for federal chartering is to look at particular recommended models. Because it represents the kind of proposal often set forth, let us examine the features of the case presented by Schwartz. He makes it clear that his proposal for federal incorporation is to "control those corporations which have a significant impact beyond their immediate vicinity." Thus, his proposal would be aimed at the giant corporations and would include at least all the companies on the *Fortune* 1000 list.[15] His model federal statute would contain four major sections — (1) Corporate Records and Reports, (2) Directors and Management, (3) Shareholders, and (4) Organic or Fundamental Changes — each of which will be reviewed briefly.

Corporate Records and Reports. The proposed changes here would make the corporation and its management more accountable to a larger constituency by putting more information in the hands of the public. The information would be included in the annual report sent to shareholders and also filed with the federal incorporation agency. To provide for maximum flexibility, the agency would have the authority to enact regulations governing both the form and substance of the reports.

Shareholders should know who has a substantial interest in the corporation; thus, all interests above 5 percent would be reported. Other disclosures might include reports on steps being taken to equalize em-

---

[12]William L. Cary, "Federalism and Corporate Law: Reflections upon Delaware," *Yale Law Journal,* March 1974, p. 663.
[13]Marcus and Walters, p. 58.
[14]Ibid., p. 60.
[15]Donald E. Schwartz, "The Case for Federal Chartering of Corporations," in Robert L. Heilbroner and Paul London (eds.), *Corporate Social Policy: Selections from Business and Society Review* (Reading, Mass.: Addison-Wesley Publishing Co., 1975), pp. 325-331.

ployment and promotion opportunities as well as information about pollution, worker safety, and corporate political activities.

Schwartz points out that such disclosures should pose no undue hardships, as the required information is already available in a well-run company. The responsibility for the report would lie with the board.[16]

Directors and Management. We will be brief here because this topic will be discussed more fully later in the chapter. The essential features Schwartz recommends in this section are designed to increase the diversity of influences on the board and to make those who run corporations more accountable.

To increase the variety of inputs into the decision-making process, a greater variety of people would be put on the board. Also, individual board members would have resources available for their use, including the ability to hire a counsel and staff to check up on management. Another way to increase input might be to create a public policy committee. Such a committee would be composed of no more than two-thirds management representatives and would be required to hold public meetings and to publish reports. (Associated with this is the suggestion of conducting a "corporate social audit," an idea we will discuss later.) Inputs could also be expanded by giving employees more of a role in management.

Directors would have to be more accountable, and directorships should be full-time jobs, or nearly so. The number of boards one could serve on would be limited. The board would also become more accountable if directors were subject to more personal liability not indemnifiable by the corporation.[17]

Shareholders. The corporation's owners would be given more influence over corporate policy. The primary way of doing so would be to end management's exclusive control of the proxy machinery. Any shareholder who could substantiate a minimal amount of support would be allowed to have his or her proposal printed on management's proxy. The shareholders would also be allowed to vote on major proposals as well as on nominees to the board of directors; this could be done instead of merely authorizing a proxy. This would tend to ensure representation of some minority interests on the board, whereas the present system merely perpetuates management by allowing it to solicit proxies and then vote them in their own interest at meetings.[18]

Organic or Fundamental Changes. A federal incorporation statute

[16]Ibid., pp. 329-330.
[17]Ibid., pp. 330-331.
[18]Ibid., p. 331.

ought to contain a stipulation calling for regulatory approval of mergers and sales. It has been seen through experience that when the standard for effecting shareholder rights is one of fairness, the courts allow considerable liberty to management. Furthermore, disclosure may be of questionable importance in protecting shareholder interest. Finally, to prevent unreasonably huge concentrations of power, advance notice is needed so that a reasoned and consistent policy can be formed.[19]

Proposals such as the model set forth by Schwartz would result in sweeping changes of current corporate law. The objectives — making the corporation more accountable, correcting management's neglect of shareholders, opening the decision-making process to accommodate community input, and requiring public disclosure on many matters for which it is not now required — are quite noble. There are many, however, who question what the true impact of federal chartering would be and hesitate at the thought of such radical proposals. Because federal chartering is the most comprehensive concept offered for controlling big business — or "taming the giant corporation," as Nader, Green and Seligman choose to call it[20] — many feel that such an effort attempts to do too much too quickly when the potential impact is so uncertain. In fact, some think federal chartering is "an idea well worth forgetting."[21]

A major problem one might have in justifying federal chartering is stated well by Marcus and Walters:

> In order to support the federal chartering proposal, one would have to conclude that the large corporation is the root of most social and economic evil. . ., that the existing widespread network of regulatory agencies of the federal and state governments is not working, and that the behavior of large corporations would be radically transformed by tying their right to continue in business to their "good behavior."[22]

In sum, there are both pros and cons to the idea of federal chartering, and the likelihood of its occurring soon is slim. What may happen is that particular parts of federal chartering proposals may be implemented in piecemeal fashion. We should not completely rule out federal chartering because it may well represent the model of the future for controlling large corporations.

---

[19]Ibid., p. 331.

[20]Ralph Nader, Mark Green, and Joel Seligman, *Taming the Giant Corporation* (New York: W. W. Norton & Co., 1976).

[21]Peter H. Aranson, "Federal Chartering of Corporations: An Idea Well Worth Forgetting," in Heilbroner and London (eds.), pp. 332-337. A good review of the pros and cons of federal chartering are included here.

[22]Marcus and Walters, p. 61.

RESTRUCTURING THE BOARD OF DIRECTORS

Though many advocates of corporate reform do not subscribe to the notion of federal chartering, practically all agree that corporate boards of directors should be restructured or recomposed to some degree.[23] Some of the reasons suggested for this need to reform the board are the concern over corporate power, the social and environmental crisis, lack of accountability, and lack of legitimacy.[24]

Though these reasons have been evolving for some time, more immediate events of the past decade have created the stimulus for closer scrutiny of boards. Recent payoff scandals that have been in the news, unlawful political contributions and bribes, the spectacular Equity Funding fraud, the collapse of the Penn Central and other corporate failures — all have combined to focus attention on the way directors of major corporations have been doing their jobs.[25] Add to this the much closer scrutiny the SEC is giving to directors, and it appears that a crisis is imminent at the board level.[26]

Historically, board members have been selected by management through solicited proxies of small shareholders, thus enabling managers to name virtually anyone they wanted to the board. Board members were frequently persons who did not have the time, expertise, or inclination to closely scrutinize management. As a result of recent revelations of corporate wrongdoing, uprecedented pressure by the SEC, social activists, and vocal shareholders is being placed on corporate directors to be more aware of what management is doing, and in whose interests they are doing it.

The following example of SEC action illustrates the kind of critique given to directors throughout the United States today:

> From the SEC: Members of the board of National Telephone Company should have awakened sooner to the 1975 credit squeeze that put the Hartford, Conn., telephone-equipment supplier into the hands of a court-appointed receiver.[27]

[23]For an interesting and insightful discussion of board reform, see John Collins and Richard Ryberg, "Corporate Board Reform as a Mechanism for Improving Corporate Social Responsiveness," unpublished paper available from authors.

[24]Philip I. Blumberg, "Reflections on Proposals for Corporate Reform Through Change in the Composition of Directors: 'Special Interest' or 'Public Directors,'" in S. Prakash Sethi (ed.), *The Unstable Ground: Corporate Social Policy in a Dynamic Society* (Los Angeles: Melville Publishing Company, 1974), pp. 112-134.

[25]B. E. Calame and E. Morganthaler, "Outside Directors Get More Careful, Tougher After Payoff Scandals," *Wall Street Journal*, March 24, 1976, p. 1.

[26]"The SEC Looks Harder at How Directors Act," *Business Week*, February 2, 1976, p. 56.

[27]Burt Schorr, "Corporate Directors Scored for Lax Scrutiny of Management's Acts," *Wall Street Journal*, April 10, 1978, pp. 1, 24.

TABLE 10-1
The Growth of Audit Committees

Year	Percent of Large Public Companies with Audit Committees
1967	25%
1973	45%
1978	90%

SOURCE: "Mr. C.P.A., Meet Mr. C.C.D." *Forbes,* May 1, 1978, p. 28.

The conclusions of the SEC in the National Telephone case demonstrate one more reason why relationships between directors and managers are under intensive scrutiny at many of the more than 10,000 companies whose stock is publicly traded. Congress, federal agencies, the courts, and the stock exchanges are thus applying pressure for tighter, more independent control of management operations. There has also been heightened interest in recent years for increased activism of board audit committees in addition to requests for more *outside* directors, more *independent* directors, and more *special interest* directors.

Audit Committees

The audit committee is a relative newcomer to board organization charts, and the SEC says they have "become the rage."[28] As their name implies, audit committees have the function of carefully auditing accounting procedures to assure the board that the company's ways and means of operating are above suspicion and that management is making ethical and wise decisions. Table 10-1 shows how audit committees have grown in popularity over recent years.

The New York Stock Exchange mandated that all its listed companies have audit committees by 1978, and the SEC appears to be headed toward requiring all public companies to establish such committees before long.

The audit committee's responsibilities seem to be growing exponentially. Not only does the committee have the responsibility to prevent a "devious management from deceiving the public," but other topics of shareholder interest become legitimate matters of investigation, too.[29] A current subject of much scrutiny by audit committees has been corporate management's "perks" (perquisites) — those extra privileges or

[28]Calame and Morganthaler, p. 25.
[29]"Mr. C.P.A., Meet Mr. C.C.D.," *Forbes,* May 1, 1978, pp. 28-29.

fringe benefits that are incidental to regular salary and are sometimes claimed by management groups to be their absolute right.

It should be noted that the New York Stock Exchange has adopted a policy that audit committees of listed companies be made up "solely of directors independent of management and free from any relationship that, in the opinion of its board of directors, would interfere with the exercise of independent judgment as a committee member. . ."[30]

Independent Outside Directors

One of the ways proposed by the SEC and others to restructure boards is to include more *independent outside directors*. These would be individuals who are not currently members of management and who have no business relationship to the company they serve. Such individuals might be college professors, former government officials, executives of unrelated concerns, "professional" directors, or representatives of civil rights and consumer groups.[31]

Robert Mundheim has stressed, moreover, that board independence can be achieved if the following three conditions exist: (1) new outside directors are nominated by existing outside directors, (2) compensation is not materially important to the outside directors, and (3) management or the chief executive officer (CEO) does not have the dominant voice in the renomination of incumbent directors.[32] Thus, not only must the directors be independent, but the method of selecting them must be independent.

The idea of an independent *nominating committee* is another feature in the trend toward more outside directors. At Phillips Petroleum, for example, a recent settlement of a shareholder lawsuit calls for a nominating committee to be composed entirely of outside directors. Consequently, directors will no longer be handpicked by the chairman — a common procedure in the past and one that could make board members beholden to management.[33] Data recently gathered suggest this idea is becoming more popular. In a survey taken in late 1977, for example, it was found that 19 percent of 501 companies surveyed had board nominating committees. By contrast, surveys in the four preceding years indicated almost no companies with such committees. These committees are regarded as key tools for recruiting more independent directors.[34]

---

[30]"The Adversarial Board," *Wall Street Journal,* October 20, 1978, p. 22.
[31]Joann S. Lublin, "Outsiders In: Firms Add More Independent Directors but Find Doing So Can Mean Headaches," *Wall Street Journal,* May 26, 1978, p. 38.
[32]Marcus and Walters, p. 63.
[33]Calame and Morgenthaler, p. 25.
[34]Schorr, p. 1.

The outside independent director is not just an idea to improve corporate governance but, as the discussion to this point has implied, a reality in the corporate world today. As stated in a *Wall Street Journal* article, "Inside directors are on the way out, and more outside directors are on the way in."[35] Nearly two-thirds of the directors named in 1977 were not current management officers of companies. This compares with fewer than half in 1976. A private economist in New York speculates, "Within the next five years, the majority of American companies' boards will be composed of independent outside directors."[36]

The hope of those who are advocating the trend toward outside directors is that these unbiased individuals will act as guardians for both shareholders' and society's interests. It should be noted, however, that this will not occur without problems. One of the major difficulties is that, in some cases, these outsiders do not even know how to read a profit-and-loss statement or a balance sheet. One solution to this is to carefully screen those nominated. Regardless of such screening, however, the result can still be a group of outside directors who vary in their knowledge and competence.

To deal with this problem, some have suggested further education in corporate directorship. Victor Earle, for example, has quite seriously suggested a special school for directors. Such schools do not now exist, but Earle argues that they should be created at two or three major universities around the country.[37] They could be adjuncts to the business and law schools and be called, perhaps, Institutes of Corporate Governance. What would the directors do once they got there? First, they would acquire the vocational skills needed to do the job. Second, they would contribute to the incremental development, in a scholarly atmosphere, of a body of jurisprudence on corporate governance. The number of problems they could study is virtually unlimited, but a few worthy ones might be the following:

1. When and on what grounds does a board remove a CEO?
2. Can bribes, or submitting to extortion, ever be tolerated?
3. How much executive compensation is too much?
4. May a director — must a director — own stock in the corporation?
5. From what ranks should a new director for a particular corporation be drawn?
6. Is a nominating committee of outside directors essential to avoid self-perpetuating oligarchies?

[35]Lublin, p. 38.
[36]Ibid.
[37]Victor M. Earle III, "A Stop at School on the Way to the Boardroom," *Fortune,* July 2, 1979, pp. 102-103.

7. How does a board balance its desire to be a good corporate citizen with the desire of the shareholders for profits when the two interests appear to collide?[38]

Special Interest Directors

In addition to the movement toward more independent, outside directors, proposals for *special interest* or *constituency directors* have been made. One purpose of these proposals is to broaden the board's perspective by adding individuals with different backgrounds and experience. Another is to place representatives of various special interest groups on the board. This idea has not caught on nearly as much as the notion of outside, independent directors, however.

In addition to current trends to include a few women and members of minorities on a board, Ralph Nader has proposed that the board consist of nine directors, each of whom would have general duties plus oversight responsibilities for one of the following: employee welfare, consumer protection, environmental protection and community relations, shareholder rights, compliance with the law, profits and financial integrity, purchasing and marketing, management efficiency, and planning and research.[39] Other proposals have called for directors who are appointed by government, directors representing employees or labor organizations, and directors representing other nonshareholder constituencies.[40]

So far, most of the proposals for special interest directors have received only negligible support. This is because the notion of board members who primarily represent specific constituencies flies in the face of the tradition that directors should govern the corporation on behalf of its shareholders. Under the present system a director is accountable to the owners of the enterprise. Should this principle be abandoned, the ultimate consequence could be directors who are responsible to no one. Marcus and Walters place this issue in perspective with the following statement:

> It is one thing to believe that intelligent managers and boards should and will keep in mind the corporation's impact on society as they make their profit-oriented decisions; it is another thing to turn the board into a parliamentary body.[41]

To be sure, a number of corporate critics continue to argue that the

[38]Ibid., p. 102.
[39]Marcus and Walters, p. 64.
[40]Reginald H. Jones, "The Relations Between the Board of Directors and Operating Management," in Dill (ed.), 1978, p. 101.
[41]Marcus and Walters, p. 64.

concept of special interest directors is one whose time has come. The weight of the evidence and practical experience does not suggest, however, a widespread movement to adopt this idea.

As a variation of the special interest director, some people have made appeals for *public directors.* These individuals would be responsible for protecting the investing public and for representing the community at large. One interesting proposal has been made by Christopher Stone, who suggests that there be two kinds of public directors — general public directors and special public directors. *General public directors* would serve as "corporate consciences"; *special public directors,* with special expertise in significant areas (for example, occupational disease) would serve where a company had a problem serious enough and unique enough to warrant such an appointment.[42]

As a matter of corporate board reform, the idea of outside, independent directors has caught on significantly. By contrast, the notion of special interest directors has not caught on well at all. This is not to say, however, that companies have refused to change the composition of their board membership by adding individuals with special characteristics. Specifically, women and representatives of ethnic minorities have increased in number in recent years.

Though they constituted only a handful of directors in 1970, one study estimated there were 700 women directors in 1977.[43] More recent data are not available, but the trend toward more women directors continues. The actual status and power of women who are on boards are mixed. Frequently they are placed on "social responsibility" units rather than on the more vital committees of the board. In fact, one woman warned, as a result of her experiences: "One of the dangers of women on the corporate board is that, in putting them there, companies sometimes think they've done their thing for women — not so."[44]

Blacks, too, are becoming part of the accepted pattern of board membership. By 1975 more than seventy major American companies had elected blacks to their boards, and that number has increased each year since then.

In sum, the notion that American corporations should restructure their boards is not just a casual part of critics' proposals to reform corporate governance. Actual changes have been and are being made to move toward a governance approach that will correct the problems of the past and give more consideration to society's views in the future. The ulti-

---

[42]Christopher D. Stone, *Where the Law Ends* (New York: Harper and Row, Publishers, 1975), Chapters 15 and 16, pp. 152-183.

[43]"A Big Jump in the Ranks of Female Directors,"*Business Week,* January 10, 1977, pp. 49-50.

[44]"Female Directors on Corporate Boards Find the Experience Mixed," *Wall Street Journal,* April 5, 1977, p. 1.

mate objective is to ensure legitimacy, and corporations should be given credit for the accomplishments they have achieved.

ROLE OF SHAREHOLDERS

Just as there have been changes in recent years in the structure and operations of boards of directors, the role of shareholders has also changed. In a word, shareholders have become socially active — no longer willing to sit on the sidelines and quietly accept management and board decisions. This has been especially true with regard to social issues: illegal campaign contributions, corporate activity in South Africa, minority hiring, questionable payments to secure business, and so on.

Shareholders in the last six to ten years have become more socially active in a number of different ways, but primarily in the filing of shareholder resolutions, social activism at corporate annual meetings, demands for shareholder participation in decision making and governance, and shareholder lawsuits.

Shareholder Resolutions and Annual Meetings

The most visible efforts of shareholder groups in the last few years have been the filing of shareholder resolutions. To file such a resolution (e.g., "The company should discontinue business in South Africa"), a shareholder or shareholder group must obtain a stated number of signatures to require management to place the resolution on the proxy, where it could be voted on by all the shareholders.

Resolutions that are defeated (fail to get a majority vote) may be repeated the following year if they receive enough votes to meet the SEC's minimum voting requirements for such resubmission. To be placed on the proxy again, the SEC requires the proposal or resolution to receive 3 percent of the votes cast the first time it is voted on, 6 percent the second time, and at least 10 percent thereafter.[45] Additional SEC regulations govern the kind of issue the resolution can deal with, the form it must take, deadlines for submission, and procedures to be followed.[46]

[45]Peter B. Roche, "Taking Management to Task: Activist Shareholders Are Pushing Drive for More Disclosure About Firm's Ethics," *Wall Street Journal,* April 5, 1976, p. 26.
[46]Stan Crock, "SEC Tries Again on Shareholder Resolution Rules," *Wall Street Journal,* June 7, 1978, p. 24.

The groups behind these challenges are usually socially-oriented, exerting pressure to make the company in which they own stock more socially responsible. Though an individual could initiate a shareholder resolution, he or she probably would not have the resources or means to obtain the required signatures to have the resolution placed on the proxy. Thus, most resolutions are initiated by large institutional investors who own large blocks of stock, or by other activist groups who own a 'few shares of stock but have financial backing from some group. Foundations, religious groups, universities, and other such large shareholders are in an ideal position to initiate resolutions. [47] Religious groups, especially in recent years, have used the strategy of shareholder resolutions. Groups prominent in this endeavor include the Episcopal Church, United Church of Christ, Lutheran Church in America, United Methodists, United Presbyterian Church, and the American Jewish Congress.

The issues on which shareholder resolutions are filed vary widely, but they typically concern some aspect of the firm's social performance. In the aftermath of the revelations of illegal campaign contributions in the 1972 national elections, resolutions were filed on that issue. In 1979, the last year information was available, corporate investments and loans in South Africa was the primary issue in terms of number of shareholder resolutions submitted. Corporate pay, perquisites, and governance were close behind. The Three Mile Island nuclear accident in Pennsylvania is likely to generate heated discussions at annual meetings and be the subject of shareholder resolutions for some time.[48] Table 10-2 summarizes some of the major social issues on which shareholder resolutions were filed during the period 1975-1979.

Because most shareholder resolutions never pass, one might well ask why groups pursue them. The main reason is that they gain national publicity, and this is what the protesting group is out to achieve.

Increasingly, companies are negotiating with groups to settle issues before a resolution ever comes up for a vote. Several years ago, in a rare reversal of attitude, Exxon Corporation's managmement even recommended shareholders vote in favor of a resolution calling for the company to provide reams of data on its strip-mining operations. Exxon had agreed ahead of time to the request of the United Presbyterian Church and several Catholic groups which sponsored the resolution, but the groups wanted the resolution to go all the way to a vote and the company acquiesced. What happened at Exxon reflects subtle changes as

[47]"Religious Groups Act on South African Loans," *Atlanta Journal,* January 24, 1977, p. C-5.
    [48]Tom Herman, "Nuclear Power Issue May Spark Liveliest Annual Meetings Since Antiwar Protests,"*Wall Street Journal,* April 12, 1979, p. 6.

TABLE 10-2
Social Issues on Which Shareholder Resolutions Have Been Filed

Year	Issues
1975	Cease illegal campaign contributions Improve minority hiring Improve environmental protection
1976	Cease illegal/unethical campaign contributions More disclosure about firm's ethics Improve minority hiring Disclose information on operations in South Africa Stop marketing infant food formula in Third World countries TV networks should have ombudsmen
1977	Provide data on company strip mining operations Disclose political contributions Cease advertising on violent TV shows
1978	Curb American loans and investments in South Africa because of apartheid Executive perquisites (use of company jets, limousines, yachts, low-cost meals in executive dining room) Nepotism Marketing of infant formula in Third World countries causing malnutrition and disease
1979	Consumer safety advocates file shareholder resolutions against planned nuclear facilities Corporate investments and loans for South Africa Corporate pay, governance and perquisites Corporate directors missing more than 25 percent of their board and committee hearings Corporate-democracy reforms: allowing employees who are shareholders to cast secret ballots at annual meetings (to avoid reprisals from management) Boycott countries that violate human rights Questionable payments and political contributions

managements, increasingly sensitive to public criticism, are becoming more willing to sit down before annual meetings and work out agreements on shareholder resolutions.[49]

Closely related to the surge in shareholder resolutions has been the increased activism at corporate annual meetings in the last decade. In addition to the groups mentioned earlier, professional "corporate gadflies" purchase a small number of shares of a company's stock and then attend its annual meetings and put pressure on managers to ex-

[49]William D. Hartley, "More Concerns Willing to Enter Negotiations on Holder Resolutions," *Wall Street Journal,* March 23, 1977, p. 1.

"We will now entertain questions from stockholders."

SOURCE: Cartoon by Fred Schrier, *Industry Week,* May 9, 1979. Reprinted by permission.

plain themselves.[50] Typical of the kind of social activism that can occur during an annual meeting is the one several years ago in which GM shareholders sought explanations for a series of embarrassing controversies surrounding the automaker. Among the many questions asked of Thomas Murphy, chairman, some people wanted to know why the company substituted Chevrolet engines in cars sold by some of its other divisions, a move that infuriated many consumers who were not notifed of the changes.[51]

The motives for bringing up these issues at annual meetings are similar to those for shareholder resolutions: to put management "on the spot" and to publicly demand some explanation or corrective action. Activism at annual meetings is one of the few methods shareholders have to demand explanations and obtain accountability from top management. Being able to defend a company at annual meetings has become such an important task of top management that several years ago Haskins and Sells put together a booklet titled "Questions at Stockholders Meetings. . ."[52]

[50]Tom Walker, "Annual Meeting Time," *Atlanta Journal,* March 11, 1976, p. D-12.
[51]Leonard Apcar and Terry Brown, "GM Reputation Is Defended by Chairman Under Barrage of Shareholder Questions," *Wall Street Journal,* May 23, 1977, p. 17.
[52]"What Stockholders May Ask at Your Annual Meeting," *Nation's Business,* April 1977, p. 6.

Shareholder Participation

Another aspect of proposals for the reform of corporate governance revolves around the role of shareholder participation in decision making. An increasing number of discussions are taking place about "shareholder democracy." These concerns arise for the reasons cited earlier in the chapter — questions about management's power and accountability. Senator Howard M. Metzenbaum (D-Ohio) has asserted in this connection:

> The power in corporations now rests far too much with management and too little with shareholders.[53]

Metzenbaum, chairman of the Judiciary Subcommittee on Citizens' and Shareholders' Rights and Remedies, is part of a group that feels that corporate governance needs to be altered to ensure more shareholder input into corporate decision making. His group has been considering what should be included in a bill of federal minimum standards. One option would be to establish federal guidelines for electing some genuine shareholder representatives as board members. Whatever the ultimate resolution is, there is growing support of this view, and it should come as no surprise if such a bill is some day passed.

ROLE OF EMPLOYEES

Though employee involvement in corporate governance has not been discussed as actively as that of the board and shareholders, some critics have called for a larger role for employees in top-level decision making. This kind of role could be viewed as simply the logical extension of human relations efforts of the past several decades to get employees more involved in decision making, to appeal to their higher-order needs, or their needs for more enriched jobs.

To date, however, such an extension of employee participation into corporate governance has not met with resounding support. Proposals of those who would like to see more employee representation range from a few employee-directors on a board to the model of codetermination used in some European countries.

One form of codetermination is seen in the 1976 Codetermination Law passed by the West German parliament to decide whose interests large West German corporations would serve. According to this law, all major private corporations with more than 2,000 employees shall have

---

[53]Steve Lohr, "When Shareholders Should Have a Say," *Business Week,* April 17, 1978, p. 35.

supervisory boards composed of equal numbers of representatives of shareholders and employees. The German supervisory board (*Aufsichtsrat*) is roughly comparable to the American board of directors, except that top-level managers are excluded by law from the board of the company that employs them.[54]

Although the law has been in force for only a brief time, it has given rise to a controversy of serious proportions. Foreign investors have threatened to boycott West Germany. The West Germany Employers Association's challenge to the new law has reached the Federal Constitutional Court.[55] The intensity of the reaction suggests that anyone who thinks this might be the model of the future, to make private corporations more responsive to employee interests, would do well to analyze the West German experience carefully.

In the United States such notions as codetermination have tended to run counter to history and experience, which has been largely dictated by the role of labor unions. Traditionally, American unions have carefully distinguished between labor issues and management issues, and have stayed out of areas typically reserved for management, such as decision making. As a result, this tradition makes codetermination culturally awkward here.

Only a few extreme reformists to date have proposed radical changes in the role of employees in corporate governance. Despite our history and given recent trends, however, this could change and become one of the major new issues for the decade. Some increase in employee roles, moreover, will likely continue to be an element in proposals for corporate reform.

A CONCLUDING REMARK

Corporate legitimacy and corporate governance will continue to be important issues. Our pluralistic social system has had significant repercussions on how business is structured and operated. Pressures will continue to emanate from external sources, and these will likely be matched by pleas for accountability and reform by shareholders and employees. The net result will be that managers will be caught in the crossfire of debate and questioning, and will probably find their already difficult task of balancing various constituency interests more complex than it has been in the past. In addition, managers will probably face

[54]Hugh Neuburger, "Codetermination: The West German Experiment at a New Stage," *Columbia Journal of World Business,* Winter 1978, pp. 104-109.

[55]Ibid., p. 104. See also Herbert Northrup, "Partners in Management?" *Wall Street Journal,* June 12, 1978, p. 16.

slow but sure usurpation of their autonomy and power, and as a consequence the management profession will never be the same.

SUMMARY

Business must not only face the disenchantment of consumerists, environmentalists, and other vocal critics outside the corporation, it must also listen and be responsive to pleas for corporate reform coming from within. Not only are its products and practices being questioned, but its basic legitimacy and mode of governance are under attack. The most basic issue pertains to business's legitimacy. Organizations are legitimate to the extent that their activities are congruent with the goals and values of the social system within which they function. Questions are thus being raised as to whether business organizations have earned the right to continue existing in their current form.

As a result of this uncertainty, proposals have been made for the revision of corporate governance. For business to maintain its legitimacy, its governance must correspond to the will of the public. Four aspects of corporate governance which have been discussed are federal chartering of corporations, restructuring the board of directors, strengthening the role of shareholders, and strengthening the role of employees.

Pleas for improvements in business's relationships with public interest groups, shareholders, and employees will continue in the future. The result will be that managers will have to give increased attention to these groups and not be content to respond just to vocal critics from the outside. The very survival of the corporate form of business as we now know it is at stake.

QUESTIONS FOR DISCUSSION

1. Outline and describe the major elements of corporate organization. Discuss the elements in terms of a hierarchy of authority. What are some questions that are being raised with respect to each of these groups?

2. Explain the concept of business legitimacy. In what way is it related to corporate governance?

3. Do the issues of legitimacy and governance have any relevance to noncorporate forms of business organization (sole proprietorships and partnerships)? Discuss.

4. Does William Dill's statement that business "never had an over-whelmingly clear endorsement as a social institution" come as a surprise to you? Discuss this statement's validity.

5. Discuss the kinds of proposals that are being made as part of corporate governance reforms.

6. Describe federal chartering of corporations and outline its advantages and disadvantages. Do you favor the concept? Why?

7. What kinds of factors have contributed to the need to reform the board of directors? Enumerate and discuss.

8. Discuss audit committees, inside versus outside directors, independent and special interest directors as concepts for improving corporate governance.

9. Describe how shareholder resolutions work. What do their proponents hope to achieve with them? Why do companies settle some of them even before they come up for a vote?

10. Is it fair that a shareholder who owns just one or two shares of a company's stock can attend the company's annual meeting and create havoc for management and the board? What do you think of professional corporate gadflies?

11. How likely is it, in your view, that a concept such as codetermination could catch on in the United States? Under what circumstances might it become popular?

Cases

Shareholders Assert Themselves

A stockholder of R. H. Macy and Company recently proposed a resolution that would rescind the company's authorization to give charitable contributions. The resolution was introduced at the company's annual meeting by a woman who is a holder of twenty shares. The woman, a professional shareholder in many companies, said that the money that normally is given to charity should be given to the shareholders as dividends, allowing shareholders to give to their favorite charities rather than those favored by the Macy board of directors. In the last fiscal year Macy's gave $704,000 to charity.

When the votes were tallied, only about 6 percent (517,619 shares) favored banning corporate charitable contributions. Opposing the motion were 94 percent of the share votes cast.[1]

QUESTIONS

1. Normally when a shareholder resolution is submitted it is to force the company to be more socially responsible. The above represents the opposite of this pattern. What message do you read into the actual vote?
2. Should a shareholder of only twenty shares have the right to submit such a resolution?

SEC: "Protect Us from These Shareholder Suits"

In these times of "buyer beware," some corporations suffer. Shareholders (the buyers) are becoming increasingly interested in the operations of the corporations in which they own stock. More and more, shareholders are bringing suits against corporations for allegedly false or misleading statements about earning projections and other information in their annual reports.

Corporate officials have now turned to the SEC for help. They say that if the SEC could protect them in some way against stockholders' suits, they would overcome their fear of making earnings projections.

An Advisory Committee on Corporate Disclosure plans to recommend to the SEC that it adopt a rule to protect company managers from liability for earnings projections if they go wrong. The corporations do not want to stop profit projection reporting, but they do want to place the burden of proof on the shoulders of the person claiming that management was liable for a projection.

The advisory panel also recommended to the SEC that it not make earnings projection reports mandatory for corporations. The committee suggested that the decision as to the disclosure of earnings projections be left up to the management. The committee added that the SEC should, however, overhaul its policy statements concerning what to include about earnings projections in annual reports to encourage disclosure.

[1]From "Macy Shareholders Decide to Continue Donations to Charity," *The Wall Street Journal*, November 29, 1978, p. 4. Reprinted by permission of *The Wall Street Journal*, © Dow Jones & Company, Inc., 1978. All rights reserved.

QUESTIONS

1. In your opinion, do corporations have the right to ask SEC protection from stockholder suits?
2. Is a corporation acting in the interest of its shareholders by not disclosing projected earnings reports?
3. As a member of the Securities and Exchange Commission, what issues would you consider before making a decision concerning the advisory committee's recommendations?

The Annual Trial

Each year during the spring most American companies hold their annual meeting of shareholders. In recent years the meetings have been lively and vitriolic. Stockholders frequently ask company executives not only about profits and dividends, but also about foreign bribes, codes of ethics, and social responsibility concerns such as equal employment opportunities, sponsorship of violent TV shows, and pollution problems. To avoid embarassing and nasty questions, executives sometimes use one of the following strategies.

In the "open the meeting with good news" approach used by many companies, the annual meeting may begin with a report that a new discovery is going to help the firm to stay in very good financial shape. This usually brings the shareholders to their feet cheering, even if later in the meeting executives have to tell them about some company problems.

A second approach is to try the "wear 'em down" game plan. Also a very common approach used by many companies, this method consists of showing lengthy movies or slides, and presenting long analyses of the various company operations by division managers. By the time the executives are through, shareholders are too exhausted to ask any further questions.

The third method is called "promise them goodies." When the time arrives to respond to questions from the floor, some member of the board will tell the shareholders that they will receive a box of gift products at the end of the meeting. Or an executive may say that it's now time for questions even though we have the latest company movie to show you. If the questions go on too long, however, we won't have time to view the film.

If these approaches fail, executives have two other ways to answer embarassing or nasty questions: (1) the very quick answer, such as "No further comments," or (2) the "attack them back" approach, "We are doing our best working day and nights to survive!"[2]

QUESTIONS

1. Are the different methods discussed above ethical approaches to dealing with shareholders? Are there any circumstances in which they might be appropriate?
2. As a shareholder, how would you react if you attended a meeting in which these kinds of strategies were used? Do you think you would realize it was happening to you?
3. What do such approaches say to you about the nature of board-management-shareholder relationships, realizing full well that not all companies use such practices.

[2]This case was inspired by Earl C. Gottshalk, "The Annual Trial by Stockholders Is About to Begin," *The Wall Street Journal*, February 7, 1977. Reprinted by permission of *The Wall Street Journal*, © Dow Jones & Company, Inc., 1977. All rights reserved.

Part IV:
Managing Corporate
Social Performance

Basic Question

How should management respond to the external and internal issues and publics it faces?

Objectives of Part IV

To illustrate how social issues must be addressed from a managerial point of view

To relate planning, organizing, controlling, and communicating functions to the realm of corporate social performance

Chapters in Part IV

11. Corporate Social Policy and Management

12. Planning and Organizing for Social Response

13. Social Performance Measurement and Reporting

14. Communicating the Business Social Role

INTRODUCTION TO PART IV

Having acquired an understanding of fundamental issues and external and internal publics, it is now appropriate to turn our attention to the topic of managing corporate social performance. Because business needs to manage its social performance just as it does its economic and financial performance, managers must prepare themselves for shaping and articulating their social role in the future. Toward that end we discuss in Chapter 11 how corporate social policy is developed as part of a company's overall corporate strategy. In Chapter 12 we extend this discussion by considering how business plans and organizes for social response. Pertinent here are social forecasting and goal setting, and developing organizational structures for accommodating business's social response. We then address the managerial control function in Chapter 13 — the use of social audits and social performance reports to assist organizations in controlling and monitoring their social performance. Finally, in Chapter 14, which was contributed by James M. Lahiff, we cover the vital topic of communicating to its major publics the social role of business. This is a function that has been neglected but is essential to business's success in the future.

Corporate Social Policy and Management

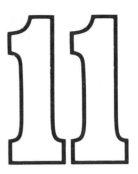

Understanding the various external and internal social issues that impinge on business is not enough. Nor is it enough to appreciate the evolution of business's changing social role, the notion of corporate social responsibility, and the intricacies of the complex business-government relationships. Though it is important — in fact, mandatory — to have such knowledge, it only provides a frame of reference for the formulation of corporate social policy and the implementation of corporate social action.

In this chapter and the next three, we undertake a closer examination of how management has responded and should respond, *in a managerial sense*, to the kinds of social issues we have been discussing up to this point. Though we have mentioned in previous chapters how business has responded with various programs and efforts, we now want to consider how the traditional processes of management have been affected by business's acceptance of the social environment as a legitimate influence in decision making.

In this chapter, attention is directed to how the concern for social responsibility and the social environment has become a management issue, and how managers have integrated social concerns into their concept of the organization and its functions. In other words, the chapter focuses on how social concern and responsiveness have become institutionalized by business, as discussed in the following topics:

- General management reorientations
- Corporate social policy: the macro view
- A corporate social performance model
- Social response process
- Corporate social policy: the micro view

GENERAL MANAGEMENT REORIENTATIONS

As a direct consequence of the current turbulent social environment and, in particular, the concern for the firm's social responsibilities, the "open system" is becoming an important characteristic of business organizations. An *open system* is one that exchanges information, energy, and material with its environment.[1] It is also one that affects and is affected by its environment. Of course, organizations always have been open systems; management just did not always view them as such.

The social turbulence organizations have been experiencing, especially throughout the 1970s and into the early 1980s, has forced corporate managers in the upper echelons to reorient their thinking toward the *systems point of view;* that is, they have been forced to think of their organizations as interdependent elements in a larger social system. The necessity for this reorientation is obvious when one thinks about the external pressures, forces, and expectations that have emanated from systems and subsystems external to the firm, especially government. This new reorientation is so pronounced that a *Business Week* magazine article not long ago referred to the chief executive officer of large firms as "Mr. Outside." (We might add that we are sure they were including the female gender in this reference.) The "outside" designation is, of course, the key point; it referred to the fact that top-level managers now spend more of their time dealing with groups, issues, pressures, and organizations outside rather than inside their various firms.

We are not saying that business has just discovered the environment in which it resides. Rather, we are pointing out the preoccupation with the social environment that has recently been demanded of managers. In fact, managers today could not operate their organizations as closed systems even if they wanted to. So many of the demands — especially those of government — necessitate some kind of business response. The question becomes, then: What will be the *nature* and *kind* of managerial response to the changing social environment?

As organizations and their management begin thinking about how they are going to respond to this question, the need for a conceptualization of corporate social policy becomes inevitable. Let us consider, therefore, what a corporate social policy is, and what role it assumes in management's overall thinking about its social performance.

---

[1]Fremont E. Kast and James E. Rosenzweig, "General Systems Theory: Applications for Organization and Management," *Academy of Management Journal,* December 1972, p. 450.

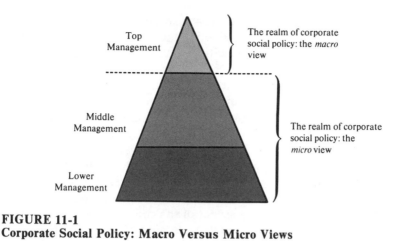

FIGURE 11-1
Corporate Social Policy: Macro Versus Micro Views

CORPORATE SOCIAL POLICY: THE MACRO VIEW

Along with the general management reorientation discussed above — a viewpoint which openly admits that social concerns are a facet of decision making that cannot be ignored — formulation of corporate social policy is also attracting the attention of top-level managers.[2] Such top-level policy formulation manifests management's philosophical position on an issue and represents one of the more mature responses to matters of managerial interest. Once an issue has been acknowledged to be an obligation (i.e., social responsibility) or to need a response, efforts are directed toward conceptualizing top management's overall posture and designing policy statements that reflect general management philosophy. Top management, then, becomes the design architect of corporate social policy.

Corporate social policy can be conceptualized at two levels. At the level of the organization's interface with its environment, where top-level strategic posturing is done, we have the *macro view*. That is our immediate concern in this section. Later in the chapter we treat the *micro view*. There we refer to specific decision-making guides that middle- and lower-level managers use as they attempt to integrate the social point of view into their daily decision making and operations. Figure 11-1 illustrates this distinction in terms of organizational levels.

[2]Archie B. Carroll, "Corporate Social Responsibility: Its Managerial Impact and Implications," *Journal of Business Research,* January 1974, pp. 75-88.

The macro perspective of corporate social policy, therefore, deals with how much consideration is given to the organization's social orientation as top management frames its overall strategic posture, of which social policy is one part.

The notion of corporate strategy refers to the top-level process of determining basic company purpose. Top management is concerned with the *business the firm is in* and the *kind of company* it chooses to be. At this level commitments are made as to the underlying character and identity of the organization. Since top management develops the company's basic character and identity — setting the tone for everyone else and for all decision making — it also has the responsibility for determining the degree to which social factors will be considered in company operations. It follows that one aspect of the company's overall strategy or strategic posture, therefore, is its statement of overall corporate social policy.

It is commonly accepted that there are three major phases in the process of developing corporate strategy: (1) strategy formulation or design, (2) strategy implementation, and (3) strategy evaluation.[3] In the first phase corporate social policy is designed and articulated. It is at this level — the level at which strategy is formulated — that macro social policy is set. In the second phase — strategy implementation — micro social policy is set and administered. Thus the basic nature of the relationship between the two types of social policy is revealed: macro social policy is established first and then micro social policy is derived from it. Figure 11-2 illustrates this relationship, and shows how the evaluation phase fits into the total scheme.

The most crucial step in the strategic process is strategy formulation or design. At this stage basic choices are made and consideration is given to the various factors that do and should impinge on the strategy decision. One way to look at corporate social policy — the macro view — is to consider it just *one* of the crucial elements or factors that goes into the organization's choice of strategy.

Several experts have taken the approach that strategy is a result of considering four factors that shape overall corporate policy:

1. The company's competencies and resources
2. Market opportunities
3. Personal values and aspirations of the management group
4. Acknowledged obligations to segments of society.[4]

---

[3]Daniel McCarthy, Robert Minichiello, and Joseph Curran, *Business Policy and Strategy: Concepts and Readings* (Homewood, Ill.: Richard D. Irwin, 1975), p. 52.

[4]C. Roland Christensen, Kenneth Andrews, and Joseph Bower, *Business Policy: Text and Cases,* 3rd ed. (Homewood, Ill.: Richard D. Irwin, 1973).

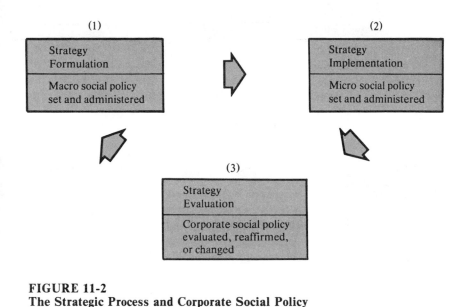

FIGURE 11-2
The Strategic Process and Corporate Social Policy

The first two factors are most fundamental; they determine what the organization can do and what the existing market opportunities are. The third factor is what the organization wants to do — or more specifically, what top management or ownership prefers as a statement of corporate strategy.

The fourth factor deals with corporate social policy. Because it refers to what management and the organization ought to do, it raises the question of how social responsibility meshes with, affects, and helps determine overall strategic choice. To some, the orderly, rational process of determining overall company direction and policy should not be subjected to such value-laden considerations as those bound to be represented by undertaking responsibilities that extend beyond legal obligations. There definitely are problems involved, hence the business person who cares about social policy must examine the impact on the public good of the policy alternatives he or she freely elected.[5] Figure 11-3 illustrates the four factors as they impinge on the strategy decision of the firm.

It is simple to draw a diagram as we have done in Figure 11-3. It is far more difficult to develop an overall business strategy that considers all the diverse factors that merit attention in the decision process. Conflicts

[5]Ibid., p. 578.

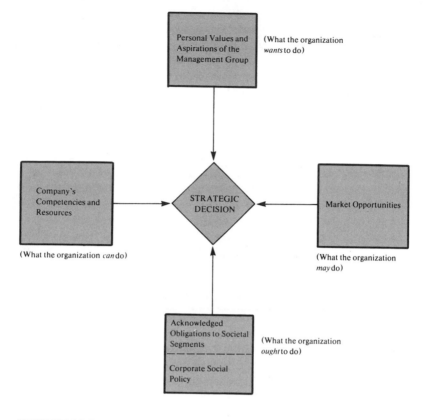

FIGURE 11-3
Factors Affecting Strategy: Role of Corporate Social Policy

are inevitable. Regardless, social trends have been established and top-level managers, if they are to be successful, must apply their knowledge of management to the social realm and devise corporate strategies which include corporate social policies that societal groups consider acceptable. Recall from our prior chapter that the very existence of business as we know it is at stake if managers fail in this pursuit.

There are at least three basic reasons why managers should examine the impact of policy decisions on the public good. First, professional managers today realize their legitimacy depends upon being responsive to the full range of their social responsibilities: economic, legal, ethical, and discretionary. Thus, a professional concern for legality, fairness, and decency has developed as a result of all that has come to be expected of managers by shareholders and the public. Second, there is the continuing and very real threat of added government regulation, which may be forthcoming if business behavior does not meet the standards that are being set for it by society. Third, it is becoming increasingly obvious that developing a sound corporate social policy just makes good managerial sense. The variables that now affect business success go far beyond the simple (by comparison) factors of the past.

Closely related to the third point is the question of business's success and, ultimately, its continued existence. At stake, then, are opportunities that, if properly addressed, could mean added success. Social issues and forces can and should have an impact on corporate strategy, at least in those cases where management is able and perceptive. George Sawyer suggests that as society changes, the resulting social forces should influence at least three types of near-term corporate strategic decisions: (1) marketplace decisions capitalizing on changing tastes and needs, (2) decisions based on protective reaction and, hopefully, on imaginative response to particular social issues, and (3) decisions anticipating fundamental change in our society.[6] Through responses of these types, modern businesses have the opportunity to "relate social issues to [their] ongoing flow of strategic decisions, and to benefit significantly as a result."[7]

In sum, though corporate social policy does not have a clearly accepted definition among management practitioners and among those who write about and study such issues,[8] it does deal with managerial philosophy, thinking, and commitment at the highest levels of the organization. The macro perspective assumes that once a social issue has been identified and acknowledged to be a social responsibility, efforts are initiated toward integrating this recognition into the firm's overall policy or strategy. Corporate social policy, therefore, embraces management's highest order of commitment to the pursuit of social goals as well as to economic goals. It mandates that management ask not just "What do we owe the shareholders?" but "What responsibilities do we have to consumers, environmentalists, minorities, government, employees, and other groups while we pursue profits?" To do less would not be in keeping with enlightened self-interest.

Figure 11-4 attempts to illustrate how social policy at the macro level is but one part of the organization's overall corporate strategy. As seen in the diagram, other major policies are developed too, but those are not of interest to us here. The corporate strategy, of course, was devel-

[6]George C. Sawyer, "Social Issues and Social Change: Impact on Strategic Decisions," *MSU Business Topics,* Summer 1973, pp. 15-20.
[7]Ibid., p. 19.
[8]George A. Steiner and John F. Steiner, "Social Policy as Business Policy," in Lee E. Preston (ed.), *Research in Corporate Social Performance and Policy,* vol. 1, (Greenwich, Conn.: JAI Press, 1978), pp. 201-221.

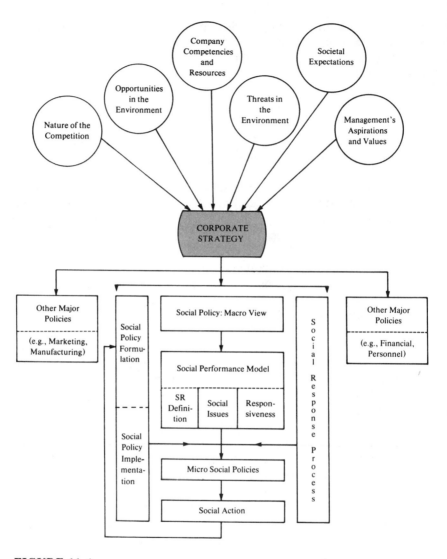

FIGURE 11-4
Corporate Strategy and Its Relation to the Social Policy Process

oped after considering a host of factors in the organization's environment.

The social performance model, which we will discuss next, helps management conceptualize, operationalize, and implement its social response process, which also encompasses social policy formulation and social policy implementation. Vital here, too, are the micro, or specific, social policies that are developed and stated to facilitate the organization's social actions. Results of these social actions then provide the basis for further refinements in social policy formulation.

A CORPORATE SOCIAL PERFORMANCE MODEL

As managers attempt to develop corporate social policy, they inevitably find a need to identify the major variables that might go into their conceptualization of what social performance entails. There are a number of different models or conceptualizations that might be chosen. The one we present here builds on the definition of social responsibility we presented in Chapter 2.[9] While any model or abstraction can only outline in broad dimensions the kinds of issues managers must face, it must provide us with an idea of the interrelated issues involved if it is to be useful.

There are at least three major factors that must be considered as management attempts to address corporate social issues:

1. A *basic definition* of social responsibility (Does our responsibility go beyond economic and legal concerns?)
2. An identification of the *issues* in which social responsibility exists and in which response is expected (what are all the social areas — environment, product safety, discrimination, etc. — in which we are expected to respond?)
3. A specification of the *philosophy and strategy of response* (Do we react or proact to the issues? Do we "fight all the way" or "lead the industry"?)

The Definition of Social Responsibility

There is no need to repeat our discussion of the first aspect of the four-part model as we defined it in Chapter 2. Recall, however, that social responsibility was defined there to include the economic, legal, ethical, and discretionary expectations placed on organizations by society.

The Social Issues Involved

In developing a conceptual framework for viewing corporate social performance, we not only have to specify the nature (economic, legal, ethi-

---

[9]The material in this section is taken from Archie B. Carroll, "A Three-Dimensional Conceptual Model of Corporate Social Performance," *Academy of Management Review,* September 1979, pp. 497-505.

cal, discretionary) of business's social responsibility, we also have to identify those social issues or topical areas in which these responsibilities are to be exercised.

No effort will be made here to discuss those social issues in which business must address its social responsibilities. The major problem is that the issues change and they also differ for companies in different industries. It is partially for this reason that the issues approach to examining business and society relationships was replaced by managerial approaches, as these were more concerned with developing generalized modes of response to all social issues that became significant to the firm.

One need not ponder at length the social issues that have evolved under the rubric of social responsibility to recognize how the issues have changed over time. Contemporary concern, for example, with product safety, occupational safety and health, and business ethics were not of major interest as recently as a decade ago. The same could be said about the degree of preoccupation with the environment, consumerism, and employment discrimination. Thus, the issues are continuously in a state of flux, especially the degree of organizational interest in the issues. As the times change, so does business's emphasis on the range of social issues it must address.

Particular social issues are also of more or less concern to firms depending on the industry in which they exist as well as other factors. A bank, for example, is not as pressed on environmental issues as a manufacturer. Likewise, a manufacturer is considerably more absorbed with the issue of recycling than an insurance company. Furthermore, companies within the same industry may also be impacted in different ways, and may adopt different social policies because of differing corporate strategies.

A multitude of factors come into play as a manager attempts to determine which social issues should be of most interest to the organization. A recent survey by Sandra Holmes illustrates this point quite well. In her queries to managers of large firms about the factors that assume a prominent role in selection of areas of social involvement by their firms, the top five factors were as follows:

1. Matching of a social need to corporate skill, need, or ability to help
2. Seriousness of social need
3. Interest of top executives
4. Public relations value of social action
5. Government pressure[10]

---

[10]Sandra L. Holmes, "Executive Perceptions of Corporate Social Responsibility," *Business Horizons,* June 1976, p. 37.

That these quite different factors should show up in response to a question of this kind suggests strongly that business executives do not have consensus on which social issues should be addressed, but rather, that their decisions take into consideration different factors or concerns.

Thus, we are left with a recognition that social issues must be identified as an important aspect of corporate social performance, but that there is no uniform agreement as to what these issues should be.

Philosophy of Responsiveness

The third aspect of our conceptual model addresses the philosophy, mode, or strategy of business (managerial) response to social responsibility and social issues. The term generally used to describe this dimension is social responsiveness.

Social responsiveness can range on a continuum from no response (do nothing) to a proactive response (do much). (The assumption is made here that business does have a social responsibility and that the prime focus is not on management accepting a moral obligation but on the degree and kind of managerial action.) In this connection, William Frederick recently articulated the responsivesness view, which he terms CSR_2, well:

> Corporate social responsiveness refers to the capacity of a corporation to respond to social pressures. The literal act of responding, or of achieving a generally responsive posture, to society is the focus ... One searches the organization for mechanisms, procedures, arrangements, and behavioral patterns that, taken collectively, would mark the organization as more or less capable of responding to social pressures.[11]

Several other writers have provided conceptual schemes that describe the responsiveness facet. Ian Wilson, for example, asserts that there are four posssible business strategies — those of reaction, defense, accommodation, and pro-action.[12] Terry McAdam has, likewise, described four social responsibility philosophies which mesh well with Wilson's and, indeed, describe the managerial approach that would characterize the range of the responsiveness dimension: "Fight all the way," "Do only what is required," "Be progressive," and "Lead the industry."[13] Davis and Blomstrom, too, describe alternative responses to societal

[11]William C. Frederick, "From CSR_1 to CSR_2: The Maturing of Business-and-Society Thought," (Graduate School of Business, University of Pittsburgh, 1978), Working Paper No. 279, p. 6.
[12]Ian Wilson, "What One Company Is Doing About Today's Demands on Business," in G. A. Steiner (ed.), *Changing Business-Society Interrelationships,* (UCLA, 1975).
[13]T. W. McAdam, "How to Put Corporate Responsibility into Practice," *Business and Society Review/Innovation,* Summer 1973, pp. 8-16.

Ian Wilson	Reaction		Defense	Accommodation	Proaction
Terry McAdam	Fight all the way		Do only what is required	Be progressive	Lead the industry
Davis and Blomstrom	Withdrawal	Public Relations Approach	Legal Approach	Bargaining	Problem Solving

DO NOTHING ◄────────────────────────────► DO MUCH

FIGURE 11-5
Social Responsiveness Categories

SOURCE: Archie B. Carroll, "A Three-Dimensional Conceptual Model of Corporate Social Performance," *Academy of Management Review,* vol. 4, no. 4, 1979, p. 502. Reprinted by permission.

pressures as follows: withdrawal, public relations approach, legal approach, bargaining, and problem-solving.[14] These correspond, essentially, with the above schemas. Figure 11-5 summarizes these three approaches on a responsiveness dimension.

The corporate social responsiveness dimension, then, which has been discussed by some as an alternate focus to that of social responsibility, is, in actuality, the action phase of management's responding in the social sphere. In a sense the responsiveness orientation enables organizations to rationalize and operationalize their social responsibilities without getting bogged down in the quagmire of definition problems, which can so easily occur if organizations try to get an exact determination of what their true responsibilities are before acting.

Figure 11-6 puts the three aspects together into a cubic conceptual social performance model.

Uses of the Model

The social performance conceptual model in Figure 11-6 is intended to be useful both to those who are studying the subject for academic purposes and to managers or prospective managers. For those studying the subject, the model is primarily helpful as an aid to distinguishing among different definitions of social responsibility that have appeared in the

[14]Keith Davis and Robert L. Blomstrom, *Business and Society: Environment and Responsibility,* 3rd ed. (New York: McGraw-Hill Book Company, 1975).

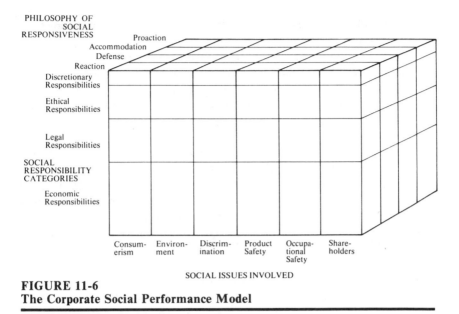

FIGURE 11-6
The Corporate Social Performance Model

SOURCE: Archie B. Carroll, "A Three-Dimensional Conceptual Model of Corporate Social Performance," *Academy of Management Review,* vol. 4, no. 4, 1979, p. 503. Reprinted by permission.

literature. What were previously regarded as separate definitions of social responsibility are suggested here to be three separate issues pertaining to corporate social performance.

One aspect pertains to what we include in our definition of social responsibility. Here we suggest that economic, legal, ethical, and discretionary components are involved in defining the entire range of responsibilities business has. The second aspect concerns the range of social issues (consumerism, environment, discrimination, etc.) management must address. Finally, a social responsiveness dimension was identified. Though some writers have suggested this as the preferred focus of social responsibility today, it is suggested here that responsiveness is but another additional aspect that must be addressed if corporate social performance is to be achieved. The three aspects of the model force us to think through the dominant questions that must be faced in analyzing social performance. Its major application to those studying the subject, therefore, is in systematizing the important issues that must be taught and understood in relation to the social responsibility concept. The model is not intended as the ultimate conceptualization. It is, however, a modest but necessary step toward understanding the major facets of social performance.

It is also intended that the conceptual model be useful to managers. It could assist the manager in understanding that social performance is not necessarily separate and distinct from economic performance but is just one part of business's total social responsibilities. The model integrates economic concerns into a social performance framework. In addition, it places ethical and discretionary expectations into an economic and legal framework that appears more rational.

From a policy standpoint the model can help the manager systematically think through major social issues that must be faced. Though it does not provide the answer to how far the organization must go, it does provide the conceptualization that could lead to a better managed social performance program. Moreover, it could be used as a planning tool and as a diagnostic problem-solving tool. The model can assist the manager by providing categories within which the organization can be situated or positioned.

An illustration will perhaps be helpful as an organization attempts to categorize what it has already done into the cubic space in Figure 11-6. Recently, Anheuser-Busch test marketed a new adult beverage called "Chelsea." Because the beverage had more alcoholic content than the average soft drink, consumer groups protested, calling the beverage "Kiddie beer" and claiming that the company was socially irresponsible in making a drink that would be available to youth. Anheuser-Busch's first reaction was defensive — attempting to claim that it was not dangerous and would not lead youngsters to stronger drink. The company's later posture was to withdraw the beverage from the marketplace and reformulate it so that it would be viewed as safe. The company concluded this was the socially responsible action to take, given the criticism.

If we conceptualize this example using the social performance model in Figure 11-6, the company found itself in the consumerism segment of the model. With respect to its total social responsibilities, the issue surfaced as an ethical issue. The product being introduced was strictly legal because it conformed to the maximum alcoholic content standard. As it became clear that so much protest might be turning an ethical issue into an economic one (as threats of product boycotts), the company moved on the responsiveness dimension from reaction and defense to accommodation.

Thus we can see by way of illustration how an actual business example can be positioned in the social performance model. The average business firm has many such controversial issues arising and could possibly use the conceptual model to analyze and evaluate its stance on these issues, and perhaps help diagnose its own motivations, actions, policies, and response strategies. Managers would thus have a systematic framework that would be helpful in thinking through the social issues they faced and the managerial response patterns contemplated.

The model could serve as a framework, too, to provide direction for criteria to be formulated in positioning the organization in the model on various social issues. These criteria, too, should be so formulated as to make sure that the organization's social policy is consistent with its overall corporate strategy. The net result might be more systematic attention being given to the whole realm of corporate social policy and performance and its relationship to corporate strategy.

THE SOCIAL RESPONSE PROCESS

The social response process might be viewed as a more detailed articulation of the social responsiveness aspect of the social performance model discussed above. Since the social responsiveness aspect embodied a concern for philosophy and mode of action, it can be viewed as a part of the process by which policy is converted into organizational action.

There are two types of social response (i.e., companies doing something in response to the social environment or social pressures), referred to by Neil Churchill as Type A and Type B patterns of action.[15] They are defined as follows:

> *Type A*   Socially related programs initiated in response to primarily external stimuli
>
> *Type B*   Socially related programs initiated in response to primarily internal stimuli

Type A corporations, in Churchill's research, typically initiated significant social activities in response to external pressures, such as a boycott of the company's products or intense public pressure. The Type A response was as follows:

$$\text{Pressure} \longrightarrow \text{Policy} \longrightarrow \text{Action Programs}$$

Type B companies were stimulated to examine their social activities from inside. The stimulus typically came from one of the top executives who was concerned with his organization and the social environment in which it existed. The Type B response was as follows:

$$\text{Investigation} \longrightarrow \text{Policy} \longrightarrow \text{Measurement} \longrightarrow \text{Action}$$

---

[15]Neil C. Churchill, "Toward a Theory for Social Accounting," *Sloan Management Review,* Spring 1974, pp. 1-17.

The initiative in these companies led to an investigation prior to the formulation of policy and then measurement (e.g., a partial inventory) prior to action. The Type B response seems more desirable on the face of it, and we would certainly advocate this *proactive* approach over the *reactive* Type A response. In actual experience, however, a thorough study would likely find more Type A companies, particularly if the study were made five to ten years ago. It is hard to speculate whether Type A or Type B would prevail today. The trend is definitely in the direction of the more planning-oriented Type B.

Whether the initiative came from within or without, the first major management effort the two types of responses have in common is that of policy. This helps us to understand and appreciate the emphasis on social policy developed early in the chapter then carried through the social performance model to where we are now — the social response process. We will use the social response process concept identified by Robert Ackerman, for his work in this area seems to be the most accepted. His research has lead to the conclusion that the social response process embraces three phases of organization involvement:

- Phase 1: A policy matter
- Phase 2: A technical problem
- Phase 3: A management problem[16]

Phase 1 — A Policy Matter

For effort to be triggered, top management must recognize the importance of a social issue. The rationalization may come as an admission of a social obligation or as simply a far-sighted self-interest. At this stage, the chief executive may begin to speak out on the issue at various public gatherings, become active along with others in studying the issue, and commit corporate resources to special experimental projects. After this the manager may perceive a need to do what managers frequently do: formulate a policy. After the policy is formulated efforts are made to articulate and communicate the policy to others in the organization. Policy having been formulated and disseminated, the mandate for further action now exists.

Phase 2 — A Technical Problem

The new phase begins when a staff executive is appointed to coordinate the company's efforts in the area of concern. The newly appointed

[16]Robert W. Ackerman, "How Companies Respond to Social Demands," *Harvard Business Review,* July-August 1973, pp. 88-98.

manager, frequently a specialist in the field, might carry a title such as Vice President for Urban Affairs, Director of Environmental Affairs, or Vice President for Minority Relations. This individual, the specialist, views the problem not as a policy matter but as a technical issue. The task here is to gather information on company operations in the social area, match these data with environmental demands, and generally do the staff work that is needed for the company to properly manage the new responsibility.

Research by Edwin Murray on the response process in commercial banks has led him to refine this second phase by speaking in terms of a Phase 2-A and Phase 2-B.[17] Phase 2-A is a *technical learning* phase in which emphasis is placed on the development of new knowledge and skills related to the social area (in his research, minority lending). Phase 2-B is concerned with *administrative learning.* Here the organization gains a better appreciation of the way in which policies, information and control systems, and reward systems relate to the implementation of company policies.

Phase 3 — A Management Problem

At this stage, the entire organization becomes involved and management, down to the lowest administrative level, becomes an active participant. The organization commits resources, designs monitoring systems, alters reward systems, and generally integrates the social goals into the organization's everyday operations. Cooperation on the part of operational managers is essential if the full institutionalization of social concern is to take place. Figure 11-7 summarizes this social response process.

It is easier to state and summarize this three-phase conversion of social responsiveness from policy to action than it is to address all the intricate issues that actually become involved in the process. Because space does not permit us to discuss these difficulties and how to avoid them, the following are a few guidelines for strategy:[18]

1. Do not overload the response process. Management cannot take on every issue that comes along, so it should give priority to those areas that are most likely to impact on the company's business.
2. Use specialists effectively. The specialist can become a multipurpose corporate change agent, but he could keep his hands in one issue too long. Managers must take over because the staff specialist's role should be temporary.

[17]Edwin A. Murray, Jr., "The Social Response Process in Commercial Banks: An Empirical Investigation," *Academy of Management Review,* July 1976, pp. 5-15.
[18]Ackerman, pp. 88-98.

ORGANIZATIONAL LEVEL	PHASES OF ORGANIZATION INVOLVEMENT		
	Phase 1	*Phase 2*	*Phase 3*
Chief Executive:	Issue: Corporate obligation ▷	Obtain knowledge ▷	Obtain organizational commitment ▷
	Action: Write and communicate policy ▷	Add staff specialists ▷	Change performance expectations ▷
	Outcome: Enriched purpose, increased awareness ▷		
Staff Specialists		Issue: Technical problem ▷	Provoke response from operating units ▷
		Action: Design data system and interpret environment ▷	Apply data system to performance measurement ▷
		Outcome: Technical and informational groundwork ▷	
Division Management			Issue: Management problem ▷
			Action: Commit resources and modify procedures ▷
			Outcome: Increased responsiveness ▷

FIGURE 11-7
Conversion of Social Responsiveness from Policy to Action

SOURCE: Reprinted by permission of the *Harvard Business Review.* Figure from "How Companies Respond to Social Demands," by Robert W. Ackerman (July-August 1973), p. 292. Copyright © 1973 by the President and Fellows of Harvard College; all rights reserved.

3. Formulate specific response strategies. Insist on a direct parallel between specific social response strategies and overall corporate strategy. Two benefits are that (a) the response becomes anticipatory and not merely reactive, and (b) the articulation provides the basis for future measurement and evaluation.

4. Make the evaluation process more sophisticated. If social performance is to be expected it must be integrated into the normal evaluation process for merit raises and promotions. This is difficult to do and one major result is that it complicates the evaluation process and

makes managerial judgment more difficult. Effective social performance will not occur, however, if it is not in some way recognized
and rewarded.[19]

Understanding the social response process is essential if management
is to effectively implement a concern for social issues. Though other
concepts of the process are available, the above is one of the most widely accepted.

CORPORATE SOCIAL POLICY:
THE MICRO VIEW

When we discussed the macro perspective of corporate social policy, we
said that *micro social policies were derived from the organization's larger
statement of social policy or strategy.* We have now traced how that larger
view of social policy has been translated into corporate action through
the development of a view of social performance and the social
response process.

The notion of micro social policies refers to *guides for decision making,*
which, as we illustrated in Figure 11-4, should help lead to corporate social action. Micro social policies are vehicles for helping operational
managers carry out the larger (macro) view of social policy held by the
firm. Social policies as we are viewing them here would likely have been
set at some middle-management staff level, perhaps during Phase 2 of
the corporate social response process. The purpose of such policies is to
channel managerial decision making and, hence, company action, in
desired directions. It would be hoped that such policies would provide
for a more rational, systematic, and uniform company social performance.

Some of the best examples of social policies have been provided by
George Steiner. Let us review a few of these and see how they might
lend a rational perspective to a company's social efforts.

> It is the policy of this company to concentrate action programs on
> limited objectives. No company can take significant action in every area
> of social responsibility. It can achieve more if it selects areas in which to
> concentrate its efforts.[20]

The theory behind this policy is that a company can do more good if it
identifies a few good social objectives and concentrates on those. The
alternative of pursuing many social objectives results in diluted effort

[19]Ackerman, pp. 88-98.
[20]George A. Steiner, "Social Policies for Business," *California Management Review,*
Winter 1972, pp. 17-24.

and limited or superficial success in each one. By limiting the objectives pursued, particularly those in the philanthropic category, the organization can achieve a unity of effort that otherwise is impossible.

> *It is the policy of this company to concentrate action programs on areas strategically related to the present and prospective economic functions of the business.*[21]

The position taken here is that if a company is going to pursue social objectives, it might as well pursue those that are also in its strategic economic best interest. Once again, this would relate most to the discretionary category of social responsibility. According to this policy, a bank would be more supportive of a United Way campaign that helps people in the community in which it exists, rather than the environmental group Friends of the Earth, which espouses causes more remote from the banking industry.

> *It is the policy of this company to begin action programs close at home before spreading out or acting in far distant regions.*[22]

Since many companies have severe financial constraints on what they do, this policy makes sense. It argues that companies should look to their own communities first in their selection of social programs. One illustration of this might be the large financial contributions the Coca-Cola Company makes to Emory University, both of which are located in the Atlanta area. Many large firms have sufficient resources that they can pursue national efforts, but this is frequently not the case.

> *It is the policy of this company to facilitate employee actions which can be taken as individuals rather than as representatives of the company.*[23]

This policy places a high premium on employees pursuing programs of their own choosing. Its position is that it is socially active or responsive to facilitate or accommodate employee efforts. In this connection, a number of companies have given employees time off with pay to serve on community benefit committees and have allowed managers to use company resources (e.g., secretarial time, reproduction facilities, postage) while pursuing social objectives.

There are many other policies that could be mentioned, but these illustrate well the point being made. Companies can add a degree of rationality and uniform effort if they are simply willing to take the time to do so. The result can be a social program that is strategically related to the economic interests of the firm, and one that is supported by sound managerial judgment as to the mutual interests of both the company

[21]Ibid., p. 23.
[22]Ibid.
[23]Ibid.

and the recipient groups. The view taken here is that management should apply its judgment and knowledge to the social realm just as it does in the economic realm. To do less is not to take advantage of managerial learning and experience, which has served business so well for so many years.

SUMMARY

As a result of the turbulent social environment, managers have become more sensitive to their social responsibilities and to social response programs. One major impact on managers has been their development of a more external orientation, causing them to think about possible ways in which they can apply their managerial knowledge and skills to the area of social performance.

One of the ways in which this has occurred has been the development of corporate social policy. As organizations enter the 1980s they are discovering that they must have a corporate position — a strategy, a policy — on the social environment they face. This social policy can be viewed in two ways — as macro social policy or micro social policy. At the macro level, social policy merges with corporate strategy as part of the firm's corporate image. Though the two merge in the organization's overall statement of corporate strategy, the social position the firm takes remains clearly identifiable.

Managers who are trying to make their larger view of social policy viable may find the corporate social performance model useful. It conceptualizes three significant issues managers must face — the definition or view of social responsibility, the categories in which this responsibility may be manifested, and the philosophy and mode of social responsiveness.

A further articulation of the social performance model requires a closer look at what is known as the social response process. Three phases are involved. First, the social issue becomes a policy matter for top management. Second, the onus is on the specialist. Third, the entire organization becomes involved in the institutionalization process.

Thus, specific managerial policies can be developed to add rationality and a unity of purpose to the company's efforts in the social area. If this is done, company efforts in both the economic and the social realm will be mutually supportive.

QUESTIONS FOR DISCUSSION

1. Describe the kind of reorientation that managers are having to undergo to deal with the social environment.

2. What is meant by corporate social policy? How does this relate to the notion of corporate strategy?

3. Distinguish between micro social policy and macro social policy. Which is most similar to corporate strategy?

4. What are the elements that comprise the corporate social performance model? Describe each carefully. Why is the model called a conceptual model? Of what value is it to managers?

5. Discuss the relationship between corporate social policy and the corporate social performance model.

6. What is the corporate social response process? Describe its phases. Does the modification of Phase 2 by Murray make sense? Discuss.

7. Discuss the relationship of the social performance model to the social response process.

8. In what sense are micro social policies derived from macro social policy? Give an example of a micro social policy.

9. Could micro social policies be of value to an individual who is attempting to lend rationality to his own social giving programs? Discuss.

Cases

They Did It All for Us

If you did not know it you'd never guess. There are no golden arches adorning this fully renovated nine-bedroom house in northeast Atlanta. From the street it appears to be the residence of a large family with a taste for keeping up their yard. In a sense the residents are a family — one bonded together by their children.

The Ronald McDonald House is home during the year for some 300 families who come from all over the Southeast to bring their children to the regional cancer diagnostic and treatment center of Emory Hospital and Egleston Children's Hospital. Many parents choose to remain close to their children during treatment, which may last from a week to a month. Before there was the House, which is in easy walking distance of the hospitals, parents and families stayed in local motels, slept in their children's hospital rooms, or slept in their cars. By themselves they faced the anxiety of serious childhood illness. While staying in the House, they find an atmosphere of mutual support, consideration, and exchange of information.

The House opened in 1979. Two years earlier, the Atlanta Area McDonald's Operators Association heard about the Ronald McDonald House program and learned that Atlanta needed such a facility. Local operators raised $42,000 in one summer week by donating the proceeds from their sales of banana shakes. After more promotional efforts the group raised their total contributions to over $100,000. Other groups in the community also helped. The Atlanta House became the fourth in the country, after those in Philadelphia, Chicago, and Denver.

QUESTIONS

1. Appraise, evaluate, and characterize the social policy of the McDonald operators who helped found this temporary residence.

2. Are the operators responding to economic, legal, ethical, or discretionary social responsibilities?

A Successful Business Social Response?

In 1978 an Yves Saint Laurent fragrance called Opium was introduced at a selling price of $100 an ounce. It was a sensual Oriental blend of essences with "slight animal notes." Very quickly opponents banded together in a Coalition Against Opium Perfume and Drug Abuse. The coalition, spearheaded by the Organization of Chinese-Americans, charged that the product's name and advertising romanticized narcotics and insulted Chinese people.

The coalition put pressure on the distributor and its parent company, the Squibb Corporation. They insisted the company change the product's name and the tone of the advertising. A boycott was threatened.

A vice president for Squibb said that the company's committee on social responsibility took two steps in response: (1) it modified the ads that were offensive, and (2) it hired a marketing research firm to find out how the public perceives the name.

The coalition thinks the company has missed the point. A spokesman argued that it is ridiculous for Squibb to think it can advertise the word Opium without it being drug-related. Further, they say there's no way it can avoid offending the Chinese. The coalition wants a new name for the product.[1]

[1]Based on "Opium Battle," *The New York Times*, June 10, 1979, p. 41. © 1979 by The New York Times Company. Reprinted by permission.

QUESTIONS

1. Analyze the company's response using the social performance model.
2. How should its social response have differed from what actually occurred?
3. Discuss this case from the standpoint of corporate social policy.

The PiBB Girl

To advertise its Mr. PiBB soft drink, Coca-Cola U.S.A. planned a promotional scheme designed to identify the "PiBB girl." The contest focused on a nationwide search for a girl who most closely resembled a composite picture of five white American actresses. The composite girl would have the eyes of Susan Anton (NBC's "Golden Girl"), the mouth of Debby Boone (the singer), the hair of Pam Dawber ("Mork and Mindy"), the face shape of Melissa Sue Anderson ("Little House on the Prairie"), and the nose of Kristy McNichol (Buddy on the TV series "Family").

The contest became controversial when a contest entry blank was seen by a principal of a black school in Chicago. His response was not surprising: "It is immediately apparent to any sensitive person that non-Anglo contestants need not apply."

Apparently some local Coca-Cola bottling officials were quicker to note the possible racial bias in the contest than the national company. The Atlanta bottlers, for example, decided not to take part in the promotional search even before the issue became a controversy. With the large proportion of blacks in the Atlanta area, they noted that a contest such as this would be like saying that half the women in Atlanta could not think about entering the contest. The Atlanta bottling company did decide to promote the contest in some of their less minority-populated areas, such as Macon and Dublin.

When officials at the national level heard of the criticism from the black principal in Chicago, they agreed to downplay the contest, but not to discontinue it. It apparently did not occur to them that the contest they had designed might have racial overtones.[2]

QUESTIONS

1. Do you think the contest had racial overtones, or do you think this is just a case of someone seeing racial implications where there are none?

[2]This case was inspired by Evan Kossoff, "Coke Bottlers Here Noticed Bias, Rejected PiBB Contest," *Atlanta Journal and Constitution*, April 20, 1980, p. 1-B. Used with permission.

2. What is your analysis of the Atlanta bottling company's response to this contest? What are the difficulties involved in one part of a company (e.g., the Atlanta bottlers) taking a different posture than the national company on an issue such as this one?
3. Has the company exhibited a Type A or Type B pattern in this case? (Refer to the chapter.)
4. What is your appraisal of the national company's social response upon hearing of the criticism of the promotional scheme? How would you, as management, respond differently?

Planning and Organizing for Social Response

As the social environment has become more turbulent, organizations have had to rely with increasing frequency on the application of traditional management methods and processes to cope with current social uncertainty. Uncertainty, of course, is relative; organizations of twenty or more years ago perhaps felt their environment was uncertain also. But as we have said throughout this book, the uncertainty that characterizes the modern business environment is unprecedented. In addition, we simply are more aware today of the degree of impact the social environment is having on organizations. We have also come to realize that the organization-environment interface is not completely unmanageable, but that we are capable of taking steps to be prepared for it.

Planning, organizing, and controlling are considered the most fundamental and important of the basic management functions. It should not be surprising, therefore, that we find it appropriate to structure part of our discussion of managing for social response around these functions. In the last chapter we dealt with corporate social policy, which is very much a planning process on a general scale. We felt that a discussion of that topic as a general management issue was desirable before discussing other aspects of planning in more detail.

Organizing, or the structuring of the firm to deal with social issues, is another crucial activity. The degree to which the organization accommodates social issues by altering its basic authority, responsibility, and reporting patterns signals its true degree of concern and maturity. It also indicates the extent to which it seriously views social issues as an integral and vital part of the organization's survival and success. This topic, too, will be discussed in the present chapter.

We are reserving the subject of controlling for discussion in the next chapter, which deals with corporate social performance reports. There we will see how difficult it is to separate planning from controlling, because the two concepts are so similar.

Our emphasis in this chapter will be on planning and organizing for business social response. We will pursue these two topics by discussing the following issues:

- An overview of the planning process
- The need for corporate social planning
- Social forecasting
- Social goal setting
- Organizing for social response

AN OVERVIEW OF THE PLANNING PROCESS

So much has been written about the planning process that it is difficult to know how far to go in an overview.[1] Our approach will be to keep it simple and introduce only in broad terms what is essential to our discussion of social response planning. To begin, we define *planning* as a process that entails an assessment of the organization, its resources, and its environment, and that encompasses the setting of objectives using the assessment as a backdrop. Planning requires looking at the past, the present, and the future. We often stress the futurity of planning to such an extent that we fail to make it clear that the past and the present are our points of departure. Using the past and the present as reference points, in planning we consider both (1) what we *anticipate* the future will be like, and (2) what we *desire* it to be like.[2]

We give consideration to anticipating what the future will be like in the forecasting process. *Forecasting* is that part of planning that embodies our estimates, projections, or speculations about what future conditions will be. These future conditions include the economic, the political, the technological, and the social environments in which we expect our organizations to reside next month, next year, and many years from now.

We give consideration to what we desire the future to be like in our view that by planning we may be able in some way to shape an environment that would be more desirable than the one that might result if left to the vagaries of societal forces. The process of "making a future happen" by active intervention now is known as *proactive* planning. Implicit in this concept is the belief that planning is a philosophy — a way of

---

[1]For a more lengthy discussion, see Chapter 5, "Planning and Controlling for Goal Accomplishment" in H. R. Smith, Archie B. Carroll, A. G. Kefalas, and Hugh J. Watson, *Management: Making Organizations Perform* (New York: Macmillan, 1980), pp. 149-187.
[2]Ibid.

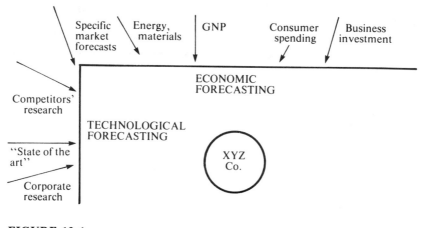

FIGURE 12-1
A Two-Sided Conceptualization of Planning

SOURCE: Ian H. Wilson, "Socio-Political Forecasting: A New Dimension to Strategic Planning," *Michigan Business Review,* July 1974, p. 163. Reprinted by permission.

thinking about managing. Indeed, planning is a philosophy of managing, only then becoming a set of steps to follow or techniques to use. One must fully internalize the spirit of planning before great success can be anticipated from the process of planning.[3]

In sum, planning is a vital managerial function that entails forecasting, goal setting, and other activities that make the organization better equipped to face the future. Though not much planning has been done with respect to the organization's social environment historically, this has changed in the past five to ten years.

THE NEED FOR CORPORATE SOCIAL PLANNING

The need for corporate social planning evolves from a concern with the growing turbulence of the social and political environments and the increasing extent to which a firm's performance in the social realm influences its legitimacy, its image, and ultimately its success.

There was a time when organizations were content to plan for the economic environment and to some extent the technological environment. This two-sided approach is seen in Figure 12-1. Today, however,

[3]Ibid.

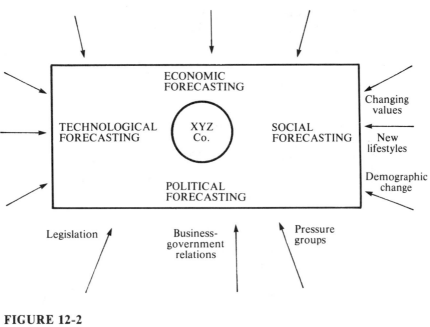

FIGURE 12-2
A Four-Sided Conceptualization of Planning

SOURCE: Ian H. Wilson, "Socio-Political Forecasting: A New Dimension to Strategic Planning," *Michigan Business Review,* July 1974, p. 164. Reprinted by permission.

concern must be given not only to these two factors but also to the social environment and the political environment. The two-sided planning conceptualization has, according to Ian Wilson, given way to the necessity of a "four-sided framework" for planning.[4] Figure 12-2 pictorially represents this more complete conceptualization.

Rapidly accelerating social and technological change carries within it the threat of obsolescence for organizations that do not adequately adapt to change. Adequate adaptation requires that the organization not only be prepared to respond once the change occurs, but also be prepared in advance of the change so that sufficient proaction can be accomplished.

Planning for the social environment is increasingly becoming the standard practice in large American corporations, according to a study done by Harry Lipson.[5] Furthermore, a number of advantages accrue to

---

[4]Ian H. Wilson, "Socio-Political Forecasting: A New Dimension to Strategic Planning," *Michigan Business Review,* July 1974. Reprinted in Archie B. Carroll (ed.), *Managing Corporate Social Responsibility* (Boston: Little, Brown and Co., 1977), pp. 159-169.

[5]Harry Lipson, "Do Corporate Executives Plan for Social Responsibility?" *Business and Society Review,* Winter 1974-1975.

those organizations that do engage in planning for the social environment. Among these advantages are the following:

1. It allows managers to *identify early* problems, threats, or opportunities which may exist in the environment.
2. It *improves decision making* by surfacing all the elements, factors, or forces which come to bear on a decision situation.
3. It *injects rationality*, analysis, system, and logic into activities and processes.
4. It provides a *focus on objectives* which should channel behaviors and decisions in directions which are agreed upon and communicated in advance.[6]

There is a dire need for planning for the social and political environments of business organizations today. No longer is the environment relatively placid. It is changing rapidly as fundamental assumptions which underlay most business decisions for years prove to be no longer acceptable. As a consequence, managers must generate new ways of looking at the environment and new approaches to forecasting what the future will bring. Figure 12-3 illustrates some of the many environmental impacts that affect company planning. An understanding of these impacts makes it clear why social forecasting and planning can be so difficult.

SOCIAL FORECASTING

We referred earlier to the crucial role of forecasting in the planning process. Of all aspects of the planning process, none is more vital in dealing with the social environment than forecasting. This is because forecasting provides the underlying premises on which strategic planning and other plans are based. Figure 12-4 illustrates how environmental forecasts relate to strategic and tactical planning in the business planning process.

We have already discussed the traditional roles of economic and technological forecasting in planning. We now want to focus on *social forecasting*, which some have called socio-political forecasting. We will use the former term, keeping in mind that many noneconomic and economic forces are intermixed in such forecasting efforts.

The definition of social forecasting proposed by Kenneth Newgren captures the essence of this relatively new approach:

[6]Smith, Carroll, Kefalas, and Watson, p. 152.

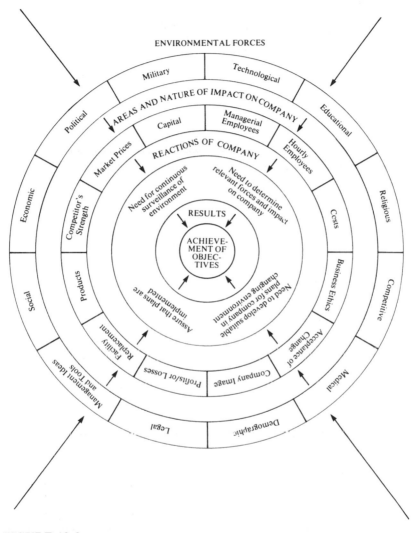

FIGURE 12-3
Environmental Impacts on Company Planning

FIGURE 12-4
The Business Planning Process

SOURCE: From Kenneth E. Newgren, "Social Forecasting: An Overview of Current Business Practices," in Archie B. Carroll (ed.), *Managing Corporate Social Responsibility,* © 1977 by Little, Brown and Company (Inc.), p. 171. Reprinted by permission.

> Social forecasting. . .is a systematic process for *identifying* social trends and their underlying attitudes, *analyzing* these social changes for their relevance to the organization, and *integrating* these findings with other forecasts to cover a time period of at least five, but preferably more, years (emphasis added).[7]

Expanding this definition slightly, it could be said that social forecasting consists of four phases: (1) *commitment* by top management to social forecasting, (2) *identification* of social trends and their underlying attitudes, (3) *analysis* of these social changes to determine their relevance to the organization, and (4) *integration* of the social forecast with other external forecasts.

Rather than social forecasting, other authorities have chosen to speak of environmental scanning as the activity or process in which managers plan to deal with environmental change.[8] *Environmental scanning* has been defined as the process that seeks "information about events and relationships in a company's outside environment, the knowledge of which would assist top management in its task of charting the company's future course of action."[9] As can be seen from the definitions, social forecasting is somewhat more precise in its focus than environmental scanning, but both terms are used frequently to refer to the same general activity.

Newgren found in his research that many companies engaged in no

---

[7] Kenneth E. Newgren, "Social Forecasting: An Overview of Current Business Practices," in Archie B. Carroll (ed.), *Managing Corporate Social Responsibility* (Boston: Little, Brown and Company, 1977), pp. 170-190.

[8] See, for example, Francis J. Aguilar, *Scanning the Business Environment* (New York: Macmillan, 1976).

[9] Ibid.

formal social forecasting, some engaged in formal identification (Phase 2) but no formal analysis (Phase 3), and some engaged in both formal identification and formal analysis of social trends. He was unable, however, to determine the degree to which companies integrated their social forecasts with other external forecasts.[10]

With respect to environmental scanning, Liam Fahey and William King found three scanning models to exist among twelve large businesses they questioned in depth. The three scanning models were: irregular, regular, and continuous.[11] The *irregular* model represented a process of ad hoc environmental study, which was likely occasioned by sóme unanticipated occurrence in the environment. An example would be the energy crisis or a new product introduced by a competitor. Thus, it was largely a reaction to a crisis. The *regular* scanning model was more comprehensive and systematic; it entailed a regular (usually annual) review of the environment or at least those components of it deemed important. This approach was typically decision- or issue-oriented. The *continuous* scanning model emphasized constant monitoring of various environmental systems — political, regulatory, competitive, and so on — rather than specific events. Its motivation and mode of operation were systems-oriented, in that regular organizations systems were used for both data processing and information utilization.[12] Quite obviously, the third model was the most sophisticated and required the highest degree of commitment to the planning process. Furthermore, most of the firms studied indicated they were moving toward more sophisticated forms of environmental scanning because of their belief in its importance. Table 12-1 summarizes the characteristics of the three scanning models.

Though systematic studies do not indicate that the large majority of business firms engage in social forecasting or environmental scanning as yet, the trends are clearly in that direction.

Techniques of Social Forecasting

All stages in the social forecasting process pose a challenge for managers. Perhaps the most difficult aspect, though, is that of identifying social trends and their underlying attitudes (Phase 2). In an effort to develop an appreciation of the various techniques that are available and have been used in this process, let us briefly review some of the most prominent ones.

[10]Newgren, p. 174.
[11]Liam Fahey and William R. King, "Environmental Scanning for Corporate Planning," *Business Horizons,* August 1977, p. 62.
[12]Ibid., pp. 62-63.

TABLE 12-1
Scanning Model Framework

| | SCANNING MODELS | | |
	Irregular	*Regular*	*Continuous*
Media for scanning activity	Ad hoc studies	Periodically updated studies	Structured data collection and processing systems
Scope of scanning	Specific events	Selected events	Broad range of environmental systems
Motivation for activity	Crisis initiated	Decision and issue oriented	Planning process oriented
Temporal nature of activity	Reactive	Proactive	Proactive
Time frame for data	Retrospective	Primarily current and retrospective	Prospective
Time frame for decision impact	Current and near-term future	Near-term	Long-term
Organizational makeup	Various staff agencies	Various staff agencies	Environmental scanning unit

SOURCE: Liam Fahey and William R. King, "Environmental Scanning for Corporate Planning," *Business Horizons,* August 1977, p. 63. Copyright, 1977, by the Foundation for the School of Business at Indiana University. Reprinted by permission.

Much of what has been done in developing techniques for social forecasting has been referred to by some as *futures research.* Though futures researchers claim their mission is not simply to predict the future, some of what they do comes in the form of predictions. According to Robert Lusch and Gene Laczniak, futures research typically pursues the following more modest objectives:

1. To make explicit the assumptions people hold about the future.
2. To anticipate alternative events or "futures."
3. To trace possible consequences of important current and past developments.
4. To shape and guide current strategies that might affect the future.[13]

[13]Robert F. Lusch and Gene R. Laczniak, "Futures Research for Managers," *Business,* January-February 1979, p. 41.

Whether they are called social forecasters, futurists, or soothsayers, these individuals hold the view that the future is at least partially controllable if it can be anticipated. Toward that end, they employ a variety of techniques, some of which are borrowed from economics, mathematics, statistics, and management. For purposes of discussion, let us use the classification scheme developed by Lusch and Laczniak. They argue that the basic methods of futures research (or social forecasting) can be grouped as follows: (1) authority methods, (2) conjecture methods, and (3) mathematical modeling. Figure 12-5 illustrates these three methods and some of the subclassifications that comprise them.

Authority Methods. One of the oldest techniques for assessing the future is eliciting the views of authorities. The Greeks had their oracles, rulers of the Middle Ages had their wizards, and various American and African tribes conferred with medicine men. And, of course, astrologers have been popular throughout recorded history.

There are basically two authority methods: the sole-source method and the polling method. The *sole-source method* entails the solicitation of the views of a single expert or authority. As an illustration, a supermarket chain may employ a leading marketing expert to draft a report on the future of food retailing. The expert uses his expertise and exist-

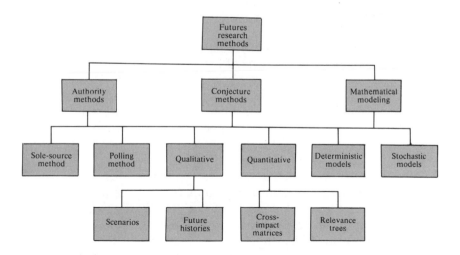

FIGURE 12-5
Futures Research Methods, or Techniques of Social Forecasting

SOURCE: Robert F. Lusch and Gene R. Laczniak, "Futures Research for Managers," *Business,* January-February 1979, p. 42. Reprinted by permission.

ing information to project developments in the macroenvironment that the retailer might face in the future.[14]

Companies may use the authority method by hiring a sole-source consultant as they need one, or they may choose to employ a social forecaster on a full-time basis to continuously scan the environment and forecast for them. Increasingly, these individuals are appearing on the organization charts of major corporations. The Gillette Company hired a futurist to be a part of the planning department and to contemplate what the social environment might be like in the years ahead. His first project was to put together a report outlining the pitfalls and prospects (threats and opportunities) for the company in the year 2000. He began by formulating a hypothesis: that the family structure by 2000 will be profoundly affected by the changing role of women. He read three newspapers each day and thirty to forty magazines and journals each month to pick up clues about the future. He then put trends into historical perspective and further tested his ideas by talking with colleagues. He posed such questions as: "Could one person's observation that few families eat meals together anymore mean that household items like fancy dishes won't be selling as well?"[15]

Polling methods of social forecasting are really just an extension of the sole-source method; they rely on a group of authorities or experts rather than just one. If several heads are better than one, this method has the advantage of not depending exclusively on one person's judgment. There are basically two polling methods: (1) the regular poll, in which a number of individuals are simply asked their opinion, and (2) the Delphi polling method.

Regular polls attempt to sample large groups to ascertain how they think or feel about an issue. One of the most well-known organizations that conducts such polls is Yankelovich, Skelly and White, Inc., a Madison Avenue public opinion and market research concern. Working for ninety-six sponsoring companies, including Procter and Gamble and GE, Yankelovich provides numbers for such seemingly nebulous social trends as "tolerance for chaos and disorder," "social pluralism," "living for today," and "focus on self."[16]

Each year Yankelovich's "Monitor" project asks 2,500 people nationwide about, for example, how important it is to plan in advance and how much they enjoy doing things on the spur of the moment. Another service of this research firm, one called "Corporate Priorities," examines how much the public and a cross-section of the leadership community really care about controlling air pollution, regulating busi-

[14]Ibid., p. 42.

[15]Liz Roman Gallese, "The Soothsayers: 'Futurists' to Discern What Is Lying Ahead," *Wall Street Journal*, March 31, 1975, p. 116.

[16]Roger Ricklefs, "Monitoring America," *Wall Street Journal*, October 2, 1978, p. 26.

ness, and other societal demands. One of the obvious values of such polling is to reveal to the sponsoring companies which social issues they must seriously address and which they can safely ignore.

As an illustration of the kind of social trend that can be identified by Monitor studies, consider the research firm's conclusion that we are becoming a more self-centered people. Once-accepted values such as sacrifice for children and general self-denial are declining, and the pursuit of individual pleasures and interests is rising, so it is not for nothing that a new magazine called *Self* is being published by *Vogue Magazine.* As the executive vice president of Yankelovich puts it, "We're now a country of 'what about me?'" Another senior vice president at the company says the social trend in general means consumers are "willing to spend on the 'me' items (from perfume to entertainment) but they look closer at the price-value relationship for the 'we' items (like family room furniture)." To obtain the detailed data on trends such as these, each Monitor sponsor pays $13,800 a year.[17]

Yankelovich's Corporate Priorities service is not as product-oriented as the Monitor studies; it attempts to measure attitudes toward thirty widely discussed public issues. Their studies find, for example, that pollution control, truth-in-advertising, fair treatment of the elderly, and privacy are deep-seated public concerns. While employee health and safety also has strong support, such issues as pressure for worker participation in management and corporate disclosure do not move the public very much. The sponsors of Corporate Priorities are mostly large, visible companies, such as Exxon, DuPont, Union Carbide, and GM.[18]

The regular polling method continues to be one of the most frequently used techniques of social forecasting. The data gathered provide management with a great deal of information about social trends and changes in values, and their probable impact on industries, companies, products, and ways of managing and doing business.

The other major polling technique is the Delphi method, developed at the Rand Corporation.[19] Though Delphi has not been used as often as the regular polling method, it is a fascinating technique for social forecasting purposes. Delphi is used to attain a consensus of opinion from a group of experts without having them confront one another in face-to-face debate, but still permitting them to know the opinions of the other experts involved.

The technique typically involves a group of experts independently

---

[17]Ibid.
[18]Ibid.
[19]See, for example, Norman Dalkey and Olaf Helmer, "An Experimental Application of the Delphi Method to the Use of Experts," *Management Sciences,* April 1963, pp. 458-467.

estimating the likelihood of some future events. The results are then tabulated and the experts are asked if they care to revise their estimates after having seen the opinions of the other experts. The procedure can then be repeated through several "rounds." Experiments have shown that over repeated trials the range of responses of the experts will decrease and that the group response, or median, will move in the direction of the "most likely" answer.[20]

Several years ago, four large companies — DuPont, Scott Paper, Lever Brothers, and Monsanto — had a preview of the 1980s through their sponsorship of Project Aware, a Delphi program run by the Institute for the Future. Each company paid $120,000 for the results of the three-year Delphi study.

The Delphi panel concluded that the quality of life was likely to decline as measured by such trends as urban decay, the depersonalization of daily activities, and distrust of major institutions. They also concluded that the energy crisis would probably be resolved by market forces as rising prices would change energy use and spur development of new energy sources. They predicted worker discontent would intensify despite improvements in working conditions and efforts to mechanize routine work.[21] Table 12-2 illustrates and summarizes some of the other predictions.

Conjecture Methods. Referring to Figure 12-5, it can be seen that conjecture methods constitute the second major grouping of social forecasting techniques or futures research methods. These are reasoned and systematic attempts to identify and characterize alternative futures that may have a bearing on a social forecast topic. In general, there are two types of conjecture methods, qualitative and quantitative. The *qualitative conjecture* is one in which the content cannot be measured or counted. Because these conjectures use words to describe, they are sometimes referred to as narrative methods. The two principal qualitative techniques are scenarios and future history construction.[22]

A *scenario* is a background narrative which describes an alternative future. It is a description of conditions at some future point in time. Thus, a scenario addressing technology in 1990 might posit a time of dramatic new developments, including some that might alleviate many of today's social problems. An alternative scenario might characterize

---

[20]Lusch and Laczniak, p. 43.
[21]"A Think Tank that Helps Companies Plan," *Business Week,* August 25, 1973, pp. 70-71.
[22]Lusch and Laczniak, p. 44.

TABLE 12-2
What's Likely to Happen by 1985

Event	Percent Probability
Many chemical pesticides phased out	95%
National health insurance enacted	90
Spending on environmental quality exceeds 6% of GNP	90
Insect hormones widely used as pesticides	80
Community review of factory locations	80
Substantial understanding of baldness and skin wrinkling	40
A modest (3%) value-added tax passed	40
Wide use of computers in elementary schools	25
Development of cold vaccines	20
Autos banned in central areas of at least seven cities	20
Breeder reactors banned for safety reasons	20

SOURCE: "A Think Tank that Helps Companies Plan," reprinted from p. 70 of the August 25, 1973, issue of *Business Week* by special permission, © 1973 by McGraw-Hill, Inc., New York, N.Y. 10020. All rights reserved.

1990 as a time when an antitechnology ethic prevailed and reduced innovation to a level below that of decades earlier.

Exhibit 12-1 illustrates a scenario that was used as a part of a Delphi panel. The scenario is primarily concerned with the future state of business-government relations.

The value of scenario construction is that it permits managers to become familiar with many alternative possibilities and helps prevent them from experiencing future shock by being caught totally unaware of what the future may be like. Lusch and Laczniak offer these guidelines to keep in mind when constructing scenarios:

1. Scenarios should be limited because the unbounded scenario is typically too broad to be of use. (For example, the scenario in Exhibit 12-1 was limited to the business-government relationship.)
2. Facts and assumptions which undergird the scenario should be closely scrutinzed.
3. Scenarios should be internally consistent.
4. The biases and prejudices of the scenario writer should be known.

When alternative future scenarios are constructed, they then give management several different conceptualizations of what the future may be like, and thus management is able to engage in contingency planning. Then, working back to the present time from the future sce-

EXHIBIT 12-1
Scenario X

The government/corporate relationship in the 1978-1987 period continued to develop along patterns established in previous decades, with no major discontinuities or radical surprises. The most far-reaching and substantial change occurred late in the period when Congress enlarged the planning authority of its budget office, setting five- and ten-year national manpower, natural resource, and other economic goals. This legislation primarily affected federal fiscal policies and contained no authority to compel action on the part of the private sector to meet the indicated goals.

Nevertheless, following the lead of West Germany, the federal government did offer some incentives to companies that acted to meet certain national objectives — for example, locating new industrial facilities in certain areas for social reasons (such as environmental or employment reasons). During the decade the government made a commitment to guaranteed jobs rather than guaranteed income.

In the environmental arena, economic incentives and penalties became the government's major tools for compliance. Effluent charges were established to internalize the costs of pollution. Other tax incentives and loans were made available to companies for the installation of pollution-control equipment. Congress also legislated a time limit for legal actions to block a construction project on environmental grounds.

In other regulatory areas, the government moved selectively, increasing requirements on some industries while reducing controls on others. For example, while moving to deregulate much of the air transport business, Congress at the same time passed a full-disclosure labeling act for prepared foods that requires the listing of all ingredients and the percentage of each ingredient. Congress also set a rule requiring that every proposal for new regulation be accompanied by a regulatory impact statement detailing the probable effects of the proposal on the economy.

Turning down proposals for federal chartering of corporations, Congress nevertheless acted to influence the internal governance of large corporations: it passed a full-disclosure law concerning most corporate activities and established a limit on the number of inside directors permitted to serve on the boards of directors. Legislation established due process and protection for whistle blowers (employees who report legal violations). The government placed stringent safeguards on corporate data banks containing information about employees and customers.

In the domain of social legislation affecting business, the minimum wage was indexed to the cost of living and Congress passed a comprehensive national health plan in which employers pay a significant portion.

SOURCE: Reprinted by permission of the *Harvard Business Review.* Exhibit from "What's Ahead for the Business-Government Relationship" by James O'Toole (March-April 1979), p. 100. Copyright © 1979 by the President and Fellows of Harvard College; all rights reserved.

narios, management can generate alternative courses of action it may choose to pursue if it becomes apparent one scenario or another is going to occur. Figure 12-6 pictorially represents this looking-forward-and-working-backward process.

Future history construction is the second type of qualitative conjecture. Unlike the scenario, it traces the course of events and developments over a time interval to explain how a set of circumstances developed out of preceding circumstances. For example, whereas a scenario might characterize the state of department store retailing in 1990, a future history might trace how computerized banking in 1975 led to a mass system of cashless transactions by 1985 and finally to an automated, cash-free department store in 1990.[23]

Two *quantitative conjecture* techniques are cross-impact matrices and relevance trees. The *cross-impact matrix* is used to assess the impact of

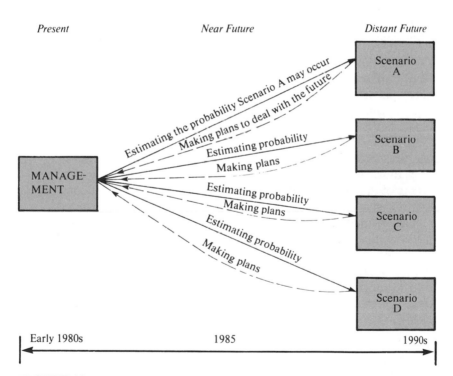

FIGURE 12-6
Management Facing Alternative Scenarios and Making Plans to Deal with Them

[23]Ibid., p. 44.

one event on the likelihood of occurrence of subsequent events.[24] The basic assumption is that the occurrence of one event will affect the likelihood of certain other events. The technique is interesting because it can be successfully used in conjunction with the Delphi technique, scenario construction, and future histories. As an illustration, a company may identify several new technologies it feels are likely by 1990. These events could then be entered as part of the matrix and analyzed in terms of which technologies most affect others.[25]

Relevance trees are constructed by establishing a possible future situation and identifying stage by stage the alternative means by which the event could be achieved. For example, suppose the United States decides on a goal of energy independence by 1985. To achieve this objective two alternative policies are established: increase energy supplies and reduce demand for energy. Several steps must then be identified to accomplish each of these alternative policies. Figure 12-7 illustrates a constructed relevance tree. Though not shown in this illustration, relevance values are assigned to the various alternatives. These are then mathematically manipulated to yield the set of actions that will most likely lead to the goal or desired event.[26]

Mathematical Model Building. Another type of futures research technique consists of mathematical modeling and equations. Using both *deterministic* models, where certain knowledge of the parameters of the model is assumed, and *stochastic* models, where the parameters of the model take on a series of possible values, the model builder constructs mathematical relationships that are assumed to portray other relationships found in the "real world."[27]

One of the most famous of the mathematical models ever constructed by futurists was by the Club of Rome. They set forth their work in a report entitled *The Limits to Growth.*[28] In that effort, a system of mathematical equations was constructed to represent the future. Portrayed in the study was the future of food production, global pollution, population growth, resource availability, and technological capacity. The model became quite renowned because under various assumptions it projected the collapse of the socioeconomic system by the year 2025.

[24]T. J. Gordon and H. Hayward, "Initial Experiments with the Cross-Impact Matrix Method of Forecasting," *Futures,* December 1968, pp. 110-116.
[25]Lusch and Laczniak, p. 45.
[26]Ibid., p. 46.
[27]Ibid.
[28]Dennis H. Meadows, et. al., *The Limits to Growth: A Report on the Club of Rome's Project on the Predicament of Mankind* (New York: Universe Books, 1972).

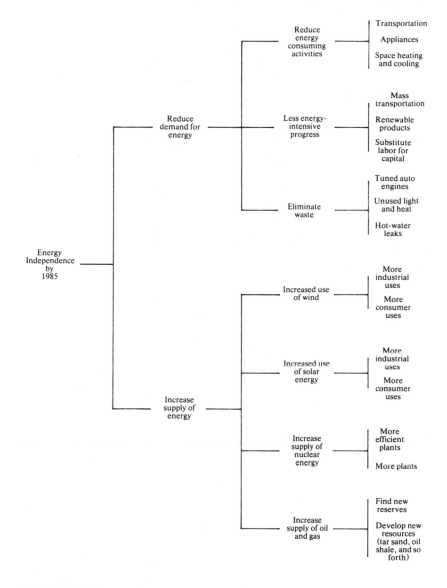

FIGURE 12-7
A Relevance Tree for Energy Independence

SOURCE: Robert F. Lusch and Gene R. Laczniak, "Futures Research for Managers," *Business,* January-February 1979, p. 47. Reprinted by permission.

Social Forecasting in Practice

The range of social forecasting techniques, as we have seen, is quite extensive, and we have by no means covered all the techniques available. With the sampling of major techniques provided, however, the reader should now have a fundamental grasp of what this aspect of planning for the social environment is all about.

It is not yet known how extensively business today engages in social forecasting. One of the best answers is offered by Kenneth Newgren, who gathered data from 183 large corporations in a national sample.[29] His purpose was to determine the extent to which businesses in the United States practice social forecasting and to ascertain the techniques they employ. Newgren found that only 34 percent of the companies studied had institutionalized their social forecasting efforts. He also found, however, that the vast majority of companies studied did anticipate initiating or expanding their social forecasting efforts within the next decade. Thus the practice of social forecasting is on the rise and appears to have a bright future.

In terms of techniques used in practice, Newgren found that the highly sophisticated approaches, such as relevance trees and network analysis, were used only infrequently. In general, the most frequently used techniques were those that were rather straightforward and simple. Newgren reported data for business firms (e.g., retailing, transportation, life insurance) and for industrial firms (e.g., electronic computing equipment, petroleum, electrical appliances/machinery) in terms of their usage of various techniques. Table 12-3 presents his survey findings by classification.

After studying various aspects of social forecasting in practice, Newgren also presented a social forecasting paradigm that embodied his empirical findings and was, therefore, an accurate description of the characteristics of social forecasting as it is done today. Table 12-4 presents this social forecasting paradigm.

As an approach to helping companies plan for the future, all the evidence indicates that social forecasting will continue to evolve. Though social forecasting is still in the early stages of its development, companies are striving to increase the frequency and quality of their efforts in its use. Eventually the social forecast will come to be viewed as a legitimate and essential input into strategic planning and policy formulation. The end result should be a comprehensive planning process based on more credible forecasts of the entire external environment, and this will be of benefit to both business and society.

[29]Newgren, pp. 170-190.

TABLE 12-3
Ranking of Techniques Used to Analyze Organizational Relevance by Industrial and Business Firms

INDUSTRIAL FIRMS	BUSINESS FIRMS	TOTAL
Rank/Technique	*Rank/Technique*	*Rank/Technique*
Most Frequent Use	**Most Frequent Use**	**Most Frequent Use**
1. Pooled opinion of executives	1. Pooled opinion of executives	1. Pooled Opinion of executives
2. Trend analysis	2. Industry sponsored activities	2. Trend analysis
3. Surveys of interest groups	3. Trend analysis	3. Industry sponsored activities
Occasional Use	**Occasional Use**	**Occasional Use**
4. Scenarios	4. Brainstorming	4. Brainstorming
5. Industry sponsored activities	5. Consultants	5. Surveys of interest groups
6. Consultants	6. Scenarios	6. Consultants
7. Brainstorming	7. Surveys of interest groups	7. Scenarios
Less Than Occasional Use	**Less Than Occasional Use**	**Less Than Occasional Use**
8. Cross-impact analysis	8. Cross-impact analysis	8. Cross-impact analysis
9. Delphi technique	9. Delphi technique	9. Delphi technique
10. Relevance trees	10. Relevance trees	10. Relevance trees

SOURCE: From Kenneth E. Newgren, "Social Forecasting: An Overview of Current Business Practices," in Archie B. Carroll (ed.), *Managing Corporate Social Responsibility,* © 1977 by Little, Brown and Company (Inc.), p. 184. Reprinted by permission.

TABLE 12-4
Revised Social Forecasting Paradigm Reflecting Empirical Findings

Phases	Time Horizon	Techniques	Personnel
Commitment to social forecasting	Analysis of social issues in both long and short run	Recognition of social relevance Allocation of resources	Chief Executive V.P. Corporate Planning
Identification of social trends and attitudes	10 years (consistent with other forecasts)	**External Sources** More frequent use: 　Public surveys 　Professional conferences 　Industry activities Occasional use: 　Consultants 　Company activities **Internal Techniques** At least two: 　Trend analysis 　Brainstorming 　Survey of executives	Corporate Planning Department (3 members) Top management assistance from 3-4 functional/staff departments

344

Analysis for relevance to the organization	8 years (consistent with other forecasts)	**Industry** More frequent use: Pooled opinion of execs. Trend analysis Interest group surveys Occasional use: Scenarios Industry activities[a] Consultants Brainstorming **Business** More frequent use: Pooled opinion of execs. Industry activities Trend analysis Occasional use: Brainstorming Consultants Scenarios Interest group surveys	Corporate Planning Department (3 members) Top management assistance from 3-4 functional/staff departments
Integration with other forecasts	8 years (consistent with other forecasts)	More frequent use: Scenarios Occasional use: Consultants reports Cross-impact analysis	Corporate Planning Department (3 members) Top management assistance from 3-4 functional/staff departments

[a]Used significantly more by business firms.

SOURCE: From Kenneth E. Newgren, "Social Forecasting: An Overview of Current Business Practices," in Archie B. Carroll (ed.), *Managing Corporate Social Responsibility,* © 1977 by Little, Brown and Company (Inc.), p. 189. Reprinted by permission.

SOCIAL GOAL SETTING

Once the social environment has been forecast and corporate social policy at the upper levels of management has been set, there remains the task of seeing that plans established at the top filter down into the organization and are eventually implemented. Quite frequently this is where the system breaks down: good intentions are not translated into specific goals which are then achieved.

It should be especially noted at this point that social goal setting is related to the corporate strategy and social policy process we discussed in the last chapter. In particular, the setting of social goals facilitates the social response process as we characterized it in Figure 11-4. Social goal setting may be seen as a specific managerial approach to ensuring that the organization's social performance is achieved.

Managers have admitted in recent years to their organizations' social responsibilities, but then have not used the management technology at their disposal to see that social goals are achieved. Indeed, specific social goals are seldom set. When goals are set they are frequently stated in such a broad, general fashion that no one really knows for sure what must be done to achieve them. This practice of not going beyond the aesthetic level of goal setting — the setting of broad, general, pleasing-to-the-eye type objectives — has also been a problem for years in other areas of business. For example, such goals as "to make the highest profit possible," "to sell the most we can," or "to achieve the lowest possible costs," seldom initiate specific action on the part of lower-level managers and personnel.[30]

To some degree managers have moved beyond the aesthetic level in these traditional business areas, but have not done so in the area of the firm's social performance. It is not altogether clear why management has chosen to remain at the level of aesthetic goals in the area of social performance, but the reasons might be: "Social responsibility is such a nebulous thing," or "Social issues are not our bread-and-butter concern."

In any event the problem is basically the unwillingness or inability of management to go beyond the level of aesthetic social objectives — objectives of the "window-dressing" variety with such platitudinous generalities as "to be a good corporate citizen," "to improve the level of ethics in our company," "to serve the community as best we can," and "to always operate with the public interest in mind." To be sure, these types of general statements are necessary for public relations pur-

---

[30]Much of the material in this section comes from Archie B. Carroll, "Setting Operational Goals for Corporate Social Responsibilty," *Long-Range Planning Journal,* April 1978, pp. 35-38.

poses and to convey management's social responsibility philosophy; however, if *goal accomplishment* is the objective, then management must move beyond aesthetic objectives.[31]

It is proposed here that management decision makers can learn much from the theory and practice of MBO (Management by Objectives), which has evolved and become more sophisticated in recent years. A number of guidelines on operationalizing goals have been established in areas where MBO may be applicable. S. J. Carroll and H. L. Tosi, for example, suggest that "one purpose of MBO is to facilitate the derivation of specific objectives from general ones. . ."[32] Indeed, this is what *operationalizing* goals or objectives means — converting general (aesthetic) objectives into specific ones for which goal attainment is readily identifiable and accomplishable.

A number of guidelines for the operationalization of objectives are available. We recommend using these guidelines to develop specific statements of social goals for the business firm. In applying these guidelines to objective writing, for instance, Carroll and Tosi suggest that the objective statement be (1) clear, concise, and unambiguous; and (2) accurate in terms of the true end state or condition sought.[33]

Dale McConkey, writing on this same subject, suggests that objectives should be "specific," "specify results to be achieved" (as opposed to activities engaged in), and should be "realistic and attainable."[34] One way of making an objective realistic and attainable, asserts McConkey, is to make sure it contains "stretch." This means that the objective "should be set at a level of difficulty and achievement that requires managers to exert more than normal effort or a business-as-usual approach."[35]

Further guidelines for operationalizing objectives are recommended by George Morrissey, who argues that a well-written objective should:

1. start with the word 'to,' followed by an action verb;
2. specify a single key result to be accomplished;
3. specify a target date by which the accomplishment is expected;
4. specify maximum cost factors involved; and
5. be as specific and quantitative (and hence measurable and verifiable) as possible.[36]

[31]Ibid., p. 36.
[32]S. J. Carroll, Jr. and H. L. Tosi, Jr., *Management by Objectives: Applications and Research* (New York: Macmillan, 1973), pp. 69-70.
[33]Ibid., p. 72.
[34]Dale D. McConkey, *MBO for Nonprofit Organizations* (New York: AMACOM, 1975), pp. 56-57.
[35]Ibid., p. 57.
[36]George L. Morrisey, *Management by Objectives and Results* (Reading, Mass.: Addison-Wesley Publishing Co., 1970), pp. 52-54.

In effect, then, it is suggested that the aesthetic social objectives that so frequently characterize social goal setting in business organizations be fashioned after the guidelines that have emerged during the last five to ten years' experience of MBO. Though MBO objectives typically are written *by* individual managers *for* individual managers, there is no valid reason why this same procedure cannot be used in operationalizing social goals.

Illustrations of Operational Social Goals

Illustrations from a number of different social performance areas can demonstrate how aesthetic objectives may be converted to specific objectives so that goals can be operationalized according to the guidelines discussed above. The objectives discussed are simply examples of some that could be used to fulfill the social response process we discussed in Chapter 11. These objectives relate to community affairs, environment and energy, and philanthropy. Though the objectives may not in every case conform to every guideline, they generally conform to the guidelines previously discussed.

- *Aesthetic Objective*: To be a good community citizen by supporting community projects.
  Operational Objectives: (a) To begin a program on improved race relations by holding the first community meeting at company headquarters on June 15, 1980, with an initial dollar support of whatever costs are necessary to fund the meeting, up to $1,000. (b) To provide ten hours a week released time for each of two executives to serve on the community's Committee on Crime Prevention for two years at a cost of $18,000 to the company. (c) To underwrite the $5,000 cost of the annual Christmas concert for 1980 put on by the Boy's Club of Athens. (d) To participate in the YWCO-sponsored day-care program by permitting their officials to disseminate promotional literature through the company's internal mail system during the months of August and February each year for the next three years.[37]
- *Aesthetic Objective*: To protect the environment and promote energy conservation.
  Operational Objectives: (a) To require that all new machinery purchased after January 1, 1981, meet all requirements laid down by the EPA for antipollution standards and energy usage. (b) To develop a formal company policy on environmental protection and energy conservation by July 15, 1982.[38]

[37]Carroll, *Long-Range Planning Journal,* p. 36.
[38]Ibid., p. 37.

- *Aesthetic Objective*: To support worthwhile organizations by contributing money to their causes.
  Operational Objectives: (a) To increase our pledge to the Urban League by 15 percent over last year's contribution. (b) To donate to education, including both secondary and higher education, 1 percent of the company's net profits for fiscal year 1981-1982. (c) To match with company funds all donations by company employees to such federated drives as the United Fund and Community Chest during the 1981 calendar year.[39]

If a social goal-setting process such as this is effectively implemented, a number of positive consequences are likely to follow. First, the integrity of the planning process is established because the process is made meaningful and functional with specific, identifiable end results. Second, improved social performance programs will result. Third, success will reinforce future efforts in the social arena. Fourth, specific goal attainment will facilitate appraisal of personnel. And, fifth, the approach will provide enhanced credibility with the organization's multiple publics.[40]

The notion of more formality in social performance planning efforts is an extremely pertinent one in today's conditions. Whether it be social forecasting or social goal setting, management will find that efforts to improve planning for the social environment will enhance the organization's quality of social and economic performance. Furthermore, a planning approach as described here will provide prima facie evidence that management is sincerely interested in providing a social response rather than debating endlessly whether it has a social responsibility or simply attempting to assuage its conscience.

ORGANIZING FOR SOCIAL RESPONSE

Just as planning for business social response is an important managerial activity, organizing is essential too. By *organizing* we refer to those decisions which set the basic pattern of structure for the organization and the establishment of its basic relationships, which includes the determination of who will have what responsibilities, to whom individuals will report, and what will be the channels of authority, responsibility, and communication.

Very early on, managers found that they had to have particular units to carry out certain responsibilities and that through the development of

[39]Ibid.
[40]Ibid.

departments and levels of management they were able to create administrative structures that could achieve the organization's objectives. They found, too, that there was no ideal organization structure — or pattern of relationships among people in the organization — and that, indeed, there was some freedom of choice as to how the organization should be arranged to deal with the many tasks it had to accomplish.[41]

As managers have become more serious about responding to social pressures and the social environment, a variety of approaches have emerged by which the organization can institutionalize its way of dealing with environmental issues and social change. In general, the different methods used range from very informal to very formal. Dow Votaw has characterized the nature of organizational adaptation to social pressures as evolving through three stages — token behavior, attitudinal changes, and substantive changes. In a very real sense this evolution depicts what has happened in the realm of organizational responses to social concerns.

An examination of five approaches companies use to organize their social responsiveness efforts shows the basic choices that are available. The five possible approaches are (1) the officer, (2) the task force, (3) the permanent board committee, (4) the permanent management committee, and (5) the permanent organization group.[42]

Officer

The corporate social responsibility officer is typically an executive who has been assigned the task of handling the company's social responsibility program. In research conducted in the early 1970s, Henry Eilbirt and Robert Parket found the position to be a relatively new one on organization charts. Their research disclosed that of the fifty-two such positions reported among the companies they surveyed, only nine (17 percent) were in existence prior to 1965.[43] Though their survey revealed that over half of the social responsibility officers reported to the president or a vice president, there were a good number who reported to lower-level managers. It is difficult to generalize, therefore, as to the status that these individuals held.

[41]H. R. Smith, Archie B. Carroll, A. G. Kefalas, and Hugh J. Watson, *Management: Making Organizations Perform* (New York: Macmillan, 1980), Chapter 6, pp. 182-222.

[42]Terry W. McAdam, "How to Put Corporate Responsibility into Practice," *Business and Society Review/Innovation,* Summer 1973, pp. 8-16.

[43]Henry Eilbirt and I. Robert Parket, "The Corporate Responsibility Officer," *Business Horizons,* February 1973, pp. 45-51.

Task Force

In a task force a number of different persons in the organization are brought together, usually to deal with a crisis-oriented social issue. The task force has less permanence than a committee, and therefore suffers from lack of continuity and an inability to deal with issues within a medium- or long-range planning framework. Though the task force is a good way to get an activity started quickly, it usually suffers from the limitation of not being able to implement changes in operating practices because few formal lines of communication exist between it and top management. Task force members are usually part-time participants because they are regular members of management or staff, with other responsibilities and duties.[44]

Permanent Board Committee

A permanent committee of members of the board of directors has the primary advantage of status and authority. At this level the organization has visibility of its efforts and high-level support for its actions. In other words, the committee has influence because of its position in the organization hierarchy. For this approach to be effective the committee must have adequate staff and have access to information generated elsewhere in the organization, on which to base its decisions and policy making. Just because a board committee exists, it does not preclude the establishment of some additional position, committee, or mechanism somewhere among the lower managerial ranks. One of the major problems the board committee may face is the heavy time demands already placed on its members.

Permanent Management Committee

Many of the characteristics of the board committee apply to the management committee as well, including the need for an adequate staff. The management committee is probably in a better position to know what information is available than those at the board level. It would also have a greater sensitivity to implementation considerations of various policies that might be adopted. One of the principal drawbacks to the management committee may be its inability to be as objective as a board committee.[45]

A slight variation to board and management committees would be one that includes both line and staff officers of the company with

[44]McAdam, p. 15.
[45]Ibid., p. 15.

perhaps several members of the board as minority members. This arrangement could have the added flexibility of including outside members from community groups or academic faculties. A major difficulty with a group like this could be that it becomes more consultative than operational in nature.[46]

Permanent Organization Group

One of the most advanced organizational responses to the social environment is to have a permanent department or group which is continuously engaged in monitoring, analyzing, planning for, and responding to social responsibility issues. Using Votaw's terms, this would represent not just token or attitudinal changes but substantive ones.

Many benefits could flow from a permanent department or group that has as its primary reason for existence the management of social affairs. First, the separate department would allow for *specialization.* No longer would it be necessary to burden already busy line or staff managers with extra duties they do not consider central to their own success. Second, the group or department could *centralize* environmental monitoring, appraisal, policy making, and action. Thus, the group could integrate the many social concerns that are impinging on the organization. Such coordination also has the advantage of organizational learning being transferred from the experience of one social issue to others. Third, *communication* could be enhanced. A group such as this can construct and nurture stronger communication lines. By way of continuous feedback it can keep managers alerted to issues and ensure continuity of analytic efforts.

For these kinds of benefits to accrue, the organizational unit must report to top management and have support and credibility at high levels. Only top management can ultimately ensure that this will be the case. Therefore, the permanent organizational department is contingent on top-level support for survival and success.

The permanent group will typically show up on the company's organization chart. It may be quite inclusive or comprehensive as to social concerns addressed, or quite differentiated into organizational units specializing in separate social issues. An inclusive group might be something like the Department of Social Affairs envisioned by Mazis and Green.[47] Such a department, with top management commitment

---

[46]Courtney C. Brown, "Organizing for Socially Responsible Management," in Melvin Anshen (ed.), *Managing the Socially Responsible Corporation* (New York: Macmillan, 1974), pp. 23-40.

[47]Michael Mazis and Robert Green, "Implementing Social Responsibility," *MSU Business Topics,* Winter 1971, pp. 68-76.

and support, would function on the corporate level. It would assist operating divisions and departments in the formulation of plans to implement social responsibility programs. With the corporate view, the department would be able to assess company resources and market opportunities and design programs to maximize both economic and social contributions. The department would act in basically a staff capacity and would encourage other departments to set specific goals and coordinate social programs in such a manner that all units in the firm would function together to achieve social objectives. As the department found it necessary, it might specialize into units dealing with environmental affairs, consumer affairs, urban affairs, and so on. In sum, the department would provide a high-level, integrative, coordinated unit that would facilitate a planned approach to managing social issues confronting the firm. Figure 12-8 illustrates the flow of social information within the firm, and Figure 12-9 illustrates the informational interfaces that may be expected when a Department of Social Affairs exists in a company.

Opposite the centralized social affairs department are organizational units that deal with social issues on a more specialized basis. For example, here we might find individual units appearing on the organization chart that deal with equal employment opportunity, environmental affairs, corporate contributions, urban and minority affairs, and so on. These, too, are permanent organization groups, but they do not entail the same degree of centralization of function as does the Department of Social Affairs. Figure 12-10 illustrates a partial organization chart of Atlantic Richfield Company. It indicates a number of different social functions being represented in various locations.

Organizational Patterns in Use

There does not appear to be one best way to organize structurally to deal with social responsibility programs and social environmental issues. We have seen a number of different approaches, all of which are in use today. The specific pattern a company chooses will depend on a number of factors, some of which include industry characteristics (e.g., the nature of technology and interface with the public), size of the firm, industry preferences or patterns,[48] social issues involved, and management philosophy.

In a survey taken to ascertain how companies organize to deal with social issues, Sandra Holmes found that organizational patterns varied somewhat depending on asset size, number of employees, and

[48]Sandra L. Holmes, "Adapting Corporate Structure for Social Responsiveness," *California Management Review,* Fall 1978, pp. 52-53.

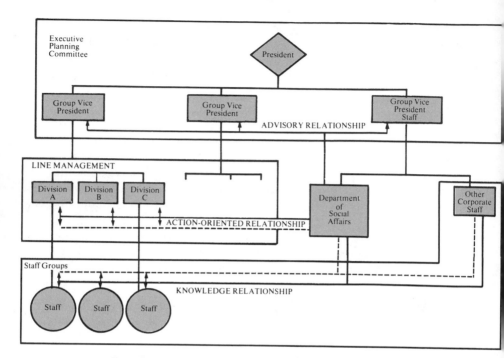

INTERFACES OF DEPARTMENT OF SOCIAL AFFAIRS

Advisory Relationship—Top Executive Committee

Input from Department of Social Affairs:
—recommendations of social objectives and goals
—evaluations of social consequences of corporate actions
—information on social affairs
—report on firm's social performance

Action-Oriented Relationship—Line Groups (day-to-day working relationship)

Input from Department of Social Affairs:
—information on social affairs
—social audit
—assistance in information to formulate programs to meet social goals
—aid in design of programs to monitor social aspects of operations (consumer review board, ecological testing, pollution control, community participation)

Output to Department of Social Affairs:
—dissemination of programs to department
—social performance plans

Knowledge Relationship—Staff Groups (two-way flow of information)

Input from Department of Social Affairs:
—information on social affairs
—advice to staff groups on desirable social actions

Output to Department of Social Affairs:
—notification of department about staff efforts which could affect social affairs
—dissemination of information which may have social consequences
—performance of special projects (market research, financial analysis, and so forth) for department

FIGURE 12-8
Flow of Social Information Within the Firm

SOURCE: Michael Mazis and Robert Green, "Implementing Social Responsibility," *MSU Business Topics,* Winter 1971, p. 72. Reprinted by permission of the publisher, Division of Research, Graduate School of Business Administration, Michigan State University.

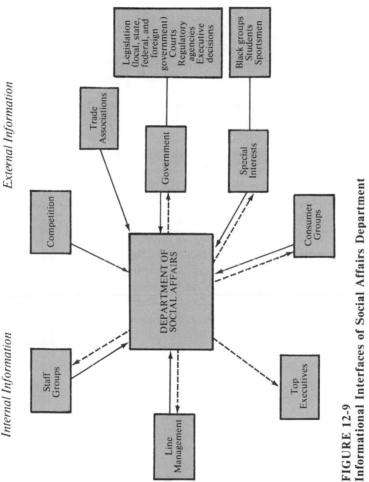

FIGURE 12-9
Informational Interfaces of Social Affairs Department

SOURCE: Michael Mazis and Robert Green, "Implementing Social Responsibility," *MSU Business Topics,* Winter 1971, p. 74. Reprinted by permission of the publisher, Division of Research, Graduate School of Business Administration, Michigan State University.

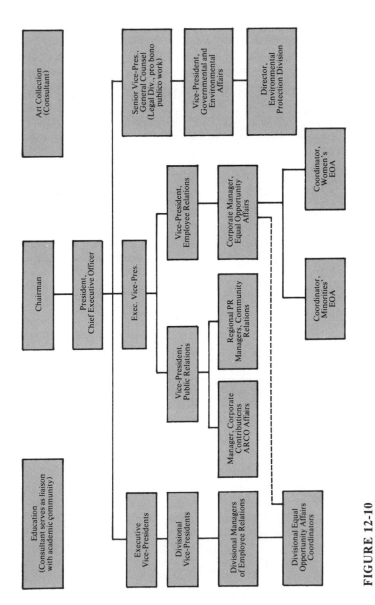

FIGURE 12-10
Partial Organization Chart of Atlantic Richfield Company

SOURCE: John L. Paluszek, "How Three Companies Organize for Social Responsibility," reprinted by permission from the *Business and Society Review/Innovation*, Summer 1973, p. 19. Copyright © 1973, Warren, Gorham and Lamont Inc., 210 South St., Boston, Mass. All rights reserved.

industrial classification. Table 12-5 presents her findings regarding preferred organizational arrangements. Her research data indicated a trend in the direction of permanent structural arrangements. In more cases than not, the permanent department stood out as the most preferred organizational arrangement.

Whether the organization selects the permanent department, individual officer, task force, or committee, one observation is clear: we find more companies are making specific organizational accommodations to deal with the ever-fluid social environment. These organizational adaptations are but one part of the increasing need to manage the social affairs of the modern organization. It should be stressed that though the method of organizing is important, the ultimate goal should not be the implementation of social policy by special departments or social issue specialists, but rather the implementation of social policy by all managers and employees within the organization. Only then will social policy be fully institutionalized and become an integral part of operations throughout the company.

In the final analysis, the company will have to design or structure itself in a way that optimizes its economic and social performance, while at the same time embracing all the other considerations that are becoming a part of its complex everyday life.

SUMMARY

As the social environment has become increasingly turbulent, the need for organizations to apply managerial approaches in dealing with the environment has also increased. In particular, planning and organizing has been deemed essential if effectiveness in the social arena is to be achieved. With respect to planning, social forecasting and social goal setting are two prominent activities. Social forecasting is necessary so that managers will have some notion of what the social future will be like. They can then integrate this forecast into their corporate policy and strategy decisions.

Social forecasting techniques may be classified into three broad categories: authority methods, conjecture methods, and mathematical modeling. Techniques in the first two categories used quite frequently for social forecasting purposes are the regular poll, the Delphi poll, and scenarios. In actual practice, the less complex approaches to social forecasting prevail.

Once the social environment has been forecast and corporate social policy at the upper levels of management has been set, there remains the task of seeing that plans established at the top filter down into the

TABLE 12-5
Preferred Organizational Arrangements for Making Decisions with Considerable Social Implication Across Five Major Industrial Classifications

Which of the following means is most often used by your firm in making decisions with considerable social implication?

	Oil and Gas	Finance, Insurance and Real Estate	Wholesale and Retail	Manufacturing	Transportation, Communication, and Utilities	Totals
			INDUSTRY*			
Number of responses	16	52	12	93	19	192
Individual executives are appointed or permitted to handle critical issues as they arise. %	19	19	0	26	32	23
A temporary task force of executives handles critical issues as they arise. %	6	2	17	6	0	5

	%					
A permanent committee of senior officers handles social decisions.	19	16	8	15	26	16
A permanent department (or departments) is assigned all recurring social decisions and recommends policies for new social decisions.	44	40	50	24	16	31
Other or a combination of the above.	12	23	25	29	26	25
Total of the percentages	100	100	100	100	100	100

*A test for significance of variations across industrial classifications was not feasible due to small sample sizes in some cells.

SOURCE: Sandra L. Holmes, "Adapting Corporate Structure for Social Responsiveness," Copyright © 1978 by the Regents of the University of California. Reprinted from *California Management Review*, Fall 1978, vol. XXI, no. 1, p. 51 (Table 2). By permission of the Regents.

organization and are eventually accomplished. Techniques of social goal setting become important at this point. In particular, operational social goals must be set; implementation then becomes more feasible.

Just as planning for business social response is vital, organizing is essential too. There exists a range of ways in which the organization can structure itself to deal with social issues. Possible arrangements include the social resonsibility officer, the task force, the permanent board committee, the permanent management committee, and the permanent organization group. Which approach the organization uses depends on such factors as company size, industry characteristics, industry patterns or preferences, social issues involved, and management philosophy. Research indicates a trend in business toward permanent structural arrangements.

Planning and organizing for business social response allow: management to identify incipient problems, threats, or opportunities that may exist in the environment, improve decision making, be more rational with respect to its social performance efforts, and focus on objectives agreed upon and communicated in advance. The net results should be enhanced social programs and a more effective overall approach to dealing with the multitude of environments the organization must face.

QUESTIONS FOR DISCUSSION

1. Provide an overview of the planning process and discuss the various environments for which the organization must plan.
2. What is proactive planning? Compare and contrast its characteristics with a reactive planning approach. What, in your view, are the benefits of proaction?
3. In what sense has the two-sided approach to planning given way to a four-sided conceptualization? Discuss.
4. Define social forecasting and indicate the phases involved in the process. What is environmental scanning and how does it compare with social forecasting?
5. Provide an overview of the three scanning models discussed. Describe the characteristics of each.
6. What are the major approaches to social forecasting? Provide a brief description of each. Which techniques are most used in business and industry today?
7. Compare and contrast the regular polling method with the Delphi technique. What, in your view, are the advantages and disadvantages of each?

8. Describe the conjecture methods of social forecasting.

9. Differentiate between an aesthetic social goal and an operational social goal. Provide illustrations of each.

10. Identify the major organizational arrangements that companies use for dealing with the social environment. What are the characteristics of each? According to research, which approaches are most often used?

11. Identify and discuss the factors that would influence the type of organization structure arrangement a company might use.

Cases

Forecasting the Future: Where Are Those 3-D TV Sets?

It recently became known that, in 1957, E. F. Hutton and Company asked twenty-five executives to predict what the future would hold for society in the year 1979. Well, 1979 arrived and the time capsule that contained the executives' predictions was opened. The results? Judge for yourself.

Some of the predictions were that railroads would dominate the nation's transportation system, most households would have three-dimensional television sets as well as three or four cars, and few people would need eyeglasses any more because pills would be available that would cure eyesight problems.

One executive even predicted that one of the most popular cars would bear the distinguished name of "Rambler," the pioneering car that reversed a trend (American Motors stopped making the Rambler more than ten years ago).

None of this happened, of course, but it is what was being predicted by business executives some twenty-two years earlier.

Besides these inaccurate predictions, some executives were correct in their forecasts. For example, some of the executives predicted that compact cars would displace bulkier autos, that Americans would be working an average 35-hour week (down from an average of 41 hours in 1957), that supersonic planes would whisk passengers from New York to Los Angeles in just several hours, and that subscription television would make a box office out of many living rooms.[1]

---

[1]This case was inspired by Richard E. Rustin, "The Future Is Now: So Where Is 3-D TV and Those 4 Cars," *The Wall Street Journal*, October 10, 1979, p. 31. Reprinted by permission of *The Wall Street Journal*, © Dow Jones & Company, Inc., 1979. All rights reserved.

QUESTIONS

1. In the light of our discussion about social forecasting, do the results of these predictions raise any doubts in your mind? Discuss.
2. What is your analysis of the results of these predictions?
3. Would it be at all helpful to you to know what the social conditions were in 1957, when these forecasts were made.

A Drink to Celebrate Your Birthday?

The director of public affairs for a major national greeting card company was taken aback by a recent article that appeared in a respected health journal. According to the study reported there, greeting cards that depict getting drunk as humorous, enjoyable, and harmless are no laughing matter.

The study went on to say that the cards may legitimize and reinforce tolerant attitudes toward alcohol abuse. Furthermore, the study suggested that the greeting cards seemed to make light of getting drunk, leaving the reader with the overall impression that the effects are either trivial, humorous, or worth the risk.

The study indicated that the popularity of the cards, with their recurring theme that drinking is a natural way to celebrate special occasions, suggests that alcohol abuse is sanctioned and promoted among certain segments of our society.

Next to cards depicting sexual behavior, the drinking theme is one of the most popular topics today, with about 4 million cards sold annually.

QUESTIONS

1. As director of public affairs for the card company, how would you respond to this information if you found it while scanning the journal in which it appeared for social issues?
2. A social issue has been identified; how would you analyze it for relevance to your organization?

The Compliance Executive

A new position appearing on the organization charts of a number of companies is frequently referred to as compliance executive.

Compliance with government regulations has become a huge task, with eighty-seven separate federal bodies having regulatory power over business (e.g., OSHA, EPA, FDA, FTC, and CPSC). In addition, there are innumerable state and local government bodies. The cost of compliance to business was estimated in 1979 to be a staggering $50 billion and around 150 million executive and personnel man-hours of work a year.

A handful of companies are pulling their widely scattered compliance programs together and placing them under the aegis of a single, high-level executive. Three major functions seem to be emerging for this new role: (1) the routine of compliance, (2) forecasting future government actions, and (3) working to head off new laws and regulations.

As for the routine of compliance, the executive must coordinate many conflicting regulations, procedures, and systems. The forecasting of future government action is as crucial a task as influencing it. The executive must gauge in advance what possible or probable effects might result from government actions. To head off new laws and regulations, the compliance executive must engage in extensive lobbying and must visit frequently with government agency officials and representatives of consumer and environmental groups.

The compliance executive is typically a powerful person and usually reports directly to the company's president or vice president.[2]

QUESTIONS

1. What do you see as the principal advantages and disadvantages of the compliance executive position? What problems might companies encounter?

2. Do you think this position might become a prototype for other organizations to copy in the future? Why? Why not?

3. Could the compliance executive position mesh well with a Department of Social Affairs? How would their functions be similiar or different?

[2]From "A New High-Level Executive," *Dun's Review*, November 1979, pp. 63-64. Reprinted with the special permission of *Dun's Review*. Copyright 1979, Dun & Bradstreet Publications Corporation.

Social Performance Measurement and Reporting

In addition to the expectations of society and societal groups for improved social performance from business in the last decade or so, pressures have also existed for business to measure and report its social responsibility efforts. The need for this reporting (frequently called social auditing) arose from a desire to document how business firms have responded to the social costs (or "externalities") that they have been creating and that are borne by society in general but are not included in business's traditional accounting systems. These social costs are the consequences to society of business's conventional methods of operation. They have included polluted streams, foul air, unsafe products, dangerous work environments, misleading advertising, and discrimination in employment.

Business has found it necessary to internalize these social costs that typically have been passed on to society by learning how to treat them as other, more direct costs have been treated traditionally. It is not surprising, therefore, that the need for business to measure the effects of its social performance has become increasingly important. The recent interest in such measurement has grown out of a desire to develop techniques that would permit a firm to understand its social costs and to report in some meaningful way the impact of its socially-oriented programs.

The impetus for the actual reporting of the firm's social performance has come from both external and internal sources. Externally, public interest and governmental groups have expressed a desire in recent years to know what the firm is actually doing in various social performance areas. Indeed, such government agencies as EPA, SEC, OSHA, CPSC, and EEOC have required businesses to report specific data on their social performance in the categories the agencies regulate.

Internally, interest in the firm's social performance has come from the management group itself and, in some instances, from shareholder groups. With the realization of how important and costly social issues have become, managers have taken an interest in social measurement and performance. Shareholders, some of whom are now concerned with business ethics and specific social issues, have also taken more of an interest in what companies are doing.

Though it is quite difficult to measure social performance (as one individual has said, "How do you measure clear blue sky?"), it has become an important part of the planning and controlling functions of management as they attempt to guide performance in the social realm. To attain a better understanding of these functions, we will discuss the following topics:

- Important definitions
- Brief history
- Purposes of social auditing
- Methods of social auditing
- Problems associated with social auditing
- Social auditing as control
- The future

IMPORTANT DEFINITIONS

The term most frequently used in recent years in referring to social performance measurement and reporting has been the *social audit.* Although this term has been used to describe a wide variety of activities, it is defined here as a systematic attempt to identify, measure, monitor, and evaluate the organization's performance with respect to its social efforts, programs, and objectives.

The *identification* function is included as a part of the definition because experience has shown that companies frequently are not completely aware of all that they are doing in the social arena. *Measurement* is important because any serious effort to determine what a company is doing requires the development of measures by which performance can be reported, analyzed, and compared. *Monitoring* and *evaluating* are significant because they stress that the effort is continuous and aimed at achieving certain standards the company may have in mind.

The term social audit has been subjected to some criticism. The foremost objection is that it implies an "independent attestation" to the company's social efforts, whereas such an independent attestation typically does not exist. The word audit as used by accountants usually means that some outside party has verified that the firm's situation is as it has been reported. Because social audits are typically conducted by people within the organization, it is obvious why this objection is raised. The criticism is also made that there exist no generally accepted social accounting principles, no professionally recognized independent auditors, and no generally agreed-upon criteria against which to measure a firm's social performance.[1]

Despite these concerns, the term social auditing continues to be used. Another term, social accounting, is frequently used in reference to this same function and has been defined as follows:

> The measurement and reporting, internal or external, of information concerning the impact of an entity and its activities on society.[2]

It is readily seen that these definitions are quite similar.

Perhaps the only term for the function we have been describing that has not been severely criticized is *corporate social performance reporting*. We will, nevertheless, use interchangeably all the terms introduced, and urge the reader to keep in mind the points we have made with respect to each. This is especially necessary in regard to social auditing, a term we will use frequently, as it is so much a part of the already existing literature on and experience of social performance measurement and reporting.

BRIEF HISTORY

The social audit as a concept for monitoring, measuring, and appraising the social performance of business dates back at least to 1940.[3] In a 1940 publication of the Temporary National Economic Committee, Theodore J. Kreps presented a monograph entitled *Measurement of the Social Performance of Business.*[4] Not only was the term social audit used in 1940 (a remarkable fact considering that a firm's social performance was hardly discussed then), but it was used in a vein similar to that employed today — as a concept for measuring the social performance of

---

[1]David H. Blake, William C. Frederick, and Mildred S. Myers, *Social Auditing: Evaluating the Impact of Corporate Programs* (New York: Praeger Publishers, 1976), p. 3.

[2]Ralph Estes, *Corporate Social Accounting* (New York: John Wiley & Sons, 1976), p. 3.

[3]Archie B. Carroll and George W. Beiler, "Landmarks in the Evolution of the Social Audit," *Academy of Management Journal,* September 1975, pp. 589-599.

[4]Theodore J. Kreps, *Measurement of the Social Performance of Business* (Monograph No. 7, "An Investigation of Concentration of Economic Power for the Temporary National Economic Committee") (Washington, D.C.: U.S. Government Printing Office, 1940).

business. In fact, Kreps introduced the term social audit in a chapter he entitled "Tests of Social Performance."[5]

Upon close examination of Kreps' monograph, however, we find that many of what he called social issues during this late Depression/pre-World War II period were closer to what we would refer to today as economic issues. For example, his measurements were of such factors as employment, production, payroll, and dividends and interest.[6]

In contrast to current social audits, the Kreps audit involved more economic-type issues, represented a governmental evaluation of business's social performance, and was to be used by society to assess business performance.

Another landmark in the development of social audits came in 1953 in a book by Howard R. Bowen.[7] Bowen's concept was that the social audit would be a high-level, independent appraisal conducted about every five years by a group of disinterested auditors. The auditors' report would be an evaluation with recommendations intended for internal use by the directors and the management of the firm audited. Some of the areas Bowen proposed auditing were similar to those of Kreps, but Bowen also included more socially oriented activities.

In contrast to these earlier landmark models, the social audit as it came of age in the early 1970s attempted to focus on such social performance categories as minority employment, pollution/environment, community relations, consumer issues, and philanthropic contributions. The audits have been undertaken for a variety of purposes and for the most part have been used internally by the organization. We will look in closer detail at the modern social audit in the material that follows; however, Table 13-1 presents in broad terms an overview and comparison of the Kreps, Bowen, and modern audits.

PURPOSES OF SOCIAL AUDITING

Modern social auditing did not evolve in a vacuum. It evolved as a response to changing expectations on the part of the public to business's social performance. Social auditing eventually came about for many of the same reasons that social issues became more important in business's scheme of things. When society no longer confined its expectations of business to the traditional ones of producing goods and

---

[5]Carroll and Beiler, pp. 590-591.
[6]Kreps, pp. 3-4.
[7]Howard R. Bowen, *Social Responsibilities of the Businessman* (New York: Harper and Row, Publishers, 1953).

Table 13-1
Three Landmark Models of the Social Audit

Subject	Kreps' 1940 Audit	Bowen's 1953 Audit	Today's Audit
Definition	Acid test of business performance	Evaluation of the performance of business from a social point of view	Measurement of companies' progress toward social goals
Purpose	Government evaluation of business's social performance	The firm's evaluation of its social performance	The firm's evaluation of its social performance
Apparent motives	Establish criteria for future evaluations Establish the technique for society to influence business performance	Bring social point of view to management	1. Satisfying the corporate conscience 2. Improving financial wisdom of social programs 3. Public relations 4. To enhance credibility of the business firm
Nature of issues audited	Quantifiable areas: 1. Employment 2. Production 3. Consumer effort commanded 4. Consumer funds absorbed 5. Payrolls 6. Dividends and interest	Company policy toward: 1. Prices 2. Wages 3. Research and development 4. Advertising 5. Public relations 6. Human relations 7. Community relations 8. Economic stabilization	Company performance in: 1. Minority employment 2. Pollution/environment 3. Working conditions 4. Community relations 5. Philanthropic contributions 6. Consumerism issues
Use	By society to assess business performance	By managment to assess its performance	Divided between two schools of thought. One group feels it should be only for management's use. Another group feels it should be a public document.
Methodology	Evaluation of public information employing economic indices	Judgmental appraisal of company policy	Monitor, measure, and appraise all aspects of social performance using various techniques—cost vs. benefit, accounting, etc.
By whom conducted	A government bureau	Internal personnel or an industry agency	Internal personnel or a consultant

SOURCE: Archie B. Carroll and George W. Beiler, "Landmarks in the Evolution of the Social Audit," *Academy of Management Journal,* vol. 18, no. 3 (September 1975), p. 598. Reprinted by permission.

services, business had to attend to the human, environmental, and other social consequences of its activities.

One very significant expectation of the public has been to know more about what business is doing with respect to the impact of its activities on society and social programs. In order to respond to specific inquiries from government, the press, consumer groups, shareholders, and social activists, business had to have a more manageable way of gathering, analyzing, and reporting such information. This need gave rise to social audits and various forms of social performance reports.

Much of the initial impetus for social audits to provide information on social performance came in the form of *external pressures.* These demands for information came from government (SEC, EPA, EEOC, etc.), public interest groups (Nader's Raiders, Sierra Club, Corporate Accountability Research Group, Common Cause, etc.), shareholders (institutional investors — foundations, churches, universities, insurance companies, banks, mutual funds), and others (news media, educators, researchers, general public).[8]

As external forces began requiring accountability and disclosure, *internal pressures* began mounting to find better ways of gathering and assimilating social performance data. The greatest need was felt at the levels of top management, board of directors, and staff. Individuals at these levels in the organization must be able to respond to social activists and a criticial press, to answer proxy challenges and stockholders' questions, and to testify knowledgeably when called on to do so by congressional committees or regulatory agencies.

Corporate directors need to know more about the firm's social performance because of their growing legal liability. They also need to be more knowledgeable about the effects of their corporations on society — especially the negative effects — for that is where criticism is bound to come from. And as directors, they must be prepared to respond, as do other top managers. In addition, the firm's social performance should be appraised, evaluated, and integrated into top-level policy decisions if a sound overall corporate strategy is to be designed and implemented. Table 13-2 summarizes the external and internal potential users of social performance information.

We have presented a number of purposes for which social audits need to be conducted. It is now worthwhile to look at the results of a specific survey that asked companies why they undertook a social audit. This survey, by John Corson and George Steiner, is one of the most comprehensive that has been conducted on the subject.[9] Of the 750 com-

[8]Estes, p. 4.
[9]John J. Corson and George A. Steiner, *Measuring Business's Social Performance: The Corporate Social Audit* (New York: Committee for Economic Development, 1974), p. 22.

TABLE 13-2
Potential Users of Corporate Social Performance Information

INTERNAL		
Directors	Other employees	Public Relations Department
Management	Union Local	Law Department

EXTERNAL

Associated
  Investors and lenders—especially churches, foundations, banks, insurance
    companies, universities, and mutual funds
  Customers
  Suppliers

Government
  Securities and Exchange Commission
  Environmental Protection Agency
  Equal Employment Opportunity Commission
  Department of Housing and Urban Development
  Internal Revenue Service
  General Accounting Office
  Congress, state legislatures, city commissions
  Law enforcement agencies
  Regulatory agencies and commissions at all levels (FTC, FCC, ICC, etc.)

Public Interest Groups

Project on Corporate Responsibility	Council for Corporate Review
Council on Economic Priorities	Citizens Action Program
Accountants for the Public Interest	Tax Action Group
Corporate Accountability Research Group	Common Cause
Agribusiness Accountability Project	Public Citizen, Inc.
Investor Responsibility Research Center	NAACP
American Civil Liberties Union	Public Communication, Inc.
San Francisco Consumer Action	Sierra Club
National Affiliation of Concerned Business Students	Wilderness Society
	Friends of the Earth

Others

News media	Financial Analysts Federation
Stock exchanges	Researchers
American Institute of Certified Public Accountants	Educators
American Accounting Association	Sudents and other potential employees
National Association of Accountants	General public

SOURCE: Realph Estes, *Corporate Social Accounting* (New York: John Wiley & Sons, 1976), p.4. Reprinted by permission.

panies sent the survey, usable replies were received from 284. Table 13-3 presents the data from this survey.

It is interesting to note the top four purposes in Table 13-3 for undertaking social audits:

1. To examine what the company is actually doing in selected areas.
2. To appraise or evaluate performance in selected areas.
3. To identify those social programs which the company feels it should be pursuing.
4. To inject into the general thinking of managers a social point of view.

Implicit in these responses is the fact that many managers were simply unaware of what their companies were doing in the social arena. Because the top four purposes are quite fundamental to the social perfor-

TABLE 13-3
Purposes that Led Companies to Undertake Social Audits

	Number	*Percent*
1. To identify those social pressures which the company feels pressured to undertake	55	5
2. To identify those social programs which the company feels it ought to be pursuing	157	14
3. To examine what the company is actually doing in selected areas	194	17
4. To appraise or evaluate performance in selected areas	162	14
5. To determine areas where our company may be vulnerable to attack	101	9
6. To inject into the general thinking of managers a social point of view	122	11
7. To ensure that specific decision-making processes incorporate a social point of view	95	8
8. To inform the public of what the company is doing	70	6
9. To offset irresponsible audits made by outside self-appointed groups	41	4
10. To meet public demands for corporate accountability in the social area	78	7
11. To increase profits	37	3
12. Other	17	2

*A total of 196 companies checked one or more purposes.

SOURCE: John J. Corson and George A. Steiner, *Measuring Business's Social Performance: The Corporate Social Audit* (New York: Committee for Economic Development, 1974), p. 33. Reprinted by permission.

mance area, they indicate, perhaps, that companies are still at a rather basic level in their social auditing efforts. In addition to those purposes listed in Table 13-3, a number of managers suggested such other purposes as the following: "as a guide to internal management," "part of long-range planning," and "to balance commitment to social activity against job activity."[10]

METHODS OF SOCIAL AUDITING

Just as there are a variety of purposes for which social auditing was undertaken, there are a number of different methods by which social audits have been conducted. Five different methods or approaches are presented here. While these do not exhaust all the possibilities, they do provide a means of characterizing most efforts.

Cost or Outlay Method

This method involves the identification and totaling of all expenditures for social activities so that the dollar costs of social programs can be tallied and reported. The approach concentrates on inputs (as measured in dollars); it makes no attempt to measure outputs. The application of this method necessitates difficult decisions regarding cost allocations. For example, what fraction of the cost of hiring and training a minority person should be attributed to the regular cost of doing business and what part should be counted as an employer undertaking a social activity? Another problem with this approach is that it provides little evaluative information.[11]

Inventory Method

This approach involves the cataloging and narrative description of what the company is doing in social areas; its end product is a massive listing (inventory) of the company's activities with little or no analysis of costs or results. Although this technique does generate a considerable amount of information, it fails to assess costs to the firm and benefits to societal groups. For this reason, it is not a significant improvement over the cost or outlay method.[12]

---

[10]Ibid., p. 34.
[11]Ibid., p. 18.
[12]Ibid., pp. 19-20. See also *Corporate Social Reporting in the United States and Western Europe,* Report of the Task Force on Corporate Social Performance (U.S. Department of Commerce, July 1979), p. 7.

Program Management Method

This approach focuses on measuring only those activities in which a company is primarily involved for social reasons. With respect to each activity, this method identifies committed resources (costs) and effectiveness of the effort. As such, it is a kind of limited cost/benefit approach.[13] In some versions of this method, comparisons are made of social performance with company goals. Thus, program management tallies the cost and benefits of social programs, though not in any fully quantitative sense. The main practitioner of this approach is the Bank of America.[14] Table 13-4 illustrates a generalized social responsibility program statement that is basically the format for one form of the program management method.

Cost/Benefit Method

Attempts to evaluate both costs and benefits have been a principal feature of some social measurement efforts. A number of different cost/benefit analyses have been tried, with none of them fully and accurately identifying and measuring all attendant costs and benefits. One approach to this is the "balance sheet" statement espoused primarily by Clark Abt. This method attempts to assess benefits to society (stated in the form of assets) and costs to society (stated in the form of liabilities) of actions taken or not taken by a firm. Critics of Abt's approach have lauded him for inventiveness but think the approach is too subjective and too complex to be of practical value at this time. Table 13-5 illustrates what one form of a cost/benefit statement might include. The cost/benefit method is perhaps the most conceptually sound of all the approaches, but its complexity considerably reduces its usefulness.[15]

Process Audit Method

The process audit was developed by Raymond Bauer and Dan Fenn.[16] Basically qualitative in nature, the process audit attempts to examine the underlying process by which a firm became involved in its social activities. It attempts to ascertain the reasons management undertook a particular activity, the goals of the activity, and the rationale for the action. It also describes what is actually being done as opposed to what the

---

[13]Ibid., p. 18.

[14]Harold L. Johnson, *Disclosure of Corporate Social Performance: Survey, Evaluation, and Prospects* (New York: Praeger Publishers, 1979), p. 83.

[15]For a further discussion of this topic, see David Novick, "Cost-Benefit Analysis and Social Responsibility," *Business Horizons*, February 1973.

[16]Raymond A. Bauer and Dan H. Fenn, "What Is a Corporate Social Audit?" *Harvard Business Review*, January-February 1973, pp. 37-48.

Table 13-4
Social Responsibility Program Statement

Program	Committed Resources	Effect on Human Behavior and/or Environment
Human resources Company medical plan	$____Health insurance contribution	____Number of employees covered
		____Claims paid during year
Job safety program	$____Expended for noncompulsory safety equipment	____Injuries/1,000 man-hours
	____Man-hours spent on safety seminars and instruction	____Ratio of employee injuries to industry average
	____Suggestions adopted	
Leisure and recreation	$____	____Employees participants in softball league
	$____Land value	____Man-hour usage of company athletic facilities
Education	____Employees participating in company courses of instruction	____Employees successfully completing company courses of instruction
	$____Tuition paid	____Credit hours financed at colleges or universities
		____Degrees awarded to employee participants in tuition reimbursement program
Physical resources Company recycle program	____Man-hours spent on special studies	____Tonnage recycled
		____Ratio of waste/final output
		____Energy usage/final output
Land reclamation program	$____	____Ratio of reclaimed/damaged land
Product or service contributions Product safety	$____	____Product safety innovations implemented
	____Product research man-hours	
Packaging reduction	$____	____Reduction in tons of nonrecyclable packaging
	____Product research man-hours	____Tons of product or packaging recycled
Community involvement Local business development	$____Funds contributed	____Businessmen receiving free consulting
	$____Loans to minority	
	$____Business averaging	
	____Man-hours spent training unemployed	____Workers trained and removed from welfare
Community fund	$____Contributions	
	____Man-hours devoted to lecture on United Fund activities	____Percentage of employees contributing fair share

SOURCE: C. H. Brandon and J. P. Matoney, Jr., "Social Responsibility Financial Statement," *Management Accounting,* November 1975, p. 33. Reprinted by permission.

Table 13-5
Social Impact Statement for the Year Ended December 31, 19xx
The Progressive Company

Social Benefits
  Products and services provided $xxx
  Payments to other elements of society
    Employment provided (salaries and wages) $xxx
    Payments for goods and other services   xxx
    Taxes paid   xxx
    Contributions   xxx
    Dividends and interest paid   xxx
    Loans and other payments   xxx   xxx

  Additional direct employee benefits   xxx
  Staff, equipment, and facility services donated   xxx
  Environmental improvements   xxx
  Other benefits   xxx

    Total Social Benefits $xxx

Social Costs
  Goods and materials acquired $xxx
  Buildings and equipment purchased   xxx
  Labor and services used   xxx
  Discrimination
    In hiring (external) $xxx
    In placement and promotion (internal)   xxx   xxx

  Work-related injuries and illness   xxx
  Public services and facilities used   xxx
  Other resources used   xxx
  Environmental damage
    Terrain damage $xxx
    Air pollution   xxx
    Water pollution   xxx
    Noise pollution   xxx
    Solid waste   xxx
    Visual and aesthetic pollution   xxx
    Other environmental damage   xxx   xxx

  Payments from other elements of society
    Payments for goods and service provided $xxx
    Additional capital investment   xxx
    Loans   xxx
    Other payments received   xxx   xxx

  Other costs   xxx

    Total Social Costs   xxx

Social Surplus (Deficit) for the Year $xxx
Accumulated Surplus (Deficit) December 31, 19xx   xxx

Accumulated Surplus (Deficit) December 31, 19xx $xxx

SOURCE: Ralph Estes, *Corporate Social Accounting* (New York: John Wiley & Sons, 1976), p. 96. Reprinted by permission.

rationale indicates should be done. Bauer and several of his associates prepared a handbook for use in the development of a process audit. In the handbook, entitled *A Management Process Audit Guide*, the authors state:

> The goal of such a process audit is to assemble the information that will make it possible for a person to intelligently assess the program, to decide whether he agrees with its goals, to decide whether the rationale is appropriate to the goals, and to judge whether the actual implementation promises to attain those goals satisfactorily.[17]

Exhibit 13-1 presents a brief description of the process audit guide prepared by its developers.

The process audit, which has become a major management tool for a number of companies, has several advantages: it is easy to understand and apply; it focuses on specific programs and goals which can be evaluated; it can be applied to a wide range of activities; and it avoids the conceptual intricacies of those methods that attempt to measure the entire range of social impacts.[18]

No single approach to social auditing has yet acquired total acceptance of those engaged in social performance reporting. In addition to the techniques described above, companies have published in the past decade a mixture of social information in annual reports and in the format of special *social reports*. Each year since 1971, for example, the accounting firm of Ernst and Ernst has reported the extent to which *Fortune* 500 companies are disclosing social information in their annual reports. When the survey series began, five categories of social performance were being reported. The report for 1978 showed a growth to twenty-seven categories during the seven years. These categories can be aggregated into seven major reporting areas as follows: (1) environment, (2) energy, (3) fair business practices, (4) human resources, (5) products, (6) community involvement, and (7) other disclosures.[19]

It must be kept in mind that the inclusion of social performance information in annual reports is not a social audit per se, but represents attempts by companies to communicate to relevant publics what they are doing in the social realm. In the next chapter we will discuss more fully business's efforts to communicate its social role to its several constituent groups.

Though there are a number of problems associated with business's attempts to report social information, particularly in annual reports and specially produced social reports, it is possible to abstract suggested criteria for effective social reporting from a number of reports that have

[17]Ibid.
[18]*Corporate Social Reporting in the United States and Western Europe*, p. 9.
[19]Ibid., p. 10.

EXHIBIT 13-1
New Manual on Social Auditing

We have developed a manual, *A Management Process Audit Guide,* which consists primarily of a series of major research questions, of suggested procedures for answering them and explanations of the reasoning behind the questions and the procedures. The guide is organized according to the following sequence:

(1) Identification of the issue or issues on which the audit will focus;

(2) Gathering of relevant background data on the industry and the firm or firms to be audited;

(3) Description and evaluation of the management and administrative system or systems for handling the issue or issues.

The heart of the audit, of course, is the description and evaluation of the management and administrative systems. It follows Ackerman's three implementation stages. It is designed, first, to be able to place the organization, at least roughly, within one of his three stages on one or more issues, next to assess progress within that stage, and finally to assess the factors which affect the probability of its moving forward.

The guide leaves a good deal to the discretion of the auditor. This is in part because situations differ so much. Sometimes the information is available in one location, sometimes it is dispersed. Time constraints or confidence in the quality of a single source of information may dictate a short chase, reverse conditions may require a long one.

Another reason for the guide's relatively loose structure is the incompleteness of our understanding of the implementation process along with our related inability to adapt it specifically to all the issues to which it may be applied. The salvation, we hope, of this incomplete structure is the "rationale" we give for each research question. This is intended to spell out the intent of the research question and thus help the auditor exercise judgment.

We hope other scholars and practitioners will want to review the guide or try to use it. We hope they will either share their reactions and experience or simply employ it as an oyster might an irritating piece of sand, namely to go off and generate a pearl of their own.

EXHIBIT 13-2
Suggested Criteria for Effective Social Reporting

- A description of the organizational structure for social-policy planning, for the company as a whole, and for each major social-performance category.
- A sense of the attitude toward and commitment to social performance at the senior management level.
- Identification and concise discussion of major social issues facing the company, including the company's position and general response.
- Identification of the company's major constituencies and how the company's activities affect each one.
- A description and concise evaluation of major social programs, broken down by issues or constituencies.
- Liberal use of meaningful data, including comparisons over time *and* against any known industry or government standards.
- A sense of candor — in other words, not focusing exclusively on favorable social performance.
- Written in an attractive, readable, and educational style.
- Publication of the names and telephone numbers of those to contact for more information in specific areas.
- Inclusion of an "outside" critique.

SOURCE: David C-H Johnston, "Corporate Approaches to Social Accounting," *Business,* July-August 1979, pp. 48-49. Reprinted by permission.

been examined. In Exhibit 13-2 we see a summary of these criteria as presented by David C-H Johnston. Most of these criteria pertain to social performance reporting of the variety that appears in annual and special reports, but some of them are applicable to social auditing as well.

PROBLEMS ASSOCIATED WITH SOCIAL AUDITING

By its very nature — as it attempts to measure what some consider to be immeasurable — social auditing has a number of problems associated with its conceptual design, implementation, and use. An examination of a select few of these difficulties will help us appreciate why social auditing has been slow to gain approval and why managers, upon learning of social audits, have not rushed to institute them. Indeed, there is some feeling that social audits had their greatest favor in the early to mid-1970s and are now of dwindling interest to managers. This need not be the case, but an awareness of the problems involved in social auditing is needed if social performance reporting instruments are to be used effectively.

The problems associated with social auditing extend beyond the obvious technical ones. Included in the list of difficulties would have to be some that are attitudinal, organizational, and political.[20]

It is not by accident that Corson and Steiner's survey of business firms found "inability to develop measures of performance which everyone will accept" as the major obstacle to social auditing. Related to this was another obstacle, "inability to make creditable cost/benefit analysis to guide company action."[21] Both of these concerns point to perhaps the single most significant technical problem associated with social auditing — the problem of *measurement.*

We are at a time when there is tremendous pressure to use measurement to form the basis for rational management actions and decisions, and the social audit has not escaped this pressure. Ideally, a measurement system would capture with a single measurement unit every effect of every action on every person in society. Such a system is, of course, unobtainable, and thus a practicable measurement scheme would have to be far more limited in scope.[22] Even allowing for a more limited notion of measurement, however, there is no universally accepted set of indices for measuring the effects of social programs and social activities.

The inability to develop generalized measures has led social measurement in the direction of qualitative and quantitative indicators specific to the social area being examined. In the area of the hiring, training, and promoting of minority and female employees, for instance, the indicators of achievement tend to rely on answers to *process* and *end results* measures, which do not truly capture all costs and benefits. Such questions as the following are typical:

Qualitative Indicators
1. Are recruiting efforts planned to maximize the possibilities of recruiting qualified women and minorities?
2. Are women and minorities encouraged to seek advancement?
3. Does the company participate wholeheartedly in private-sector and government-sponsored incentive programs to train and hire women, minorities, and other protected-group individuals?

Quantitative Indicators
1. Number of interviews with minority and female candidates, as a percentage of all such interviews.
2. Number of protected-group persons hired, by job category.
3. Number of protected-group persons promoted, by job category into which promotions occurred.
4. Number and type of EEO complaints.

[20]Blake, Frederick, and Myers, pp. 23-49.
[21]Corson and Steiner, p. 36.
[22]Neil C. Churchill, "Toward a Theory for Social Accounting," *Sloan Management Review,* Spring 1974, pp. 1-17.

Most serious attempts to develop measurement schemes that social auditors would accept have failed. As a result, many companies have used approaches similar to the process audit discussed earlier. Though the process audit is considered an acceptable beginning approach to social auditing, those interested in social performance still hope that social accounting techniques will become more refined in the future. In the interim, measurement problems will continue to plague efforts to develop generally acceptable social audits. In addition, though companies will strive to develop acceptable measurement methods, the government continues to demand quantitative statistics. This is especially true in such areas as pollution control and minority/female employment.

Though it appears that measurement problems are the most serious obstacle to social auditing, there are other major difficulties as well. One very significant question is that of *determining what should be audited.* Once again, Corson and Steiner found "inability to develop consensus as to what activities should be covered" to be a major obstacle to social auditing.[23]

Determining what areas of social performance or impact should be audited poses a major conceptual problem for management. The choice of what to include and exclude, in a sense, provides the company with its own operational definition of social responsibility. At a minimum, it provides the company with a list of areas it views as important. Some companies may choose to include social performance areas in which legal mandates now exist (for example, pollution, minority hiring and promotion, product safety). Other companies may feel that since these are legally mandated, they do not need to be included in social audits.

Another problem area concerns *what constitutes success* in the social realm.[24] This critical question presupposes that the company knows which areas it wants to measure and has developed at least rudimentary approaches to measurement. The basic question is: How does the company know whether its social performance has been successful? This determination is quite difficult because the organization frequently will not have any standards or criteria against which to measure its success. The company will have to at least develop objectives to aspire toward. These objectives (see the discussion on social goal setting in Chapter 12) may reflect improvements on past experience, industry standards where available, or competitors' performance. Regardless of which approach is used, the result will be quite value laden.

A very practical problem companies face when they undertake a social audit is *getting the data.*[25] Significant difficulties here include the

[23]Corson and Steiner, p. 36.
[24]Bauer and Fenn, pp. 37-48.
[25]Ibid.

feasibility, expense, and time involved in collecting, summarizing, and analyzing social information. In large, diversified organizations, collecting data about social programs and impacts poses an almost insurmountable problem. Experience reveals that individuals conducting social audits have trouble comparing data from various sections of the organization. Also, social auditors frequently encounter stubborn internal resistance by some managers when they are required to divulge social performance information. This is not difficult to understand. Because, traditionally, managers have not been evaluated on social performance, they have a negative attitude when someone wants to gather this type of information from them.

In sum, the problems associated with social auditing are numerous. Though some problems are technical (most notably the measurement problem), there are conceptual or definitional difficulties, bad attitudes to overcome, and continuing practical issues which must be faced as the company attempts to gather, summarize, analyze, and report social performance information. The next difficult question is what the company should do with the results.

SOCIAL AUDITING AS CONTROL

As one contemplates what an organization might do with the results of a social auditing experience, thinking might evolve in the direction of better efforts to plan and control the company's social performance. When we discussed planning issues earlier, we provided a broad context in which to see social objectives and efforts as a part of overall organizational strategy. Now it is worthwhile to focus on the managerial process of control.

Though planning and control are two inseparable management functions, control tends to focus on keeping management activities in conformance with plans. Control traditionally has subsumed three essential steps: setting standards against which performance can be compared, comparing actual performance with what was planned (the standard), and taking corrective action to bring the two back into alignment.

In the context of social performance, it is suggested here that a social audit or social performance report represents an effort to measure, monitor, or compare actual company performance with that which was desired. In the case of a company just starting out, it probably does not have any social objectives; and its measurement effort, however crude it might be, simply provides useful information about how the company is doing. For the company that has attempted to manage its social performance programs and impacts, the social audit supplies information needed for control purposes. The performance information permits the organization to compare its actual performance with stated plans, thus providing a foundation for any corrective efforts that are seen as necessary. Figure 13-1 illustrates this social performance control process diagrammatically.

As seen in Figure 13-1, the control process is embedded in a larger management system. This system necessitated a study of the environment for social issues and matters of concern, and the development of an overall corporate strategy. Next were derived a social policy and social objectives (standards); these formed the linkage between the planning system and the social performance control system. The resulting schematic provides a conceptualization of the way social auditing fits into the larger concern for planning and controlling the organization's social performance.

THE FUTURE

There is a temptation to say that social auditing has a bright future and that eventually the federal government will mandate a comprehensive social audit of all firms' social performance. Indeed, there has been some speculation that this would happen. Some argue that the federal government already requires a social audit, albeit a rather fragmented one, in the form of specific performance reports to such agencies as OSHA, EEOC, and EPA.

We do not anticipate, however, that the federal government will require a comprehensive social audit any time soon, even though there does exist a Task Force on Corporate Social Performance within the Department of Commerce. This task force issued a report in 1979, but the report turned out to be an overview of social reporting practices throughout the United States and abroad rather than a call for social auditing by the federal government.[26]

At the level of specific companies, social audits and social performance reporting will undergo continued experimentation and improvement in quality. Society's concern for quality social performance from the business community remains high, and this will serve as a continuing incentive for companies to strive to improve their social measurement and reporting efforts. As companies continue in their pursuit of improved management of the business and society relationship, social measurement and reporting will remain essential ingredients in business's quest for efficiency and effectiveness in the social realm.

[26] *Corporate Social Reporting in the United States and Western Europe.*

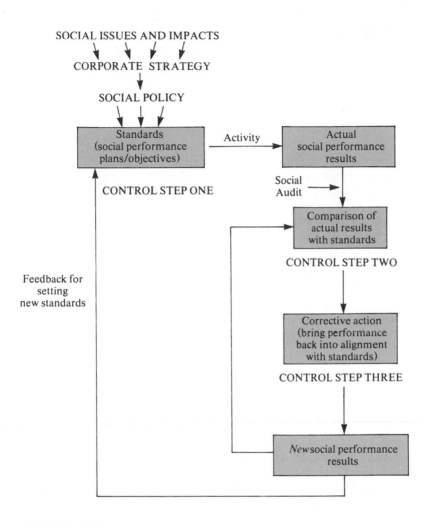

FIGURE 13-1
The Social Audit and Social Performance Control

SUMMARY

Pressure on businesses for continued improvement in their social performance has led to considerable experimentation with social auditing and other forms of social performance measurement and reporting. Though these efforts began almost forty years ago, the 1970s marked the period during which recent concern for social reporting took hold. In the 1970s companies began turning their attention to the management of social issues, and monitoring, measuring, and appraising became natural activities.

The purposes for which companies initially undertook social auditing are varied, as are the techniques of social auditing. Among the many different methods are the cost or outlay approach, the inventory method, the program management approach, cost/benefit analysis, and the process audit. The process audit has been the most popular because it aims to scrutinize the overall process by which social performance occurs, thus avoiding some of the difficult measurement problems that complicate the other approaches.

Social auditing or reporting does not come easily; there are numerous problems associated with its conceptual design and implementation. These problems are not only technical, they are conceptual, attitudinal, organizational, and political as well.

Social auditing can be conceived as part of a larger effort to plan for and control the organization's social performance. Because the need to improve planning and control will be with us for as long as management desires to improve the managing of the business and society relationship, social auditing and social performance reporting will likely also be with us for some time. The net result of continued experimentation should be improved corporate social performance and enhanced credibility of business in the eyes of the public.

QUESTIONS FOR DISCUSSION

1. Define social auditing, social accounting, and social performance reporting. Why do some object to use of the term social auditing?
2. Provide a brief overview of the history of social auditing.
3. Compare and contrast the Kreps audit with the Bowen audit. Compare and contrast both of these with the modern social audit.
4. Discuss the underlying reasons for or purposes of social auditing. Be sure to differentiate between internal and external reasons for social auditing.
5. What are the basic methods or approaches to social auditing? Describe their main features.
6. Outline the principal features of the process audit. How does it avoid some of the problems inherent in other forms of social audits?
7. Identify and discuss the problems associated with the successful design and use of social audits.

8. Identify and discuss five suggested criteria for effective social reporting.
9. Discuss social auditing as a control effort, being sure to illustrate the role the social audit plays in the social performance control process.

Cases

Getting Started on the Social Audit

Rusty Wade was pleased that as a second-year MBA student he had been selected for the summer management intern program at B&C Bank in a nearby metropolitan area. He anticipated that he would receive valuable experience during his three months at B&C.

He spent the first day getting acquainted with people in the bank, and the second morning he anxiously entered the office of Herbert Book, one of the bank's vice presidents, to get his assignment for the summer. Following is his brief conversation with Book.

Book: I think I've got an interesting assignment for you, Rusty. We want you to conduct our first-ever social audit. We want to know what the bank is doing in the social responsibility area and how well we're doing it.

Wade: That's fine, Mr. Book, but I know very little about social auditing. What is it?

Book: Fear not, Rusty, I've got a book and two articles for you to read before getting started.

Wade: Fine. But are your people in the bank ready to have someone closely scrutinize their social responsibility efforts?

Book: Well, probably not. But you've been highly recommended to us, and I think that if anyone can pull it off, you can.

Wade: I'll give it my best shot, but it'll take me awhile to figure out where to begin.

Book: Take your time. You've got all summer to complete this. Oh, by the way, don't look too closely at what we are doing in the area of granting mortgage loans to potential residents of low-income areas. Bob Biggers, our president, views that as a sensitive issue.

QUESTIONS

1. Evaluate the approach Herbert Book and the B&C Bank have taken to conduct their first-ever social audit.
2. What problems do you anticipate Rusty Wade will encounter?

3. Do you think B&C is really ready for a social audit?
4. If you think the approach used should have been different, suggest what it might have been.

A Social Accounting Proposal

A professor at a large business school in the Midwest proposed the following as a format for a social accounting of corporate social activity.

Item	Points Possible	Points Earned
1. The Free Enterprise Orientation	1,000	
2. Public Relations Policies	1,000	
3. Management and the Individual	1,000	
4. Response to Protest Movements	1,000	
5. Ethical Stance	1,000	
6. Creeds and Philosophies	1,000	
7. Labor-Management Relations	1,000	
8. Social Action Programs	1,000	
9. Future Responsibilities	1,000	
10. Social Responsibilities	1,000	
Total Possible	10,000	Total Earned

QUESTIONS

1. Critique the above format as a possible device for social accounting or auditing.
2. What merit do you see to an approach such as this one? Discuss.
3. What refinements could be made to the above system to make it a better one?

Memo to Mr. Bradley

TO: Bruce C. Bradley, Vice President
        Personnel Services

FROM: Angela Duxbury
        Administrative Assistant

RE: Recently Completed Social Audit

As you requested, Mr. Bradley, I have conducted a social audit of National Life Insurance Company and I'm pleased to report to you that National Life spent $5,400,000 being "good guys" last year. Below is a summary of what I considered to be our socially related expenditures:

Item	Amount
Corporate Contributions (Note: $25,000 for employee welfare was excluded from this.)	$ 560,000
Department of Social Affairs (Note: This amount represents 60% of total expenditures. The other 40% was on compliance activities—not purely social responsibility activities.)	750,000
Research Data for Education (Charts, maps, statistics, etc., that we supply to educators on an annual basis—upon request.)	150,000
Mortgage Department (This amount is the yield loss and money lost due to making loans to normally unqualified applicants.)	1,680,000
Deposits in Minority-Owned Banks (This is money maintained on account in 14 minority-owned banks. The figure represents loss of interest as we receive no interest on this money.)	68,000
Medical Department Expenditures (This includes booklets, demonstrations, and other health-related education expenditures. I took only two-thirds of the total amount. I considered the rest business expense.)	480,000
Minority Vendors (I estimate this is how much we lost due to placing orders with minority vendors rather than the vendor with the lowest price. It is an estimate.)	65,000
Expenditures on Minority Affairs (This is an estimate of salaries and overhead associated with special hiring and training efforts for minorities.)	350,000

Item	Amount
Advertising	1,297,000
(Two-thirds of the total amount was included here because I felt this much was for public service programs and promotional efforts.)	
TOTAL	$5,400,000

I hope this is what you wanted, Mr. Bradley. Would you like me to write up a press release to let everyone in the metro area know how socially responsible we are?

QUESTIONS

1. Evaluate on an item-by-item basis the above expenditures of National Life. Does each seem valid? Discuss. What additional information would you need about each to know if they were valid?

2. What concept or definition of social responsibility expenditures does Ms. Duxbury seem to be using? Has she been inconsistent anywhere?

3. Would you feel confident enough about this social audit to instruct Ms. Duxbury to release a press notice? If not, how and to whom should the information be communicated?

Communicating the Business Social Role

One very neglected aspect of managing the business and society relationship is the communication of business's role. This should not be surprising for it has only been in recent years that companies have begun to concern themselves in a systematic way with corporate social policy, planning and organizing for social response, and developing and using social performance reports. These important managerial activities typically need to be accomplished before an organization has a sound basis for communicating its position on social issues.

If such planning and policy development does not take place, the best an organization can hope for is haphazard and sporadic communication of its position. This is unfortunate, because many companies that have taken their social performance seriously frequently are lumped together, in the public's mind, with those that have little regard for their social impacts.

The subject of this chapter is, therefore, quite important, and it is placed with other managerial topics because effective communication to both external and internal publics is truly a managerial challenge of the highest magnitude.

To date there has been little development of principles and concepts to point managers in the direction of effective communication with various publics of social responsibility positions and philosophies. Nevertheless, we should discuss what some of these essential publics are, some business concerns with respect to each, and what some organizations are doing (and what others ought to be doing) to improve this vital facet of their communcation responsibility.

One point should be made quite clear as we embark on this topic: Business communicates as much by its activities and by its silence as it does by its public statements and other specific communication efforts.[1] For the organization in which planned communication is not a reality,

This chapter was contributed by James M. Lahiff, University of Georgia.
[1]James M. Lahiff and William T. Greenwood, "Planning for the Optimal Corporate Image," *Managerial Planning*, July-August 1977, p. 34.

the public's knowledge of its social efforts is determined almost by accident. Whatever information the public receives about the organization is dictated by the interests of the public rather than by the intent of the organization. The lack of a specific effort to communicate, therefore, leaves the company at the mercy of the public's perceptions of its activities. It is ironic that some of the organizations that may be the most forceful in marketing and advertising their products display a complete lack of these qualities when it comes to communicating their social positions. Passivity can lead to a distorted public view of the organization.

In this chapter we will first discuss the role of public relations firms, which, historically, business has relied upon to help communicate with various publics. We will see how the public relations function has changed. Then we will examine organizational efforts to communicate with several major publics — shareholders, employees, the general public, and the media. We will then look at advocacy advertising, a special kind of communication approach which has become popular recently, and close out the chapter with several selected guidelines for improving business social communication.

In sum, we will consider the following topics:

- The role of public relations firms
- Communicating with shareholders: annual meetings
- Communicating with shareholders: reports
- Communicating with employees
- Communicating with the public
- Business and the media
- Advocacy advertising
- Guidelines for improved corporate communication

THE ROLE OF PUBLIC RELATIONS FIRMS

In many organizations the only time any attention is directed at planned communication is when there is a crisis. It is at this point that public relations specialists are recruited to remedy the problem or at least to help save face. Public relations firms are used to help an organization cope with a crisis — even those large organizations that have their own public relations staffs are beginning to rely on outside public relations advisers also. When a corporation is confronted with a new problem, an outside agency may have already faced the same problem and thus be better prepared to cope with it than the organization's own public relations staff.

The activities of the Bechtel Corporation in response to public pressures typify business's increased emphasis on public relations. After this multibillion-dollar construction firm was widely criticized for cost overruns and delays on major projects, the company went on the offensive. It began running institutional ads in national media; it made its executives more available to the press; it began to actively support political candidates sympathetic to its interests; and it expanded its own public relations staff.[2]

Such examples show that the role of the public relations practitioner has undergone considerable change in recent years. The stereotype of the PR specialist has long been one of a fast-talking, manipulative "con artist" who made up with polish what he lacked in ethics. Whether the description was in any way accurate or not, business has been slow to acknowledge the importance of the public relations function because public relations was so often equated with press-agentry. Merely getting a client's name in the paper was a major purpose of public relations, even in the recent past.

Public Relations Redesigned

The expanding role of public relations is also suggested by the ways the designation of the function have changed. In many business organizations "public relations" has been superseded by "public affairs" or "corporate communication." It has become increasingly common in larger organizations to assign responsibility for this function to a vice-president; this new designation suggests the importance now attached to the function.

Because public relations practitioners have long been accused of being more concerned with cosmetics than with substance, many people have viewed redesignation of titles as more of the same. Charges that the only changes are semantic ones, however, appear not to be completely valid. Although the public relations role may have once been to present the company line to the public, organizations now recognize that there are multiple publics with which there must be realistic communication. If a corporation is to transmit the information necessary to influence public opinion, differing interests of the various segments of the public must be attended to. It is only by appealing to the interests of the different publics that a corporation is likely to create a climate more favorable to its own interests.

Having observed what effective public relations can accomplish, business is beginning to see the value of an ongoing communication

[2]"The Corporate Image: PR to the Rescue," *Business Week,* January 22, 1979, pp. 47-61.

program. Rather than alert the public relations forces when a rescue is required, the business organization increasingly relies on its public relations staff to be a bellwether and to anticipate problems. As one public relations specialist explains it to his clients, "Every problem shouldn't have to be an unexpected pie in the face."[3]

In presenting an outsider's image of America, Paul Theroux explained why he felt the image was largely negative. "If America were a military power instead of a commercial empire, people would look up to it. Who respects businessmen? No one. People look at America and all they see are traveling salesmen. So they laugh."[4] While Theroux's feelings may not be identical to those of the American public, it is well documented that there is considerable public skepticism concerning business.

We will now look at some of the efforts of business to make its publics aware of what the corporation is doing to meet its social responsibilities. We will examine communications with stockholders, employees, the public, and the media.

COMMUNICATION WITH SHAREHOLDERS: THE ANNUAL MEETING

According to one public relations consultant, some corporations look upon shareholders as "their best salesmen."[5] The fact that much more attention is being directed to the annual shareholders' meeting than was formerly the case bears out the enhanced importance of these persons.

For years communicating with stockholders seemed to be of secondary importance and hardly the reason for the meeting being held. Instead of being viewed as simply something to get through, though, stockholders' meetings are increasingly seen as an opportunity to brighten the organization's image.

In the past there have been numerous charges that stockholders' meetings were a sham and, indeed, many corporate officials would readily agree that a brief stockholders' meeting was a good meeting. It was alleged that meetings were scheduled for times when they would be unlikely to attract a crowd. Questions of those stockholders who did bother to attend were given short shrift. If questioners persisted, chances were good that they would be ejected from the meeting.

[3]Ibid., p. 50.

[4]Paul Theroux, *The Old Patagonian Express* (Boston: Houghton Miffin Company, 1979), as quoted in "The Bookshelf," *Wall Street Journal,* August 31, 1979, p. 6.

[5]Youssef M. Ibrahim, "Metamorphosis of the Stockholders' Meeting," *New York Times,* April 9, 1979, sec. 3, p. 1.

Corporations now appear to recognize that stockholders have a right to know more than they have been told in the past. Rather than make it difficult for stockholders to attend, some corporations seek meeting times convenient to a large number of stockholders. Organizations such as E. I. du Pont de Nemours and Company sometimes hold stockholders' meetings in addition to the statutory annual meeting. Such "satellite" meetings are held at various sites and help the corporation to get in closer touch with its stockholders. Since there is no official business to transact at such meetings, more time is available for questions and answers. AT&T seeks to become more accessible to its stockholders by broadcasting the annual meeting via closed-circuit television to other sites.[6]

Accompanying the new openness at stockholders' meetings is a widening range of issues being debated there. Many of these issues, once thought to be outside the realm of stockholder involvement, now occupy a significant segment of stockholder meetings. As we discussed in Chapter 10, consumer safety, investments in South Africa, and corporate pay and governance are some of the more prominent social issues stockholders are being asked to consider today.

Stockholders are more likely now to request detailed information concerning a corporation's charitable contributions. Exxon and Con Edison stockholders recently considered, for example, whether the firms should continue to contribute to organizations that engage in experimentation with animals without having a veterinarian on the premises to look after the animals' well-being.[7]

Stockholders attending such meetings represent a much broader spectrum of society than was formerly true. Representatives of unions and church groups, institutional investors, and university officials can regularly be found at these meetings. The efforts of organized groups such as the Interfaith Center on Corporate Reponsibility have ensured that a corporation's level of social consciousness will be publicly examined and evaluated.

In summary, business is more concerned with communicating with stockholders than ever before. Due in part to various social pressures, corporations are not only developing positions regarding social issues but they carefully plan the way in which they communicate their positions. The stockholders' meeting is one format through which a corporation communicates to its stockholders. In the past such meetings were little more than a formality. Now that is changing. Substantive issues are being discussed, and their impact on the organization is being considered.

[6]Ibrahim, p. 9.
[7]Judith Miller, "New Activist Tactics," *New York Times,* April 9, 1978, sec. 3, p. 8.

COMMUNICATION WITH SHAREHOLDERS: REPORTS

Although stockholders' meetings have acquired a broader purpose than in the past, less money is being spent on them and more is being spent on providing information to stockholders in other ways. Yearly and quarterly reports are providing more information than ever before. The 1978 reports of many companies were 10 percent to 40 percent more lengthy than those of the year before.[8]

Rather than simply transmitting the basic financial information in annual reports, some companies have sought to translate the jargon-laden financial information into "plain English,"[9] in order to communicate complex financial information more effectively and, in short, to get stockholders to read it.

While presenting financial data more intelligibly accounts for some of the increased size of the reports, there has been an even more significant change. *Business Week* reported that about half of the 120 big corporations whose reports it surveyed in 1979 discussed such matters as corporate social responsibility and political and environmental issues. According to the previous research of *Business Week*, two-thirds of the reports surveyed in earlier years ignored such topics.[10] Some aspects of social responsibility, however, continue to go unmentioned in business reports. Barnhill-Hayes, Inc., a Milwaukee consulting firm, reported that only 20 percent of the 500 largest industrial companies commented on affirmative action programs in 1978 annual reports.[11]

The formats for communication with stockholders remain largely unchanged. The annual meeting and the report continue to be the most common means used to reach stockholders. The former was once more cosmetic than substantial. The latter was once little more than a collection of complex financial data. Both are now increasingly used to present corporate thought and involvement concerning matters of social responsibility.

COMMUNICATING WITH EMPLOYEES

For many years management believed the only kind of information it was necessary to provide its employees was that which dealt directly with their duties. In the 1930s, however, corporations began to recog-

---

[8]"The Annual Report 1978: Thick and Innovative," *Business Week,* April 16, 1979, pp. 114-118.
[9]Ibid., p. 116.
[10]Ibid., p. 114.
[11]"Labor Letter," *The Wall Street Journal,* September 25, 1979, p. 1.

TABLE 14-1
The Eras of Management-Employee Communication

Era	Date	Purpose of Communication	Sample Topics
I	1940s	Entertainment	Social news features about employees
II	1950s	Information	Company policy; product markets
III	1960s	Persuasion	Company viewpoint on controversial issues

nize the value of giving employees some information about the firm and its activities.

Some researchers believe that communication patterns from management to employees in each of several decades can be clearly identified. Table 14-1 describes the identifiable eras of communication. During the 1940s, Era I, the purpose was entertainment; the 1950s constituted Era II, when the purpose was information; the purpose of Era III, the 1960s, was persuasion.[12]

From the 1930s to the present there has been an evolution in management's efforts to communicate with its employees. As indicated in Table 14-1, management has been motivated to share more information with its employees. This evolution has not occurred at the same pace in all organizations. In fact, some organizations still appear to be mired in Era I, as is evident in many company newspapers or magazines — house organs — published by organizations for their employees.

Employee publications in Era II responded more directly to the information needs of employees. With growing unionization and union publications responding to these needs, company house organs began including articles on such topics as company policy and the future of the company.

Since the advent of Era III in the 1960s, the limits of employees' knowledge of company activities have been considerably expanded. Controversial topics once considered inappropriate are more likely to be communicated to employees. No longer content with presenting information and assuming that the facts speak for themselves, the Era III communicator seeks to persuade individuals by advocating a position.

[12]C. J. Dover, "The Three Eras of Management Communication," *Business and Industrial Communication: A Source Book,* edited by W. Charles Redding and George A. Sanborn (New York: Harper and Row, Publishers, 1964), pp. 61-65.

The Role of House Organs

Today's publications for employees range from mimeographed sheets distributed irregularly to slick monthly magazines. House organs are a widely used means of employee communication. It is estimated that the total circulation of house organs in the United States is over 200 million, more than three times the country's total daily newspaper circulation of 62 million.[13]

Many house organs are still characterized by an absence of controversial company-related issues and by an abundance of items emphasizing management's benevolence. The employee at work and play is a frequent subject of articles.

After working two days for Atlantic Richfield Corporation as a business communicator, humorist George Plimpton devised the following "rules" for those who edit house organs:

1. Do not on Friday write an article complete with pictures about an employee who is fired the following Monday.
2. Do not run a picture of an individual who has just won a substantial lawsuit against the company.
3. Do not run baby pictures of the company president.
4. Do not run favorable reviews of publications or movies with views in opposition to those of the company.
5. Do not include a regular department titled "Accident Corner" where employees tell their own stories.
6. Do not print stories on topics which may be of interest to you but to no one else at the company.
7. Do not ignore a strike if the company's main gate has been smashed flat.[14]

Plimpton's rules notwithstanding, it appears that the thrust of the house organ is changing. A comparison of the content of employee publications of 1975 with those of 1977 found that information on company policies jumped from nineteenth place to fourth place while personals dropped from fourth to twenty-first. According to the researcher, "Babies, bowling scores, and babble are diminishing" as major topics in employee publications.[15]

Atlantic Richfield's house organ, *Arco Spark*, is one employee pub-

---

[13]"Most Firms' House Organs Emphasize Employee News and Avoid Controversy," *Wall Street Journal*, November 7, 1978, p. 19.

[14]"Plimpton Tells ARCO Tale," *iabc News*, July 1979, vol. 9, no. 1, p. 7. Reprinted by permission.

[15]"Most Firms' House Organs Emphasize Employee News and Avoid Controversy," p. 19.

lication that does not shun controversy. Subjects such as company-related accidents and resultant deaths or injuries are covered in detail. Suits filed against the company are considered newsworthy and are thus included, as are the company's operational problems. *Flagship News,* the house organ of American Airlines, is also noted for its openness to news that does not always reflect positively on the company. For example, it published details concerning the $75,000 in illegal contributions paid by company officers to former President Richard Nixon's reelection campaign in 1972.

The Zone of Management Silence

Because a house organ is developed exclusively for the employees of an organization, it is an ideal medium for the transmission of information that is especially relevant to them. Instead, however, it is often used solely for the presentation of that which is innocuous and of little interest to the reader. In 1965 a researcher described a "zone of management silence" consisting of a wide variety of controversial subjects about which management does not communicate with its employees.[16] Three main reasons are commonly given by management for not communicating more issue-related information to employees:

1. Corporations fear that their communications may be labeled propaganda.
2. Some corporations feel that their credibility may be lost if they communicate.
3. Some corporations feel that the prestige of the corporate image may be compromised by communication.[17]

The zone of silence appears to be shrinking. A growing number of house organs have expanded their coverage and are now including articles on what the company is and is not doing to meet its social responsibilities. When more companies recognize their employees' right to such information, more viable house organs will result. New approaches may also be taken to disseminating such information to employees. The *Wall Street Journal* reports that in-house corporate television newscasts, for example, are growing in popularity.[18] It is estimated that more than 300 major companies in the United States are using this medium to communicate with employees.

---

[16]"C. J. Dover, *Management Communication on Controversial Issues* (Washington, D.C.: Bureau of National Affairs, 1965), p. 3.

[17]C. J. Dover, "Silence — An Employee Relations Pitfall," *Vital Speeches,* February 1, 1957, pp. 249-252.

[18]"Hottest New Tool in Employee Relations Is the In-House, Corporate TV Newscast," *Wall Street Journal,* April 13, 1979, p. 7.

COMMUNICATING WITH THE PUBLIC

A wide variety of approaches have been taken in recent years to improve the relationship between business and the public. Many efforts have been devoted to simply preaching the gospel of free enterprise. In some quarters it is felt that the distrust and suspicion with which much of the public views business is due to ignorance of the free enterprise system.

With financial support from various business organizations, the efforts of various free enterprise missionaries have not lacked creativity. There are musical groups that rock to the beat of free enterprise. The repertoire of one such group includes a song with these lyrics:[19]

> *You know I could never be happy*
> *just working some nine-to-five.*
> *I'd rather spend my life poor*
> *than living it as a lie.*
> *If I could just save my money*
> *or maybe get a loan,*
> *I could start my own business*
> *and make it on my own.*

A national organization called Students in Free Enterprise is devoted to selling the free enterprise system. Members at the University of Cincinnati wrote a probusiness jingle, set it to disco music, and had it played on radio and television stations in that area as a public service announcement. The project at another school featured seminars on free enterprise geared especially to clergymen. Called Dollars & Saints, it was hoped that the seminars would stimulate clergymen to incorporate free enterprise concepts into their sermons or Sunday School classes. A puppet show was the means used by another group to teach school children that corporate profits are lower than many believe.[20] Projects such as these are intended to publicize the virtues of the free enterprise system in general.

We criticized business earlier in the book for not effectively telling its story, especially with regard to educating the public to its view of profit. Recently, however, business has been trying very hard to communicate by way of magazine ads that its profits are not excessive. Indeed, there has been a spate of such ads in the last several years. Exhibits 14-1 and 14-2 are ads from the Mobil Corporation and Chevron that illustrate these communication efforts.

---

[19]"Corporations Back Campus Missionaries for Free Enterprise," *Wall Street Journal,* June 21, 1979, p. 1.
[20]Ibid., p. 33.

...il customers, we thank you for our $47.9 billion in sales. ...thought you'd like to know where each dollar went.

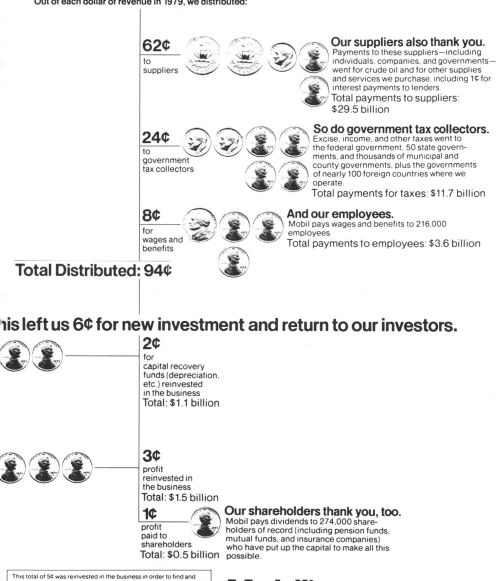

ONE DOLLAR OF REVENUE

Out of each dollar of revenue in 1979, we distributed:

62¢
to suppliers

Our suppliers also thank you.
Payments to these suppliers—including individuals, companies, and governments—went for crude oil and for other supplies and services we purchase, including 1¢ for interest payments to lenders.
Total payments to suppliers: $29.5 billion

24¢
to government tax collectors

So do government tax collectors.
Excise, income, and other taxes went to the federal government, 50 state governments, and thousands of municipal and county governments, plus the governments of nearly 100 foreign countries where we operate.
Total payments for taxes: $11.7 billion

8¢
for wages and benefits

And our employees.
Mobil pays wages and benefits to 216,000 employees.
Total payments to employees: $3.6 billion

Total Distributed: 94¢

...is left us 6¢ for new investment and return to our investors.

2¢
for capital recovery funds (depreciation, etc.) reinvested in the business
Total: $1.1 billion

3¢
profit reinvested in the business
Total: $1.5 billion

1¢
profit paid to shareholders
Total: $0.5 billion

Our shareholders thank you, too.
Mobil pays dividends to 274,000 shareholders of record (including pension funds, mutual funds, and insurance companies) who have put up the capital to make all this possible.

This total of 5¢ was reinvested in the business in order to find and develop new energy sources and provide other products and services people need. In 1979, it took 49¢ of assets to generate one dollar of revenue.

...bil Corporation

Based on estimated unaudited results.

...ted by permission.

EXHIBIT 14-2

No. 4 *America's energy problem is complex. This is the fourth in a series in which we will discuss each of the individual factors affecting the energy situation.*

Profits: Friend or Foe?

In the enormously expensive job of energy development, profit is one of the most important factors. Simply put, profits produce energy.

Fact is, after paying stockholder dividends, Chevron historically has invested its remaining profits . . . and more . . . in the development of energy.

What's Chevron's profit on a dollar?

While our profits appear large in total dollars, the amount we earn on each sales dollar is less than you may think. This year, Chevron averaged about 5½ cents profit on each dollar worldwide . . . about 3½ cents in the U.S.

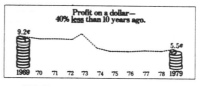

Profit on a dollar—
40% less than 10 years ago.

9.2¢

5.5¢

1969 70 71 72 73 74 75 76 77 78 1979

'79 Profits will help provide more energy.

Increases in Chevron's profits this year make it possible to spend about $400 million more than originally planned for energy development . . . 75% in the U.S.

Profits are vital to the development of America's own energy sources. And just as important, all of us must do an even better job of conserving the energy we have now.

Thank you for listening.

Chevron U.S.A. Inc.

Speakers' Bureaus

An increasing number of organizations are beginning to recognize the importance of gaining public understanding and support on significant issues. Speakers' bureaus are often used as a means of accomplishing those ends. A speakers' bureau consists of employees who are available to speak before groups about various subjects, usually related to the employer's interests. Unlike most of the other approaches to communicating with the public, the speakers' bureau format allows face-to-face contact. Typically, there is also the opportunity for audience members to ask questions of the speaker.

Because public scrutiny of business organizations has increased, much care is now taken in the preparation of those employees who participate in the firm's speakers' bureau. In many organizations the training of speakers is done by outside professionals hired by the company. The company gives each speaker material on the most relevant topics. An oil company, for example, might provide materials on such topics as energy supply and demand, environment, divestiture, imports, decontrol, and profits.

The importance that organizations attach to such public contacts is evident in the lengths to which they will go to ensure effective communication. Some companies even provide their speakers with slide presentations and movies. Ordinarily the company schedules and coordinates the speaking engagements and, if speaking schedules grow light, the company may publicize the availability of its speakers.

Traditionally, speakers' bureaus have been staffed by executives. But Continental Oil Company (CONOCO) has recruited rank and file workers also — in addition to the usual corps of executives. Their speakers also include economists, engineers, geologists, lawyers, secretaries, and pipeliners.

By making such nontraditional types of representatives available for public contacts a company may be able to overcome a significant barrier to general acceptance of the speaker's message. It is often felt that what an executive presents to a group is nothing more than the "party line" of the organization. An organization might enhance its credibility by providing a broader spectrum of company representatives.

In the public communication formats thus far described, the organization is able to control the situation. Even though the public might not completely accept the message as intended, the message and the situation in which it is presented are carefully planned — the communication is characterized by organizational planning and control.

Crisis Communication

Control and planning are not possible, however, in all instances of communication between the organization and the public. Very often some unexpected crisis or incident necessitates immediate communication. Variables over which the organization was formerly able to exert control are suddenly beyond its control.

What *Fortune* magazine has termed the "Firestone Fracas" is a good example of what sometimes occurs when an organization must respond publicly to a crisis.[21] From the time Firestone was first accused of selling defective radial tires, the image it conveyed to the public was not a positive one. It attempted to thwart the investigation of the National Highway Traffic Safety Administration (NHTSA) and, in the process, attracted more negative publicity than might otherwise have been the case. The result was that considerable negative communication concerning the company's view of its social responsibilities took place.

As reported in *Fortune*, Firestone held a major clearance sale of their 500-series radials while the government was quietly investigating the safety of the tire. When the investigation later became common knowledge, it appeared that Firestone's sale had actually been an attempt to unload damaged and unsafe goods. Even though Firestone later claimed that the clearance sale was routine in all respects, it is unlikely that the public perceived it in that way. By its actions the company communicated to much of the public its concern for making a profit, even at the possible expense of consumer safety. As the investigation gathered momentum, Firestone gained further questionable publicity by charging that the investigating agency bore a grudge against it, and that the investigation was all a part of a Naderite conspiracy.

When the NHTSA conducted a survey of tire owners, Firestone learned that its products had made the worst showing. It then went to court and secured a restraining order to prevent the agency from making the results public. The end result of this order was to further publicize Firestone's recalcitrance in the matter as well as its apparent indifference to the public good. Ironically, despite the restraining order, the survey results were inadvertently released and published. Thus, Firestone received a double dose of bad publicity: first, by opposing the release of the survey findings, and second, by the actual findings, which reflected poorly on the company's 500-series radials.

As the investigation progressed, Firestone balked at providing information regarding such matters as complaints against its radials and the

[21]Arthus M. Louis, "Lessons from the Firestone Fracas," *Fortune,* August 28, 1978, p. 45.

manufacturing methods used. Additional court action was necessary to gain the cooperation of the company. Throughout this episode Firestone sought to obstruct an orderly investigation of an apparent problem. It conveyed to the public a disregard for human safety and an arrogance toward both government and public. Because the concept of social responsibility was ignored so completely, this case history affords an excellent example of how not to cope with a public crisis.

BUSINESS AND THE MEDIA

The relationship between business and the media has been the subject of much speculation. One business executive compares the relationship between business and the press to "two strange dogs circling each other warily, suspicious of each other's intentions." Another describes the relationship as "tentative." Business executives have two main complaints against the press: (1) the press is prejudiced against business; and (2) the press is not competent to report business and economic news. Media representatives, on the other hand, claim that what business actually wants is simply a more favorable press.

Causes of Tensions

Robert A. Beck, chairman and chief executive officer of the Prudential Insurance Company, cites six dilemmas to explain the tension and misunderstandings that exist between business and the media.[22]

1. The Question Dilemma. Because questions from the press are often considered evidence of mistrust, business representatives often respond with anger or at least with extreme wariness. Questions and an inquiring mind, however, are major tools in the reporter's toolchest. Without the inquisitiveness which business finds threatening, the reporter is impotent. When a reporter ceases to be skeptical, he or she becomes gullible.

2. The Object/Process Dilemma. While reporters consider the business process to be of interest to the public, business emphasizes results rather than the means employed to accomplish them. While the reader may be interested in the steps followed and the obstacles encountered in pursuing a goal, the business person avoids discussing such information because it might be of value to the competition.

3. The Consensus/Conflict Dilemma. Reporters seek evidence of

[22]Robert A. Beck, "The Forum," *Dun's Review,* December 1978, pp. 87-91.

conflict because conflict interests readers. Business people strive for consensus because that is the route to unified action. While the media may highlight disagreement as newsworthy, business people view it as counterproductive and certainly not appropriate for public exposure. In short, from the reporter's standpoint conflict is exciting; consensus is dull.

4. The Secrecy Dilemma. Secrecy is viewed by many business people as being vital to the efficient performance of business. Research and development plans, sales figures, marketing projections, and details about manufacturing processes are kinds of information that must be guarded from competitors.

From the viewpoint of the media, however, such secrecy suggests either conspiracy or questionable business practices. After all, the suspicious person reasons, if a company were doing business in an honest and ethical fashion there would be no need for secrecy. In these post-Watergate times such attitudes seem more reasonable than they might have at an earlier time.

5. The Expansiveness Dilemma. When a business person is expansive to the media, that person's colleagues view it as grandstanding or publicity seeking. Such a person might be accused of seeking to gain power within an organization by developing support of the public.

As perceived by a news person, expansiveness indicates honesty. An individual who has nothing to hide will be open and expansive. An unwillingness to talk freely indicates to the news person either willful deceit or, perhaps, ignorance.

6. The Complexity/Simplicity Dilemma. An ongoing complaint by business is that the media frequently reduces the complex to the simplistic. Time and space demands constrain the media from devoting as much attention to complex issues as these issues merit. Business people usually acknowledge that compression in the media is inevitable; what they do complain about is the distortion that may accompany such compression. The press maintains that business people routinely inflate the simple to the very complex. This practice thus makes it necessary, in the view of the news people, to deflate the content accordingly.

Beck believes that the business/media tensions are caused not only by these dilemmas but also by a problem of stereotyping. Each side, for example, views the other as irresponsible. Business people see journalists as responsible to no one, least of all the truth. In the journalist's view, business people operate completely free from control. These dilemmas and various outworn stereotypes are responsible for many of the misunderstandings that exist between business and the media.

There is little doubt that misunderstandings and the resulting tensions between business and the media have created an adversary relationship between the two. In the minds of many on either side of the issue, it has become "we" versus "they." Evidence abounds about the caution with which the two sides view each other, as well as the perceptions of third parties. A professor writes of "the visceral hatred and contempt that most businessmen have for the media."[23] A journalist maintains that American news people are hostile to business. Referring to television, she writes: "The antagonism to capitalism on the nation's airwaves, the deeply entrenched prejudice in favor of state control over the productive machinery of the nation, is not a subjective assessment. It is a hard cultural fact."[24]

Executives as Communicators

A significant aspect of the stressful relationship between business and the media concerns the role played by the business executive. Corporate presidents, for example, may be selected on the basis of managerial, financial, or legal expertise; they are not selected for their ability to explain the corporate stance to lay persons unfamiliar with the organization. The skills required of an executive are different from those necessary to deal with the media.

It often happens that a person who is a very competent manager is not at all competent in dealing with media people. Consequently, a new occupation has developed to remedy such shortcomings. Communication consultants are now being hired to coach executives on how to handle questions, whether from reporters or stockholders, and how to speak with clarity and directness. Giving the executives stage presence is the general thrust of much of such training, and these coaching services are being purchased by many major corporations. One such service is reported to charge $4,000 for a twelve-hour seminar.[25]

Because many executives are unskilled in effective communication, they are at a severe disadvantage when confronted by a skilled interviewer. The increased use of communication consultants represents an attempt to make the executive a more even match for the reporter.

There are some who believe that most executives are already too

---

[23]Louis Banks, "Taking on the Hostile Media," *Harvard Business Review,* March-April 1978, p. 123.

[24]Edith Efron, as quoted by Chester Burger, "How to Meet the Press," *Harvard Business Review,* July-August 1975, p. 62.

[25]James C. Condon, "Coaching Executives on Stage Presence," *New York Times,* February 6, 1977, p. F-2.

highly polished as communicators. Columnist Art Buchwald has written of the way "corporate gobbledygook" may be used when a person tries to befog an issue.[26] According to Buchwald, corporate spokespersons often do not say what they mean. He provides translations for what he considers to be typical messages:

When a Person Says . . .	*That Person Means . . .*
"We have no comment on the charges until we can study them."	"Maybe by next week the reporter won't call back."
"There is no truth to the government's charges that our product is unsafe. Under normal conditions it is accident-proof. But we 'can't guarantee it where the consumer doesn't follow the instructions.' "	"Maybe by next week the reporter won't call back."
"We have decided to plead 'no contest' to avoid an expensive legal battle which we are certain we would win."	"Our lawyers have advised us we don't have a chance in hell of winning the case."

Although Buchwald is a satirist, he reflects some commonly held perceptions of the business executive. It is a stereotype that may have some basis in fact. Because the image of business held by the public is determined in part by the media, it is crucial that business strengthen its relationship with the media.

ADVOCACY ADVERTISING

Although business recognizes the need for improved media relations, it also recognizes constraints which would persist even with the betterment of relations. The advent of improved relations will not alter the basic function of the media, which will continue to be to investigate and to publish that which is newsworthy. Even if business/media relations were to become absolutely harmonious, business-as-usual would continue to lack newsworthiness.

As a means of ensuring that their concern for the public interest receives public exposure, some large corporations have turned to advocacy advertising. In advocacy advertisements an organization presents its views on one or more public-policy issues. According to Sethi, an authority on the subject, advocacy advertising is "concerned with the propagation of ideas and elucidation of controversial social issues of public importance in a manner that supports the position and interests

---

[26]Art Buchwald, "Corporate Gobbledygook," *Atlanta Journal,* September 24, 1978, p. 3-C. Reprinted by permission.

of the sponsor while expressly denying the accuracy of facts and downgrading the sponsor's opponents."[27] More simply defined, advocacy advertising is "the purchase of advertising space to express a viewpoint on controversial issues of social importance."[28] To illustrate the concept of advocacy advertising, Exhibits 14-3 and 14-4 are ads published by Champion International and Bethlehem Steel.

Advertising: Image and Advocacy

Organizations have long engaged in traditional corporate image advertising, which has as its purpose keeping the corporate name in the public eye. While the function of product or service advertising is obvious, corporate image advertising is less so. Corporate image advertising simply deals with the characteristics of the corporation.

The objective of corporate image advertising is to make friends for the company. It often does this by relating the company to activities that are considered socially desirable. The company's efforts to control pollution or to conserve natural resources might be the subject of an advertisement, the aim of which is good public relations. Corporate image advertising is usually somewhat bland, and its impact is probably minimal.

In contrast to corporate image advertising, advocacy advertising does not shun controversy. It deals with controversial matters while promoting the interests of the sponsor. The American Electric Power System, for example, conducted a media campaign over a several-year period. The ads touched on a variety of energy-related issues; they brought public attention to the battle between utilities and groups regarded by the utilities as unsympathetic to their cause. Among these groups are the federal government, conservationists, state legislatures, and government regulators at every level.

Purposes of Advocacy Advertising

Sethi suggests four main reasons for using advocacy advertising.[29] When a business organization uses advocacy advertising, it is for one or more of these purposes:

1. To counteract public hostility to corporate activities because of ignorance or misinformation.

---

[27]S. Prakash Sethi, *Advocacy Advertising and Large Corporations,* (Lexington, Mass.: D.C. Heath and Company, 1977), p. 7.

[28]S. Prakash Sethi, "Business and the News Media," *California Management Review,* Spring 1977, p. 52.

[29]Sethi, *Advocacy Advertising and Large Corporations,* p. 57.

EXHIBIT 14-3

The future is coming. And with it will come great benefits for mankind. And a whole new set of problems. Because we are a forest products company, and plant seeds that take up to 50 years to become mature trees, Champion International has to think a lot about the future. We'd like to share some of the things we've learned with you—to help you make intelligent choices in the years to come. Here is something you might want to think about.

In the future, electronic information gathering and analysis techniques could be used to find out more about you, and what you think and feel, than you may want others to know.

How will we prevent our heads from turning into open books?

Are your thoughts and feelings *your* property? Or do they belong to any organization that has the skill, technology and *intent* to collect whatever personal data they want about you?

This is a major question concerning many of the world's leading lawmakers today. And with advancing technology, it will become even more of an issue in the future.

Futurist David Goodman believes that ours could become "the most snooped-on society in history" unless we take steps to prevent it.

The issue of personal privacy is a very complex one.

First of all, there is no commonly accepted definition of privacy.

Is privacy "the right to be let alone"? Or is it "the right of the individual to determine when, how, and to what extent there should be a disclosure of information about himself"?

To dramatize how difficult it is to find an appropriate definition, after two years of study and debate a government commission called The Privacy Protection Study Commission finally concluded that *privacy* was not even a good label for many of the issues they were considering, and settled, for lack of a better term, on "fair informational practices."

Many legislators understand that while personal privacy must be meaningfully protected, restrictions on the gathering and analysis of personal data could seriously hamper our society's ability to make import decisions.

As our society becomes more complex, w need to rely on the accurate large-scale gath ing and analysis of information to help us w rational decision-making about important public issues like allocation of resources, hot ing and food supply and health care needs.

Accurate information gathering would a be invaluable in such critical personal decisi as choice of careers, habitats—even mates.

Obviously, information will be one of our most important products in the future. Already, one job in two in the U.S. is related the handling of information.

The Privacy Protection Study Commis-sion has recommended that Congress establ an independent Federal Privacy Board with the government to protect personal privacy in The Age of Information, with its omnidir tional microphones, its lasers, its incredible data banks, etc.

Obviously, there are legitimate needs on both sides of the privacy issue. What we nov do about the use of personal information ca have a profound effect on our future. It's something to think about.

But if you'd like to do more than just thi about it, write to:

Champion International Corporation, Box 10126, 1 Landmark Square, Stamford, Connecticut 06921.

Champion, a forest products company with its roots planted firmly in the future.

We are in the forest products business. We plant trees and harvest trees. We produce wood and paper. And we make things out of wood and paper.

Because we make our living from the forest, our success depends, in one way or another, on the future These are our operating divisions that are planning for the future:

CHAMPION TIMBERLANDS
CHAMPION BUILDING PRODUCTS
CHAMPION PAPERS
CHAMPION PACKAGING (HOERNER WALDORF)

Champion

Champion International Corporation

Planting seeds for the future

SOURCE: ©1979 Champion International Corporation. Reprinted by permission.

EXHIBIT 14-4

Fuel for the future–will America have enough?

Tell Congress what you think it should do to conserve and develop energy.

The space opposite belongs to you. Use it to spur Congress to enact a much-needed energy policy for our nation.

Tell your Congressman—in your own words and for your own reasons—what you think America must do to develop the energy we need for the future. Energy to keep our lights burning. Our homes heated. Our automobiles running. Our factories working.

Conservation can help

All of us must seek new and better ways to save energy —right now and for years to come. But conservation is no cure-all. If America is to grow, and to become less dependent on foreign fuel, reliable sources of domestic energy must be developed.

Coal and nuclear power are practical answers

America sits squarely on top of one of the largest supplies of coal on earth—enough to last hundreds of years, even if we double or triple present levels of consumption.

As a nation, we should expand coal production and substitute this fuel for dwindling supplies of gas and oil.

Coal, for example, can help replace oil and gas to generate electricity.

Reliance on coal is one answer. Increasing the share of the nation's electric power that comes from nuclear energy is another answer. Without continued expansion of safe, large-scale nuclear power, there's a good chance America will face energy shortages year after year as demand rises.

Tell Washington to act

Your ideas on energy may differ from ours. What matters is that you let Washington know what you think. And that you want action.

Write your Congressman today. Your message—along with the messages of thousands of other voters—won't go unheeded.

Bethlehem

Bethlehem Steel
Corporation
Bethlehem, PA 18016

SOURCE: Courtesy Bethlehem Steel Corporation.

2. To counteract the spread of misleading information by the critics of business and to fill the need for greater explication of complex issues.
3. To foster the values of the free enterprise system.
4. To counteract inadequate access to and bias in the news media.

Counteracting Public Hostility. While research substantiates the presence of public hostility toward business, there is less agreement on the causes of the hostility. Business leaders contend that such hostility stems from two factors: (1) ignorance on the part of the general public of the function of business and of business's contributions to society; and (2) misinformation received and accepted by the general public regarding such matters.

Surveys indicate that the public thinks that after-tax profits average 28 percent. They also feel that such profits should be limited by such government regulations as price control.[30] In order to counteract such ignorance and to refute such misinformation, business turns to advocacy advertising.

Because business is a social institution which derives its right to exist from society, it follows that public hostility could destroy it. Business employs advocacy advertising to reduce public hostility. Few question the right of business to take the advocacy approach but some question the value of it, as the effectiveness of advocacy advertising is still largely undetermined.

Counteracting Misleading Information. Business alleges that its antagonists often oversimplify complex issues and that the media adds to the problem by providing one-sided coverage. The public is then provided with misleading information.

Theoretically, advocacy advertising will explain the company's side of the story and thereby balance information that the public has received elsewhere. It is thought that individuals who are exposed to these advertisements will recognize the various sides of complex issues. Advocacy advertisements themselves, however, usually provide only the company's side. If the public is to acquire a balanced perspective, it will not come from a steady diet of advocacy advertisements. As Sethi explains it:

> Thus, the information balance is achieved in the marketplace, where everyone has an opportunity to express his or her viewpoint. It is not in the nature of advocacy advertising to present a balanced picture since one of its premises is to answer the arguments made by opponents. In an admittedly controversial issue,

[30]Ibid., p. 58.

the sponsor is not likely to present the opposition view in a sympathetic light, because to do so would be to reduce the credibility of his own message.[31]

Critics of advocacy advertising claim that much of it attempts to reduce the complex to the overly simple. Thus it appears that business organizations, in their advocacy campaigns, engage in the same practices they fault their adversaries for using. Critics also allege that advocacy advertisements are not actually intended for the general public, as business claims. The media selected by business for advocacy advertisements are not the media on which the general public relies. Rather than attempting to educate the general public through advocacy campaigns, it appears that the intended audience is actually composed of opinion leaders.[32]

Fostering Values of the Free Enterprise System. There is a firmly held conviction among many business leaders that public suspicion of business is due to a basic misunderstanding of the free enterprise system. For that reason much advocacy advertising is aimed at reacquainting the public with traditional American values of free enterprise, individualism, freedom, and the work ethic. Sethi questions the wisdom of such an approach because the relationship between the modern corporation and its marketplace bears so little resemblance to the classical model of the free enterprise system.[33]

Even if an advocacy advertising campaign successfully convinces readers of the merits of free enterprise, such ads may be dysfunctional in the long run. It is conceivable that the increased awareness of the system that may result from advocacy advertising may also increase public awareness of existing diferences between free enterprise in its pure form and the contemporary version. In such a case it would be unlikely that public confidence in business would grow.

John Steiner believes that there is no need to sell the public on free enterprise because the public is already sold. As evidence he cites a survey by Yankelovich which showed that 91 percent of the public does not favor government control of large corporations. The same survey showed that over two-thirds of Americans said they are willing to make sacrifices to preserve the free enterprise system.[34]

It is a fact that much advocacy advertising is aimed at promoting free enterprise. The wisdom of such an approach is disputable, as is the actual need for it.

---

[31]Ibid., p. 65.
[32]S. Prakash Sethi, "Business and the News Media," *California Management Review,* Spring 1977, p. 52.
[33]Sethi, *Advocacy Advertising and Large Corporations,* p. 67.
[34]John F. Steiner, "The Business Response to Public Distrust," *Business Horizons,* April 1977, p. 77.

Counteracting Inadequate Access and Bias

> They (the press) want to cut your throat one day, then be buddy-buddy with you the next. The only thing our news media wants is negative. That's all they want to print. They don't want to applaud the positive; they have to look for the negative. . .[35]

These remarks were part of a speech given by a football coach. They might have been made by a business executive because many business people share this same sentiment. Corporate executives routinely castigate the news media for failure to provide balanced reporting. While some attribute it to unwillingness, the more charitable critics blame it on incompetency. In either case, the media are viewed as being a major cause of the problem.

> Too often a member of Congress, a consumer advocate, an environmentalist — or other adversary — can make sensational charges to which there are factual, sober answers that are anything but sensational. Alas, these answers rarely get much attention. It takes time to assemble facts. Once the facts are in hand, the definition of "news" today militates against their widespread exposure in the news media. . .
>
> Sixty seconds on the evening news tonight is all that is required to ruin a reputation, turn a politician out of office, or impair a company's profitability. The power of the press with today's methods of mass communication has become, in short, the power to destroy.[36]

One newspaper executive responded to such charges with a combination of sympathy and a request for self-evaluation:

> Let me note, first, that as a manager I can sympathize with some of the recurrent complaints that executives make about the press. News coverage of the press as a business is not all it ought to be. I, too, have felt victimized by headlines such as those proclaiming that profits are up 50 percent — when profits rose from 2 to 3 percent. I have been irked by some reporting on labor disputes, production problems and EEO complaints when stories failed to reflect what I thought were important factors or constraints on management.[37]
>
> But if a reporter phones your office with a question, does he get a prompt answer from someone who really knows? Some of you, I know, can say without hesitation: yes. To others, I can only say that complaining to each other about the press is not very helpful to you, or to us. Why not complain to us? When you see explanations that seem to you incomplete or misleading, why not let us

[35]"Carlen Blasts Press," *Atlanta Journal*, September 25, 1975, p. D-2.
[36]Sethi, *Advocacy Advertising and Large Corporations*, p. 75.
[37]Katherine Graham, "Business and the Press," *University of Michigan Business Review*, January 1976, pp. 22-23.

know about it? Why not tell us how to call for expert advice the next time the issue comes up?[38]

Business feels that inadequate access to the media, whatever the cause, is a genuine problem. Even when access is allowed business by the media, so many constraints are imposed, executives complain, that it is not possible to present one's side in adequate detail. *Advertising Age* magazine described some of the constraints in reporting that led Mobil Oil to resort to advocacy advertising. Mobil saw advocacy advertising as a means of refuting certain parts of a news series on the oil industry which was presented on a New York City television station. According to *Advertising Age*, the station offered to allow a Mobil spokesperson to appear on a live newscast or to make a short statement in response to the news series. However, the station refused to relinquish its right to edit what Mobil might have to say.[39] Advocacy advertising is looked on by business as a means of gaining access to the media. Some executives consider it the only approach in which the corporate viewpoint can be presented with enough detail and clarity.

Impact of Advocacy Advertisements

Major organizations such as IBM, Citibank, Bethlehem Steel, Diamond Shamrock, and Boise Cascade now run advocacy ads on various issues. The most prominent exponent of advocacy advertising, however, is Mobil Oil, which budgeted four million dollars for it in 1978.

Yankelovich, Skelly, and White conducted a survey to determine the effectiveness of Mobil's ads on energy deregulation. These are some of their findings:

- 90 percent of the government leaders polled had read them;
- 66 percent of the government leaders thought the ads were of little or no use to them in understanding energy deregulation issues, and they said that the ads did not influence their opinion on any policy matter;
- 9 percent of those surveyed felt that Mobil is "seriously concerned" about doing something to solve the energy problem;
- Many readers are irritated by the tone of these ads, which they describe as "abrasive," "unpersuasive," and "antagonistic."[40]

[38]Ibid., p. 24.
[39]Maurine Christopher, "Mobil Presses WNBC for Paid 'Rebuttal' Time," *Advertising Age,* March 15, 1976, p. 3.
[40]Lynn Adkins, "How Good Are Advocacy Ads?", *Dun's Review,* June 1978, pp. 76-77. Reprinted by permission.

TABLE 14-2
Credibility of Sources of Information Regarding Public Issues

	Very Credible	Not Credible
Advocacy Advertisements	6%	53%
Corporate Executives	12%	39%
Union Leaders	13%	42%

SOURCE: Lynn Adkins, "How Good Are Advocacy Ads?" *Dun's Review*, June 1978, pp. 76-77. Reprinted by permission.

Based on the survey findings, it appears that the penetration of Mobil's campaign is impressive. The ads are high in visibility. One might question the value of visibility, though, when so many respondents find the ads of little or no use.

The low percentage of respondents who consider Mobil "seriously concerned" about the energy problem is surprising considering the penetration of the ads. According to Adkins, this percentage represents virtually no improvement over the previous four years.[41] During the same period, according to Yankelovich, other major oil companies registered gains of up to 6 percent on the question. Also, among the nine companies tested, only one was ranked lower by the public than Mobil.

Regarding advocacy or public-issue ads in general, Yankelovich found that 53 percent of the respondents said they were "not credible." Only 6 percent of the public considered advocacy ads "very credible." In Table 14-2 a comparison is made in credibility of advocacy advertisements and some other possible sources of information.

Mobil Oil Corporation began using advocacy advertisements in 1970 but, as the Yankelovich findings indicate, the impact of the campaign is questionable. If visibility were the sole criterion, their advocacy advertising appears effective. When one considers such criteria as credibility and persuasiveness, the effectiveness of their advocacy advertising is more dubious. The fact remains, however, that many companies are ensuring that their views on social issues are publicly aired through advocacy advertising.

AEP Company's Advocacy Campaign

American Electric Power Company (AEP) spent 3.6 million dollars on an advocacy advertising campaign. The company's campaign included a

[41]Ibid.

TABLE 14-3
AEP's Advocacy Advertisements

Theme	Number of Ads*
Criticism of scrubber systems	13
Criticism of EPA, Clean Air Act, and pollution control standards	8
Encourage and allow greater usage of coal	6
Defending AEP's record in conservation and pollution control	6
Imported oil and gas makes U.S. more vulnerable to foreign pressure	3
Less energy means less employment	2
Urging government to release more federal land for coal mining	2
Criticism of coal exports	2

*Some copy themes are included in more than one category.

SOURCE: Reprinted by permission of the publisher, from *Advocacy Advertising and Large Corporations* by S. Prakash Sethi (Lexington, Mass.: Lexington Books, D. C. Heath and Company, Copyright 1977, D. C. Heath and Company), p. 122.

total of thirty-six advertisements which appeared from February 1974 to December 1974 in major national magazines and national newspapers. The ads also appeared in sixty-nine daily and 192 weekly newspapers located in AEP's marketing area.[42]

In its campaign AEP sought to attract public attention to several controversial issues regarding the energy problem. Table 14-3 lists the main themes of the ads and the number of ads that appeared on each theme.

The effectiveness of AEP's campaign is debatable. As was true of Mobil's campaign, AEP's efforts appeared to succeed in making the public aware of the company. It also may have focused public attention on various significant issues. At least company executives "feel" that the campaign accomplished those purposes. The extent to which the campaign educated or persuaded is not known. Despite the costliness of AEP's campaign, no attempt was made to measure its effectiveness.

Bethlehem Steel has systematically employed readership attitude surveys and analyses to learn which publications offer the company the greatest benefits versus the cost of running advocacy advertisements. Bethlehem was able to identify, on the basis of specific publications, the percentage of "swayables" on each of the three issues addressed in

[42]Sethi, *Advocacy Advertising and Large Corporations,* p. 115.

their ads. The issues were capital formation, environment, and energy. Respondents were identified as swayable if their responses to the survey placed them in one of these categories: moderately in favor of conservative position (probusiness); neutral; moderately in favor of liberal position (antibusiness). These swayables became the target audience for Bethlehem's ads, and the magazines they read became the media used to reach them.[43]

Some advertising executives have estimated that $500 million was spent on advocacy campaigns in 1978.[44] The substantial investment notwithstanding, advocacy advertising, unlike product or service advertising, remains an area in which measurement of results is not routinely attempted.

Legal Implications

Advocacy advertising is not closely regulated at present. There are three governmental agencies, however, that could exert control over such advertising.

Regulations of the Internal Revenue Service allow deductions for advertising that presents views on economic, financial, social, or other questions of a general nature. When such advertising involves outright lobbying, however, deductions are prohibited.[45] The distinction between messages that are informational and those that are persuasive is not a clear one. As corporations increase their advocacy advertising budgets, it seems likely that pressure will mount for a definitive answer to the question of deductions.

In a 1949 amendment to the Communications Act of 1934, Congress approved the fairness doctrine by recognizing "the obligation imposed upon broadcasters ... to operate in the public interest and to afford reasonable opportunity for the discussion of conflicting views on issues of public importance."[46] The Federal Communications Commission has found several institutional or advocacy advertisements to be subject to the fairness doctrine. The FCC decided in favor of applying the fairness doctrine to the National Broadcasting Company for running Esso ads concerning oil development in Alaska. The FCC ruled the same way in the Media Access Project case, which involved Georgia Power Company ads concerning rate increases.[47]

---

[43]William A. Latshaw, "Target Group Research: New Tool for Advocacy Advertising, *Public Relations Journal,* November 1977, pp. 28-33.

[44]Bernice Kanner, "Public Skepticism Fuels Growth of Corporate Ads," *Advertising Age,* February 27, 1978, p. 42.

[45]S. Prakash Sethi, "Economic Scene: Tax Deductability and Business Ads," *New York Times,* July 18, 1978, p. D-2.

[46]Sethi, *Advocacy Advertising and Large Corporations,* p. 105.

[47]Ibid., p. 107.

While the Federal Trade Commission has the authority to require substantiation of product-related advertisements, it has thus far declined involvement in the area of advocacy ads. An FTC staff report does, however, present guidelines for determining whether advocacy ads have a "dominant commercial appeal," in which case the FTC could require substantiation of an ad's claims.

Advocacy advertising is presently viewed by business as an ideal medium through which to provide the corporate viewpoint on controversial issues. As the volume of advocacy advertising increases, so also will the attention paid to it by the public. It also seems likely that governmental regulatory agencies will become increasingly involved.

GUIDELINES FOR IMPROVED CORPORATE COMMUNICATION

The business organization has several options regarding the selection of media for communicating its position on social issues. Regardless of the intended audience, there are certain principles that, if heeded, will result in better communication.

Need for a Proactive Approach. As long as a corporation's communication is limited to responding to the questions and allegations of others, the organization's role in creating its image will be a passive one. The proactive approach allows an organization to develop and pursue a strategy likely to result in the desired image.

Planning Communication in Advance. These are some of the questions that must be asked in planning corporate communication: Exactly what is to be accomplished? How will it be accomplished? What schedule must be followed? How will performance be measured?

Too much of corporate communication is a response to a crisis. It is relatively unplanned and usually defensive in nature. Figure 14-1 describes the success, as perceived by executives, of firms having explicit external affairs objectives compared to those firms without objectives. It is obvious that those organizations that have explicit external affairs objectives are considered to be more successful than those without objectives. This also confirms a point we were making in Chapter 12 concerning the importance of social responsibility goals or objectives.

Willingness to Talk with Journalists. The corporation should provide executives with whatever training is necessary and should encourage contacts with journalists.

Organizations with Objectives ☐

Organizations Without Objectives ☐

FIGURE 14-1
Perceived Success of Firms with Specific Objectives Compared to Firms Without Objectives

SOURCE: W. Harvey Hegarty, John C. Aplin, and Richard A. Cosier, "Achieving Corporate Success in External Affairs," *Business Horizons,* October 1978, p. 71. Copyright © 1978 by the Foundation for the School of Business at Indiana University. Reprinted by permission.

Addressing Issues from the Standpoint of the Public Rather than from that of the Company. It is virtually impossible to arouse public sympathy for a faceless corporation. Unless it can be shown that the corporate viewpoint is supporting the public good, little public support will be forthcoming.

Obtaining Systematic Feedback from Target Audiences. In the absence of feedback there is no way of learning the extent to which the company has elicited the desired response from the public.

Maintaining Ongoing Communication with the Various Publics. More public contacts should be made by corporate representatives from all levels of the organization. The greater the diversity of spokespersons, the easier it will be for the public to identify with them. Ongoing communication will result in a greater voluntary disclosure of information by the company. Presenting negative as well as positive information will enchance the organization's credibility.

Gearing Messages to the Level of the Target Audience. Special efforts must be made to inform the public about topics that are especially subject to distortion and misunderstanding. Corporate profits are such a topic. Many public announcements of corporate profits do little but provide fuel for the charges of excess profits. The public's level of understanding must be recognized when preparing a message.

SUMMARY

Business organizations are now beset by social pressures which heretofore were virtually nonexistent. Corporate executives devote considerable time and effort to developing an organization's position regarding various social issues. Not enough attention is paid, however, to the way in which this information is communicated.

The public relations function has become more important as organizations seek to cope with the pressure exerted by the various publics to which the organization is accountable. The importance of public relations is attested to by the growing number of organizations in which public relations responsibility is placed at the vice-presidential level.

At one time the annual stockholders' meeting was viewed as a necessary but rather meaningless ritual. Now these meetings are actually being used to keep stockholders informed of a wide range of organizational activities. Included in the matters now being discussed at stockholders' meetings are social issues and the company's stance on them.

Companies are also using annual and quarterly reports for multiple purposes. At one time such reports were little more than collections of complex financial data. Now the financial data are made understandable for the average person. In addition to the financial picture, the reader is also often presented with corporate thinking on matters of social responsibility.

Employers today recognize the value of keeping employees informed of corporate thought, even on controversial topics. House organs are widely used for organizational communication. Until recent years, however, house organs dealt only with innocuous topics. Now social issues and corporate responsibility are regarded as appropriate fare.

Business organizations have been innovative in seeking to make the public aware of the ways in which business meets its social obligations. Some organizations concentrate on publicizing the virtues of the free enterprise system; other organizations publicize the ways in which they are being socially responsible. Many companies sponsor speakers' bureaus as a means of getting the corporate message before the public.

Much of the information the public receives from and about business is the result of a crisis. When a business organization is in the midst of a crisis, much of the information the public receives is of a negative nature.

The relationship between business and the media is a stormy one. Each side suspects the motives of the other. Because many otherwise competent executives are poor communicators, they are not effective representatives of their organizations.

Some business organizations try to convey their stand on controversial issues to the public through advocacy advertising. The main purposes of advocacy advertising are: (1) to counteract public hostility; (2) to counteract the spread of misleading information; (3) to foster the values of free enterprise; and (4) to counteract access and bias problems with the media.

QUESTIONS FOR DISCUSSION

1. For what reasons has the public relations function become more important? Which do you consider to be the most important reason? Why?

2. Explain why the annual meeting was not regarded as a significant communication event until recent years.

3. What are the strengths and shortcomings of annual or quarterly reports for communicating with stockholders? (Compare the annual reports from several corporations according to the attention devoted to corporate social responsibility.)

4. Considering the eras of management-employee communication in Table 14-1, do you believe that we are still in Era III (persuasion) or have we entered a new era? If it is new, how would you describe it?

5. For what reasons has management not wanted to communicate issue-related information to employees? Do you believe that there is still a "zone of management silence"? If so, what topics do you believe are presently included in it?

6. Several innovative approaches for communicating with the public are described in this chapter. What are some other possible approaches?

7. What principles should guide corporate spokespersons when obligated to communicate due to a crisis?

8. Of the dilemmas cited as causes of the tension between business and the media, which one do you consider to be most significant? Can you think of any dilemmas in addition to the ones cited?

9. What are the purposes of advocacy advertising? Which one do you feel is the main purpose? Why?
10. What is your overall assessment of advocacy campaigns as a means of presenting to the public the corporate stand on issues? What are the strengths and shortcomings of the advocacy approach?

Cases

Why Advocacy Advertising?

Companies like Mobil are always asked: Why do you do it? Why the high profile and readiness to comment on almost any topic, no matter how socially sensitive? These questions, of course, are asked in reference to Mobil's advocacy advertising program.

Mobil's commitment to dialogue led to the well-known weekly advertising messages that appeared in the *New York Times* and in other leading newspapers. The subjects of the ads have included better television fare, First Amendment rights of business, charities, and so on. They have appeared since 1970.

Mobil's answer to why they do it is twofold. First, they say they are committed to dialogue because a pluralistic society necessitates a vigorous discussion of ideas. Second, they believe that companies, like people, should have an opportunity to manifest their personalities, which in their case includes a demonstration of sensitivity to the environment in which they operate.

Their print messages, which in the late 1970s were budgeted for about $4 million annually, are written entirely by in-house writers who confer on a regular basis with management.

Answering their critics quickly has become one of Mobil's hallmarks. Several years ago, for example, a New York television station carried a series that attacked the oil companies. Mobil responded within a week with a full-page ad in New York newspapers and the *Wall Street Journal*.[1]

QUESTIONS

1. What is your analysis of advocacy advertising, especially of the type Mobil publishes?
2. Is advocacy advertising socially constructive or destructive?

---

[1]Based on Herbert Schmertz, "Mobil's Motives," *The Wall Street Journal*, April 10, 1978, p. 18. Reprinted by permission of *The Wall Street Journal*, © Dow Jones & Company, Inc., 1978. All rights reserved.

3. Is advocacy advertising an effective instrument for communicating the business position on social issues? What alternatives are available?

Communicating Social Performance Information

In the past five years or so companies have used a variety of approaches to communicate social performance information to their various publics. Hundreds of companies have dedicated two or more pages of their annual reports to presentations on social responsibility. Some companies have published special annual reports on their social efforts. These special documents chronicle a company's efforts in areas such as minority hiring and promotion, energy conservation, ethics, and product safety. Other, more ambitious companies have developed special public and social policy goals and publish regular reports of how the organization is progressing toward those goals.

Several companies have also engaged extensively in advocacy advertising. In some cases the issue addressed was related to the firm or industry supporting the ad. In other cases the message was just a general discussion of a current social issue that had no specific relation to the company or the industry sponsoring the ad. Other companies have conducted social audits and made the results available to the public.

QUESTIONS

1. What do you think business expects to achieve by these reporting and communication efforts? What do you think they are achieving? Evaluate each of the above approaches to communicating social performance information.
2. Is social performance reporting really of value?
3. Are the above approaches really worthwhile or is it simply what a company does that is important?

Criticizing Government Through Ads

One of the favorite targets of advocacy ads is government. Many companies have used such ads to criticize excessive government regulation. A good illustration of such advertising appears in the ad reproduced here that was published by Gould Inc.

Technology and overregulation: Or, why our standard of living might not get better.

Determining exactly how much government should regulate American life and industry is an extremely difficult problem. In our past, government intervention was spawned by serious and genuine desires to protect the public good against threatened erosion of the quality of American life. Regulation, then, was intended to *improve* our standard of life by intelligent control.

Today the pendulum of regulation has swung too far. The results of overregulation have become as much a threat to the public good as the original evils they were intended to exorcise.

Overregulation now punishes the public more than it protects.

Today, 87 government agencies have been created to regulate some aspect of business. They regulate product safety, food and package labels, and advertising. They establish hiring, firing, and working conditions. They control the environment, speed limits, and community relations.

As the noose of overregulation tightens, it threatens to strangle creativity and invention—and, therefore, productivity and increased employment. To discourage risk and investment in capital expansion. To discourage increasing investment in research and development. To erode our standard of living. And, ultimately, to stifle progress.

Government overregulation doesn't dampen inflation. It fuels it.

During this fiscal year, Professor Murray Weidenbaum of Washington University estimates that compliance with federal regulations will cost nearly $103 billion, 20% of the entire federal budget. Or about $440 for every U.S. citizen.

Put another way, current regulations increase the price of a new house by $1500 to $2500 and the price of an average new car by $666.

Professor Weidenbaum points out that business must invest about $10 billion in new capital spending merely to meet government regulations each year.

It is expensive, time-consuming, and wasteful to do business in America today.

Overregulation reduces the amount of capital and resources available for the

development and extension of new technologies and higher productivity.

But there is a more subtle effect. Since regulations tend to be so complex, comprehensive, and contradictory, meaningful technological development isn't likely to happen. Companies are so confused and so uncertain whether or not a new process or technology will meet existing or future regulations that they prefer to wait for an age of clarity and rely on more primitive, more proven technologies that simply maintain the status quo.

We must solve our problems—not regulate them into more serious problems.

Economic freedom—the free enterprise system—is still a far more effective arbiter of constituency needs than the tangled bureaucratic maze on the banks of the Potomac. Our competitive economic system—if allowed to work—will work. But it must be given the opportunity.

We do not suggest doing away with all regulation. Only those regulations and agencies that are conflicting, unnecessary, and counterproductive. And the regulators who sanctimoniously believe that they, and they alone, are the last, best hope of the public welfare.

Unless the regulatory house is thoroughly cleaned, the public may become so contemptuous of "Big Brother" government that the regulatory process will cease to be effective.

Fortunately, attitudes are changing. Both business and Congress are beginning to do something about overregulation. But there is a good deal more to be done.

1. **We must eliminate conflicts within the regulatory process itself.**
2. **We need to eliminate overlapping regulatory jurisdiction.**
3. **We need to stop trying to regulate everything in existence and concentrate on those abuses that threaten the public good—realistically.**
4. **We need to determine the cost-benefit effectiveness of the regulatory process.**
5. **We need to place "checks and balances" on the regulators themselves.**

But before we do so, we must understand that tinkering is not the answer. We cannot look at only the worst regulations on a piecemeal basis. We cannot try to regulate the regulators. The problem is the system and the process. And that is where we all should begin.

Business, too, must play a constructive role.

Business must take the initiative and help define the difference between regulation that is necessary and overregulation. Business must also better regulate itself, removing the opportunities and need for government intervention and regulation. It is not too late to undo the damage that overregulation has wrought. For America's businessmen have the courage, creativity, knowledge, and ability to balance the scales.

It really is not an option. Something that Thoreau wrote in 1848 now seems alarmingly prophetic: "If we are left solely to the wordy wit of legislators in Congress for our guidance, uncorrected by the reasonable experience and reasonable complaints of its people, America will not long retain her rank among nations." What we need now is a unified voice of resistance, coupled with a sincere commitment to technological progress. And a better standard of living in the future.

Science and technology can solve many problems. If they don't, what else will?

SOURCE: Courtesy Gould Inc., Rolling Meadows, Ill.

QUESTIONS

1. What is your opinion of business taking government to task in advocacy advertising? Read the Gould ad carefully before responding.

2. Does advocacy advertising of this type create an adversary relationship that would be impossible to overcome? Discuss.

Part V: Epilogue

INTRODUCTION TO PART V

We close out the book with a rather broad discussion of the future social role of business. As we have stated earlier, it is difficult to predict precisely what the business-social issues of the future are going to be, but that should not inhibit our discussion of what the future may be like. The future social role of business will probably be an expanded one, and the emerging trends discussed here should form the basis for some intelligent and reflective thought on what that future might hold. Looking forward, even when the glimpse ahead is not clear, will continue to be the hallmark of the successful manager of business social performance. No less than the very survival of business is at stake.

The Future Social Role of Business

It seems appropriate as we finish the book to consider what the future social role of business is likely to be. At this stage it is still easier to ask the right questions and identify crucial issues than to provide the appropriate answers. We should not be discouraged by this, however. In fact, one corporate planner, recently commenting on the future of business, summed up the changing trend in this way:

> The ruling scepter is passing from those with the answers to those who ask the questions. The best questioners will run the most successful corporations.[1]

It should be added that there have been so many predictions of what business in the future will be like that it would be an impossible task to summarize and construct an appropriate scenario in this brief, final chapter. One principal reason for this is that so much thinking has been done but so little consensus has been reached. Furthermore, as we attempt to limit our comments to business's future *social* role, we have to isolate as best we can many of the economic, technological, and political factors that we know are vital to a comprehensive picture of the future. It is safer and probably fairer to suggest some of the trends that are likely to shape the future social role of business than to construct a scenario that could be superceded in a short time by events in the rapidly changing social scene.

Business's future social role will be a function of the trends (particularly social trends) that emerge and develop, and of what business perceives as its need to respond to these trends as well as to expectations and pressures. Despite the qualification that we will not make specific predictions, one trend seems clear enough to be offered as a foundation to this chapter: Business will have an expanded rather than a contracted social role in the future. Also, because it is risky to speak of

---

[1]"An Expanded Role for Big Corporations," *Business Week*, September 3, 1979, p. 194.

the future in open-ended terms, we will confine our discussion to roughly the next two decades — until the year 2000.

Though there is no absolute consensus that the future social role of business will be expanded, the bulk of writing, thinking, and predicting done today invite this conclusion. What is not so clear is *how expanded* business's future social role will be. In an effort to imagine some of the features of this expanded role, we will discuss a few prominent developments and trends under the following topics:

- Changing societal values
- Role of government
- Work life in the future
- Limits to growth
- Global consciousness

CHANGING SOCIETAL VALUES

It is perhaps proper to discuss changing values first because this factor forms the basis for many of the developments that are now under way. While our discussion here will be limited to the effect of changing societal values on business, we should keep in mind that these values are important in other trends as well.

Values are obviously in a state of transition. In recent years it has been apparent, at least in industrialized countries, that social and personal goals (quality of life issues) have been competing with economic goals as major concerns of the citizenry.[2] New attitudes have developed and are continuing to develop with respect to the environment, interpersonal relations, institutional authority, welfare, and "entitlements" of societal members.[3] There is every indication that these value changes will continue.

A very complex situation for business stems from the expectation that, though social values are increasing in importance, the demand for higher levels of material comfort, more jobs, etc., will continue to strengthen also.[4] The major consequence of this condition is that business cannot relax its economic and technological progress while also continuing to perform successfully in the social arena. One way of depicting this new condition for business can be seen in Figure 15-1,

[2]"The Changing Expectations of Society in the Next Thirty Years," a joint project of the American Assembly of Collegiate Schools of Business (AACSB) and the European Foundation for Management Development (EFMD) (Washington, D.C.: AACSB, 1979), p. 25.
[3]Theodore Gordon, "A View of the World in 2000," in William H. Newman (ed.), *Managers for the Year 2000* (Englewood Cliffs, N.J.: Prentice-Hall, 1978), p. 31.
[4]"The Changing Expectations of Society in the Next Thirty Years," p. 25.

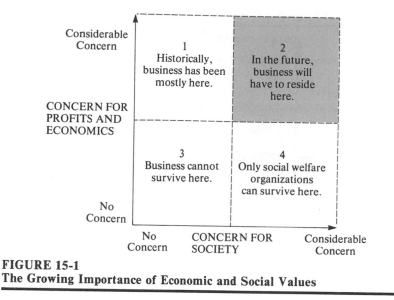

FIGURE 15-1
The Growing Importance of Economic and Social Values

which shows that business's future survival and success lie in quadrant 2. There business will have to put an enormous amount of time and effort into creating not only the traditional economic outputs but social outputs as well. What is not shown is where within quadrant 2 there will be an equilibrium between economic and social concerns.

Changing values are resulting not only in a growing concern for a cleaner environment, limited population and business growth, safer and purer products, equal rights in the workplace, and so on, they are also causing managerial behavior to be more in conformance with increasingly higher ethical expectations. Indeed, in recent years managers have become more sensitive to the ethics of their conduct.

One other value shift that business will have to be sensitive to in the future is the increasing questioning of the capitalist system itself. Capitalism has been criticized historically on two grounds: pragmatics and ethics.[5] Criticism of business on pragmatic grounds reached its zenith during the Great Depression, when it appeared for awhile that the system was not going to work. Today ethical questions are being raised about the system: how it functions; how it allocates goods, serices, and other forms of wealth; and what its social consequences are. Fortunately, whereas business people of years past used to make a pragmatic defense for every ethical attack, they now are more receptive to

[5]Max Ways, *The Corporation and Society* (Austin, Texas: The Institute for Constructive Capitalism, 1979), p. 11.

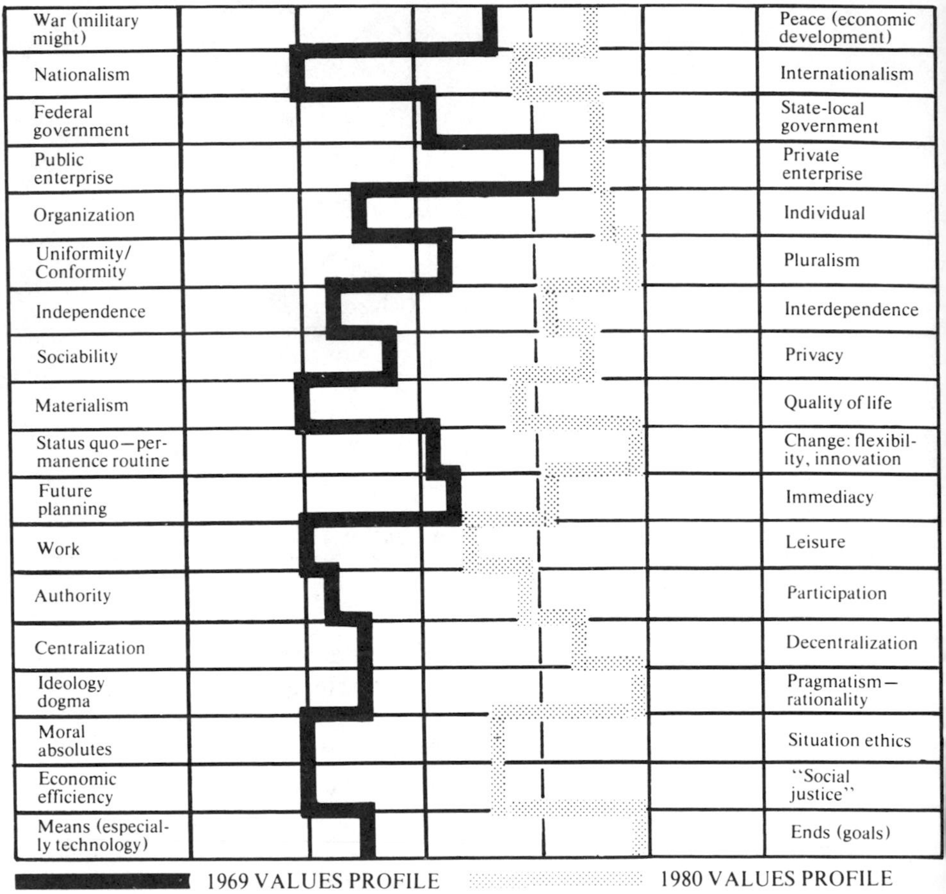

| 1969 VALUES PROFILE | 1980 VALUES PROFILE |

FIGURE 15-2
Profile of Significant Value-System Changes: 1969-1980 (as seen by General Electric's Business Environment Section)

SOURCE: Ian H. Wilson, "Socio-Political Forecasting: A New Dimension to Strategic Planning," *Michigan Business Review,* July 1974, p. 168. Reprinted by permission.

ethical criticism and more willing to institute reforms and accept reformist public policy.[6] They now understand that the future of our system as we now know it is at stake.

To illustrate some of the value shifts business is concerned with and is attempting to anticipate, Figure 15-2 presents some of the changes that the Business Environment Studies staff of the General Electric Company had expected would occur between 1969 and 1980.

[6]Ibid., p. 12.

ROLE OF GOVERNMENT

From an operational standpoint, no trend more precisely helps to specify business's social role than government involvement. With the ever-present threat of its taking ethical and discretionary issues and converting them into legal issues, government's power looms large as business faces the future. In view of the rapidly increasing role government has had in the past decade, it becomes difficult to guess whether this trend will continue for the next twenty years. It is also hard to predict whether the basically adversary relationship between business and government which flourished in the 1970s will continue into the 1980s and 1990s.

Both business and government pay lip service to the notion of a partnership for the future, but there is no evidence available that such a partnership is plausible or forthcoming. In 1979, for example, Thomas A. Murphy, chairman of the board of General Motors, argued in a speech that:

> We in business are calling on the government to end its adversary relationship to us; in return we have a responsibility to be just as cooperative and constructive in our relationship with government, in order to serve the public interest.[7]

Though Mr. Murphy effectively invoked the cases of the Japanese and the West Germans as examples of successful business/government partnerships, very little on the horizon suggests that this model will become a reality soon in the United States.

In Chapter 4 we made clear that what is basically at stake here is a competition between two ideologies. On the one hand is the collectivistic ethic or ideology which is consistent with a larger role for government. On the other hand is the individualistic ethic which business generally embraces and which argues for a restrained involvement of government in business. The extent to which business will become involved with social issues is largely a function of which of these two ideologies emerges as the public choice.

Two fairly recent studies offer somewhat contradictory findings as to what the future holds with respect to business and government. First, William F. Martin and George Cabot Lodge conducted a survey in 1975 to ascertain business managers' views on what 1985 would be like. They reported their findings in an article entitled "Our Society in 1985 — Business May Not Like It."[8] Basically, they questioned managers to

---

[7]Thomas A. Murphy, "Is America Ready for the Eighties?" a speech at the National Coal Association Conference, Colorado Springs, Colorado, June 22, 1979, p. 7.

[8]W. F. Martin and G. C. Lodge, "Our Society in 1985 — Business May Not Like It," *Harvard Business Review,* November-December 1975, pp. 143-152.

determine which of two opposing ideologies they preferred. The first was the traditional American emphasis on individual rights — the individualistic ideology. The second stressed the idea that the group is most important — the communitarianism ideology. The managers surveyed preferred the first ideology but predicted the latter would prevail by 1985. The latter ideology, of course, is more conducive to a larger role for government.

In a second and more recent study, James O'Toole in 1979 attempted to determine, using a Delphi panel of experts, what is ahead for the business-government relationship.[9] He found that — at least in the 1980s — there would be no radical change in the freedom of business to profitably and efficiently produce goods and services.

Several futurists have taken the view that an increased social role for business is inevitable. Howard V. Perlmutter, for example, thinks that government reporting requirements are moving business toward what might be called a "glass-walled corporation."[10] Roy C. Amara, president of the Institute for the Future, puts it this way: "Inevitably, there will be more public involvement in corporations. . ." Amara predicts we will see the rise of the "corporate state" within fifty years. This will be a time in which ". . .allegiance to the company may be more important than to the state."[11]

Some futurists see an even larger social role for business than that so far described. The corporation, it is suggested, could take over certain activities now considered the domain of government. For example, business's participation in education would seem natural, inasmuch as the modern corporation already is deeply involved in such educational activities as day care centers for preschoolers and postgraduate training for executives.[12]

Predictions seem to vary considerably as to what government's role in business will be. The majority of opinion sees government taking on a larger social role in business, but this may be moderated somewhat as business moves on its own in response to societal expectations and pressures. As this occurs, government's role as an intermediary between business and society is only likely to increase to the extent that business does not proact and be responsive to the public will.

[9]James O'Toole, "What's Ahead for the Business-Government Relationship," *Harvard Business Review*, March-April 1979, pp. 94-105. For further information on this survey, see John E. Fleming, "A Possible Future of Government-Corporate Relations," *Business Horizons*, December 1979, pp. 43-47.

[10]*Business Week*, September 3, 1979, p. 194.

[11]Ibid., p. 195.

[12]Ibid., p. 195.

WORK LIFE IN THE FUTURE

Changing population factors suggest difficult times for business in the future as it attempts to absorb a larger and more educated work force into its daily operations. The immediate problem, and probably the biggest employment problem business will face in the 1980s, is to produce the quantity and quality of jobs that will accommodate this new work force. Figure 15-3 portrays population growth by age groups through the year 1990.

Between 1975 and 1985 the increase in the 20-44 age group is signifi-

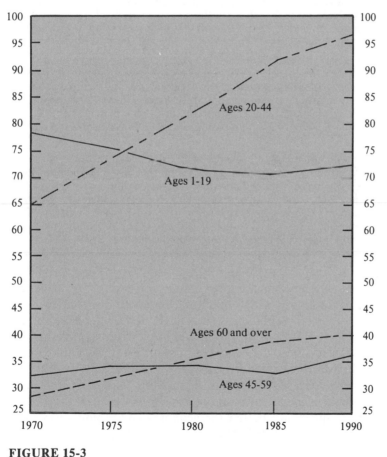

FIGURE 15-3
Population Growth by Age Group (in Millions)

SOURCE: Bureau of the Census, U.S. Department of Commerce.

EXHIBIT 15-1
Employees Will Have a Stronger Voice

It seems almost a given: Employees in 2029 will expect — and get — a much greater say in how they do their jobs. But how far the move toward participatory management will go remains open. Labor leaders normally prefer the role of senior gadfly to junior board member. Thus, while tomorrow's employees will help decide their working conditions and procedures, strategic decisions will still come from the top.

U.S. corporations will seek the best of both worlds. American businessmen think that the Japanese method of filtering all information downward, and weighing all responses equally, leads to agonizingly slow decisions. But they envy the instantaneous implementation of decisions that Japanese "consensus management" provides. American corporations will probably try to ease resistance to fiats by bringing such techniques as management by objectives further down the managerial ladder. And they will continue to beef up internal communications programs.

Decision by oracle. "We will allow a limited group of managers to build a set of objectives that they believe everyone agrees with," predicts James B. Farley, chairman of Booz, Allen & Hamilton Inc. Hank E. Koehn, vice-president of futures research at Security Pacific National Bank, sees that sort of agreement springing from a "Delphi-type" system under which management would retain the ultimate role of oracle, but would consistently poll workers for their views.

Executives who do not accept this will fall by the wayside. "The autocractic instincts of many American executives are such that they'd rather go under than become more democratic," states James J. O'Toole, a writer on work organization and head of the 20-year forecast project for the Center for Futures Research. Yet even O'Toole admits that some democratization is critical. "The only way to increase efficiency is to get workers to be more responsible," he says. "You don't order people to be more responsible."

---

cant. Because this represents the most employable group, the challenge to business to absorb and satisfy it should be enormous. This will be greatly due to the competitive pressures generated by the sheer numbers of individuals in this group. Compounding the problem is the fact that this is the best educated group in our nation's history, with over 40 percent estimated to have attended college by the time they are thirty.[13]

Some experts see severe social disruptions ahead as business attempts to make available meaningful jobs for this burgeoning group. There is serious question whether the economy and business will ever supply enough high-level jobs to match the educational attainments and aspirations of this baby-boom group.[14] Besides a probable shortage of jobs for this group, pressures will continue to make those jobs that are

[13]"Americans Change," *Business Week,* February 20, 1978, pp. 66-67.
[14]Ibid., p. 67.

Nor can people be ordered to be more productive, and participatory management may be one way of getting clerical and managerial workers to pull their weight in the effort. A recent study showed that middle-level managers spend 25% of their time on "clerical" duties. Word-processing centers and other methods of automating offices will help, but most important will be learning to measure managerial productivity.

Although the U.S. is nowhere near having such a system, most experts are optimistic. "Companies are very willing to share productivity data," notes C. Jackson Grayson Jr., head of the American Productivity Center. And business can be sure of public support for improving productivity, adds Theodore J. Gordon, head of The Futures Group. "Profits have become a dirty word — productivity is still clean," he says.

Employee loyalty. Productive workers are not necessarily loyal workers, however, U.S. companies are unlikely ever to attain the intense degree of employee loyalty that the Japanese corporations take almost for granted. However, even today, American businesses have instituted fringe benefits and systems that are suspiciously reminiscent of the Japanese view of corporate morality. Employee-assistance programs, for example, guarantee an employee's job while he is treated for alcoholism, emotional disorders, or other diseases. Tuition assistance, housing allowances, and other executive perks will filter down through the ranks, making employees less impatient to leave jobs.

But they still will leave jobs — and probably in Japan as well. Japanese worker loyalty is already eroding. American businessmen can take consolation in the fact that, 50 years from now, job-hopping may be a global and not just an American problem.

SOURCE: Reprinted from p. 198 of the September 3, 1979 issue of *Business Week* by special permission, © 1979 by McGraw-Hill, Inc., New York, N.Y. 10020. All rights reserved.

available more in keeping with society's new concept of job satisfaction and employees' rights. Workers will increasingly demand meaningful and challenging work, greater individual responsibility, and an opportunity to assume a role in decision making. Exhibit 15-1 is one view of what may happen in the area of employee involvement in decision making by the year 2029.

Though it is difficult to predict how business will cope with the growing numbers of educated workers, it may deal with the employees' new concept of the workplace by extending a number of management techniques and strategies that are now being tried. Among these new approaches are efforts toward job enrichment and restructuring work time. The purpose of job enrichment plans, of course, is to make jobs more meaningful to the jobholder. Restructuring work time is done to give workers more control over their time and to help accommodate their desire for more flexibility than the traditional eight-hour day, fourty-hour workweek schedule allows. Two examples of the restructuring of work time which will undoubtedly continue are the shorter work week and flex-time programs, which allow workers to start and stop work at times that are more convenient than the traditional daily schedules of the past. Exhibits 15-2 and 15-3 present two scenarios of work life in 1998 that were developed by the American Council of Life Insurance.

LIMITS TO GROWTH

The recent acknowledgment that there are limits to business growth is not merely a reflection of changing values about the environment and pollution, but represents a realization of the stark reality of an energy shortage and limited resources. This new awareness is in striking contrast to the traditional business view that "big is better" and that continuous growth should be the ultimate objective.

Historically, business has been able to operate under the assumption that "bigness is goodness" without difficulty. It is only the recent awareness of the environmental conditions in which business exists that has generated the view that there are and must be limits to growth. As business faces the future, its approach to dealing with growth will characterize in a significant way its social or societal role. Societal and world conditions are dictating that business view the notion of growth differently, and the way business responds to this mandate will in a dramatic way shape our future. Stated in another way, business has a very important social responsibility to manage its growth so that the quality of life is not further diminished.

The primary reasons business will have to alter its concept of growth include increasing world population, resource shortages, and environmental pollution. Of particular importance among these is the availability and scarcity of resources, the future status of which business has not yet been able to determine. At least three attitudes illustrate the varying assumptions that are being made concerning the availability of resources:

1. *Doomsday.* This view holds that all resources are being depleted and pollution is increasing at an accelerating rate. Ecological disaster is inevitable.
2. *No Problem.* This view holds that technological ingenuity and the price mechanism working through the normal supply and demand interactions will provide substitutes and solutions as the need arises.
3. *Constructive Realism.* This view holds that sensible planning and

EXHIBIT 15-2
Work in the Future: Scenario A, 1998

Scenarios attempt to provide credible paths to alternative futures. There are two scenarios in this report; one focuses on the changes that might result from major shifts in attitudes toward work and the other focuses on changes that could result from the rapid development of certain technologies. In reality, these variables will interact with many others to determine trends in the world of work.

These simple scenarios are not predictions, but rather aids to help the reader visualize the results of today's decisions.

Combined with the fulcrum of continued affluence, attitudes toward work were the levers that pushed the workplace off balance. Unaware that these new attitudes could act as such a powerful agent of change, many organizations were unprepared for a decade of workplace transition.

The whispers of worker restlessness grew louder during the 1980s as the availability of promotions and other financial incentives became limited. By mid-decade, workers were shouting for redistribution of authority and the compensation that accompanies it, for a re-evaluation of the rights and responsibilities of workers and supervisors, and for the opportunity to perform meaningful work and to restructure the workplace in accordance with changing societal definitions of fair treatment.

Some managers, attuned to the implications of these developments, tried to modify existing policies to demonstrate that their organizations were malleable enough to cope with change. Perhaps it was a case of too little, too late. Workers put their muscle behind legislative proposals.

Co-determinism Acts, modeled on European bills of the 1970s, passed in over half the states. Under the provisions of this legislation, workers won the right to choose their supervisors and to hold half the seats on boards of directors. In many localities, employers were legally required to provide exercise facilities, family centers (including day care), counseling or other stress management technique sessions.

About the same time, supporters of the Employee Bill of Rights put together an unexpected coalition of interest groups, including unions, professional organizations and public interests groups, some of which everyone else seemed to think were splintered beyond repair. After a minor setback (the right to refuse to work under hazardous conditions was defined to exclude mental hazards), the bill passed.

And yet by the mid-1990s, it became apparent that behavioral changes resulting from changing attitudes toward work would have greater impact on society than all the legislated worker participation combined.

Flexible work patterns, increasingly valued as workers sought autonomy and control over their lives, became the norm. This one change gave most Americans the opportunity to exercise more choice in the way they structured their daily lives. Child care responsibilities could be more evenly divided, so even more women entered the labor market. Exurbs and rural areas bristled with construction as new housing went up to accommodate those who could now live further from the city. In the cities, new "families" of affinity groups with common interests shared both work and home tasks. Energy consumption patterns, shopping patterns and transportation systems were dramatically altered. Government policy, at both the Federal and local level, was shifted from the family to emphasize the individual.

Knowing they would enjoy a longer life than their counterparts a few decades ago, many Americans set aside their late middle years to prepare for a new career. The scarcity of labor for entry-level jobs in the 1990s never materialized, as so many "older" Americans chose to exploit these opportunities to start over in another field. In the same fashion, the burden on retirement programs eased when Americans started taking leisure time earlier in life and then returned to work in their later years.

SOURCE: American Council of Life Insurance, "Work in the Future, Scenario A, 1998," *TAP 17: The Changing Nature of Work*, p. 12. Reprinted by permission.

EXHIBIT 15-3
Work in the Future: Scenario B, 1998

It is clear that fewer and fewer people need to work to support the needs of Americans and Canadians. Industrial robots, advanced micro-computer capabilities in almost every home and the capacity to reproduce matter without using traditional manufacturing processes (through replicators or plazma enzyme production) are making human labor obsolete.

Policymakers call the lack of work the most serious problem of the century. Stop-gap solutions include several legislative efforts to assign value to housework and other socially useful leisure activities, so that fewer people will seek paid employment away from the home.

Public debate over the allocation of jobs has revolved around the following options: creating a government job lottery; establishing a national meritocracy system for all jobs; assigning jobs to those most in need of them; encouraging emigration; selling jobs and gearing educational efforts to convince students that while productivity is important, jobs are not.

To some degree, a meritocracy is already in place. At early ages, children undergo intelligence testing, muscle fiber analysis and tests to determine their potential ability to exercise control over the "involuntary" muscle systems and the emission of hormones. This information (along with intelligence evaluations) determines the education students receive and, to a great degree, their employment. Databanks are routinely used to match job specifications to test results of applicants. A counter-trend to the development of an absolute meritocracy is the widespread concern that genetic experiments will be used to design the ideal worker for specific jobs.

Consciousness experiments and technologies began to receive increased attention in the 1980s as a way to cope with systems complexity. It is expected that these new technologies will make a direct brain and computer hook-up possible within the next decade. There are fears, however, that this synthesis will further reduce the need for knowledgeable workers and would make it possible for a few of the new expanded brains to exert incredible influence over the activities of others.

Even though Federal cash grants provide everyone financial security at a minimum level, the growing class of unemployed is expected to grow even more restless. Global unemployment has pushed record numbers of undocumented workers across American borders. Displaced workers make minimal attempts to find new jobs. Crime rates are staggering; it seems that criminals are engaging in acts of violence merely to relieve boredom. Terrorist groups show the potential of strangling several major cities.

People no longer identified themselves foremost as workers, as working hours shrank and offices were replaced by communication systems. For many mobile, multi-married Americans, work identity had provided the last solid link to a sense of community. When this final link to traditional communities was severed, the resulting individual isolation and the responsibilities that came with it were too disorienting for most people to handle.

As a result, closely knit groups—with their implicit promise of continuity and support—flourished. Religious institutions, particularly those who rejected many technologies, recruited massive followings. Political showmen put together feverish rallies. Remaining workers looked for ways to share tasks; labor saving devices were rejected in favor of labor-intensive methods.

This wave of anti-technology has saddened many Americans, since they fear that by saying no to the challenge of leisure, humankind may be losing its only chance for undreamed of evolution and trans-formation.

SOURCE: American Council of Life Insurance, "Work in the Future, Scenario B, 1998," *TAP 17: The Changing Nature of Work,* p. 13. Reprinted by permission.

ecological prudence will help us to develop more effective resource strategies ahead of time.[15]

Which of these views, or others not listed, should business hold about the future? Not knowing the answer, it should not be too surprising that many experts think business should take a conservative posture. Questions such as the following are frequently raised: "Can we have an economically growing society which uses less energy and resources? What trade-offs will people make between levels of consumption (of energy and other resources) and rising prices, pollution or loss of amenity, risk of catastrophe (e.g., from nuclear power), [and/or] undesirable working conditions (e.g., in coal mines)?"[16]

To assume this new social role of managing and controlling the earth's resources and the possible polluting effects of their use, business must learn to differentiate between good growth and bad growth, and must develop a responsible growth strategy. With respect to good versus bad growth, Peter Drucker has recently argued that business does not understand that "there is no virtue in business growth."[17] He goes on to state that a company is not necessarily better because it is bigger any more than an elephant is "better" because it is bigger than a honeybee. With respect to a responsible growth strategy, Drucker argues that every business needs one and that it must have ways of knowing whether it is really growing or merely getting obese.[18] Pursuing this concept of a responsible growth strategy, A. G. Kefalas reasons that business cannot accept or afford anything but a growth pattern that keeps a firm's increase in output and productive capacity in line with increases in its external environment. He terms this a "sustainable growth strategy."[19]

The notion of limits extends beyond the ultimate global or physical limits to growth. As never before our society, and indeed the world society, is being forced to make choices among priorities. No longer can we have everything. Business will assume a vital social role in these decisions, as they inevitably involve business exerting its efforts in one direction or another. The full force of this notion of limits has not yet been absorbed by the public consciousness, but it will in the future.[20]

[15]"The Changing Expectations of Society in the Next Thirty Years," p. 22.
[16]Ibid., p. 22.
[17]Peter F. Drucker, "Good Growth and Bad Growth," *Wall Street Journal,* April 10, 1979.
[18]Ibid.
[19]A. G. Kefalas, "Toward a Sustainable Growth Strategy," *Business Horizons,* April 1979, p. 40.
[20]Roy Amara, "Issues of the 1980s: Society's Five-Sided Attack on Management," *Planning Review,* March 1978, p. 13.

GLOBAL CONSCIOUSNESS

Most of the issues we have been discussing have pertained to our domestic society, but the future social role of business will extend beyond national boundaries. The changing international order is dictating that business no longer consider its role on simply a national scale. A global consciousness is forming and taking hold. Interdependence among nations is becoming more obvious. As a consequence, business — especially American business — has to think through its role in and impact on the international scene.

Many of the effects of business operations on the national level have become social issues at the global level. Business is slowly but surely realizing that multinational corporations (MNCs) have worldwide social impacts and responsibilities. Whether the issue be the power of the MNCs in developing countries, usage of world energy and other resources, international competition, or international business ethics, the concept of business's social responsibility and responsiveness has entered a new dimension.

The future of international relations is intimately connected to business's social as well as economic performance at the global level. Because the distribution of resources throughout the world is affected by business actions, such actions influence to a great extent our country's status and position in the world. As American business seeks international markets in which to expand, it must also assume special social responsibilities as a representative of our country in a foreign land. More than anything else, business represents economic power, a power that must be exercised in a responsible fashion. As business does this, it helps fulfill its role as one of America's most effective instruments of economic as well as social advancement. Thus, the relatively less difficult task of being responsive to society's needs at home becomes quite complex as that society is expanded to the world level. And the many different value systems that business will encounter make the international domain one of the most challenging opportunities business will have to demonstrate its economic and social responsiveness.

CONCLUDING REMARKS

It is difficult to know where to stop when one addresses the future social role of business. Five trends or factors have been discussed that will probably assume a special place in shaping this role: changing values, the role of government, future work life, limits to growth, and global consciousness. Patterns in each of these areas seem to confirm what we stated at the outset: The future social role of business will be an expanded one. Whether we are talking about consumerism, equal employment opportunity, the environment, corporate governanace, employees' rights, or business ethics, well-established trends indicate that society will be expecting more of business than in the past. At the same time business faces increasing pressures to perform in the economic realm, one which very few would call healthy and fertile for business success, profitability, and growth during the present period.

With public expectations ranging from economic performance to social performance, business faces the problem of how to do all these things for all these people. As the "societized corporation" — one which people expect to be a multipurpose social organization — emerges, some of the most significant challenges managers have ever faced loom on the horizon. To make the situation even more difficult, business looks to these challenges with full realization that public mistrust of business is at an all-time high and that the public is skeptical of practically every step that business takes. Can the management of any other organization in society today say that it faces the future with such uncertainty? Probably not. In any event, perhaps the most difficult task of the 1980s for the business organization will be the managing of its social performance. If business fails in this pursuit, it will no longer be a viable institution in our society. Management must and will respond to the challenge.

QUESTIONS FOR DISCUSSION

1. Discuss the changes in societal values that are now taking place or are expected to take place in the future. What impacts will these value shifts have on the future social role of business?

2. On what grounds has the capitalist system been criticized? Discuss.

3. To what extent will government shape the future social role of business? Will government assume a greater or a lesser role in the future?

4. Differentiate between the collectivistic and individualistic ethics. Which do you think will prevail by 1990?

5. Describe the effect population trends are having and will continue to have on work life in the future. How might society reconcile the problem of more educated people and fewer meaningful jobs?

6. What is meant by limits to business growth? What are the factors that have brought the limits issue to the forefront? How does a "sustainable growth strategy" relate to the above issues?

7. Describe global consciousness. How does it relate to the future social role of business?
8. What other arguments exist to suggest a larger business social role in the future? Discuss.

Cases

Does Nader Shift in Priorities Suggest Issues for the Future?

Ralph Nader, the self-appointed, self-styled consumer advocate, became famous because of his continuous attacks on companies for producing unsafe and impure products or otherwise neglecting the consumer. Consumerism, a movement initiated by Nader and others, resulted in significant changes in business behavior toward consumers throughout the 1960s and 1970s. In 1978, however, Congress failed to pass a Nader-backed consumer protection agency.

Though Nader has continued his efforts on behalf of the consumer, he now appears to be turning his attention to other priorities. Among these are increased rights of shareholders, worker ownership, broader disclosure of social activities by business, and the responsibilities of a business when it decides to shut down a plant and leave the community. In addition, he seems to enjoy analyzing potential candidates for public office.

Among business people, Nader is one of the most disliked of the social activists. Many business people think his opinions no longer reflect how the average citizen in this country really feels about business. As a result, they object to his expounding upon what the citizenry doesn't like about American business.

QUESTIONS

1. Do you think Nader's concerns represent those of most Americans? Discuss.
2. As business faces the future, how should it assess Nader's ability to continue his antibusiness activities?
3. Do you think some of the issues Nader is now turning to give us a hint of those social issues that business will have to cope with in the future?
4. Is it possible that business's future social role can be shaped by social activists such as Ralph Nader? Has business lost control of its future?

Work Life in the Future

In attempting to assess the future social role of business, some studies see more social responsiveness occurring in the realm of employees' work lives. One study, for example, suggested that in the last twenty-five years of the twentieth century we will see increased business activity in response to changing aspirations of minorities and females, more job enrichment programs, increased employee involvement in decision making, and improvements in physical working environments.

QUESTIONS

1. Do these trends concur with your anticipation of business's future social role? Discuss why or why not.
2. In addition to those mentioned above, what other internal social responsibilities do you see on the horizon?

Will Awards Stimulate Greater Social Awareness in the Future?

At least one foundation is now granting awards to business firms that engage in activities that reflect positive social and ethical values. The Phillips Awards represent such a program. Supported by the Ellis Laurimore Phillips Foundation, the Phillips Awards seek out business programs in five categories:

1. Management-Employee Relations
2. Company Relations with Customers and Suppliers
3. Community Involvement
4. Concern for the Physical Environment
5. Company Awareness of Values

The concept of the awards is to go "beyond the bottom line" to see how a successful and profitable business enterprise can implement positive social and ethical values in its daily operations. Reproduced here is the letter that is sent to businesses to solicit entries for the awards; also reproduced here is a detailed description of the award categories.

QUESTIONS

1. What is your appraisal of these awards? Do you think the award categories are appropriate?
2. Do you think such awards will stimulate business organizations to improve their social performance? Discuss.
3. Can you envision a future in which awards such as these will assume an important role for business? Discuss.

The Phillips Awards
Value Decisions in / Business Management

C.W. POST CENTER
LONG ISLAND UNIVERSITY
GREENVALE. N.Y. 11548
516 299-2827

To the President:

The environment for the business firm has changed markedly in recent years.
Today managers can no longer afford to be content with achieving profits and
growth. They must also face up to dealing with a range of issues touching
employee discontent, consumer sensitivity, concern for the physical environment
and many new government regulations. In this changing scene managers must develop a
new sensitivity to ethical and value-centered issues in order to be successful.

The Phillips Awards Committee has studied the changing scene and is aware of the
problems confronting management; and is continuing its search for exemplifications
of recent management decision making with special regard for social and ethical
values.

Business firms contribute more to society than just making a product or providing
a service. In the Phillips Awards Program we are looking "beyond the bottom line"
to find outstanding examples of how successful, profitable firms implement positive
social and ethical values in business.

Would you please furnish us with information about any of your company's business
activities which we may consider for the Phillips Awards for Value Decisions in
Business? Enclosed is a description of the Phillips Awards and information on how
to submit nominations for the Awards. These Awards are intended to recognize
outstanding accomplishments and to provide inspiration to others through example.
Only a brief description is required to initiate the consideration of your firm's
accomplishments by the Awards Committee. What is your firm doing which deserves
this recognition?

Sincerely,

THE PHILLIPS AWARDS COMMITTEE
Dr. Armand J. Prusmack, Chairman

Enclosures: Explanation of Awards Program
            and Nomination Form
            Reply Envelope

This Program is funded by the Ellis Laurimore Phillips Foundation to foster a greater awareness of social and ethical values in Business Management.

AWARDS CATEGORIES

There are hundreds of different activities and programs a business organization may be involved in which reflect the social and ethical values of that firm. However, the impact of the organization's values falls in the first four categories of the Awards. The fifth category is the formulation and awareness of values by the organization itself.

The following explanation is designed to help the person nominating a company select the relevent awards category.

1. *Management-Employee Relations*
    How does the organization seek to enable employees to realize their full potential? Included in this category would be programs involving career development, equal opportunity, recruitment of the disadvantaged, etc.

2. *Company Relations with Customers and Suppliers*
    How do the firm's values affect those it does business with? In dealing with customers, what standards of quality and service does the firm intend to render to the customer, and how does the firm organize to implement this ideal in practice? In dealing with suppliers, what standards are set by the firm, and how does the firm implement them?

3. *Community Involvement*
    How does the firm contribute to the quality of life in the communities in which it operates? How do the organization and its members enhance the social, cultural, educational, governmental, recreational, or moral life of the community? In this category the Awards Committee is looking for programs which involve a significant number of members of that organization, not a list of cash contributions to worthy community activities.

4. *Concern for the Physical Environment*
    How does the firm conserve and maintain the physical environment? Included in this category would be programs to conserve energy and other scarce natural resources, pollution control, restoration or improvement of the environment, etc.

5. *Company Awareness of Values*
    How does the firm formulate and communicate a sense of values to all members of the organization? Recently many fine firms managed by idealistic executives who thought they hired individuals of "good character" have uncovered bribery, corruption, falsification of records, and other misdeeds. Possibly the most valuable contribution the Phillips Awards could make to the business community would be to discover and publicize an effective corporate program to communicate a sense of values to all members of a firm so that these individuals could withstand the pressures applied to them both abroad and at home by a competitive world.

SOURCE: Reprinted by permission of The Phillips Awards.

Index